Construction Achievement of China-ASEAN Institute
of Modern Craftsmanship: Series of Textbooks

中国-东盟现代工匠学院建设成果系列教材

风力与光伏发电技术及应用（中英双语）

Technology and Application of Wind & Photovoltaic Power Generation

(Chinese - English)

主　编　罗宇强　王江伟　张宝芳
参　编　高凤玉　蒙耀全

中国水利水电出版社
www.waterpub.com.cn
·北京·

内 容 提 要

本教材以现行工程实践中涉及的太阳能光伏发电技术和风力发电技术基础理论为主，以典型实践工作任务为载体，按照"任务引领、行动导向"的职业教育教学理念，将太阳能光伏发电系统的构成、安装、运行、调试和维护，以及风力发电技术系统的组成、选型、运行和维护相关知识与技能有机融合，让学习者在完成典型的工作任务过程中，掌握太阳能光伏发电技术和风力发电技术相关知识。全教材涵盖了太阳能光伏发电、风力发电的相关设计、安装、运行和维护方面内容。

本教材可供高职高专院校电气类相关专业作为太阳能光伏发电技术及应用、风力发电技术及应用课程使用，也可供工程技术人员参考。

图书在版编目（CIP）数据

风力与光伏发电技术及应用：汉、英 / 罗宇强，王江伟，张宝芳主编. -- 北京：中国水利水电出版社, 2025. 7. -- ISBN 978-7-5226-2780-9
Ⅰ. TM614；TM615
中国国家版本馆CIP数据核字第2024YP2134号

书　　名	**风力与光伏发电技术及应用（中英双语）** FENGLI YU GUANGFU FADIAN JISHU JI YINGYONG (ZHONG - YING SHUANGYU)
作　　者	主编　罗宇强　王江伟　张宝芳
出版发行	中国水利水电出版社 （北京市海淀区玉渊潭南路1号D座　100038） 网址：www.waterpub.com.cn E - mail：sales@mwr.gov.cn 电话：（010）68545888（营销中心）
经　　售	北京科水图书销售有限公司 电话：（010）68545874、63202643 全国各地新华书店和相关出版物销售网点
排　　版	中国水利水电出版社微机排版中心
印　　刷	清淞永业（天津）印刷有限公司
规　　格	184mm×260mm　16开本　18.25印张　511千字
版　　次	2025年7月第1版　2025年7月第1次印刷
印　　数	0001—1000册
定　　价	**72.00元**

凡购买我社图书，如有缺页、倒页、脱页的，本社营销中心负责调换
版权所有·侵权必究

Summary

This textbook focuses on the fundamental theories of solar photovoltaic power generation technology and wind power generation technology involved in current engineering practice, takes typical practical tasks as its core framework, and organically integrates the knowledge and skills related to the composition, installation, operation, commissioning and maintenance of solar photovoltaic power generation systems. It also covers the composition, selection, operation and maintenance of wind power generation technology systems and all in accordance with the "task-guiding and action-oriented" vocational education teaching concept. This allows the learners to master relevant knowledge of solar photovoltaic power generation technology and wind power generation technology while completing typical tasks. This textbook covers the design, installation, operation and maintenance of both solar photovoltaic power generation and wind power generation technologies.

The textbook is designed for the course on technology and application of solar photovoltaic power generation and wind power generation for students majoring in electric power in higher vocational colleges. It can also serve as a reference for engineers and technicians.

前　言

电能发展至今已有上百年历史，电能技术的每一次变革和创新，都带来社会生产力的快速进步、生活质量的大幅度改善与生存环境的巨大变化，现已成为人类生存与发展的重要载体。目前，全球90%的能源是由不可再生的传统能源供给，据专家分析，以目前世界已探明的蕴藏量看，煤炭存量剩余二百余年，石油储量、核能发电的铀矿、天然气仅剩余数十年，全球面临着能源枯竭的趋势！传统能源的使用，显露出了较为严重的环境污染问题。党的二十大指出，积极稳妥推进"碳中和"和"碳达峰"，要实现国家这一"双碳"战略发展目标，能源领域必然是"主战场"，而新能源又是这一领域的"先锋队"和"主力军"，未来新能源发电将成为我国新增能源供给的核心力量，包括风力、光伏发电等新能源每年必然有稳定的装机目标。

在今后20年，目前光伏发电建设主要包括：集中式光伏电站、与建筑结合的分布式光伏电站，以及与农业种植、水产养殖结合的各类"农光互补""渔光互补"等分布式光伏电站。大量的光伏电站开展建设和投入运行，势必推动对具有光伏发电相关专业技术人才需求的增长，光伏发电技术人员所需的专业知识与技能主要聚焦于光伏电站项目设计、施工建设、调试验收，以及电站运行与维护等方面，同时还要能够使用先进信息化设备和仪器开展相关专业技术工作，如无人机光伏电站巡检、光伏组件EL测试等，这将要求对光伏发电专业领域技术人才培养是综合化和全面化的。

风力发电技术主要包含电气和机械两个部分，且随着风电场运行与维护岗一体化，要求专业技术人员掌握风力发电机组运行原理、风力发电的控制原理、风电机组的运行与维护等相关知识与技能，并能够分析和解决风电机组常见故障。

随着能源革命的政策推动和新能源发电技术的不断成熟，包含风力、光伏发电等新能源融合发展的模式创新不断涌现出，同时针对风力、光伏等新能源出力波动性和间歇性的特点，配套建设抽水蓄能、储能电站等各类可控储能系统来保障新能源接入电网并稳定运行，在许多海岛或一定范围开发区也建设"风-光-柴-储"等多能源互补示范系统，有效促进了新能源大规模开发建设和消纳。在"双碳"战略目标下，新能源产业以其节能环保优势，迎来了更大的发展空间和机遇，据统计，采用风力、光伏等新能源每发1度（千瓦时）电，就相应节约了0.328kg标准煤，同时减少污染排放 0.272kg 碳粉尘、0.997kg 二氧化碳、0.03kg 二氧化硫、0.015kg 氮氧化物。

本教材从项目学习角度介绍对风力、光伏发电技术，融合风电场运维岗、光伏电站运维岗等岗位工作要求，结合全国职业院校技能大赛技术技能要求，以及职业技能等级证书"光伏电站运维"的知识与技能要求，使学习者能够掌握风电产业、太阳能光伏发电的所需知识与技能，同时兼顾储能技术、风光互补系统和微电网技术前沿。

本教材由罗宇强、王江伟、张宝芳主编，广西龙源风力发电有限公司的高凤玉、南方电网综合能源广西有限公司的蒙耀全深入参与了教材编写。

由于编者的水平有限，书中难免存在疏漏和不妥之处，恳请广大读者和专家批评指正。

编　者

2024 年 6 月

Preface

To date, electrical energy has witnessed hundreds of years of development. Every single reformation and innovation in electrical energy technology has brought about rapid progress in social productivity, substantial improvement in the quality of life, and dramatic change in the living environment. Electrical energy has become a critical carrier of human survival and development. Currently, 90% of the world's energy is supplied by non-renewable traditional energy sources. According to expert analysis, in terms of the world's current proven reserves, coal stocks can sustain humans for more than 200 years, while oil reserves, uranium mine for nuclear power generation, and natural gas can only sustain humans for a few decades. The world is facing the trend of energy depletion! The utilization of traditional energy sources has revealed serious environmental pollution problems. The 20th CPC National Congress states that we will actively and prudently work toward "peaking carbon dioxide emissions" and "achieving carbon neutrality". To achieve this "carbon peaking and carbon neutrality" strategic development goal of the country, energy is bound to be the "main battlefield", and new energy is the "vanguard" and "main force" in this field. In the future, new energy power generation will become the core force of China's new energy supply, and wind power, photovoltaic power and other new energy sources are bound to witness stable installed capacity targets year by year.

In the next one to two decades, the construction of photovoltaic power generation will be dominated by the following types of photovoltaic power stations: centralized photovoltaic power stations, distributed photovoltaic power stations combined with buildings, and various distributed photovoltaic power stations in the modes of "agriculture-photovoltaic complementarity" (photovoltaic power combined with farming) and "fishery-photovoltaic complementarity" (photovoltaic power combined with aquaculture). A large number of photovoltaic power stations are under construction and put into operation, which will inevitably promote the demand for technical talents with photovoltaic power generation related expertise. The expertise and skills expected from photovoltaic power generation technicians mainly focus on the design, construction, commissioning and acceptance of photovoltaic power station projects, as well as the operation and maintenance of power stations. Meanwhile, such technicians are expected to use advanced informatics equipment and instruments to carry out relevant professional and technical work, e. g. , photovoltaic power station inspection using unmanned aerial vehicles (UAV), and photovoltaic module EL testing. This leads to the expectation of integrated and comprehensive training for technical talents in the field of photovoltaic power generation.

Wind power generation technology consists of two main aspects: electrical and mechanical. With the integration of operation and maintenance positions of wind power generation plants, professional and technical personnel are expected to master the operating principle of wind turbines, the control principle of wind power generation, the operation and maintenance of wind turbines, as well as other related knowledge and skills, and analyze and solve common faults of wind turbines. With the promotion of energy revolution policy and the continuous maturity of new energy power generation technology, as well as the emergence of integrated development and model innovation of new energy sources such as wind and photovoltaic power, and also considering the volatility and intermittency of the electrical power of new energy sources such as wind and photovoltaic power, supporting facilities like pumped storage power stations, energy storage power stations, and other types of controllable energy storage systems are constructed to ensure that new energy sources gain access into the power grid with stable operation. Many islands or a certain range of development zones have also constructed multi-energy complementary demonstration systems, such as "wind-solar-diesel-storage", effectively promoting the massive development, construction and consumption of new energy sources. Under the "carbon peaking and carbon neutrality" strategic goal, the new energy industry, with its advantages of energy saving and environmental friendliness, has ushered in greater development space and opportunities. According to statistics, wind, photovoltaic power and other new energy sources used to generate 1kW·h of electricity contributes to a corresponding saving of 0.328kg of standard coal, while reducing pollution emissions by 0.272kg of carbon dust, 0.997kg of carbon dioxide, 0.03kg of sulphur dioxide, and 0.015kg of nitrogen oxides.

This textbook is written from the perspective of project-based learning on wind and photovoltaic power generation technologies. It integrates the job requirements for positions such as wind farm operations and maintenance, and photovoltaic power station operations and maintenance. It also aligns with the technical and skill requirements of the National Vocational College Skills Competition and the knowledge and skill requirements of the "Photovoltaic Power Station Operation and Maintenance" vocational skill level certificate. This enables learners to master the necessary knowledge and skills for the wind power industry and the solar photovoltaic power generation industry, while also considering advanced topics in energy storage technology, wind-solar hybrid systems, and microgrid technology.

This textbook is edited by LuoYuqiang, Wang Jiangwei and Zhang Baofang. Gao Fengyu from Guangxi Longyuan Wind Power Co., Ltd. and Meng Yaoquan from China Southern Power Grid Integrated Energy (Guangxi) Co., Ltd. were deeply involved in the revision and preparation of the textbook.

In view of the constraints of our personal expertise, we sincerely ask readers' and experts' kind indulgence for any omissions and inaccuracies that may possibly occur in this textbook.

Editors
June 2024

目 录

前言
Preface

项目1 认识太阳能光伏电池特性 …………………………………………… 1
   任务1.1 测试太阳能光伏电池性能 …………………………………………… 1
   任务1.2 调试光伏组件最大功率点跟踪方法 ………………………………… 7

Project 1 Understand the Characteristic of Solar Photovoltaic Cells // **15**
   Task 1.1 Performing Performance Testing of Solar Photovoltaic Cells // 15
   Task 1.2 Commission Methods for Tracking the Maximum Power of Photovoltaic Modules // 23

项目2 跟踪计算光伏发电系统发电量 ………………………………………… 35
   任务2.1 计算光伏发电年发电量 ……………………………………………… 35
   任务2.2 调试光伏组件跟踪太阳方法 ………………………………………… 38

Project 2 Tracking and Calculating Power Generation Capacity of Photovoltaic Power Generation Systems // **41**
   Task 2.1 Calculating Annual Photovoltaic Power Generation Capacity // 41
   Task 2.2 Commission Methods of Tracking the Sun by Photovoltaic Modules // 45

项目3 设计太阳能光伏发电系统 …………………………………………… 50
   任务3.1 设计独立光伏发电系统 ……………………………………………… 50
   任务3.2 设计并网光伏发电系统 ……………………………………………… 58

Project 3 Designing Solar Photovoltaic Power Generation Systems // **66**
   Task 3.1 Designing Stand-Alone Photovoltaic Power Generation Systems // 66
   Task 3.2 Designing Grid-Connected Photovoltaic Power Generation Systems // 79

项目 4　安装与运维太阳能光伏发电系统 …………………………………………………… 90
　　任务 4.1　安装太阳能光伏发电系统 ………………………………………………… 90
　　任务 4.2　太阳能光伏发电系统的运维 ……………………………………………… 102

Project 4　Installing, Operating and Maintaining Solar Photovoltaic Power
　　　　　　Generation Systems　// 114
　　Task 4.1　Installing Solar Photovoltaic Power Generation Systems　// 114
　　Task 4.2　Operating and Maintaining Solar Photovoltaic Power Generation Systems　// 133

项目 5　勘察风资源与选址风电场 ……………………………………………………… 153
　　任务 5.1　勘察风资源 ……………………………………………………………… 153
　　任务 5.2　选址风电场 ……………………………………………………………… 158

Project 5　Survey on Wind Resources and Selecting Sites for Wind Farms　// 162
　　Task 5.1　Survey on Wind Resources　// 162
　　Task 5.2　Selecting Sites for Wind Farms　// 170

项目 6　认识与选型风力发电机组 ……………………………………………………… 176
　　任务 6.1　掌握风力发电系统组成 ………………………………………………… 176
　　任务 6.2　选型风力发电机组 ……………………………………………………… 184

Project 6　Understanding Selecting Sites for Wind Turbine Generator Systems　// 191
　　Task 6.1　Mastering Composition of Wind Power Generation　// 191
　　Task 6.2　Selecting Wind Turbine Generator Systems　// 203

项目 7　调节与安装风力发电机组 ……………………………………………………… 211
　　任务 7.1　掌握风轮机的调向、调速和保护装置 ………………………………… 211
　　任务 7.2　安装风力发电机组 ……………………………………………………… 217

Project 7　Adjusting and Installing Wind Turbine Generator Systems　// 223
　　Task 7.1　Mastering the Yaw, Speed Control, and Protection Devices of Wind Turbines　// 223
　　Task 7.2　Installing Wind Turbine Units　// 231

项目 8　运行与维护风力发电系统 ……………………………………………………… 240
　　任务 8.1　掌握风电场变电站倒闸操作 …………………………………………… 240
　　任务 8.2　运行风力发电系统 ……………………………………………………… 243
　　任务 8.3　维护风力发电系统 ……………………………………………………… 249

Project 8　Operation and Maintenance of Wind Power Systems　// 256
　　Task 8.1　Mastering Switching Operations in Wind Farm Substations　// 256
　　Task 8.2　Operation of Wind Power Generation Systems　// 260
　　Task 8.3　Maintenance of Wind Power Systems　// 268

参考文献 ··· 278

项目 1　认识太阳能光伏电池特性

任务 1.1　测试太阳能光伏电池性能

【学习目标】

　　知识目标：了解太阳能光伏电池的类型和光生伏特效应。
　　能力目标：能对比分析每种类型太阳能光伏电池的特征。
　　素质目标：培养精益求精、追求卓越的工匠精神。
　　重点：太阳能光伏电池的类型。
　　难点：太阳能光伏电池的特征。

【任务分析】

　　太阳能光伏电池又称太阳能电池、光伏电池，是一种将光能直接转化为电能的发电装置。不同的太阳能光伏电池具有不同的特性，性能参数也不尽相同，了解太阳能光伏电池的类型、特征，以及性能参数，才能更好利用太阳能光伏电池。
　　本任务依托全国职业院校技能大赛设备平台，对应光伏生产检测、光伏电站运维岗位等工作内容，利用不同类型光伏组件，完成太阳能光伏电池的功能测试实操内容，包括太阳能光伏组件绝缘耐压测试、老化测试。

【知识学习】

1.1.1　硅系太阳能光伏电池分类与性能

　　硅系太阳能光伏电池大致可以分为以下几种。
　　1. 单晶硅太阳能光伏电池
　　单晶硅太阳能光伏电池是最早发展起来的，主要用单晶硅片来制造。与其他种类的电池相比，单晶硅太阳能光伏电池的转换效率最高。作为原料的高纯单晶硅片多是从电子工业半导体器件加工中退出的产品，以往在市场上可大量以较便宜的价格得到，因此单晶硅太阳能光伏电池能够以相对较低的成本来生产。
　　单晶硅太阳能光伏电池曾经长时期占领最大的市场份额，只是在 1998 年后才退居多晶硅电池之后，位于第二位。由于近几年太阳能电池工业高速发展，导致高纯多晶硅原料紧缺，在 2004 年单晶硅太阳能光伏电池成本又略有上升。在以后的若干年内，单晶硅太阳能光伏电池仍会继续发展，并保持较高的市场份额。最新的趋势是单晶硅太阳能光伏电池将向超薄、高效发展，不久的将来，可有 $100\mu m$ 左右甚至更薄的单晶硅太阳能光伏电池问世。德国的研究已经证实 $40\mu m$ 厚的单晶硅电池的效率可达到 20%，有可能借助改进的生产工艺实现超薄单晶硅太阳能光伏电池的工业化生产，并可能达到已在实验室获得的效率。

单晶硅太阳能光伏电池的基本结构多为 N^+/P 型，多以 P 型单晶硅片为基片，其电阻率范围一般为 $1\sim 3\Omega\cdot cm$，厚度一般为 $200\sim 300\mu m$，由于单晶硅材料大都来自半导体工业退出的废次品，因而，一些厂家利用的硅片厚度可达到 $0.5\sim 0.7mm$，由于这些硅片的质量完全满足太阳能光伏电池的要求，用来制作太阳能光伏电池可得到很好的效果，一般很容易使效率达到 15% 以上。

单晶硅太阳能光伏电池制作过程首先是表面绒面结构的制作，其次与多晶硅太阳能光伏电池不同的是所用的减反膜主要为 SiO_2 或 TiO_2 薄膜。制备 SiO_2 和 TiO_2 薄膜通常采用热氧化或常压化学气相沉积工艺。

单晶硅太阳能光伏电池（如图 1.1 所示）主要用于光伏电站，特别是通信电站，也可用于航空器电源，或用于聚焦光伏发电系统。单晶硅太阳能光伏电池的光学、电学和力学性能均匀一致，电池的颜色多为黑色或深色，特别适合切割成小片制作小型消费产品，如太阳能庭院灯等。

图 1.1 单晶硅太阳能光伏电池

单晶硅太阳能光伏电池在实验室实现的转换效率可达到 24.7%，为澳大利亚新南威尔士大学创造并保持。代表性的单晶硅电池商品主要由荷兰 Shell Solar、西班牙 Isafoton、印度 Microsol 等厂家生产。单晶硅太阳能光伏电池是目前除了砷化镓（GaAs）化合物电池以外效率最高的太阳能光伏电池产品。

2. 多晶硅太阳能光伏电池

在制作多晶硅太阳能光伏电池时，作为原料的高纯硅不是拉成单晶，而是熔化后形的硅锭，然后像加工单晶硅太阳能光伏电池一样切成薄片和进行类似的电池加工。从多晶硅太阳能光伏电池易辨认，硅片是由大量不同大小结晶区域组成的（如图 1.2 所示）。这样结晶区域

图 1.2 多晶硅太阳能光伏电池

（晶粒）里的光电转换机制和单晶硅电池完全相同。由于硅片由多个不同大小、不同取向的晶粒组成，在晶粒界面（晶界）处光电转换易受到干扰，因而多晶硅的转换效率相对较低。同时，多晶硅太阳能光伏电池的电学、力学和光学性能一致性不如单晶硅太阳能光伏电池。多晶硅太阳能光伏电池的基本结构都为 N^+/P 型，都用 P 型单晶硅片，电阻率为 $0.5\sim2\Omega\cdot cm$，厚度为 $220\sim300\mu m$，有些厂家正在向 $180\mu m$ 甚至更薄方向发展，以节约价格昂贵的高纯硅材料。

多晶硅太阳能光伏电池制作过程的主要特点是以氮化硅为减反射薄膜，商业化电池的效率多为 13%～15%，主要特点是多晶硅太阳能光伏电池为正方片，在制作电池组件时有最高的填充率。由于多晶硅的生产工艺简单，可大规模生产，所以多晶硅太阳能光伏电池的产量和市场占有率最大。

多晶硅太阳能光伏电池的实验室最高效率达到 20.3%，为德国研究机构创造，具有代表性的商品为 Q-Cell、Motech、Suntech 等公司生产的产品。

3. 非晶硅薄膜太阳能光伏电池

非晶硅薄膜太阳能光伏电池是至今取得成功的薄膜太阳能光伏电池（如图 1.3 所示）。由于目前晶体硅太阳能光伏电池供应短缺，人们试图通过非晶硅薄膜太阳能光伏电池来补充。非晶硅薄膜太阳能光伏电池之所以不能大规模使用，主要是因为光致衰减效应。非晶硅薄膜太阳能光伏电池的基本结构为 N-I-P 型，主要用 PECVD 工艺沉积在具有 $SnO_2(F)$ 的导电玻璃上制成。现在也有发展为 2 个 PN 结甚至 3 个 PN 结的非晶硅电池，基片采用导电玻璃甚至不锈钢作为衬底材料。商品

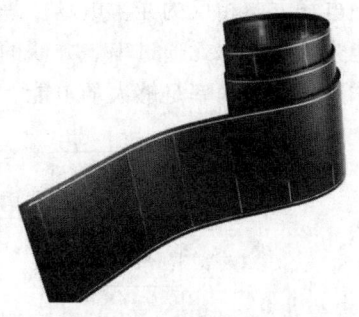

图 1.3 薄膜太阳能光伏电池

化的非晶硅薄膜太阳能光伏电池产品稳定的效率为 5%～7%，非晶硅薄膜太阳能光伏电池材料厚度在微米级。非晶硅为准直接带隙半导体，吸收系数大，可节省大量高纯硅材料，制作过程采用化学气相沉积，原材料为硅烷、硼烷和磷烷等，其过程需要在真空条件下进行。非晶硅薄膜太阳能光伏电池基本独霸消费市场，如手表、计算器和玩具等使用非晶硅电池。此外，其作为半透明光伏组件也可用于门窗或天窗，因此非晶硅薄膜太阳能光伏电池也很适合用作建筑材料。

1.1.2 单晶硅与多晶硅电池片的区别

单晶硅太阳能光伏电池和多晶硅太阳能光伏电池的寿命都很长，稳定性都很好。单晶硅太阳能光伏电池的平均转换效率比多晶硅太阳能光伏电池的平均转换效率要高（高 1% 左右），但是从占有有效面积来看单晶硅太阳能光伏电池和多晶硅太阳能光伏电池平均转换效率是没有太大区别的，这是因为单晶硅电池只能做成准正方形（其 4 个角是圆弧），所以组成太阳能光伏电池组件时（相互紧密连接时）就有一部分面积填不满。但多晶硅太阳能光伏电池是正方形，不存在一部分面积填不满的问题。单晶硅太阳能光伏电池和多晶硅太阳能光伏电池的寿命都很长，稳定性都很好。

从外观上看：单晶硅电池片四个角呈圆弧状，表面没有花纹；多晶硅电池片四个角为

方角，表面有类似冰花一样的花纹。

1.1.3 光生伏特效应

太阳能光伏发电的能量转换器是太阳能光伏电池，又称光伏电池。太阳能光伏电池发电的原理是基于半导体的光生伏特效应。光伏电池是以半导体 PN 结上接受太阳光照产生光生伏特效应为基础，直接将光能转换成电能的能量转换器。其工作原理是：当太阳光照射到半导体表面，半导体内部 N 区和 P 区中原子的价电子受到太阳光子的冲击，通过光辐射获取到超过禁带宽度 E_g 的能量，脱离共价键的束缚从价带激发到导带，由此在半导体材料内部产生出很多处于非平衡状态的电子-空穴对。这些被光激发的电子和空穴，或自由碰撞，或在半导体中复合恢复到平衡状态。其中复合过程对外不呈现导电作用，用于光伏电池能量自动损耗部分。一般希望有更多的光激发载流子中的少数载流子能运动到 PN 结区，通过 PN 结对少数载流子的牵引作用而漂移到对方区域，对外形成与 PN 结势垒电场方向相反的光生电场。一旦接通外电路，即可有电能输出。当把众多这样小的太阳能光伏电池单元通过串、并联的方式组合在一起，就构成光伏电池组件，可以在太阳能的作用下输出功率足够大的电能。光生伏特效应产生过程如图 1.4 所示。

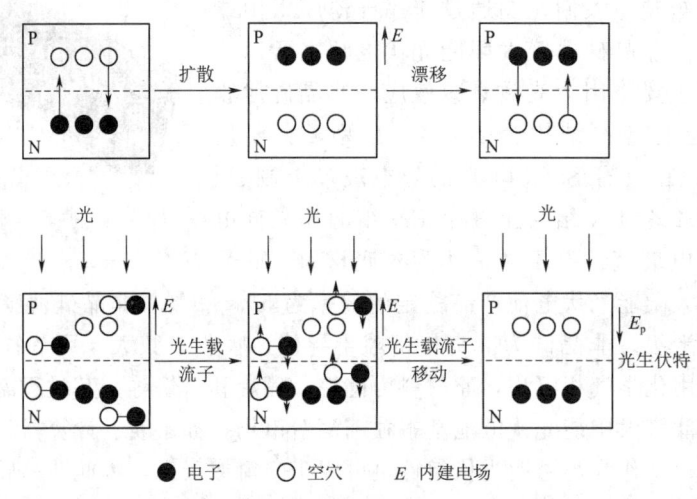

图 1.4 光生伏特效应产生过程

图 1.5 形象地示意了照射到光伏电池表面的太阳光线的各种作用情况。图 1.5 中①是指在电池表面被反射回去的一部分光线。图 1.5 中②是指刚进电池表面被吸收生成电子-空穴对的光线，其中大部分是吸收系数较大的短波光线。但它们来不及达到 PN 结就很快地被复合还原，所以它们对产生光生电动势没有贡献。图 1.5 中③是指在 PN 结附近被吸收生成电子-空穴对的那部分光线，它们是使光伏电池能够有效发电的有用光线。这些光生非平衡少数载流子在 PN 结特有的漂移作用下产生光生电动势。图 1.5 中④是指辐射到电池片深

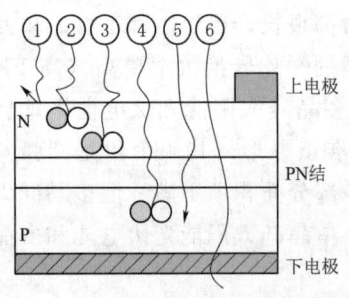

图 1.5 光伏电池受光照情况

处,距离 PN 结较远的地方才被吸收的光线,它们与光线②的情况相同,虽能产生电子-空穴对,但在到达 PN 结之前已被复合,只有极少部分能产生光生电动势。图 1.5 中⑤是指被电池吸收,但是由于能量较小不能产生电子-空穴对的那部分光线,它们的能量只能使光伏电池加热,温度上升。图 1.5 中⑥是指没有被电池吸收而透射过去的少部分光线。

由此可见,能够产生光生电动势的主要是光线③,所以应该尽可能地增加它的比例数量,才能提高光伏电池的光电转换效率。所谓光电转换效率,是指受光照的光伏电池所产生的最大输出电功率与入射到该电池受光几何面积上全部光辐射功率的百分比。

图 1.6 说明了当光伏电池的上电极和下电极接上负载电路后,光线③部分如何在外电路上形成电流的过程。

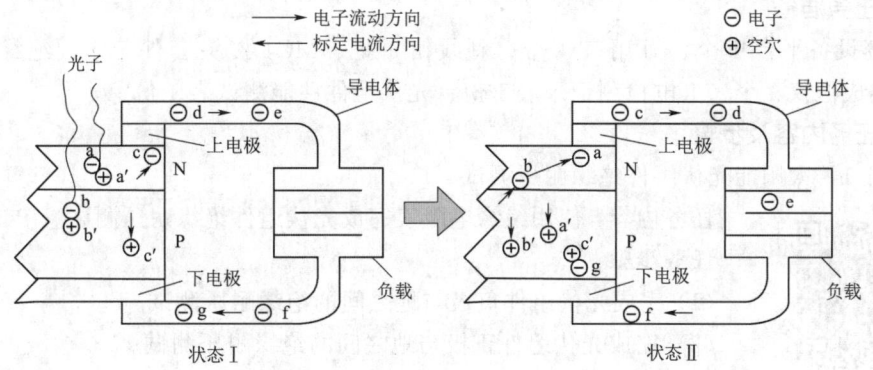

图 1.6 光伏电池产生电流示意图

如上所述,正是由于这些靠近 PN 结的光生少数载流子,在 PN 结的漂移作用下,N 区的电子留在 N 区,空穴流向 P 区;P 区的空穴留在 P 区,电子流向 N 区,构成光生电场;从外电路看,P 区为正,N 区为负,一旦接通负载,N 区的电子通过外电路负载通向 P 区形成电子流;电子进入 P 区后与空穴复合,变回成中性,直到另一个光子再次分离出电子-空穴对为止。约定电流的方向与正电荷的流向相同,与负电荷的流向相反。于是光伏电池与负载接通后,电流是从 P 区流出,通过负载从 N 区流回电池。

半导体材料在不同的温度和光辐射下,产生的电子-空穴对的数量是不同的。利用光伏效应原理制成的光伏电池,PN 结是其核心。光伏电池可制成 P^+/N 型结构或 N^+/P 型结构。其中,P^+/N 表示光伏电池正面光照层半导体材料的导电类型;N^+/P 表示光伏电池背面衬底半导体材料的导电类型。光伏电池的电性能与制造电池所用的半导体材料的特性有关。在太阳光照射时,光伏电池输出电压的极性是 P 型侧电极为正,N 型侧电极为负。

照射到光伏电池表面的太阳辐射光含有各种不同的波长,各波长光的能量和其在光伏电池中的穿透深度也随之不同。也就是说,光伏电池对光能的吸收,随光波波长的不同而不同。它对短波的吸收系数较大,对长波的吸收系数则较小。而对于射入电池材料内部的太阳光来说,只有那些光子能量 $\varepsilon \geqslant E_g$ 的光线,才能激发出电子-空穴对,而那些 $\varepsilon < E_g$ 的光线,则不能激发出电子-空穴对,只能使光伏电池自身加热。此外,已产生的电子-空

穴对,也有一部分被过早地复合还原,对光生电流没有起作用,造成光能的一部分损失。所以说太阳光能不可能全部转变成电能。

当一束太阳光辐射到物体表面,除了一部分光穿透物体表面进入物体内部外,还有一部分被物体表面反射回去。反射光强度与入射光强度之比称为反射系数 ρ,穿透光强度与入射光强度之比称为透射系数 τ。根据能量守恒定律,入射光应等于透射光与反射光之和:$\rho+\tau=1$。从制造高效率的光伏电池的角度来说,反射系数越小越好。因而在制造光伏电池时,常使用减反射膜技术或其他技术(如绒面技术)尽可能地减少反射光的比例。

【任务实施】

1. 任务准备

竞赛设备平台1个、万用表1个、剥线钳1把、MC4接头套件若干、绝缘电阻表1个、热成像仪1个、上电检测记录表1份、光伏组件性能测试表1份。

2. 任务内容及步骤

任务1:太阳能光伏组件绝缘耐压测试

任务1.1 相关实施图表

任务内容:使用绝缘电阻表完成光伏组件绝缘耐压测试。

任务步骤:

(1)完成光伏组件负极与地之间的绝缘耐压测试。

(2)完成光伏组件正极与地之间的绝缘耐压测试。

(3)完成光伏组件正负极短路时,光伏电极与地之间的绝缘测试。

任务2:太阳能光伏组件老化测试

任务内容:完成光伏组件的老化性能测试。

任务步骤:

(1)使用热成像仪查找光伏组件危险源。

(2)完成光伏组件老化衰减状况下的电气性能测试。

(3)使用绝缘电阻表完成老化的光伏组件绝缘耐压测试。

3. 技能要求

(1)太阳能光伏组件绝缘耐压测试和老化性能测试时,在符合安全规范的前提下,允许相关测试人员进入测试现场,禁止其他人员进入现场。

(2)绝缘耐压测试测量时,必须穿戴绝缘手套等防护器具。

(3)绝缘耐压测试测量时,绝缘电阻表须平放。以120r/min的匀速转动手柄,使指针逐渐上升直至出现稳定值,然后读取绝缘电阻值,严禁在正在工作的光伏组件上测量。

(4)使用热成像仪,应当避免太阳直射、建筑反射等干扰因素的影响。

4. 任务成果及考核评价

(1)太阳能光伏组件绝缘耐压测试和老化性能测试步骤正确、数据正确,占90%。

(2)操作过程展现较好职业素养,做到7S管理,占10%(7S内容包括在实验过程中对实验器材及实验的整理、整顿、清扫、清洁、素养、安全、节约)。

项目 1 认识太阳能光伏电池特性

【练习】

1. 什么是多晶硅与单晶硅？多晶硅与单晶硅的差异主要表现在哪些方面？
2. 如何区别单晶硅与多晶硅电池片？
3. 什么叫作光生伏特效应？

任务 1.2 调试光伏组件最大功率点跟踪方法

【学习目标】

知识目标：掌握光伏最大功率点跟踪概念、原理和方法。

能力目标：能完成常用的光伏最大功率点跟踪方法的调试；能够对光伏电站进行运维数据分析、运营分析。

素质目标：培养专注认真、精益求精的职业精神。

重点：光伏最大功率点跟踪概念和原理。

难点：光伏最大功率点跟踪工况下的运维数据分析和运营分析。

【任务分析】

光伏系统中的最大功率点跟踪是保证其获得最大功率、提高系统效率的有效方式。最大功率点跟踪具有较多方法，每种方法各有优势，根据系统实际情况选择最合适方法，更好地发挥太阳能光伏电池的效率。

本任务依托职业技能等级证书设备平台，对接跟踪式光伏电站的运行岗位工作内容，在光伏电站光伏组件最大功率工况下，完成运维数据分析、运营分析实操内容。

【知识学习】

1.2.1 太阳能光伏电池模型

光伏电池是光电转换器件，能够通过光伏电池将光能转换成电能的太阳辐射波长范围在 $0.2\sim1.25\mu m$ 之间。以禁带宽度为 2eV 的半导体材料制成的光伏电池为例，在太阳辐射能量中，只有波长小于 $0.62\mu m$ 的光能可激发产生电流，而这个波长的能量只占太阳辐射总能量的 58%。光伏电池因为对太阳光线的选择性吸收的特性，还要考虑其他的光电损失，使得这种材料制成的光伏电池，其光伏电池转换效率最多也只有 58% 的一半。理论分析表明，从光电转换效率来看，制造光伏电池的最佳材料是禁带宽度为 1.5eV 的半导体，而禁带宽度在 $1.1\sim2.0eV$ 范围内的材料均可以制出效率比较高的光伏电池。

根据硅型光伏电池的光电特性分析，理论上它的最大光电转换效率为 22%，而常规的硅型光伏电池效率只有 12% 左右，高效硅型光伏电池效率也只有 18% 左右。这是因为硅对光线不能做到 100% 的吸收，存在一定的折射和反射；进入硅晶体的光能也受到硅禁带宽度的限制，有一部分变为热能损失掉了，再加上电子-空穴对的复合损失和串、并联电阻的损失，使硅型光伏电池的光电转换效率进一步下降。

光伏电池按基底材料不同分为 2DR 型和 2CR 型。2DR 型硅光伏电池是以 P 型硅作为基底（即在本征型材料中掺入三价元素硼、镓等），然后在基底上扩散磷而形成 N 型并作为受光面。2CR 型硅光伏电池则是以 N 型硅作为基底（在本征型硅材料中掺入五价元素磷、砷等），然后在基底上扩散硼而形成 P 型并作为受光面。构成 PN 结后，再经过各种工艺处理，分别在基底和光敏面上制作、输出电极，涂上二氧化硅作为保护膜，即形成光伏电池，如图 1.7 所示。

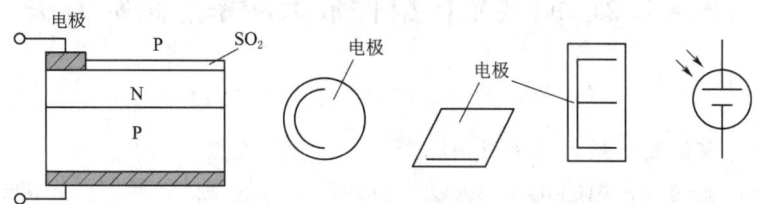

图 1.7 硅光伏电池结构及符号示意图

一般硅光伏电池受光面上的输出电极多做成梳齿状，有时也做成 π 字形，目的是便于透光和减小串联电阻。在光敏面上涂一层二氧化硅透明层，一方面起防潮保护作用，另一方面对入射光起抗反射作用，以增加对光的吸收。

太阳能光伏电池的主要功能是在不加偏置的情况下将光信号转换成电信号。其工作原理如图 1.8（a）所示，流经负载的电流为

$$I_L = I_P - I_D = I_P - I_S(e^{eU/kT} - 1) \tag{1.1}$$

式中，I_P 为光生电流，A；I_D 为 PN 结反向电流，A；U 为 PN 结两端电压（包括外加电压或光生电压），V；I_S 为 PN 结的反向饱和电流，A；e 为电子电荷 $e = 1.602176634 \times 10^{-19}$ C；k 为玻耳兹曼常数 $k = 1.380649 \times 10^{-23}$ J/K；T 为绝对温度，K。

光伏电池特性测量曲线讲解

由上式可画出光伏电池的等效电路如图 1.8（b）所示。图中，I_P 为恒流源，流出与入射光照成正比的电流，VD 为等效二极管，R_{sh} 为动态结电阻，$R_{sh} = dU/dI$。在线性测量中，R_{sh} 值越大越好，目前可达 $10^8 \sim 10^{10}$ Ω/cm，计算时可看成开路，R_S 是串联电阻，通常很小，可忽略。C_j（结电容）直流计算时可不予考虑，R_L 为负载电阻，I_L 为流过负载电阻 R_L 的电流。若进一步简化，图 1.8（b）可画成如图 1.8（c）所示的等效电路。

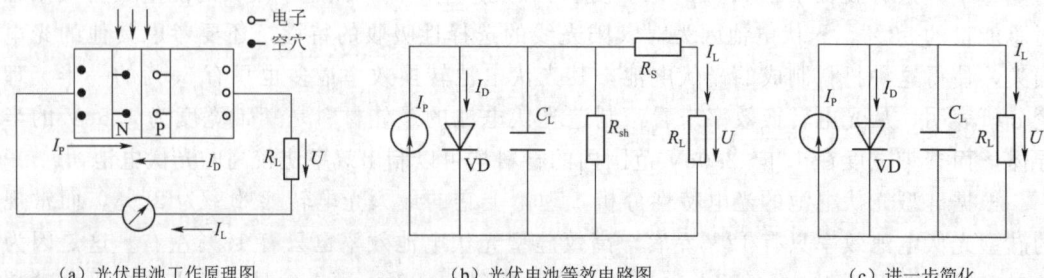

（a）光伏电池工作原理图　　　（b）光伏电池等效电路图　　　（c）进一步简化

图 1.8 光伏电池的工作原理图和等效电路

1.2.2 最大功率点跟踪概念

为了更好地发挥太阳能光伏电池的效率，有必要了解最大功率点跟踪控制的知识。太阳能光伏电池本身是极不稳定的电源，其输出功率往往是变化的。这是因为太阳能光伏电池工作时的输出功率随日照强弱、天空阴晴、环境温度（电池方阵表面温度）的变化而变化。为了得到最大的能量利用效率，就必须使电池的输出功率自动跟踪气候的变化条件，使光能尽可能地转换为电能，提高系统效率。因此需要及时跟踪太阳，使太阳能光伏电池获取最大输出功率或达到最大功率点附近处的运行状态，即最大功率点跟踪 MPPT（maximum power point tracking）控制。

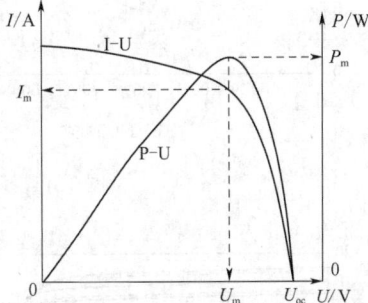

图 1.9　光伏电池阵列的特性曲线

1.2.3 最大功率点跟踪原理

光伏电池阵列的特性曲线如图 1.9 所示。

如果阵列运行在 I-U 曲线的任何一个电压 U 和电流 I，那么发出的功率为 $P=UI$。如果运行点从先前的点移动到电流 $I+\Delta I$ 和电压 $U+\Delta U$，那么新的功率为

$$P+\Delta P=(U+\Delta U)(I+\Delta I)$$

忽略小项后，简化为下式：

$$\Delta P=\Delta U I+U\Delta I$$

阵列在峰值功率点运行时，$\Delta P = \mathrm{d}P/\mathrm{d}U \approx 0$，因此，在最大功率点处以下公式成立：

$$\frac{\mathrm{d}U}{\mathrm{d}I}=-\frac{U}{I}$$

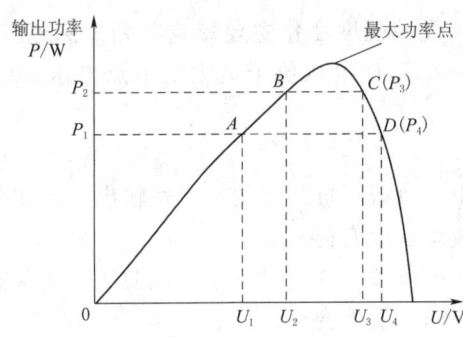

图 1.10　最大功率点跟踪控制

只要 $\mathrm{d}P/\mathrm{d}U$ 是正的，就增加运行电压，或者说，只要能获得更大的功率，就增加电压。

如果测得 $\mathrm{d}P/\mathrm{d}U$ 是负的，就降低运行电压，如果 $\mathrm{d}P/\mathrm{d}U$ 在 0 附近的预置死区内，那么电压保持不变。

如图 1.10 所示，当光伏电池阵列工作在最大功率点电压右边的 D 点时，因离最大功率点较远，可以将电压值减小，即功率增加；当光伏电池阵列工作在最大功率点电压左边时，可以将电压值调大。在给定的运行条件下，太阳能光伏电池阵列必须运行在与峰值功率点相对应的某个电压值上。

图 1.11、图 1.12 分别给出了当光照强度和电池温度变化时，光伏阵列的输出特性曲线（I-U、P-U 曲线）。

由图 1.11、图 1.12 可知，当外界自然条件改变时，光伏阵列的输出特性将随之改

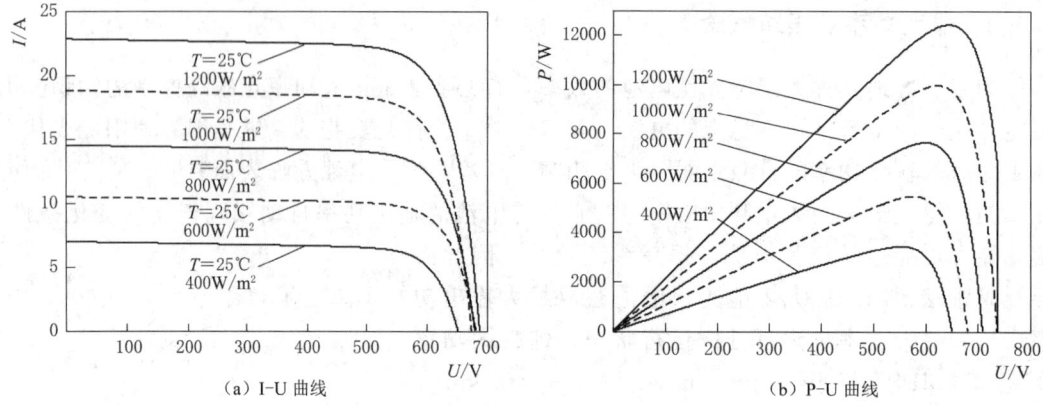

(a) I-U 曲线　　　　　　　　　　　(b) P-U 曲线

图 1.11　不同光照强度下光伏阵列的输出特性

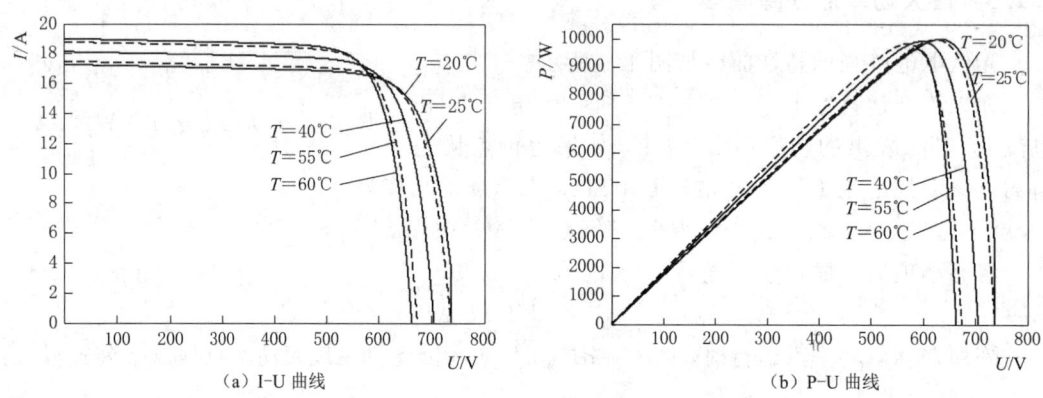

(a) I-U 曲线　　　　　　　　　　　(b) P-U 曲线

图 1.12　不同电池温度下光伏阵列的输出特性

变,其输出功率及最大功率点也相应改变。并且,光照强度变化主要影响阵列短路电流,而电池温度的变化主要影响开路电压。当光伏阵列的工作电压位于最大功率点电压 U_{max} 时,光伏阵列就会输出最大功率 P_{max}。

光伏电池输出改变存在两种情况:

(1) 假设光照和温度等外界条件不变化时,由于负载阻抗的变化,光伏输出电压和电流关系在同一条特性曲线上变动,此时电压和电流均发生变化。

(2) 当外界条件发生变化时,光伏输出电压和电流关系变成另一条特性曲线,光伏输出电压(或电流)有可能不变,而只是电流(或电压)发生变化。

因此,首先用 $U_k - U_{k-1}$ 来判断,其值等于 0 则表示输出特性不变或者已转移到另一条特性曲线上,此时由于电压保持不变,故只需检测电流变化即可判断功率变化方向。电流不变表示系统输出特性不变,此时维持占空比不变;电流增加表示系统工作点朝最大功率点方向移动,此时应增加占空比使得电流进一步增加,否则若电流降低则减小占空比。当 $U_k - U_{k-1} \neq 0$ 时,则可以利用 dP/dU 的情况来判断工作点落在最大功率点的左侧还是右侧,然后相应调整占空比的值。理论上,该方法最终可以在最大功率点处稳定运行,但是在数字处理上由于采样时间的存在,工作点可能会在最大功率点左右波动,采样时间越短,波动越小。

1.2.4 常用最大功率点跟踪方法

当日照强度和环境温度变化时,光伏电池输出电压和电流呈非线性变化关系,其输出功率也随之改变。而且,当光伏电池应用于不同负载时,由于光伏电池输出阻抗和负载阻抗不匹配,也使得光伏系统输出功率下降。目前解决这一问题的有效方法是在光伏电池输出端与负载之间加入开关变换电路,利用开关变换电路中阻抗的变化原理,使得负载的等效阻抗跟随光伏电池的输出阻抗,从而使得光伏电池输出功率最大。常用最大功率点跟踪方法有定电压跟踪法、扰动观测法、导纳增量法等。

1. 定电压跟踪法(Constant Voltage Tracking,CVT)

观察图 1.11 (b) 所示的特性曲线发现在一定的温度下,光照强度变化时,其最大功率点几乎在一条垂直线的两侧,即 P_{max} 大致对应于某一恒定电压。基于此,CVT 控制法的思想就是:将光伏阵列的输出电压恒定控制在 U_{max} 处,使阵列近似工作在最大功率点状态。实际控制中,仅需从生产厂商处获得数据 U_{max},并将工作电压钳定在 U_{max},将 MPPT 控制简化为稳压控制。

CVT 控制法的跟踪器制造及控制比较简单,易实现,造价低,可靠性高,系统工作电压具有良好的稳定性,比一般光伏系统可望多获得 20% 的电能。

但这种控制方式忽略了温度对阵列输出电压的影响,以常规的单晶硅光伏电池为例,当环境温度每升高 1℃ 时,其开路电压下降 0.35%~0.45%。这种控制方式并不是实质上的最大功率点跟踪,对于四季温度或者日温变化比较大的地区,CVT 控制法并不能完全地跟踪 P_{max},导致控制精度差,系统工作电压的设置对系统工作效率的影响较大。

为克服 CVT 控制法适应性差的缺点,可以采用手工调节的方式进行改进,即根据实际温度,手动设置相对应的 U_{max} 值,此种方法比较麻烦,结果相对粗糙。也可以通过微处理器离线查询数据表格的方式改进,事先将不同温度下的 U_{max} 值存储在 EPROM(可擦除可编程只读存储器)中,微处理器通过光伏阵列上的温度传感器获取电池温度,通过查表确定当前的 U_{max} 值。

由于 CVT 控制法良好的可靠性和稳定性,目前在光伏系统中仍被较多地采用,特别是在光伏水泵系统中,随着光伏系统控制技术的计算机及微处理器化,该方法逐渐被新方法所替代。

2. 扰动观测法(perturbation and observation,P&O)

扰动观测法也称登山法,是目前研究最多也是实现 MPPT 最常用的方法之一。其原理是:对光伏阵列的输出电压施加周期性的扰动,并检测输出功率值相对于前一周期的变化情况,如果功率增加了,则下一周期继续对电压施加相同方向的扰动,否则改变扰动的方向。扰动观测法算法流程如图 1.13 所示。

P&O 法具有控制思想简单、被测参数少、易实现等优点,与 CVT 控制法相比,它是一种真正的最大功率点跟踪。但此法最大的缺点是:在最大功率点处会有振荡现象,导致部分功率损失。因此,扰动步长的选择很重要,较小的步长能减小最大功率点处的振荡,但是会降低跟踪速度,无法适应迅速变化的环境,可能使光伏阵列长时间工作于低功率输出区。在非常低的太阳光辐射下，如日出和日落的时候，功率曲线变得非常平滑，这就使得找到最大功率值变得非常困难。并且，当外部环境发生较快变化时，程序在运行中会发生误判现象。

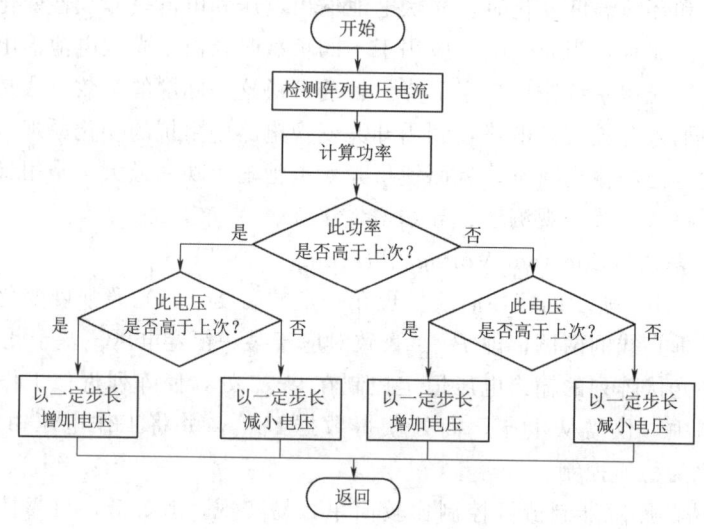

图1.13 扰动观测法算法流程

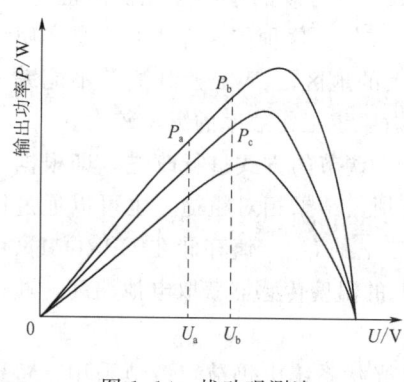

图1.14 扰动观测法

由于在一天中光照是时刻变化的，特别是早晚和有云的天气，因此对于光伏电池阵列来说，其P-U曲线是不停变化的。当光伏系统用扰动观测法进行MPPT时，假设系统已经工作在MPPT附近，如图1.14所示，当前工作电压记为U_a，光伏电池阵列输出功率记为P_a。当电压扰动方向往右移至U_b，如果日照没有变化，阵列输出功率为$P_b > P_a$，控制系统工作正确。但如果日照强度下降，则对应U_b的输出功率$P_c < P_a$，系统会误判电压扰动方向错误，从而控制工作电压往左移回U_a。如果日照持续下降，则可能出现控制系统不断误判，使工作点电压在U_a和U_b间来回移动振荡，而无法跟踪到阵列的最大功率点。对于这种由于日照强度影响造成的系统误判，可以通过加大扰动频率和减小扰动的步长来尽可能地消除。

3. 导纳增量法

导纳增量法是对扰动观测法的改进，它通过比较光伏阵列的瞬时电导和电导的变化率，并改变转换器的占空比，来实现最大功率点跟踪。光伏阵列的P-U曲线是个单峰值曲线，在最大功率点处有$\Delta P = dP/dU = 0$，若$\Delta P = dP/dU > 0$，工作点处于最大功率点左侧；若$\Delta P = dP/dU < 0$，工作点处于最大功率点右侧。

最大功率点处，以下公式成立：

$$\frac{dI}{dU} = -\frac{I}{U}$$

当 $\frac{dI}{dU} > -\frac{I}{U}$，光伏阵列工作于最大功率点左侧，此时应增大输出电压 U。

当 $\frac{dI}{dU} < -\frac{I}{U}$，光伏阵列工作于最大功率点右侧，此时应减小输出电压 U。

算法流程如图 1.15 所示。其中 U_{k-1} 和 I_{k-1} 分别为前一个采样点的光伏电池输出电压和电流，U_{ref} 和 ΔU 分别为参考电压和电压增量步长。

导纳增量法的优点是控制效果好，当外界环境变化时，能平稳地追踪光伏阵列输出电压的变化，控制稳定度高，与阵列的功率特性曲线及其参数无关。但其缺点是控制算法比较复杂，对控制系统要求较高，且检测精度和速度在一定程度上会影响跟踪的精度和速度。

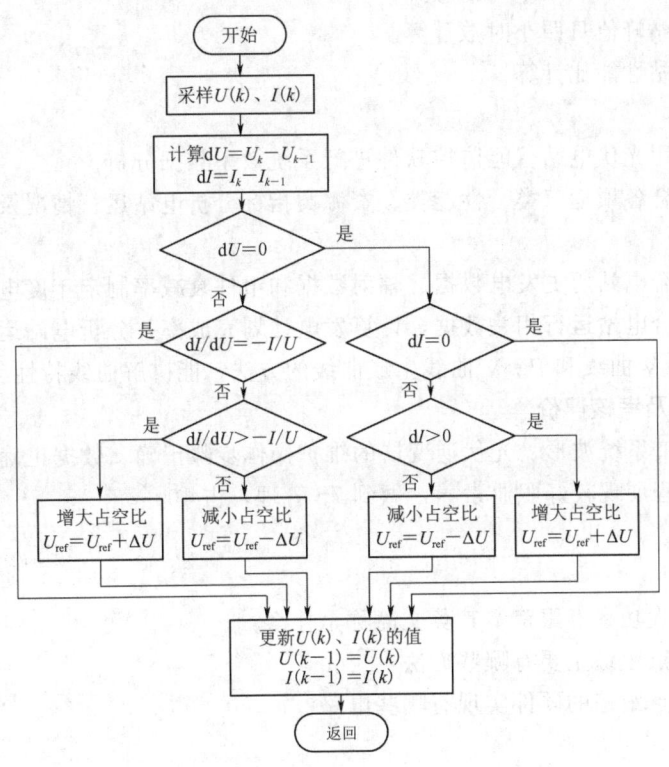

图 1.15 导纳增量法算法流程

MPPT 还有三点重心比较插值法、最优梯度法、模糊控制、神经网络控制等算法，这些方法在系统复杂度、实现难易、跟踪速度精度、硬件要求等方面各有优缺点，但控制的基本思想类似。

【任务实施】

1. 任务准备

职业技能等级证书设备平台 1 个、电脑主机 1 套、万用表 1 个、上电检查记录表 1 份、光伏运营记录表 1 份。

任务 1.2 相关实施图表

2. 任务内容及步骤

任务1：小容量光伏电站的特性测试

任务内容：完成小容量光伏电站组串的特性测试。

任务步骤：在完成光伏电池组串的调试接线的基础上，完成以下实训。

（1）智能万用表检测电压电流。

（2）采集数据，绘制I-V和P-V曲线。

（3）改变光照条件进行测试。

任务2：运营分析

任务内容：光伏组件最大功率点工况下光伏电站运营分析。

任务步骤：

（1）完成光伏等效利用小时数计算。

（2）完成电站峰值日照小时数计算。

（3）完成电站性能比计算。

3. 技能要求

（1）能够运用光伏电站智能监控软件进行系统效率数据分析。

（2）能够结合各项运营类、性能类、资源类指标分析电站运行情况及提出电站优化方案或建议。

（3）能够结合电站历史发电数据、辐射数据和组件衰减率制定年度电站发电量指标。

（4）能够结合电站运行相关数据，计算发电计划完成率并分析电站运营情况。

（5）掌握I-V曲线和P-V曲线生成曲线的方法，能讲解曲线特性。

4. 任务成果及考核评价

（1）测试逆变系统波形、光伏逆变器的维护操作步骤正确、数据正确，占90%。

（2）操作过程展现较好职业素养，做到7S管理，占10%。

【练习】

1. 什么是最大功率点跟踪？其英文简称是什么？

2. 最大功率点跟踪主要有哪些方法？

3. 最大功率点跟踪的硬件实现有哪些电路？

Project 1   Understand the Characteristic of Solar Photovoltaic Cells

Task 1.1   Performing Performance Testing of Solar Photovoltaic Cells

【Learning objectives】

Knowledge objective: To understand the types of solar photovoltaic cells and photovoltaic effect.

Ability objective: To be able to compare and analyze the characteristics of each type of solar photovoltaic cells.

Qualification objective: To cultivate the craftsmanship of striving for perfection and pursuing excellence.

Learning priority: Types of solar photovoltaic cells

Learning challenge: Characteristics of solar photovoltaic cells

【Task analysis】

Solar photovoltatic cells, also known as solar cells or photovoltaic cells, are power generation devices that directly convert light energy into electrical energy. Different solar photovoltaic cells have different properties and performance parameters. The only way to make better use of solar photovoltaic cells is to understand their types, characteristics, and performance parameters.

This task relies on the equipment platform of the National Vocational College Skills Competition. It corresponds to various work tasks of front-line positions in photovoltaic production testing, as well as the operation and maintenance of photovoltaic power stations. The task involves hands-on activities using different types of photovoltaic modules to complete the functional testing of solar photovoltaic cells, including insulation and withstand voltage testing and aging testing of solar photovoltaic modules.

【Knowledge learning】

1.1.1   Classification and performance of silicon-based solar photovoltaic cells

Silicon-based solar cells can be broadly classified as follows.

1. Monocrystalline silicon solar cells

Monocrystalline silicon solar cells were the first silicon-based solar cells to be developed and were mainly manufactured with monocrystalline silicon wafers. Compared with other types of cells, monocrystalline silicon cells feature the highest conversion efficiency. As raw materials, high-purity monocrystalline silicon wafers are mostly products withdrawn from semiconductor device processing in the electronics industry, which were previously available on the market in large quantities and at cheaper prices. Thus, monocrystalline silicon cells can be manufactured at relatively favourable costs.

Monocrystalline silicon cells used to hold the largest market share for a long time and only took second place behind polycrystalline silicon cells after 1998. The rapid development of the solar cells industry in recent years resulted in a shortage of high-purity polycrystalline silicon, as well as a slight increase in the market share of monocrystalline silicon cells in 2004. It can be expected that monocrystalline silicon solar cells will continue to grow and maintain a high market share in the coming years. The latest trend is that monocrystalline silicon cells will move towards ultra-thinness and high efficiency. In the near future, thinner monocrystalline silicon cells down to approximately 100 μm or even less are expected to come out. German research has demonstrated that monocrystalline silicon cells with a thickness of 40 μm can reach a conversion efficiency of 20%, making it possible to realize industrial production of ultra-thin monocrystalline silicon solar cells through improved production process, and achieve efficiencies comparable to those in laboratories.

The basic structure of monocrystalline silicon cells is mostly of N^+/P type, typically using P-type monocrystalline silicon wafers as the substrate, with a general resistivity range of $1-3\Omega \cdot cm$ and a typical thickness of $200-300\mu m$. Since most of the monocrystalline silicon material comes from scrap and defective products withdrawn from the semiconductor industry, some manufacturers use silicon wafers with a thickness of up to 0.5 - 0.7mm. As the quality of these silicon wafers fully meets the requirements of solar cells, they can be used to manufacture solar cells with good results: it is generally easy to achieve a conversion efficiency of more than 15%.

The production process of monocrystalline silicon cells involves, firstly, the production of surface textured structures, and secondly, the application of SiO_2 or TiO_2 films as antireflective coating, which is different from those used in polycrystalline silicon cells. The preparation of SiO_2 and TiO_2 films generally adopts the process of thermal oxidation or atmospheric pressure chemical vapor deposition.

Monocrystalline silicon solar cells (as shown in Figure 1.1) are mainly used in photovoltaic power stations, particularly in communication power stations, but also in aircraft power supplies, or in concentrating photovoltaic power generation systems. The optical, electrical and mechanical performance of monocrystalline silicon cells are uniform and consistent. The cells are mostly black or dark in color, making them particularly suitable for being sliced into small pieces to manufacture small consumer products, e. g. , solar garden lights.

Figure 1.1 Monocrystalline silicon solar cell

The conversion efficiency of monocrystalline silicon cells achieved in laboratories can reach up to 24.7%, a record created and maintained by the University of New South Wales, Australia. Representative commodities of monocrystalline silicon cells are mainly manufactured by manufacturers such as Shell Solar in the Netherlands, Isafoton in Spain, and Microsol in India. Monocrystalline silicon cells are currently the most efficient solar cell product other than gallium arsenide (GaAs) compound cells.

2. Polycrystalline silicon solar cells

During the production of polycrystalline silicon solar cells, high-purity silicon, as the raw material, is not drawn into single crystals, but melted and shaped into silicon ingots, these ingots are then sliced into thin wafers and subjected to similar cell processing as monocrystalline silicon. Polycrystalline silicon cells are easily recognizable: their silicon wafers are composed of a large number of crystalline regions of different sizes (as shown in Figure 1.2). The photovoltaic conversion mechanism in these crystalline regions (grains) is same as that of monocrystalline silicon cells. However because the silicon wafers consist of multiple grains of different sizes and orientations and because photoelectric conversion at the grain interface

Figure 1.2 Diagram of polycrystalline silicon solar cell

(grain boundary) is susceptible to interference, the conversion efficiency of polycrystalline silicon is relatively low. Moreover, the electrical, mechanical and optical performance of polycrystalline silicon is less consistent than that of monocrystalline silicon cells. The basic structure of polycrystalline silicon solar cells is of the N^+/P type, using P-type monocrystalline silicon wafers as the substrate, with a resistivity range of $0.5 - 2\Omega \cdot cm$ and a thickness of $220 - 300\mu m$. Some manufacturers are working to reduce the thickness to 180 μm or even thinner to save on the expensive high-purity silicon materials.

The production process of polycrystalline silicon solar cells is mainly characterized by the utilization of silicon nitride as an antireflective coating. The conversion efficiency of commercial cells is mostly 13%-15%. The main feature is that polycrystalline silicon cells are square wafers, leading to the highest fill rate during the production of cell modules. Thanks to the simple production process of polycrystalline silicon, allowing for massive production, polycrystalline silicon cells have the largest yield and market share.

The highest laboratory conversion efficiency of polycrystalline silicon cells reaches 20.3%, created by German research institutes, with products manufactured by Q-Cell, Motech, Suntech and other companies as representative commodities.

3. Amorphous silicon thin-film solar cells

Amorphous silicon cells are the most successful thin-film solar cells to date (as shown in Figure 1.3). Due to the current supply shortage of crystalline silicon cells, attempts have been made to supplement them with amorphous silicon cells. The main obstacle to the widespread use of amorphous silicon cells is light-induced degradation. The basic structure of amorphous silicon cells is of N-I-P type, mainly produced on conductive glass with SnO_2 (F) using the PECVD deposition process. Currently, amorphous silicon cells developed into 2 PN junctions or even 3 PN

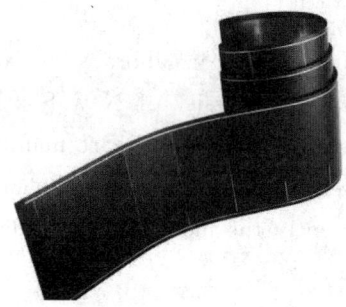

Figure 1.3 Thin-film solar cell

junctions are also available, using conductive glass or even stainless steel as a substrate materials. Commercial amorphous silicon cell products mostly have a stable efficiency of 5%-7%. Materials for amorphous silicon cells feature micrometer-level thicknesses. Amorphous silicon is a type of quasi-direct bandgap semiconductor. Thanks to its high absorption coefficient, amorphous silicon can save large quantities of high-purity silicon materials. The production process adopts chemical vapor deposition, using silane, borane, phosphorane, etc., as raw materials, and needs to be performed in vacuum conditions. Amorphous silicon cells generally dominate the consumer market, including applications in watches, calculators and toys. In addition, as translucent photovoltaic modules can be used for windows, doors or skylights, amorphous silicon cells are also well suited to be used as building materials.

1.1.2 Differences between monocrystalline and polycrystalline silicon cells

Both monocrystalline and polycrystalline silicon cells have a long lifetime and good stability. The average conversion efficiency of monocrystalline silicon cells is higher than that of polycrystalline silicon cells (by approximately 1%). However, from the perspective of effective occupied area, there is no significant difference between their average conversion efficiency. This is because monocrystalline silicon cells can only be made into a quasi-square shape (with four rounded corners). Thus, during the composition of solar cell modules (when closely connected to each other), partial areas remain unfilled. On the contrary, polycrystalline silicon cells are square, thus eliminating the problem of partially unfilled areas. Both monocrystalline and polycrystalline silicon cells have a long lifetime and good stability.

In terms of appearance, the four corners of monocrystalline silicon cells are rounded, without any pattern on the surface, while the four corners of polycrystalline silicon cells are square, with an ice flower-like pattern on the surface.

1.1.3 Photovoltaic effect

The energy converter for solar photovoltaic power generation is the solar cell, also known as photovoltaic cells. The principle of solar cell power generation is based on the photovoltaic effect of semiconductors. Photovoltaic cells operate based on the photovoltaic effect at the semiconductor PN junction exposed to sunlight. Therefore, photovoltaic cells are a type of energy converter that directly converts light energy into electrical energy. Its working principle is as follows. When sunlight hits the semiconductor surface, the valence electrons of atoms in the N- and P-regions inside the semiconductor are impacted by solar photons, acquire energy in excess of the band gap E_g through optical radiation, break away from covalent bonds, and excite from the valence band to the conduction band. In this way, many electron-hole pairs in a non-equilibrium state are generated inside the semiconductor material. These photo-excited electrons and holes either collide freely or are recombined in the semiconductor to return to equilibrium. The recombining process does not externally present a conductive effect, and results in energy loss within photovoltaic cells. Ideally, minority carriers among the photo-excited carriers move to the PN junction region, drift to the other side of the region through the traction of minority carriers by the PN junction, and externally form a photovoltaic electric field in the direction opposite to the potential energy barrier electric field of the PN junction. Once the external circuit is connected, electrical energy output is available. When a number of such small solar photovoltaic cell units are combined together via series and parallel connection, they constitute a photovoltaic module which can output electrical energy with sufficient power in the presence of solar energy. Generation process of the photovoltaic effect is shown in Figure 1.4.

Figure 1.5 graphically illustrates various effects of solar rays exposed to the surface of a photovoltaic cell.

In Figure 1.5, ①Refers to part of the rays reflected back on the surface of the cell. ②Refers to the rays absorbed immediately when they hit the surface of the cell to generate electron-hole pairs, most of which are short-wave rays with large absorption coefficients. However, such rays are quickly recombined and reduced before reaching the PN junction,

Project 1　Understand the Characteristic of Solar Photovoltaic Cells

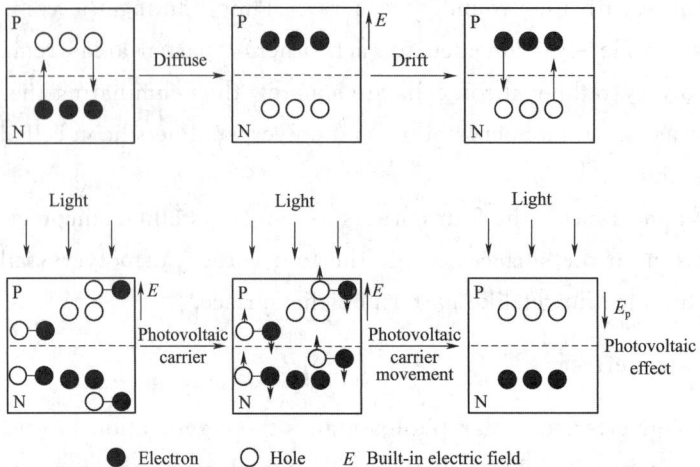

Figure 1.4　Generation process of photovoltaic effect

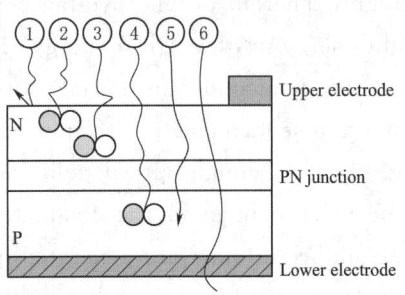

Figure 1.5　Light exposure of photovoltaic cells

so they do not contribute to the generation of photovoltaic electromotive force. ③ Refers to the portion of rays absorbed near the PN junction to generate electron-hole pairs. These are useful rays that enable the photovoltaic cell to generate electricity efficiently. These photovoltaic non-equilibrium minority carriers generate photovoltaic electromotive force under the drift effect specific to the PN junction. ④Refers to the rays that penetrate deep into the cell and are absorbed only at a distance from the PN junction. Such rays are similar to rays ②: although they can generate electron-hole pairs, they are recombined before reaching the PN junction, and only a small minority can generate photovoltaic electromotive force. ⑤Refers to the portion of rays that are absorbed by the cell but cannot generate electron-hole pairs due to limited energy. Their energy can only heat up the photovoltaic cell and increase the temperature. ⑥Refers to the small portion of rays not absorbed by the cell and transmit through it.

It can be seen that the principal rays that can generate photovoltaic electromotive force are Rays③. Thus, its proportion should be increased as much as possible to improve the photoelectric conversion efficiency of photovoltaic cells. The so-called photoelectric conversion efficiency refers to the percentage of the maximum output electric power generated by a photovoltaic cell exposed to light relative to the total optical radiation power incident on the geometric area of the cell exposed to light.

Figure 1.6 illustrates how Rays ③ generate an electrical current on an external circuit when the upper and lower electrodes of the photovoltaic cell are connected to a load circuit.

As mentioned above, thanks to the presence of these photovoltaic minority carriers close to the PN junction and under the drift effect of the PN junction, electrons in the N-region stay in the N-region and holes flow to the P-region, while holes in the P-region stay in the P-region and electrons flow to the N-region, thus constituting photovoltaic electric field. Seen from the external circuit, the P-region is positive, and the N-region is negative. Once the load is connected, electrons in the N-region pass through the external circuit load to the P-region to form an electron flow; electrons enter the P-region, combine with holes, and return to neutrality, until electron-hole pairs are separated from another photon. The direction of the conventional current is the same as the flow of positive charges and opposite to the flow of negative charges. Thus, when the photovoltaic cell is connected to the load, the electrical current flows out of the P-region, passes through the load, and returns to the cell from the N-region.

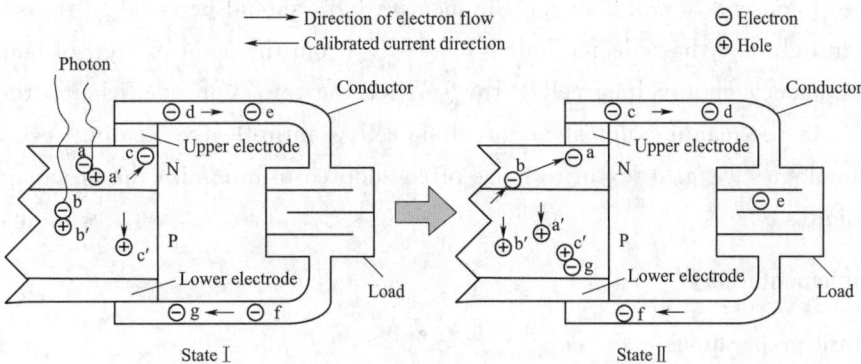

Figure 1.6　Schematic diagram of electrical current generated by photovoltaic cells

Semiconductor materials generate different numbers of electron-hole pairs at different temperatures and under different optical radiation. The PN junction is at the heart of the working principle of a photovoltaic cell, made based on the photovoltaic effect principle. The structure of photovoltaic cells can be constructed into P^+/N type or N^+/P type, where the first symbol, "P^+/N", indicates the conductivity type of the semiconductor material of the photovoltaic cell's front light layer, while the second symbol, "N^+/P", indicates the conductivity type of the semiconductor material of the photovoltaic cell's back substrate. The electrical performance of photovoltaic cells is related to the properties of semiconductor materials used to manufacture the cells. In the presence of solar exposure, the polarity of the output voltage of photovoltaic cells is positive for P-type side electrodes and negative for N-type side electrodes.

Solar rays exposed to the surface of photovoltaic cells have various wavelengths, and the energy of the rays of different wavelengths and their depth of penetration in photovoltaic cells vary accordingly. That is to say, the absorption of light energy by photovoltaic cells varies with the wavelength of the rays. To be specific, photovoltaic cells have a larger absorption coefficient for short waves and a smaller absorption coefficient for long waves. In terms of solar rays incident inside cell materials, only rays whose photon energy satisfies $\varepsilon \geqslant E_g$ can excite electron-hole pairs, while those rays whose photon energy meets $\varepsilon \geqslant E_g$ can only allow photovoltaic cells to heat themselves, rather than excite electron-hole pairs. In addition, part of the generated electron-hole pairs are prematurely recombined and reduced, without playing a role in photovoltaic currents, resulting in a loss of some light energy. Therefore, it is impossible to convert all solar energy into electrical energy.

When a beam of solar rays hits the surface of an object, part of the rays penetrate the surface of the object into its inside, and the other part are reflected back by the surface of the object. The ratio of the intensity of the reflected light to the intensity of the incident light is called the reflection coefficient ρ, and the ratio of the intensity of the transmitted light to the intensity of the incident light is called the transmission coefficient τ. According to the law of conservation of energy, the incident light should be equal to the sum of the transmitted light and the reflected light: $\rho + \tau = 1$. From the point of view of manufacturing high-efficiency photovoltaic cells, the smaller the reflection coefficient, the better. Therefore, in the manufacture of photovoltaic cells, antireflective coating technology or other technologies (e.g., texturing) are often adopted to minimize the proportion of the reflected light.

【Task implementation】

Ⅰ. Task preparations

1 competition equipment platform, 1 multimeter, 1 wire stripping plier, a number of MC4 connector kits, 1 insulation resistance meter, 1 thermal imager, 1 copy of record sheet for power-up inspection, and 1 copy of performance test form for photovoltaic modules.

Ⅱ. Task content and procedures

(ⅰ) Task 1: Insulation and withstand voltage testing of solar photovoltaic modules

Task content: Complete insulation and withstand voltage testing of the photovoltaic module using the insulation resistance meter

Task procedures:

(1) Complete insulation and withstand voltage testing between the negative electrode of the photovoltaic module and the ground.

(2) Complete insulation and withstand voltage testing between the positive electrode of the photovoltaic module and the ground.

(3) Complete insulation and withstand voltage testing between photovoltaic electrodes and the ground when the positive and negative electrodes of the photovoltaic module are short-circuited.

(ⅱ) Task 2: Aging testing of solar photovoltaic modules

Task content: Complete aging performance testing of the photovoltaic module.

Task 1.1 Related implementation charts

Project 1 Understand the Characteristic of Solar Photovoltaic Cells

Task procedures:

(1) Use the thermal imager to identify the source of hazards in the photovoltaic module.

(2) Complete electrical performance testing of the photovoltaic module under aging and decay conditions.

(3) Complete insulation and withstand voltage testing of the aging photovoltaic module using the insulation resistance meter.

III. Skill requirements

(1) During insulation and withstand voltage testing and aging performance testing of the solar photovoltaic module, relevant personnel performing testing are allowed to enter the test site, provided they comply with safety practices. All other personnel are prohibited from entering the site.

(2) During insulation and withstand voltage testing measurement, insulating glovesand other protective equipment must be worn.

(3) During insulation and withstand voltage testing measurement, the insulation resistance meter should be placed flat. Turn the handle at a constant speed of 120 r/min, so that the watch hand gradually rises until a stable value appears. Then, read the insulation resistance value. It is strictly prohibited to measure the photovoltaic module while it is operating.

(4) When using the thermal imager, the influence of direct sunlight, building reflection and other disturbing factors should be avoided.

IV. Task results, appraisal and evaluation

(1) Both procedures and data of insulation and withstand voltage testing and aging performance testing of the solar photovoltaic module are correct (accounting for 90%).

(2) The operator exhibits good professional quality during the operation process and follows 7S management model (accounting for 10%) (The 7S methodology encompasses Sort, Set in Order, Shine, Standardize, Sustain, and Save, which are implemented in the organization and maintenance of laboratory equipment and facilities during experimental processes).

【Exercises】

1. What are polycrystalline silicon and monocrystalline silicon? What are the main differences between polycrystalline and monocrystalline silicon?

2. How can you distinguish between monocrystalline and polycrystalline silicon cells?

3. What is photovoltaic effect?

Task 1.2　Commission Methods for Tracking the Maximum Power of Photovoltaic Modules

【Learning objectives】

Knowledge objective: To master the concept and principles of photovoltaic maximum power point tracking, as well as commonly used methods for photovoltaic maximum power point tracking

Ability objective: To be able to commission commonly used methods for photovoltaic maximum power point tracking; to be able to perform maintenance data analysis and operation analysis of photovoltaic power stations

Qualification objective: To cultivate the professional spirit of focusing on seriousness and striving for perfection

Learning priority: Concept and principles of photovoltaic maximum power point tracking

Learning challenge: Maintenance data analysis and operation analysis under the working condition of photovoltaic maximum power point tracking

【Task analysis】

Maximum power point tracking in the photovoltaic system is an effective way to ensure the system obtains maximum power and to improve its efficiency. Many methods are available for maximum power point tracking, and each method has its own advantages. Thus, the most appropriate method should be chosen according to the actual situation of the system to achieve better efficiency in solar cells.

This task relies on the equipment platform of the vocational skills certificate, corresponds to various work contents of operation positions at tracking photovoltaic power stations, and involves various hands-on tasks of completing maintenance data analysis and operation analysis under the maximum power working condition of photovoltaic modules in photovoltaic power stations.

【Knowledge learning】

1.2.1 Solar cell model

Photovoltaic cells are a type of photoelectric conversion device, which can convert light energy into electrical energy via photovoltaic cells in the wavelength range of solar radiation between 0.2 and 1.25 μm. Taking photovoltaic cells made of semiconductor materials with a band gap of 2 eV as an example, among solar radiation energy, only light energy with a wavelength of less than 0.62 μm can excite the generation of an electrical current, and the energy at this wavelength only accounts for 58% of the total solar radiation energy. Considering other photoelectric losses, the conversion efficiency of photovoltaic cells made of such materials is only half of 58% at most. Theoretical analysis shows that, from the point of view of photoelectric conversion efficiency, the best material for manufacturing photovoltaic cells is semiconductors with a band gap of 1.5 eV, while all materials with a band gap of 1.1 – 2.0 eV can be used to manufacture high-efficiency photovoltaic cells.

According to the analysis of photoelectric properties of silicon-based photovoltaic cells, in theory, the maximum photoelectric conversion efficiency of such cells is 22%, while the efficiency of conventional silicon-based photovoltaic cells is only about 12%, and that of high-efficiency silicon-based photovoltaic cells is only about 18%. The reasons are as follows. Silicon cannot absorb 100% of light due to the presence of certain refraction and reflection. Light energy entering the silicon crystal is also subject to silicon band gap limitations, resulting in a loss of part of the light energy as heat. This loss, together with the composite loss of electron-hole pairs and the series and parallel resistance loss, leads to a further decline in the photoelectric conversion efficiency of silicon-based photovoltaic cells.

Photovoltaic cells are divided into 2DR type and 2CR type according to their substrate materials. In terms of the production of 2DR-type silicon photovoltaic cells, P-type silicon is used as the substrate (i. e., adding boron, gallium and other trivalent elements into intrinsic materials). Then, phosphorus is diffused on the substrate to form the N-type structure as the light receiving surface. In terms of the production of 2CR-type silicon photovoltaic cells, N-type silicon is used as the substrate (i. e., adding phosphorus, arsenic and other pentavalent elements into intrinsic materials). Then, boron is diffused on the substrate to form the P-type structure as the light receiving surface. Following the formation of the PN junction and various subsequent processes, electrodes are produced and output on the substrate and the photosensitive surface, respectively, coated with silicon dioxide as a protective film, thus leading to the formation of a photovoltaic cell, as shown in Figure 1.7.

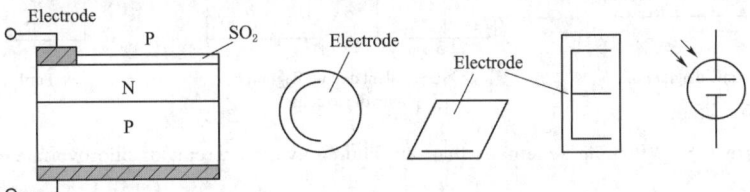

Figure 1.7 Schematic diagram of structure and symbols of silicon photovoltaic cells

The output electrodes on the light receiving surface of silicon photovoltaic cells are made into a comb-tooth shape generally and a "π" shape occasionally. The purpose is to facilitate light transmission and reduce series resistance. The photosensitive surface is coated with a transparent layer of silicon dioxide, for the moisture-proofing on the one hand, and for the antireflective effect against the incident light on the other hand to increase light absorption.

The main function of solar cells is to convert optical signals into electrical signals without the addition of any bias. The working principle is shown in Figure 1.8 (a), where the electrical current flowing through the load is

$$I_L = I_P - I_D = I_P - I_S(e^{eU/kT} - 1) \tag{1.1}$$

In the formula, I_P is the photovoltaic current, A; I_D is the reverse current of the PN junction, A; U is the voltage at both ends of the PN junction (including applied voltage or photovoltaic voltage), V; I_S is the reverse saturation current of the PN junction, A; e is the electron charge $e = 1.602176634 \times 10^{-19}$ C; k is the Boltzmann constant $k = 1.380649 \times 10^{-23}$ J/K; T is the absolute temperature, K.

Review of characteristic curves of photovoltaic cells

According to the above formula, the equivalent circuit of the photovoltaic cell can be drawn, as shown in Figure 1.8 (b). In the figure, I_P is the constant current source, which flows a current proportional to the incident illumination; VD is the equivalent diode; R_{sh} is the dynamic junction resistance; $R_{sh} = dU/dI$. In linear measurements, the larger the value of R_{sh} (currently reaching up to $10^8 - 10^{10}$ Ω/cm), the better. During calculation, the circuit can be viewed as an open circuit. R_S is the series resistance, which is generally negligible. During calculation, C_j (junction capacitance) direct current can be ignored; R_L is the load resistance; I_L is the current flowing through the load resistance R_L. With further simplification, Figure 1.8 (b) can be drawn as an equivalent circuit as shown in Figure 1.8 (c).

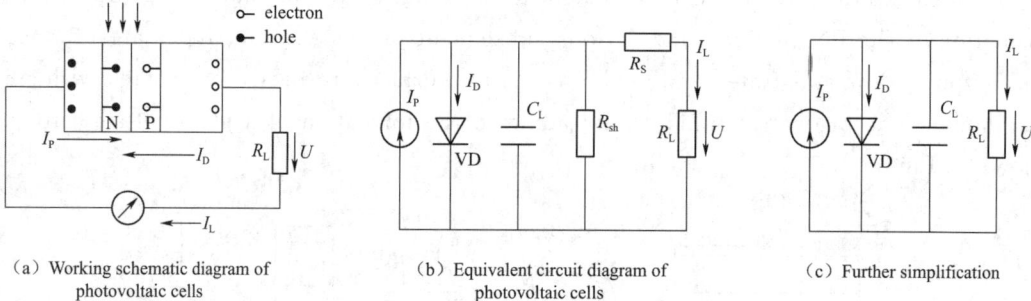

(a) Working schematic diagram of photovoltaic cells

(b) Equivalent circuit diagram of photovoltaic cells

(c) Further simplification

Figure 1.8 Working schematic diagram and equivalent circuit of photovoltaic cells

1.2.2 Concept of Maximum Power Point Tracking

To achieve better efficiency of solar cells, it is necessary to understand the principles of maximum power point tracking control. Solar cells are an extremely unstable power source in nature, and their output power tends to vary. The reason is that when solar cells work, their output power changes with the intensity of solar radiation, clear or cloudy skies, and the ambient temperature (the surface temperature of the cell array). To achieve the maximum efficiency of energy utilization, it is necessary to make the output power of the cells automatically track the changing conditions of the climate, so that light energy can be converted into electrical energy as much as possible to improve the efficiency of the system. Therefore, it is necessary to track the sun in real-time, so that solar cells operate at the maximum power or the value at the vicinity of the maximum power, i. e., MPPT (Maximum Power Point Tracking) control.

1.2.3 Principle of Maximum Power Point Tracking

The characteristic curve of the photovoltaic cell array is shown in Figure 1.9.

If the array operates at any of the voltages U and currents I of the I-U curve, the power generated is $P=UI$. If the operating point is shifted from the previous point to current $I+\Delta I$ and voltage $U+\Delta U$, the new power is

$$P+\Delta P=(U+\Delta U)(I+\Delta I)$$

After ignoring the minor terms, the formula is simplified as:

$$\Delta P=\Delta UI+U\Delta I$$

When the array operates at the peak power point, $\Delta P = dP/dU \approx 0$. Therefore, at the maximum power point, the following formula holds:

$$\frac{dU}{dI}=-\frac{U}{I}$$

Increase the operating voltage as long as dP/dU is positive, or as long as higher power is available.

If the measured dP/dU is negative, decrease the operating voltage; if dP/dU is within the preset dead zone around zero, the voltage remains unchanged.

As shown in Figure 1.10, when the photovoltaic array operates at point D to the right of the maximum power point voltage, the voltage value can be decreased (because point D is far from the maximum power point), i. e., the power is increased. When the photovoltaic array operates to the left of the maximum power point voltage, the voltage value can be adjusted upward. Under given operating conditions, the solar cell array must operate at a certain voltage value corresponding to the peak power point.

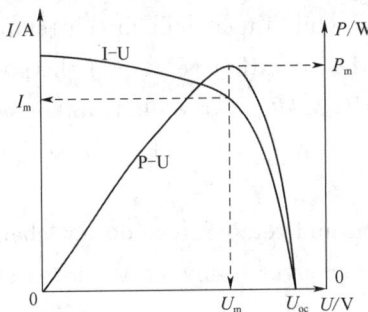

Figure 1.9 Characteristic curve of photovoltaic cell array

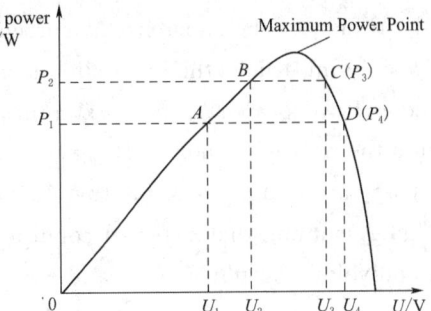

Figure 1.10 Maximum power tracking control

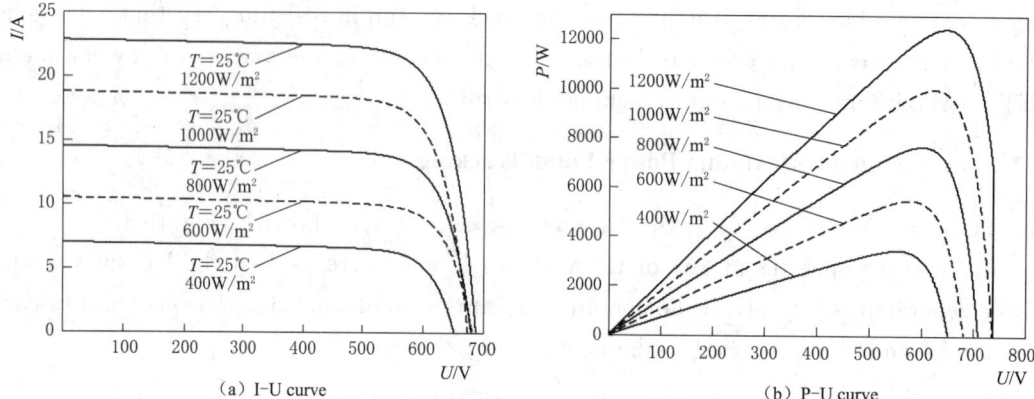

Figure 1.11 Output characteristics of photovoltaic array at different light intensities

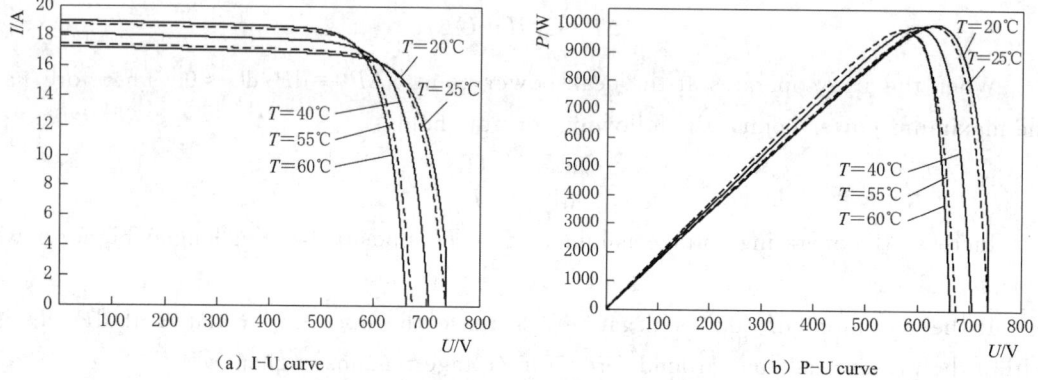

Figure 1.12 Output characteristics of photovoltaic array at different cell temperatures

Figures 1.11 and 1.12 show the output characteristic curves (I-U and P-U curves) of the photovoltaic array, respectively, when light intensity and cell temperature change.

From Figures 1.11 and 1.12, it can be seen that when external natural conditions change, the output characteristics of the photovoltaic array, as well as the output power and maximum power point, change accordingly. Moreover, the change in light intensity mainly influences the short-circuit current of the array, while the change in cell temperature mainly influences the open-circuit voltage. When the operating voltage of the photovoltaic array is located at the maximum power point voltage U_{max}, the photovoltaic array outputs the maximum power P_{max}.

There are two cases of photovoltaic cell output change:

(1) Assuming that external conditions such as light and temperature do not change, the photovoltaic output voltage and current relationship changes following the same characteristic curvedue to the change in the load impedance. At this time both the voltage and current change.

(2) When external conditions change, the photovoltaic output voltage and current relationship follows another characteristic curve. The photovoltaic output voltage (or cur-

rent) may remain unchanged, and only the current (or voltage) changes.

Therefore, first of all, $U_k - U_{k-1}$ is used for judgment. If its value is equal to 0, it means output characteristics remain unchanged or have transferred to another characteristic curve. At this time, as the voltage remains unchanged, only current change needs to be detected to judge the direction of power change. If the current remains unchanged, it means output characteristics of the system remain unchanged; at this time, the duty cycle should be maintained. If the current increases, it means the operating point of the system is shifted towards the direction of the maximum power point; at this time, the duty cycle should be increased to further increase the current.. Otherwise, if the current is decreased, the duty cycle should be reduced. When $U_k - U_{k-1} \neq 0$, the case of dP/dU can be used to determine whether the operating point falls to the left or right of the maximum power point, and then adjust the value of the duty cycle accordingly. Theoretically, this method can eventually lead to stable operation at the maximum power point. However, in terms of digital processing, due to the presence of sampling time, the operating point may fluctuate around the maximum power point, and the shorter the sampling time, the smaller the fluctuation.

1.2.4 Commonly used methods for maximum power tracking

As we know, when sunlight intensity and ambient temperature change, the photovoltaic cell output voltage and current change non-linearly, and the output power changes accordingly. Moreover, when photovoltaic cells are applied to different loads, the mismatch between the photovoltaic cell output impedance and the load impedance also makes the photovoltaic system output power decrease. Currently, the effective way to solve this problem is to add a switching conversion circuit between the output of photovoltaic cells and the load, and follow the principle of the switching conversion circuit on the change of impedance. This circuit adjusts the equivalent impedance of the load to match the output impedance of the photovoltaic cells, thereby maximizing the photovoltaic cell output power. Commonly used methods for maximum power tracking include the constant voltage tracking method, the perturbation and observation method, the incremental conductance method, etc.

1. Constant Voltage Tracking (CVT) method

Observation of the characteristic curve shown in Figure 1.11 (b) shows that, at a certain temperature, the maximum power point is nearly aligned with a constant voltage as light intensity changes, i. e. , P_{max} roughly corresponds to a certain constant voltage. Based on this, the idea of the CVT control method is as follow: Constantly control the output voltage of the photovoltaic array at U_{max}, so that the array operates approximately at the maximum power point state. In practical control, only U_{max} is the data that needs to be obtained from the manufacturer, and the operating voltage should be maintained at

U_{max} to simplify MPPT control to voltage stabilization control.

The CVT control method for tracker manufacture and control is relatively simple. Its advantages also include easy implementation, low cost, high reliability, good stability of the system operating voltage, and the potential to obtain additional 20% of electrical energy compared to general photovoltaic systems.

However, this control method ignores the influence of temperature on the array output voltage. Taking conventional monocrystalline silicon photovoltaic cells as an example, when ambient temperature rises by 1℃, the open-circuit voltage decreases by approximately 0.35%–0.45%. This control method does not constitute maximum power tracking, and for regions where change in temperatures of the four seasons or daily temperatures is relatively large, CVT control method cannot fully track P_{max}, resulting in poor control accuracy. Besides, the setting of the system operating voltage has a great impact on system working efficiency.

To overcome the shortcoming of poor adaptability of CVT control, improvement can be made via manual adjustment, i.e., manually setting the U_{max} value according to the actual temperature. Yet, this manual method is relatively cumbersome and imprecise. Improvement can also be achieved by using a microprocessor to query data sheets offline. The U_{max} values at different temperatures are stored in EPROM beforehand; the microprocessor obtains the cell temperature via the temperature sensor on the photovoltaic array, and determines the current U_{max} value by referring to the sheet.

Thanks to its good reliability and stability, the CVT Control method is still frequently adopted in photovoltaic systems, photovoltaic water pumping systems in particular. Yet, with advances in computer and microprocessor technologies of photovoltaic system control, this method is gradually replaced by more advanced techniques.

2. Perturbation and observation method

The perturbation and observation (P&O) method, also known as the hill climbing method, is one of the most researched and commonly used methods for realizing MPPT. The principle is as follows: Apply a periodic perturbation to the output voltage of the photovoltaic array and detect the change in the output power value compared to the previous cycle; if the power increases, continue to apply the perturbation in the same direction to the voltage in the next cycle; otherwise, change the direction of the perturbation. The flowchart of the algorithm is shown in Figure 1.13.

The P&O method has many advantages: simple control idea, few parameters to be measured, easy implementation, etc. It realizes real maximum power point tracking compared to the CVT control method. However, the biggest disadvantage of this method is the occurrence of oscillation at the maximum power point, resulting in partial power loss. Therefore, the choice of the perturbation step size is important. A smaller step size can reduce the oscillation at the maximum power point, but will reduce the tracking

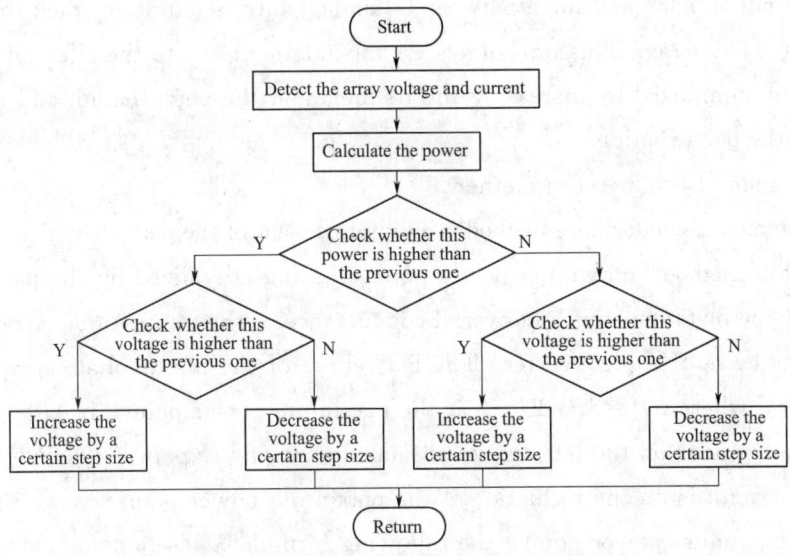

Figure 1.13   Algorithm flowchart of perturbation and observation method

speed. This prevents the tracking from adapting to the rapidly changing environment, which may cause the photovoltaic array to operate in the low power output region for a long time. At extremely low solar radiation, e.g., sunrise and sunset, the power curve becomes very smooth, making it difficult to find the maximum power value. Moreover, when the external environment changes rapidly, the program can misjudge the conditions during operation.

Light is changing all the time during the day, especially in the morning, evening, and cloudy days. Thus, for the photovoltaic cell array, the P-U curve is constantly changing. Assuming that the photovoltaic system performs MPPT with the perturbation and observation method, and that the system is already operating near the MPPT, as shown in Figure 1.14, the current operating voltage is expressed as U_a, and the output power of the photovoltaic cell array is expressed as P_a. When the direction of voltage perturbation is shifted rightwards to U_b, if there is no change in sunlight, the array output power is $P_b > P_a$, and the control system operates correctly. However, if sunlight intensity decreases, the output power corresponding to U_b is $P_c < P_a$. At this time, the system will misjudge that the voltage perturbation direction is wrong, and thus control the operating voltage leftwards to return to U_a. If sunlight intensity continues to decrease, there may be a constant misjudgment by the control system, causing the operating point

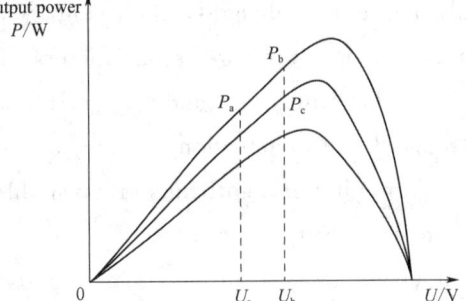

Figure 1.14   Perturbation and observation method

voltage to oscillate back and forth between U_a and U_b, thus failing to track the maximum power point of the array. This type of system misjudgment due to the effect of sunlight intensity can be minimized by increasing the frequency of the perturbation and reducing the step size of the perturbation.

3. Incremental conductance method

The incremental conductance method is an improvement of the perturbation and observation method. In this method, maximum power point tracking is realized by comparing the rate of change of the instantaneous and overall conductance of the photovoltaic array and changing the duty cycle of the converter. The P-U curve of the photovoltaic array is a single peaked curve, where $\Delta P = dP/dU = 0$ at the maximum power point; if $\Delta P = dP/dU > 0$, the operating point is on the left side of the maximum power point; if $\Delta P = dP/dU < 0$, the operating point is on the right side of the maximum power point.

At the maximum power point, the following formula holds:

$$\frac{dI}{dU} = -\frac{I}{U}$$

When $\frac{dI}{dU} > -\frac{I}{U}$, the photovoltaic array operates on the left side of the maximum power point. At this time, the output voltage U should be increased.

When $\frac{dI}{dU} < -\frac{I}{U}$, the photovoltaic array operates on the right side of the maximum power point. At this time, the output voltage U should be reduced.

The flowchart of the algorithm is shown in Figure 1.15. In this chart, U_{k-1} and I_{k-1} refer to the output voltage and current of the photovoltaic cell at the previous sampling point, respectively; U_{ref} and ΔU refer to the reference voltage and the voltage incremental step size, respectively.

The advantages of the incremental conductance method include good control effect, smooth tracking of changes in the photovoltaic array's output voltage even when the external environment changes, high control stability, and independence of the array's power characteristic curve and its parameters. However, it has several disadvantages: complex control algorithm, demanding control system, and adverse effects on tracking accuracy and speed due to detection accuracy and speed.

A number of algorithms are available for MPPT, includingbarycentric interpolation, gradient descent, fuzzy control, and neural network control. These methods have their own advantages and disadvantages in terms of system complexity, ease of implementation, tracking speed and accuracy, hardware requirements, etc., but their underlying control principle is similar.

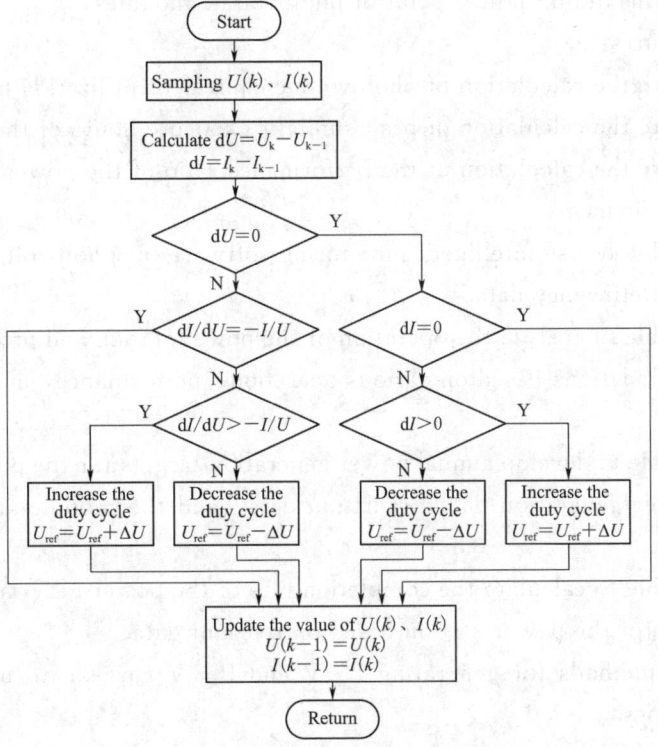

Figure 1.15 Algorithm flowchart of incremental conductance method

【Task implementation】

I . Task preparations

1 equipment platform of the vocational skills certificate, 1 set of computer mainframe, 1multimeter, 1 copy of record sheet for power-up inspection, and 1 copy of record sheet for photovoltaic operation.

II . Task content and procedures

(i) Task 1: Perform property testing of small-capacity photovoltaic power stations

Task content: Complete property testing of photovoltaic modules in small-capacity photovoltaic power stations

Task 1.2 Related implementation charts

Task procedures: Complete the following practical training procedures after the completion of commissioning and wiring of photovoltaic modules:

(1) Determine the voltage and current by using the intelligent multimeter.

(2) Collect data and draw I - V and P - V curves;

(3) Change light conditions for testing.

(ii) Task 2: Operation analysis

Task content: Operation analysis of the photovoltaic power station under the working conditions of the maximum power point of photovoltaic modules.

Task procedures:

(1) Complete the calculation of photovoltaic equivalent utilization hours;

(2) Complete the calculation of peak sunlight exposure hours of the power station;

(3) Complete the calculation of the performance ratio of the power station.

III. Skill requirements

(1) To be able to use intelligent monitoring software for photovoltaic power stations to analyze system efficiency data.

(2) To be able to analyze the operation of the power station and propose optimization plans or recommendations based on various operation, performance, and resource indicators.

(3) To be able to develop annual power generation targets for the power station based on historical power generation data, radiation data, and the module attenuation rate of the power station.

(4) To be able to calculate the completion rate of the power generation plan and analyze the operation of the power station based on relevant data.

(5) Master methods for generating I - V and P - V curves; to be able to explain curve characteristics.

IV. Task results, appraisal and evaluation

(1) Both procedures and data of testing contra variant system waveforms and maintaining and operating photovoltaic inverters are correct (accounting for 90%).

(2) The operator exhibits good professional quality during the operation process and follows 7S management model (accounting for 10%).

【Exercises】

1. What is maximum power tracking? What is its abbreviation in English?

2. What are the main methods for maximum power tracking?

3. What circuits are available for hardware implementation of maximum power tracking?

项目 2　跟踪计算光伏发电系统发电量

任务 2.1　计算光伏发电年发电量

【学习目标】

　　知识目标：了解我国太阳能资源分区；掌握辐射量的内涵。
　　能力目标：能正确计算光伏发电量。
　　素质目标：培养节约能源意识。
　　重点：太阳辐射量的内涵。
　　难点：光伏发电量的计算过程。

【任务分析】

　　能够根据不同地区的太阳能资源数据，换算相应的辐照度，并计算一定容量光伏发电系统的发电量。
　　依托全国职业院校技能大赛设备平台，在监控组态中完成光伏发电量计算程序编写，并搭建监控界面实时监控光伏发电量的值和曲线。

【知识学习】

2.1.1　太阳能资源计算

　　对于太阳能利用来说，了解国内各地的太阳能资源状况是十分必要的。但是，由于太阳辐射测量站点稀疏，仅靠实测数据远不能满足各方面的需求。国际上通行的解决办法是借助现有的太阳辐射测量站点的实测数据，与一些同日射有关且广泛观测的其他气象要素建立统计关系，然后再将这些定量关系应用到无日射观测的地区，计算出相应的日射数据来。
　　应当指出，影响日射的气象要素有很多，重要的有云量、云状、大气透明度等。此外，海拔、地理纬度、季节、时刻等因素的影响也不容忽视。云量、云状和大气透明度可以说是变化多端，难以计量。大多数计算方法也都是限定于晴天，实用价值受到限制。下面所讨论的方法仅限于多年平均状况，即气候学意义上的年或月平均曝辐量 H。
　　计算总日射曝辐量的方法种类繁多，若用通式可表达为

$$H = H_0 f(s_1, n) \tag{2.1}$$

式中，H_0 为基础总日射曝辐量值；$f(s_1, n)$ 为表征天空遮蔽程度的函数；s_1 为日照百分率；n 为云量。

式（2.1）中，s_1 和 n 可任选一，也可兼用；H_0 的选择则可分成以下三种：

（1）天文辐射。天文辐射是指大气上界的日射。由于大气上界已不存在空气，因此就没有散射，实际上只剩下直接日射，且只随纬度和时间的不同而有变化。由于天文辐射对不同海拔没有响应，因此不利于用来解决像我国这样地区辽阔、地势起伏明显的情况。

（2）晴天辐射。为了获得此值，需要将各太阳辐射测量站点的多年实测资料逐日地点绘到以日期为横坐标的图上，最后绘出全部点的外廓线，再求出响应时段（月）内，外廓线下的面积，即月内的晴天曝辐量。这样做不仅工作量大，且外廓线所代表的往往是大气处于极端透明情况下的曝辐量，其值偏高。另外，由于实测站点稀少且分布不均，因此这样得出的结果无法兼顾到不同海拔和纬度的情况。

（3）理想大气中的总日射曝辐量。该曝辐量具有如下优点：①可以通过计算精确求出，无须整理有限站点的大量原始实测数据；②可以得到不同海拔和纬度的分布值。

所谓理想大气，又称干洁大气，顾名思义，就其成分而言，除了没有水汽和气溶胶外，与一般大气无异。这样就可以把大气中的不确定因素排除，从而可以计算出大气固定成分对日射的散射和吸收。

至于 $f(s_1, n)$ 的具体表达式，国内外的大量研究现已明确，用日照百分率的效果优于使用云量。因为日照百分率毕竟是连续记录的结果，而云量靠的是目测，且一日内仅有 4 次观测，其中还包括 1 次夜间的记录（其对日射而言，毫无意义）。目前公认的最佳表达式的形式为

$$H = H_0(a + bs_1) \tag{2.2}$$

式中：a 与 b 为回归系数，可根据实测数据用最小二乘法求出；其他符号意义同前。

需要指出的是，太阳能资源相关工作并不是一项做了一次就可以一劳永逸的事。近年来的研究发现，随着空气污染的加重，各地太阳辐射普遍呈现下降趋势。近年来国外普遍使用气象卫星提供的资料开展太阳能资源的研究，这是今后应当努力的方向。

2.1.2　年发电量计算

光伏发电站的设计规范

光伏发电系统的年发电量是光伏发电系统设计必须包含的一个内容，特别是在进行可研报告编制时，就要作详细的讲解，可扫一扫二维码详细了解光伏电站的设计规范要求。

光伏发电系统的年发电量计算公式如下：

年发电量＝辐照度×系统效率×组件的衰减系数×组件功率（kW·h），其中辐照度单位为 kW·h/m²，组件功率单位为 kW。

若只有辐射量（MJ/m²）数据，则可以先转换为辐照度（kW·h/m²）数据，单位转换公式为 1MJ＝1000000W·s＝0.278 kW·h。

节能指标可以按照以下公式计算：

二氧化碳排放量＝年发电量×0.997（t）；

二氧化硫排放量＝年发电量×0.03（t）；

氮氧化物排放量＝年发电量×0.015（t）。

【例】 某地全年辐照度为 1455 kW·h/m²，光伏发电系统的容量为 400W，系统转换效率 82%，首年衰减 2.1%，首年之后光伏电池组件每年衰减 0.65%，计算此光伏发电系统 25 年总共发电量是多少，总共减少排放的二氧化碳、二氧化硫和氮氧化物分别为多少？

解：首年发电量＝1455×0.82×(1－0.021)×0.4＝467.22 （kW·h）；

第 2 年发电量＝1455×0.82×(1－0.021－0.0065)×0.4＝464.12 （kW·h）；

第 3 年发电量＝1455×0.82×(1－0.021－2×0.0065)×0.4＝461.01 （kW·h）；

第 4 年发电量＝1455×0.82×(1－0.021－3×0.0065)×0.4＝457.91 （kW·h）；

第 5 年发电量＝1455×0.82×(1－0.021－4×0.0065)×0.4＝454.81 （kW·h）；

以此类推可得各年的发电量

……

第 25 年发电量＝1455×0.82×(1－0.021－24×0.0065)×0.4＝392.77 （kW·h）；

故 25 年总共发电量＝467.22＋464.12＋461.01＋…＋392.77＝10749.83 （kW·h）；

二氧化碳排放量＝10749.83×0.997＝10717.58 （t）；

二氧化硫排放量＝10749.83×0.03＝322.5 （t）；

氮氧化物排放量＝10749.83×0.015＝161.25 （t）

【任务实施】

1. 任务准备

竞赛设备平台 1 个、上电检查记录表 1 份、光伏发电系统发电量记录表 1 份、万用表 1 个。

2. 任务内容及步骤

任务：光伏发电系统发电量计算与实时显示

任务内容：完成光伏发电系统的发电量实时显示界面设计。

任务步骤：

(1) 在工控机力控组态中完成年发量的程序编写。

(2) 搭建 25 年光伏发电系统发电量实时显示文本和曲线。

(3) 完成系统上电前的检查，并填写上电检查记录表。

(4) 系统上电运行，调节改变系统辐照度，填写光伏发电系统发电量记录表。

任务 2.1 相关实施表格

3. 技能要求

(1) 正确使用万用表挡位进行不同参数的测量，操作规范，无短路、无错挡测量。

(2) 对设备运行数据观察到位，记录正确，记录参数数据包含数值和单位。

(3) 监控界面布局美观，元件尺寸大小适当，颜色配置协调，功能控件齐全，元件标注和名称正确，无漏项。

4. 任务成果及考核评价

(1) 系统调试正确且成功并网、数据界面运行数据正确，能记录运行数据，占 90%。

(2) 操作过程展现较好职业素养，做到 7S 管理，占 10%。

【练习】

1. 计算总日射曝辐量的通式中 H_0 可分成几种?

2. 某地全年辐照度为 1400kW·h/m², 光伏发电系统的容量为 800W, 系统转率 85%, 首年衰减 2.2%, 首年之后光伏电池组件每年衰减 0.75%, 计算此光伏发电系统 20 年总共发电量是多少, 总共减少排放的二氧化碳、二氧化硫和氮氧化物分别为多少?

任务 2.2　调试光伏组件跟踪太阳方法

【学习目标】

知识目标: 掌握太阳能光伏电池组件跟踪太阳的方式。
能力目标: 能调试、维护太阳能光伏电池组件跟踪太阳。
素质目标: 培养良好的团队协作意识; 培养精益求精的工匠精神。
重点: 光伏电站跟踪程序的调试。
难点: 光伏电站跟踪程序的维护。

【任务分析】

为提高太阳能的利用效率, 采用太阳自动跟踪系统进行光线追踪, 相比固定式系统, 能够增加 30% 以上的功率输出, 调试跟踪系统时需要对光线采集信号进行判断, 并执行相应的跟踪动作, 相反方向应设互锁程序。

本任务依托全国职业院校技能大赛设备平台, 对接光伏电池方阵的设计、维护岗位工作内容, 完成光伏电站跟踪程序的设计与调试、光伏逐日系统维护实操内容。

【知识学习】

2.2.1　跟踪方式

太阳能是已知的最原始的能源, 干净、可再生、丰富, 而且分布范围广, 具有非常广阔的利用前景。但太阳能利用效率低, 这一问题一直影响和阻碍着太阳能技术的普及, 如何提高太阳能利用装置的效率, 始终是人们关心的话题, 太阳自动跟踪系统(如图 2.1 所示)的设计为解决这一问题提供了新途径, 从而大幅提高了太阳能的利用效率。

采用太阳自动跟踪系统比固定式系统能增加 30% 以上的功率输出。

跟踪太阳的方法可概括为两种方式: 光电跟踪和根据视日运动轨迹跟踪。光电跟踪是由光电传感器件根据入射光线的强弱变化产生反馈信号到计算机, 计算机运行程序调整采光板的角度实现对太阳的跟踪(如图 2.1 所示)。光电跟踪的优点是灵敏度高, 结构设计较为方便; 缺点是受天气的影响很大, 如果在稍长时间段里出现乌云遮住太阳的情况, 会导致跟踪装置无法跟踪太阳, 甚至引起执行机构的误动作。

视日运动轨迹跟踪是由控制器根据相关的公式和参数计算出白天太阳的位置, 再将高

项目 2 跟踪计算光伏发电系统发电量

度角和方位角转化成相应的脉冲发给驱动器，驱动电动机使太阳能光伏电池板随着太阳轨迹的变化而变化，从而获得最大的太阳能。

按被控制量对控制量是否产生反馈，常见的太阳自动跟踪系统也可划分为三类：闭环控制、开环控制、混合环控制。

1. 开环控制

开环控制要先确定一个初始位置，根据某时刻太阳相对位置的差值，计算出电动机转过该差值所需的脉冲数。该跟踪控制方式又分为定时跟踪和程序跟踪方式。这种跟踪方式控制简单、易于实现，但当电动机失步或堵转时，跟踪就不准确。

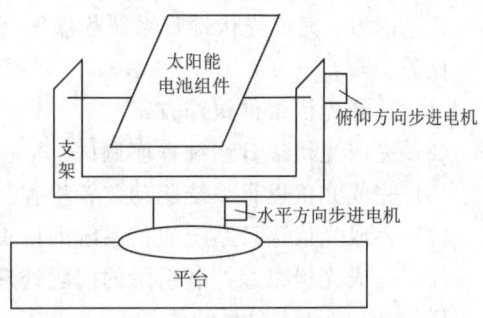

图 2.1 太阳自动跟踪系统

（1）定时跟踪。根据太阳在天空中每分钟的运动角度，计算出太阳能光伏电池板每分钟应转动的角度，从而确定出电动机的转速，使得太阳能光伏电池板根据太阳的位置而相应变动。这种跟踪可以看作对太阳运动的时角进行跟踪，也可称为时角跟踪。该方法的优点是电路简单，但由于不同季节日出日落的时间不同，会降低该系统调整的精确度。

（2）程序跟踪。这种控制方式需要与计算机或处理器相结合，首先利用一套公式算出在给定时间太阳的位置，再计算出跟踪装置被要求的位置，最后通过计算机或处理器去控制电机转动装置，实现对太阳高度角和方位角的跟踪。

2. 闭环控制

闭环控制方式就是使用一个传感器来测定入射太阳光线和系统光轴间的偏差，当偏差超过一个阈值时，通过电动机驱动机械部分转动，减小偏差直到使太阳光线与系统光轴重新平行，实现对太阳高度角和方位角的跟踪。闭环系统控制原理如图 2.2 所示。常用的传感器有太阳能光电池、光敏电阻、光电管、一维 PSD 和二维 PSD 光电位置传感器、光电角度探测器等。闭环控制能够克服开环的缺陷，但需要位置检测信号。

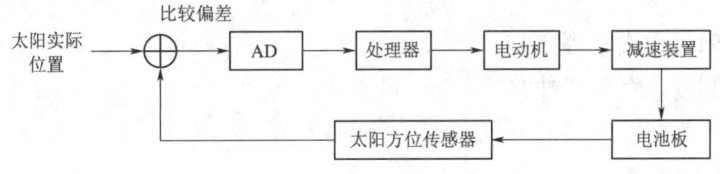

图 2.2 闭环系统控制原理

【任务实施】

1. 任务准备

竞赛设备平台 1 个、一字螺丝刀 1 把、十字螺丝刀 1 把、万用表 1 把、剥线钳 1 把、双芯屏蔽线 10m、上电检查记录表 1 份、光伏跟踪调试记录表 1 份。

2. 任务内容及步骤

任务 1：光伏电站跟踪程序调试

任务 2.2 相关实施图表

任务内容：完成光伏逐日系统程序编写与调试。

任务步骤：

（1）选择光伏组件跟踪方案。

（2）完成光伏逐日系统程序调试。

（3）完成光伏逐日系统驱动装置检查。

（4）完成光伏逐日系统通信系统的检查。

（5）完成光伏跟踪控制系统的问题处理。

任务 2：光伏逐日系统维护

任务内容：完成光伏逐日系统的设计与维护。

任务步骤：

（1）完成光伏逐日系统的故障处理。

（2）完成光伏逐日系统的跟踪范围、精度检验。

（3）完成光伏逐日系统的防雷和保护接地的检查和问题处理。

3. 技能要求

（1）能够进行光伏逐日系统的调试。

（2）能够进行光伏逐日系统的驱动装置检查和问题处理。

（3）能够进行光伏逐日系统的通信系统的检查和故障处理。

（4）能够进行光伏逐日系统的跟踪范围、精度检验和问题处理。

（5）能够进行光伏逐日系统的防雷和保护接地的完好、可靠性检查和问题处理。

4. 任务成果及考核评价

（1）光伏电站跟踪程序的调试、光伏逐日系统维护操作步骤正确、数据正确，占 90%。

（2）操作过程展现较好职业素养，做到 7S 管理，占 10%。

【练习】

1. 跟踪太阳的方式有哪些？
2. 光电探测方式有哪几种？

Project 2 Tracking and Calculating Power Generation Capacity of Photovoltaic Power Generation Systems

Task 2.1 Calculating Annual Photovoltaic Power Generation Capacity

【Learning objectives】

Knowledge objective: To understand China's solar resource zoning; to master the connotation of radiant exposure

Ability objective: To be able to correctly calculate photovoltaic power generation capacity

Qualification objective: To cultivate the awareness of energy conservation

Learning priority: Connotation of solar radiation

Learning challenge: Calculation process of photovoltaic power generation capacity

【Task analysis】

To be able to convert corresponding irradiance according to solar resource data of different regions; calculate the amount of electricity generated by a photovoltaic power generation system with certain capacity.

This task relies on the equipment platform of the National Vocational College Skills Competition and involves the following tasks: programming the calculation of photovoltaic power generation capacity via supervisory control and data acquisition; constructing a monitoring interface to monitor the value and curve of photovoltaic power generation capacity in real time.

【Knowledge learning】

2.1.1 Calculation of solar resources

For the utilization of solar energy, it is necessary to understand the status of solar resources in various Chinese regions. However, due to the sparseness of solar radiation measurement sites, measured data alone are far from satisfying various needs. The internationally recognized solution is to use measured data obtained from existing insolation sites to establish statistical relationships with other meteorological elements that are related to insolation and widely observed. These quantitative relationships are then applied to regions where insolation observation is not available, allowing for the calculation of corresponding insolation data.

It should be noted that many meteorological elements have an influence on insolation, including the following important ones: cloud amount, cloud form, atmospheric transparency, etc. In addition, the influence of altitude, geographic latitude, season, time, and other factors should not be ignored. Cloud amount, cloud form, and atmospheric transparency are, so to say, variable and difficult to measure. Therefore, most calculation methods are only applicable for clear days with limited practical value. The method discussed below is limited to multi-year averages, i.e., annual or monthly average radiant exposure H in the climatological sense.

Various methods are available for calculating total insolation exposure, which can be expressed by the following general formula:

$$H = H_0 f(s_1, n) \tag{2.1}$$

where H_0 is base total insolation exposure; $f(s_1, n)$ is a function of the degree of sky obscuration; s_1 is insolation percentage; n refers to cloud amount.

In formula (2.1), either s_1 or n, or both of them, can be used, while the following three options are available for H_0.

(1) Astronomical radiation. Astronomical radiation refers to insolation at the upper atmospheric boundary. Since the air is very thin at the upper atmospheric boundary, there is no scattering. In fact, there is only direct insolation, changing with latitude and time. Since astronomical radiation does not respond to different altitudes, it is not favorable for use in China with vast areas and markedly undulating terrains.

(2) Clear-sky radiation. To obtain this value, it is necessary to plot the multi-year measured data of each insolation site day by day on a map with date as the abscissa, then plot the outer contour of all points, and finally determine the area under the outer contour in the response period (month), i.e., the amount of clear-sky radiation in the month. This not only leads to considerable work, but also results in a high value, as the outer contour line tends to represent the exposure of the atmosphere in extreme transparency. In addition, due to the scarcity and uneven distribution of actual measurement sites, results obtained using this method cannot take into account different altitudes and latitudes.

(3) Total insolation exposure in an ideal atmosphere. This exposure has the following advantages: ①The exposure can be determined accurately by calculation, eliminating the need to collate a large amount of raw measured data from a limited number of sites; ②Distribution values can be obtained for different altitudes and latitudes.

The so-called ideal atmosphere, also known as dry clean air, is, as its name implies, no different from the general atmosphere in terms of its composition, except for the absence of water vapor and aerosols. This allows uncertainties in the atmosphere to be eliminated and the scattering and absorption of insolation by fixed components of the atmosphere to be calculated.

As for the specific expression of $f(s_1, n)$, a large number of studies locally and internationally have now made it clear that insolation percentage is superior to cloud amount in terms of their using effect. This is not difficult to understand, because the insolation percentage is, after all, the result of a continuous record, whereas the application of cloud amount depends on visual observation, and there are only four observations in a day, including a night observation (which is meaningless for insolation). The currently recognized formula of the best expression is

$$H = H_0(a + bs_1) \qquad (2.2)$$

In formula (2.2), a and b are regression coefficients, which can be determined by the least squares method based on measured data.

It should be noted that the utilization of solar resources is not a thing that can be done once and for all. Research in recent years has revealed that, with the aggravation of air pollution, there is a general downward trend in solar radiation in various regions. In recent years, data provided by meteorological satellites are generally used internationally to carry out research on solar resources. This is a direction that should be worked on in the future.

Code for design of photovoltaic power station

2.1.2 Calculation of annual power generation capacity

The annual power generation capacity of photovoltaic power generation systems is a content that must be included in the design of photovoltaic power generation systems. In particular, detailed explanation is required during the preparation of the feasibility study report. Detailed design specification requirements of photovoltaic power stations are available by scanning the QR code.

The formula for calculating the annual power generation capacity of photovoltaic power generation systems is as follows:

Annual power generation capacity = Irradiance × System efficiency × Attenuation coefficient of modules × Module power (kW·h), where irradiance is expressed in kW·h/m² and module power is expressed in kW.

If only radiant exposure (MJ/m²) is available, it can be converted to irradiance (kW·h/m²) first by the following unit conversion formula: 1MJ = 1,000,000 W·s = 0.278 kW·h.

Energy saving indicators can be calculated by the following formula:

Carbon dioxide emissions = Annual power generation capacity × 0.997 (tonnes);
Sulphur dioxide emissions = Annual power generation capacity × 0.03 (tonnes);
Nitrogen oxide emissions = Annual power generation capacity × 0.015 (tonnes).

Example: Assuming the following conditions: The annual irradiance of a region is $1455 kW \cdot h/m^2$; the capacity of the photovoltaic power generation system is 400 W; the conversion efficiency of the system is 82%; the attenuation in the first year is 2.1%; the attenuation of the photovoltaic cell module is 0.65% in the second and following years. Please calculate the total power generation capacity of the photovoltaic power generation system in 25 years. What are the total reduced emissions of carbon dioxide, sulphur dioxide, and nitrogen oxides, respectively?

Solution: Power generation capacity in the 1st year $= 1455 \times 0.82 \times (1 - 0.021) \times 0.4 = 467.22 \ kW \cdot h$;

Power generation capacity in the 2nd year $= 1455 \times 0.82 \times (1 - 0.021 - 0.0065) \times 0.4 = 464.12 \ kW \cdot h$;

Power generation capacity in the 3rd year $= 1455 \times 0.82 \times (1 - 0.021 - 2 \times 0.0065) \times 0.4 = 461.01 \ kW \cdot h$;

Power generation capacity in the 4th year $= 1455 \times 0.82 \times (1 - 0.021 - 3 \times 0.0065) \times 0.4 = 457.91 \ kW \cdot h$;

Power generation capacity in the 5th year $= 1455 \times 0.82 \times (1 - 0.021 - 4 \times 0.0065) \times 0.4 = 454.81 \ kW \cdot h$;

By analogy, power generation capacity in each year can be calculated.

...

Power generation capacity in the 25th year $= 1455 \times 0.82 \times (1 - 0.021 - 24 \times 0.0065) \times 0.4 = 392.77 \ kW \cdot h$;

Therefore, total power generation capacity in 25 years $= 467.22 + 464.12 + 461.01 + \ldots + 392.77 = 10749.83 kW \cdot h$;

Carbon dioxide emissions reduced $= 10749.83 \times 0.997 = 10717.58$ (tonnes);

Sulphur dioxide emissions reduced $= 10749.83 \times 0.03 = 322.5$ (tonnes);

Nitrogen oxide emissions reduced $= 10749.83 \times 0.015 = 161.25$ (tonnes).

【Task implementation】

I. Task preparations

1 competition equipment platform, 1 copy of record sheet for power-up inspection, and 1 copy of record sheet for power generation capacity of photovoltaic power generation systems, and a multimeter

Task 2.1 Related implementation charts

II. Task content and procedures

Task 1: Calculation of power generation capacity and real-time display of photovoltaic power generation systems

Task content: Design the real-time display interface for the power generation capacity of photovoltaic power generation systems.

Task procedures:

(1) Complete the programming of annual power generation capacity via supervisory control and data acquisition.

(2) Construct the real-time display text and curve of 25-year power generation capacity of the photovoltaic power generation system.

(3) Complete system power-up inspection and fill in the record sheet for power-up inspection.

(4) Perform system power-up operation, adjust the system irradiance, and fill in the record sheet for power generation capacity of the photovoltaic power generation system.

Ⅲ. Skill requirements

(1) Correctly use the multimeter gears for the measurement of different parameters; observe operation specifications; avoid short circuit or wrong gear measurement.

(2) Properly observe equipment operation data; make correct records; the recorded parameter data include numerical values and units.

(3) The monitoring interface layout is aesthetic; the dimensions of the components are appropriate; the color configuration is coordinated; the functional controls are complete; the components are correctly labeled and named; there are no missing items.

Ⅳ. Task results, appraisal and evaluation

(1) The system is correctly commissioned and successfully connected to the grid; the data interface runs correctly; operation data is recorded (accounting for 90%).

(2) The operator exhibits good professional quality during the operation process and follows 7S management model (accounting for 10%).

【Exercises】

1. What are the options available for H_0 in the general formula for calculating total insolation exposure?

2. Assuming the following conditions: The annual irradiance of a region is 1400 kW · h/m^2; the capacity of the photovoltaic power generation system is 800 W; the conversion efficiency of the system is 85%; the attenuation in the first year is 2.2%; the attenuation of the photovoltaic cell module is 0.75% in the second and following years. Please calculate the total power generation capacity of the photovoltaic power generation system in 20 years. What are the total reduced emissions of carbon dioxide, sulphur dioxide, and nitrogen oxides, respectively?

Task 2.2　Commission Methods of Tracking the Sun by Photovoltaic Modules

【Learning objectives】

Knowledge objective: To master the way solar photovoltaic cell modules track the sun

Ability objective: To be able to commission and maintain solar photovoltaic cell modules tracking the sun

Qualification objective: To cultivate a good sense of teamwork and the craftsmanship of striving for perfection

Learning priority: Commissioning of photovoltaic power station tracking programs

Learning challenge: Maintenance of photovoltaic power station tracking programs

【Task analysis】

To improve the utilization efficiency of solar energy, the application of automatic solar tracking systems for light tracking can increase power output by more than 30%, compared with fixed systems. While commissioning tracking systems, it is necessary to determine light collection signals, perform corresponding tracking actions, and set up interlocking procedures in the opposite direction.

This task relies on the equipment platform of the National Vocational College Skills Competition. It corresponds to various tasks of design and maintenance positions at photovoltaic power stations, and involves various hands-on activities of completing the design and commissioning of photovoltaic power station tracking programs and the maintenance of photovoltaic day-by-day systems.

【Knowledge learning】

2.2.1　Tracking methods

Solar energy is the most primitive energy known. It is clean, renewable, abundant, and widely distributed, with very broad prospects for use. However, the low utilization efficiency of solar energy has been affecting and hindering the popularity of solar energy technology. How to improve the efficiency of solar energy devices has always been a topic of concern. The design of automatic solar tracking systems (as shown in Figure 2.1) provides a new way of solving this problem, thus significantly increasing the utilization efficiency of solar energy.

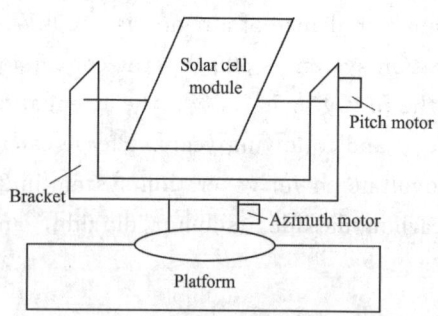

Figure 2.1　Automatic solar tracking system

The application of automatic solar tracking systems can increase power output by more than 30% compared with fixed systems.

Methods of tracking the sun can be summarized in two ways: photoelectric tracking and tracking based on apparent motions of the sun. For photoelectric tracking, photoelectric sensor devices generate feedback signals to the computer based on various intensities of the incident light, and the computer runs programs to adjust the angle of the light collecting panel to track the sun (as shown in Figure

2.1). The advantages of photoelectric tracking are high sensitivity and convenient structural design. The disadvantage is that it is greatly affected by the weather: If clouds cover the sun for an extended period of time, it will make the tracking device fail to track the sun, and even cause the actuator's malfunction.

For tracking based on apparent motions of the sun, the controller calculates the position of the sun during the day according to relevant formulas and parameters, and converts solar elevation angles and azimuth angles into corresponding pulses to be sent to the driver, the controller then drives the motor to adjust the solar cell panel with the change of the sun's trajectory, so as to obtain maximum solar energy.

According to whether the controlled variable generates feedback to the control variable, common automatic solar tracking systems can also be divided into three categories: closed-loop control, open-loop control, and hybrid loop control.

1. Open-loop control

For open-loop control, an initial position should be determined first. Based on the difference of the relative position of the sun at a certain moment, the number of pulses required for the motor to adjust for this difference is calculated. This tracking control method is subdivided into timed tracking and programmed tracking. This tracking control is simple and easy to implement. However, when missed steps or a locked rotor occur in the motor, the tracking is inaccurate.

(1) Timed tracking. According to the angle of the sun's motion in the sky every minute, the angle of rotation of the solar cell panel every minute is calculated to determine the rotation speed of the motor, so that the solar cell panel moves with the position of the sun accordingly. This tracking can be viewed as tracking the hour angle of the sun's motion, thus also known as hour-angle tracking. The advantage of this method is having simple circuits. However, as the sun rises and sets at different times in different seasons, it reduces the adjustment accuracy of the system.

(2) Programed tracking. This control method needs to be used in combination with a computer or processor. Firstly, a set of formulas are used to calculate the position of the sun at a given time. Then, the desired position of the tracking device is calculated. Finally, the computer or processor controls the motor rotation device to track the sun's elevation and azimuth angle.

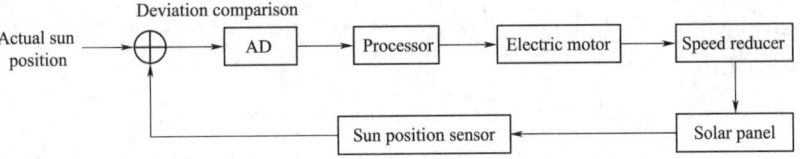

Figure 2.2 Control principle of closed-loop systems

2. Closed-loop control

For closed-loop control, a sensor is used to determine the deviation between the incident sun rays and the optical axis of the system. When the deviation exceeds a threshold value, the mechanical part is rotated by an electric motor to reduce the deviation until the sun rays are re-parallel to the optical axis of the system, so as to achieve tracking of the sun's elevation angle and azimuth angle. The control principle is shown in Figure 2.2. Commonly used sensors include photovoltaic cells, photoresistors, phototubes, one-dimensional PSD and two-dimensional PSD photoelectric position sensors, and photoelectric angle detectors. Closed-loop control can overcome the shortcomings of open-loop control, but requires position detection signals.

【Task implementation】

Ⅰ. Task preparations

1 competition equipment platform, 1 slotted screwdriver, 1philips screwdriver, 1 multimeter, 1 wire stripping plier, 10 meters of double-core shielded wires, 1 copy of record sheet for power-up inspection, and 1 copy of record sheet for photovoltaic tracking commissioning.

Task 2.2 Related implementation charts

Ⅱ. Task content and procedures

(ⅰ) Task 1: Commissioning of photovoltaic power station tracking programs

Task content: Complete the writing and commissioning of photovoltaic tracking control system programs

Task procedures:

(1) Select a proper photovoltaic module tracking plan.

(2) Complete the commissioning of photovoltaic tracking control system programs.

(3) Complete the inspection of the driving device of the photovoltaic tracking control system.

(4) Complete the inspection of the communication system of the photovoltaic tracking control system.

(5) Complete the troubleshooting of the photovoltaic tracking control system.

(ⅱ) Task 2: Maintenance of photovoltaic day-by-day systems

Task content: Complete the design and maintenance of the photovoltaic day-by-day system

Task procedures:

(1) Complete the troubleshooting of the photovoltaic tracking control system.

(2) Complete the inspection of the tracking range and accuracy of the photovoltaic tracking control system.

(3) Complete the inspection and troubleshooting of the lightning protection and pro-

tective earthing of the photovoltaic tracking control system.

III. Skill requirements

(1) To be able to carry out the commissioning of the photovoltaic tracking control system.

(2) To be able to carry out the inspection and troubleshooting of the driving device of the photovoltaic tracking control system.

(3) To be able to carry out the inspection and troubleshooting of the communication system of the photovoltaic tracking control system.

(4) To be able to carry out the inspection and troubleshooting of the tracking range and accuracy of the photovoltaic tracking control system.

(5) To be able to carry out the inspection and troubleshooting of the integrity and reliability of lightning protection and protective earthing of the photovoltaic tracking control system.

IV. Task results, appraisal and evaluation

(1) Both procedures and data of commissioning photovoltaic power station tracking programs and maintaining and operating the photovoltaic day-by-day system are correct (accounting for 90%).

(2) The operator exhibits good professional quality during the operation process and follows 7S management model (accounting for 10%).

【Exercises】

1. What are the tracking methods for tracking the sun?
2. What are photoelectric detection methods?

项目3 设计太阳能光伏发电系统

任务3.1 设计独立光伏发电系统

【学习目标】

知识目标：掌握独立光伏发电系统的设计需求。
能力目标：能设计独立光伏发电系统的光伏电池方阵、蓄电池组和负载容量；能完成监控系统和汇流箱通信调试。
素质目标：培养对我国光伏行业的自豪感和使命感。
重点：独立光伏发电系统的设计要点。
难点：独立光伏发电系统监控系统和通信调试。

【任务分析】

独立光伏发电系统的组成因负载的不同而不同，其中光伏电池是不可缺少部分，蓄电池是常见部分，必须根据负载对电能的需求情况来设计光伏发电系统的容量和串并联方案。

本任务依托全国职业院校技能大赛设备平台，对接光伏发电系统的设计岗位工作内容，以部分设计装调为任务，学习光伏发电系统的设计实操，包括智能离网微逆变系统触摸屏界面设计、汇流箱通信装调实操内容。

【知识学习】

3.1.1 设计总述

光伏发电系统的设计包括两方面：容量设计和硬件设计。

光伏发电系统容量设计的主要目的就是要计算出系统在全年内能够可靠工作所需的太阳能光伏电池组件和蓄电池的数量。同时要注意协调系统工作的最大可靠性和系统成本两者之间的关系，在满足系统工作的最大可靠性基础上尽量减少系统成本。

光伏发电系统硬件设计的主要目的是根据实际情况选择合适的硬件设备，包括太阳能光伏电池组件的选型、支架的设计、逆变器的选择、电缆的选择、控制测量系统的设计、防雷设计和配电系统设计等。在进行系统设计的时候需要综合考虑系统的软件和硬件两个方面。

在进行光伏发电系统的设计之前,需要了解并获取一些计算和选择必需的基本数据:光伏发电系统现场的地理位置,包括地点、纬度、经度和海拔;该地区的气象资料,包括逐月的太阳能总辐射量、直接辐射量以及散射辐射量,年平均气温和最高、最低气温,最长连续阴雨天数,最大风速以及冰雹、降雪等特殊气象情况等。

独立光伏发电系统是指太阳能光伏发电不与电网连接的发电方式,典型特征为需要用蓄电池来存储能量。独立光伏发电系统主要用于家庭、村级太阳能光伏电站、光伏照明系统、通信基站、太阳能水泵等;在具备风力发电和小水电的地区还可以组成混合发电系统,如风力发电与太阳能发电互补系统等。

如图 3.1 所示,独立光伏发电系统的组成包含以下几部分:光伏电池方阵、控制器、逆变器、蓄电池、交流负载、直流负载。系统各部分功能如下:

(1) 光伏电池方阵:光伏电池是组成太阳能光伏发电系统最基本的单位。但单体光伏电池发出的电能很小,工作电压为 $0.45 \sim 0.5V$,工作电流为 $20 \sim 25 mA/cm^2$,在大多数情况下很难满足实际应用的需要。一般都将电池组经串联或并联组成太阳能光伏电池组件,以提高其输出电压和电流来满足负载工作要求。

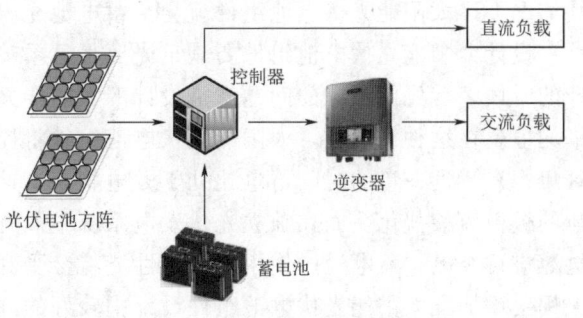

图 3.1 独立光伏发电系统

(2) 控制器:控制器是光伏发电系统的核心部件之一,主要用于实现整套系统的充、放电管理,可以防止蓄电池过充电和过放电。太阳能光伏阵列发出的直流电能经过控制器对蓄电池充电,在蓄电池未充满时,控制器的作用是最大限度地对蓄电池充电;当蓄电池被充满时,控制太阳能充电,使蓄电池处于浮充状态。当蓄电池放电至接近蓄电池过放电电压时,控制器将发出蓄电池电量不足报警并切断蓄电池的放电回路,以保护蓄电池。随着光伏产业的发展,控制器的功能越来越强大,有将传统的控制器、逆变器以及监测系统集成的趋势。

(3) 逆变器:将直流电转换为交流电的设备。对逆变器的基本要求如下:

1) 能输出一个电压稳定、频率稳定的交流电,无论输入电压发生波动还是负载发生变换,都要能达到一定的电压精度。

2) 具有一定的过载能力,一般能过载 125%~150%。

3) 输出电压波形所含的谐波成分应尽量少。

4) 具有短路、过载、过热、过电压、欠电压等保护功能和报警功能,且具有快速的动态响应。

(4) 蓄电池:太阳能发电系统只能在日间有阳光的时候才能发电,而多数在夜间大量用电,所以需要存储太阳能光伏电池方阵发出的电能并随时向负载供电维护铅酸蓄电池作为储能装置。其基本要求是:自放电率低,使用寿命长,深充电效率高,少维护或免维护,工作温度范围宽,价格低廉。

(5) 交流/直流负载:系统中的主要耗能元件,包含各种用电器。

3.1.2 设计基本原则

太阳能光伏电池组件设计的一个主要原则就是要满足平均天气条件下负载的每日用电需求。因为天气条件有低于和高于平均值的情况,所以要保证太阳能光伏电池组件和蓄电池在天气条件有别于平均值的情况下协调工作;蓄电池在连续数天的恶劣气候条件下,其荷电状态(state of charge,SOC)将会降低很多。在太阳能光伏电池组件大小的设计中,如果按照快速充满蓄电池的要求设计光伏方阵容量,结果将会得到一个容量很大的太阳能光伏电池方阵,使得系统成本过高;而在一年中的绝大部分时间里太阳能光伏电池组件的发电量会远远大于负载的使用量,从而造成太阳能光伏电池组件不必要的浪费;蓄电池的主要作用是在太阳辐射低于平均值的情况下给负载供电;在随后太阳辐射高于平均值的天气情况下,太阳能光伏电池组件就会给蓄电池充电。

设计太阳能光伏电池组件要满足光照最差季节的需要。在进行太阳能光伏电池组件设计的时候,首先要考虑的问题就是设计的太阳能光伏电池组件输出要等于全年负载需求的平均值。在这种情况下,太阳能光伏电池组件将提供负载所需的所有能量。但这也意味着每年都有将近一半的时间蓄电池处于亏电状态。蓄电池长时间内处于亏电状态将使得蓄电池的极板硫酸盐化。而在独立光伏发电系统中没有备用电源,若在天气较差的情况下给蓄电池进行充电,蓄电池的使用寿命和性能将会受到很大的影响,整个系统的运行费用也将大幅度增加。太阳能光伏电池组件设计中较好的办法是使太阳能光伏电池组件能满足光照最恶劣季节里的负载需要,也就是要保证在光照情况最差的情况下蓄电池也能够被完全地充满电。这样蓄电池全年都能达到全满状态,可延长蓄电池的使用寿命,减少维护费用。

如果在全年光照最差的季节,光照度大大低于平均值,在这种情况下仍然按照最差情况考虑设计太阳能光伏电池组件大小,那么所设计的太阳能光伏电池组件在一年中的其他时候就会远远超过实际所需,而且成本高昂。这时就可以考虑使用带有备用电源的混合系统。但是对于很小的系统,安装混合系统的成本会很高;而在偏远地区,使用备用电源的操作和维护费用也相当高,所以设计独立光伏发电系统的关键就是选择成本效益最好的方案。

3.1.3 蓄电池设计

蓄电池的设计思路是保证在太阳光照连续低于平均值的情况下负载仍可以正常工作。可以设想蓄电池是充满电的,在光照度低于平均值的情况下,太阳能光伏电池组件产生的电能不能完全填满由于负载从蓄电池中消耗能量而产生的空缺,这样在第一天结束的时候,蓄电池就会处于未充满状态。如果第二天光照度仍然低于平均值,蓄电池就仍然要放电以供给负载的需要,蓄电池的荷电状态继续下降。也许接下来的第三天、第四天会有同样的情况发生。但是为了避免蓄电池的损坏,这样的放电过程只能够允许持续一定的时间,直到蓄电池的荷电状态到达指定的危险值。为了量化评估这种太阳光照连续低于平均值的情况,在进行蓄电池设计时,需要引入一个重要的参数——自给天数,即系统在没有任何外来能源的情况下负载仍能正常工作的天数。这个参数让系统设计者能够选择所需使用的蓄电池容量大小。一般来讲,自给天数的确定与两个因素有关:负载对电源的要求程度；光伏发电系统安装地点的气象条件，即最大连续阴雨天数。通常可以将光伏发电系统安装地点的最大连续阴雨天数作为系统设计中使用的自给天数，但还要综合考虑负载对电源的要求。对于负载对电源要求不是很严格的光伏应用，在设计中通常取自给天数为3～5天。对于负载要求很严格的光伏应用系统，在设计中通常取自给天数为7～14天。所谓负载要求不严格的系统，通常是指用户可以稍微调节一下负载需求，从而适应恶劣天气带来的不便。而负载要求严格的系统指的是用电负载比较重要，例如，常用于通信、导航或者重要的健康设施（如医院、诊所里的设施等）。此外，还要考虑光伏发电系统的安装地点，如果在很偏远的地区，必须设计较大的蓄电池容量，因为维护人员要到达现场需要花费很长时间。

光伏发电系统中使用的蓄电池有镍氢、镍镉电池和铅酸蓄电池，但是在较大的系统中考虑到技术成熟性和成本等因素，通常使用铅酸蓄电池。在下面内容中涉及的蓄电池若没有特别说明指的都是铅酸蓄电池。

蓄电池的设计包括蓄电池容量的设计计算和蓄电池组的串并联设计。计算蓄电池容量的基本方法如下。

1. 基本公式

（1）将每天负载需要的用电量乘以根据实际情况确定的自给天数就可以得到初步的蓄电池容量。

（2）将第一步得到的蓄电池容量除以蓄电池的允许最大放电深度。因为不能让蓄电池在自给天数中完全放电，所以需要除以最大放电深度，得到所需要的蓄电池容量。最大放电深度的选择需要参考光伏发电系统中使用的蓄电池的性能参数，可以从蓄电池供应商处得到有关该蓄电池最大放电深度的详细资料。通常情况下，如果使用的是深循环型蓄电池，推荐使用80%放电深度（depth of discharge, DOD）；如果使用的是浅循环蓄电池，推荐使用50%放电深度。设计蓄电池容量的基本公式为

$$蓄电池容量 = \frac{自给天数 \times 日平均负载}{最大放电深度} \tag{3.1}$$

下面介绍确定蓄电池串并联的方法。每个蓄电池都有它的标称电压。为了达到负载工作的标称电压，将蓄电池串联起来给负载供电，需要串联的蓄电池的个数等于负载的标称电压除以蓄电池的标称电压。

$$串联蓄电池数 = \frac{负载标称电压}{蓄电池标称电压} \tag{3.2}$$

为了说明上述基本公式的应用，这里用一个小型的交流光伏应用系统作为范例。假设该光伏发电系统交流负载的耗电量为10kW·h/天，如果在该光伏发电系统中，选择使用的逆变器的效率为90%，输入电压为24V，那么可得所需的直流负载需求为462.96A·h/天（10000W·h÷0.9÷24V＝462.96A·h）。假设这是一个负载对电源要求并不是很严格的系统，使用者可以比较灵活地根据天气情况调整用电。选择5天的自给天数，并使用深循环电池，放电深度为80%。那么有

蓄电池容量： 5d×462.96A·h/0.8＝2893.51A·h

如果选用2V/400A·h的单体蓄电池，那么需要串联的电池数为

串联蓄电池数：　　　　　　　24V/2V＝12（个）

需要并联的蓄电池组数为

并联蓄电池组数：　　　　　　2893.51/400＝ 7.23

取整数为8。所以该系统需要使用2V/400A·h的蓄电池个数为12串联×8并联＝96个。

下面以一个纯直流系统——乡村小屋的光伏供电系统为例。该小屋只是在周末使用，可以使用低成本的浅循环蓄电池以降低系统成本。该乡村小屋的负载为90A·h/天，系统电压为24V。选择自给天数为2天，蓄电池允许的最大放电深度为50%，那么有

蓄电池容量：　　　　　　　2天×90A·h/0.5＝360A·h

如果选用12V/100A·h的蓄电池，那么需要该蓄电池2串联×4并联＝8个。

2. 设计修正

以上给出的只是蓄电池容量的基本估算方法，在实际情况中还有很多性能参数会对蓄电池容量和使用寿命产生很大的影响。为了得到正确的蓄电池容量设计，上面的基本公式必须加以修正。

对于蓄电池来说，其容量不是一成不变的，蓄电池的容量与两个重要因素相关：蓄电池的放电率和环境温度。

放电率有两种表示方法：时率和倍率。

时率是以放电时间表示的放电速率，即以某电流放至规定终止电压所经历的时间。例如，某电池额定容量是20A·h，放电时间为12h，即电池应以 $12 \div 20 = 0.6A$ 的电流放电，连续达到20h者即为合格。

倍率是指电池放电电流的数值为额定数值的倍数，如放电电流表示为 $0.1C_{20}$，对于一个 $12A·h$（C_{20}）的电池，即以 $0.1 \times 12 = 1.2A$ 的电流放电，$3C_{20}$ 是指以36A的电流放电，C的下标表示放电时率。

3. 蓄电池组并联设计

当计算出了所需的蓄电池的容量后，下一步就是要决定选择多少个单体蓄电池加以并联得到所需的蓄电池容量。可以有多种选择，例如，如果计算出来的蓄电池容量为500A·h，那么可以选择一个500A·h的单体蓄电池，也可以选择两个250A·h的蓄电池并联，还可以选择5个100A·h的蓄电池并联。从理论上讲，这些选择都可以满足要求，但是在实际应用当中，要尽量减少并联数目。也就是说，最好是选择大容量的蓄电池以减少所需的并联数目。这样做的目的就是尽量减少蓄电池之间的不平衡所造成的影响，所谓不平衡是指蓄电池之间相互进行充放电。并联的组数越多，发生蓄电池不平衡的可能性就越大。一般来讲，建议并联的数目不要超过4组。

目前，很多光伏发电系统采用的是两组并联模式。这样，如果有一组蓄电池出现故障，不能正常工作，就可以将该组蓄电池断开进行维修，而使用另外一组正常的蓄电池，虽然电流有所下降，但系统还能保持在标称电压正常工作。总之，蓄电池组的并联设计需要考虑不同的实际情况，根据不同的需要作出不同的选择。

3.1.4　光伏组件方阵设计

如何设计光伏组件的大小以及光伏组件的排布连接，是光伏发电系统设计中最重要的

一个环节。这个步骤决定了用户60%的成本投入是否产生浪费或者不足。

1. 基本公式

太阳能光伏电池组件设计的基本思想就是满足年平均日负载的用电需求。计算太阳能光伏电池组件的基本方法是用负载平均每天所需要的能量（安时数）除以一块太阳能光伏电池组件在一天中可以产生的能量（安时数），这样就可以算出系统需要并联的太阳能光伏电池组件数，使用这些组件并联就可以产生系统负载所需要的电流。将系统的标称电压除以太阳能光伏电池组件的标称电压，就可以得到太阳能光伏电池组件需要串联的太阳能光伏电池组件数，使用这些太阳能光伏电池组件串联就可以产生系统负载所需要的电压。基本计算公式如下：

$$并联的组件数量 = \frac{日平均负载(A \cdot h)}{组件日输出(A \cdot h)} \tag{3.3}$$

$$串联组件数量 = \frac{系统电压(V)}{组件电压(V)} \tag{3.4}$$

2. 设计修正

太阳能光伏电池组件的输出会受到一些外在因素的影响而降低，根据上述基本公式计算出的太阳能光伏电池组件，在实际情况下通常不能满足光伏发电系统的用电需求。为了得到更加正确的结果，有必要对上述基本公式进行修正。

（1）将太阳能光伏电池组件的输出降低10%。在实际工作中，太阳能光伏电池组件的输出会受到外在环境的影响而降低。泥土、灰尘的覆盖和组件性能的慢慢衰变都会降低太阳能光伏电池组件的输出。通常的做法就是在计算的时候，减少太阳能光伏电池组件10%的输出功率，来解决上述不可预知和不可量化的因素。可以将这看成是光伏发电系统设计时需要考虑的工程上的安全系数。又因为光伏供电系统的运行还依赖于天气状况，所以有必要对这些因素进行评估和技术估计，因此设计上留有一定的裕量将使得系统可以长期正常使用。

（2）将负载增加10%以应对蓄电池的库仑效率。在蓄电池的充放电过程中，铅酸蓄电池会电解水，产生气体逸出，也就是说，太阳能光伏电池组件产生的电流中将有一部分不能转化并储存起来而是被耗散掉。所以可以认为必须有一小部分电流用来补偿损失，用蓄电池的库仑效率来评估这种电流损失。不同的蓄电池其库仑效率不同，通常可以认为有5%~10%的损失，所以保守设计中有必要将太阳能光伏电池组件的功率增加10%以抵消蓄电池的耗散损失。

3. 完整的光伏组件设计

考虑到上述因素，必须修正简单的光伏组件设计公式，将每天的负载除以蓄电池的库仑效率，这样就增加了每天的负载，实际上给出了光伏组件需要负担的真正负载；将衰减因子乘以光伏组件的日输出，这样就考虑了环境因素和组件自身衰减造成的光伏组件日输出的减少，给出了一个在实际情况下光伏组件输出的保守估计值。综合考虑以上因素，可以得到

$$并联的组件数量 = \frac{日平均负载(A \cdot h)}{库仑效率 \times 组件日输出(A \cdot h) \times 衰减因子} \tag{3.5}$$

该方法是将实际的倾斜面上的太阳辐射转换成等同的利用标准太阳辐射$1000W/m^2$照射的小时数。将该小时数乘以光伏组件的峰值输出就可以估算出光伏组件每天输出的安

时数。光伏组件的输出为峰值日照时数×峰值电流 I_{mpp}。

例如，如果一个月的平均辐射为 5.0kW·h/m^2，则可以将其写成 5.0h×1000W/m^2，而 1000W/m^2 正好也就是用来标定光伏组件功率的标准辐射量，那么平均辐射为 5.0kW·h/m^2 就基本等同于光伏组件在标准辐射下照射 5.0h。这当然不是实际情况，但是可以用来简化计算。

因为 1000W/m^2 是生产商用来标定光伏组件功率的辐射量，所以在该辐射情况下的组件输出数值可以很容易从生产商处得到。为了计算光伏组件每天产生的安时数，可以使用峰值日照时数×光伏组件的峰值电流 I_{mpp}。

例如，假设在某个地区倾角为 30°的斜面上按月平均每天的辐射量为 5.0kW·h/m^2，可以将其写成 5.0h×1000W·h/m^2。对于一个典型的 75W 光伏组件，I_{mpp} 为 75W/17V=4.4A，就可得出每天发电的安时数为 5.0h×4.4A=22.0A·h。

总的来说，在已知本地倾斜斜面上光伏辐射数据的情况下，峰值日照时数估计方法是一种对光伏组件输出进行快速估算很有效的方法。

下面举例说明如何使用上述方法计算光伏供电系统需要的光伏组件数。

一个偏远地区建设的光伏供电系统，使用直流负载，负载为 24V，400A·h/d。该地区最低的光照辐射是 1 月，如果采用 30°的倾角，斜面上的平均日太阳辐射为 3.0kWh/m^2，也就是相当于 3 个标准峰值日照时。对于一个典型的 75W 光伏组件，每天的输出为

组件日输出：　　　　3.0峰值日照时×4.4A=13.2A·h/d

假设蓄电池的库仑效率为 90%，光伏组件的输出衰减为 10%。根据式（3.5）、式（3.4）有

$$并联的组件数量 = \frac{日平均负载(A·h)}{库仑效率×组件日输(A·h)×衰减因子} = \frac{400}{0.9×13.2×0.9}$$
$$=37.4（取整数38）$$

$$串联组件数量 = \frac{系统电压(V)}{组件电压(V)} = \frac{24}{17} = 1.4（取整数2）$$

根据以上计算数据，可以选择并联组件数量为 38，串联组件数量为 2，所需的光伏组件数为 2 串×38 并=76 块。

3.1.5　独立光伏发电系统负载的计算

负载是独立光伏发电系统的主要设计依据，是独立光伏发电系统设计和定价的关键因素之一。它通常由用户给出，但有时设计者可根据具体情况加以修正或提出更为合理的方案。负载最重要是要考虑采用直流负载还是交流负载。交流负载中哪些是电阻性负载，哪些是浪涌电流冲击的电感性负载，哪些重要负载必须保障供电，哪些是一般负载。电阻性交流负载如白炽灯、电子节能灯、电热器等，特点是无浪涌电流。电感性交流负载如电动机、电冰箱、水泵、电视机、带电子镇流器的荧光灯等，特点是有浪涌电流。通常，电动机和电冰箱的浪涌电流是额定电流的 5~8 倍，电视机的浪涌电流是额定电流的 2~5 倍，在配置逆变器时要给予充分重视。另外，为了降低发电光伏系统的配置和成本，应合理安排负载的用电时间，较大功率的负载最好能分时分区使用。

通常列出所有负载的名称、功率要求、额定工作电压和每天用电时间。对于交流和直流负载都要同样列出，功率因数在交流功率计算中不要考虑。将负载分类和按工作电压分组，计算每一组的总的功率要求。接着，选定系统工作电压，计算整个系统在这一电压下所要求的平均安培·小时（A·h）数，也就是算出所有负载的每天平均耗电量之和。关于系统工作电压的选择，经常是选最大功率负载所要求的电压。在以交流负载为主的系统中，直流系统电压应当考虑与选用的逆变器输入电压相适应。通常，独立运行的太阳能光伏发电系统，其交流负载工作在 220V，直流负载工作为 12V 或 12V 的倍数，即 24V 或 48V 等。从理论上说，负载的确定是直接的，而实际上负载的要求却往往并不确定。例如，家用电器所要求的功率可从制造厂商的资料上得知，但对它们的工作时间却并不知道，每天、每周和每月的使用时间很可能估算过高，其累计的效果会导致光伏发电系统的设计容量和造价上升。实际上，某些较大功率的负载可安排在不同的时间内使用。在严格的设计中，必须掌握独立光伏发电系统的负载特性，即每天 24h 中不同时间的负载功率，特别是对于集中的供电系统，了解用电规律后即可适时地加以控制。

另外，光伏发电系统设计时，采用怎样的馈线对整个系统的影响也是非常大。在这里馈线可以看作负载的一部分加以计算。例如，设直流负载功率为 P_0，额定工作电压为 U_0，工作电流为 I_0，输电线路的电阻、长度、截面积和材料的电阻率分别为 R、L、S 和 ρ，则输电线路上的降压 ΔU 和功率损失 ΔP 分别为

$$\Delta U = I_0 R = \frac{P_0}{U_0} \cdot \frac{\rho L}{S} \tag{3.6}$$

$$\Delta P = I_0 \Delta U = \left(\frac{P_0}{U_0}\right)^2 \cdot \frac{\rho L}{S} \tag{3.7}$$

输电线路上的降压 ΔU 是由蓄电池输出电压和负载最低启动工作电压决定的，通常不能超过 2V，而输电线路上的功率损失 ΔP 一般不要超过光伏阵列额定输出功率的 2%～5%，可以以此来确定系统输电导线的线径或截面积。铜和铝导线的电阻率分别为 $1.75 \times 10^{-8} \Omega \cdot m$ 和 $2.90 \times 10^{-8} \Omega \cdot m$。一根直径为 1mm；长度为 10m 的铜导线的电阻为 0.223Ω，那么 10A 直流电流的降压就有 2.23V，功率损失可高达 22.3W。如果直径为 2mm、长度为 10m 的铜导线的电阻就为 0.0557Ω，10A 直流电流的降压为 0.557V，功率损失为 5.57W。可见，较大的直流电流在导线上的功率损失是相当可观的。采用横截面积更大的导线固然可以降低损耗，但是也会导致整个系统的费用上升。另外，馈线的长度也需要仔细考虑计算，并和光伏阵列的放置方式进行整合优化。

【任务实施】

1. 任务准备

竞赛设备平台 1 个、一字螺丝刀 1 把、十字螺丝刀 1 把、RS485 转 USB 接头 1 个、通信原理图 1 张、组串式逆变器及其配件 1 套、电脑主机 1 套、上电检查记录表 1 份、离网光伏发电系统设计与调试记录表 1 份。

2. 任务内容及步骤

任务 1：智能离网微逆变系统触摸屏界面设计

任务 3.1 相关实施图表

任务内容：智能离网微逆变系统监控系统触摸屏界面设计。

任务步骤：

（1）完成"设置"界面功能。

（2）完成"数据监控"界面设计。

（3）完成"逆变控制"界面设计。

任务2：汇流箱通信装调

任务内容：离网微逆变系统汇流箱通信装调

任务步骤：

（1）光伏汇流箱智能监控单元通信接线。

（2）检查智能监控单元工作状态。

（3）完成智能监控单元工位号、COM端口编号、设备地址码、16进制地址码、波特率、校验位、发送地址编码、反馈编码调试和记录。

3. 技能要求

（1）能够制作四个监控界面，一个主界面和三个子界面，监控界面要求在主界面中制作三个按钮控件用于切换到三个子界面。

（2）三个子界面分别命名为"设置"、"数据监控"及"逆变控制"，并在每个子界面中制作一个按钮控件置于左下角，控件命名"返回"，此按键功能为返回到主界面。

（3）能够完成汇流箱通信模块安装与接线，包括主控模块与电流传感器模块的安装、电流传感器FMB排线连接、直流母线供电端子接线、RS485通信端子接线、直流24V供电端子接线。

（4）能够对汇流箱完成通信模块调试，并且能够分析独立光伏发电系统其他部件的调试方法。

4. 任务成果及考核评价

（1）智能离网微逆变系统触摸屏界面设计、汇流箱通信装调操作步骤正确、数据正确，占90%。

（2）操作过程展现较好职业素养，做到7S管理，占10%。

【练习】

1. 独立光伏发电系统的组成一般包含哪些部分？
2. 在进行光伏组件方阵计算时，串联的太阳能光伏电池组件数怎么计算？并联的太阳能光伏电池组件数怎么计算？
3. 光伏供电系统使用了255W太阳能光伏电池组件100块（25并联×4串联），工作电压24V，配备4500A·h的蓄电池，最大充电率为多少？

任务3.2　设计并网光伏发电系统

【学习目标】

知识目标：掌握并网光伏发电系统的设计需求。

能力目标：能设计并网光伏发电系统的光伏电池串并联方案、电网接入方案、并网方式。

素质目标：培养对严谨细致、精益求精的职业精神。

重点：并网光伏发电系统的设计要点。

难点：并网光伏发电系统交流系统设计调试。

【任务分析】

并网光伏发电系统的组成是根据电站容量情况而不同，具有多种形式并网方案，必须根据实际情况设计光伏电池容量、串并联方案和电网接入方案。

本任务依托职业技能等级证书设备平台，对接维护光伏电站交流系统岗位工作内容，以交流系统部分设计装调为任务，学习光伏发电系统的设计实操，完成光伏电站规划设计方案、逆变器通信装调实操内容。

【知识学习】

3.2.1 光伏并网发电系统组成

如图3.2所示，光伏并网发电系统主要组成如下：

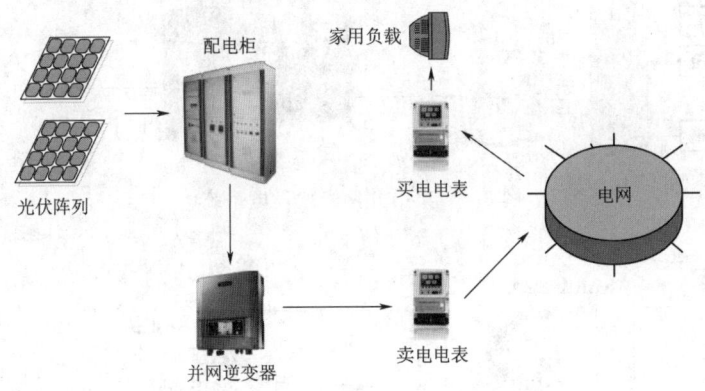

图3.2 并网光伏发电系统

（1）光伏电池组件及其支架。

（2）光伏阵列汇流箱。

（3）直流配电柜。

（4）光伏并网逆变器。

（5）接入系统设备。

（6）系统的通信监控装置。

（7）系统的防雷及接地装置。

（8）土建、配电房等基础设施。

（9）系统的连接电缆及防护材料。

项目3　设计太阳能光伏发电系统

3.2.2　并网发电系统分类

根据光伏电站与建筑结合的形式，并网发电方式可分两种：集中并网光伏发电系统（如图3.3所示）、组串并网光伏发电系统（如图3.4所示）。

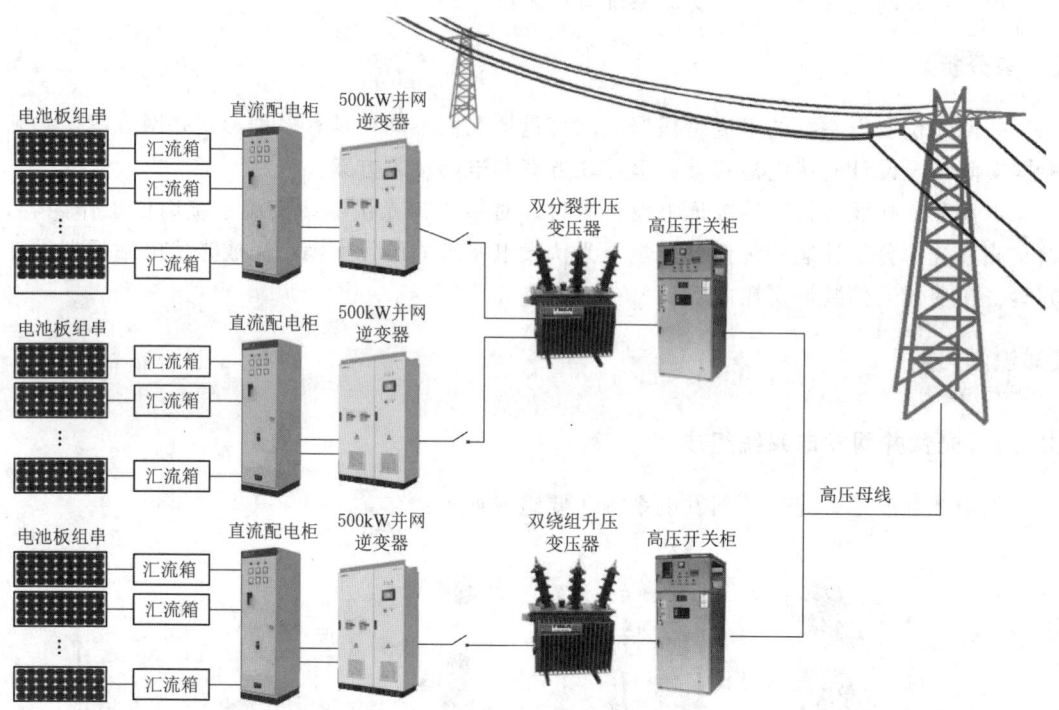

图3.3　集中并网光伏发电系统

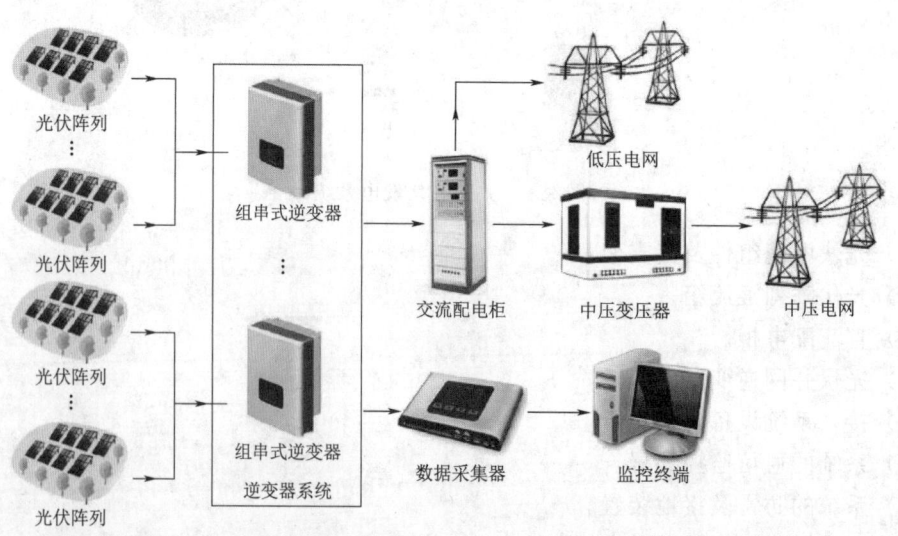

图3.4　组串并网光伏发电系统

1. 集中并网发电

集中逆变技术是若干个并行的光伏组串被连到同一台集中逆变器的直流输入端，一般功率大的使用三相的 IGBT 功率模块，功率较小的使用场效应晶体管，同时使用 DSP 转换控制器来改善所产出电能的质量，使它非常接近于正弦波电流，多用于大型光伏发电站（>10kW）的系统中。在电气设计时，采用单台逆变器集中并网发电方案实现联网功能。最大特点是系统的功率高，成本低，但由于不同光伏组串的输出电压、电流往往不完全匹配（特别是光伏组串因多云、树荫、污渍等原因被部分遮挡时），采用集中逆变的方式会导致逆变过程的效率降低和电能的下降。同时整个光伏发电系统的发电可靠性会受某一光伏单元组工作状态不良的影响。

2. 组串并网发电

组串逆变器是基于模块化概念基础上的，每个光伏组串（1～5kW）通过一个逆变器，在直流端具有最大功率峰值跟踪，在交流端并联并网，已成为现在国际市场上最流行的逆变器。

许多大型光伏电厂使用组串逆变器。优点是不受组串间模块差异和遮影的影响，同时减少了光伏组件最佳工作点与逆变器不匹配的情况，从而增加了发电量。技术上的这些优势不仅降低了系统成本，也增加了系统的可靠性。同时，在组串间引入"主-从"概念，使得系统在单串组件发出的电能不能满足维持单个逆变器工作的情况下，将几组光伏组串联系在一起，让其中一个或几个工作，从而产出更多的电能。

最新的概念为几个逆变器相互组成一个"团队"来代替"主-从"概念，使得系统具备更高的可靠性。目前，无变压器式组串逆变器已占了主导地位。

并网光伏发电系统最大的特点就是太阳能光伏电池组件产生的直流电经过并网逆变器转换成符合市电电网要求的交流电之后直接接入公共电网，并网系统中光伏方阵所产生的电力除了供给交流负载外，多余的电力反馈给电网。在阴雨天或夜晚，太阳能光伏电池组件没有产生电能或者产生的电能不能满足负载需求时就由电网供电。因为直接将电能输入电网，免除了配置蓄电池，省掉了蓄电池储能和释放的过程，所以太阳能光伏电池方阵的安装倾角应该是以全年能接收到最大太阳辐射量所对应的角度，这样可以充分利用光伏方阵所发的电力，从而减小了能量的损耗，并降低了系统的成本。但是系统中需要专用的并网逆变器，以保证输出的电力满足电网电力对电压、频率等电性能指标的要求。因为逆变器效率的问题，还是会有部分的能量损失。这种系统通常能够并行使用市电和太阳能光伏电池组件阵列作为本地交流负载的电源，降低了整个系统的负载缺电率，而且并网光伏发电系统可以对公用电网起到调峰作用。

3.2.3 并网逆变器的设计选型

1. 可靠的"孤岛效应"防护手段

所谓"孤岛效应"，即指并入公共电网中的发电装置，在电网断电的情况下，这个发电装置却不能检测到或根本没有相应检测手段，仍然向公共电网馈送电量。

一般来说，孤岛效应可能对整个配电系统设备及用户端的设备造成如下不利的影响：

（1）危害电力维修人员的生命安全。

(2) 影响配电系统上的保护开关动作程序。

(3) 孤岛区域所发生的供电电压与频率的不稳定性质会对用电设备带来破坏。

(4) 当供电恢复时造成的电压相位不同步会产生浪涌电流，可能引起再次跳闸或对光伏发电系统、负载和供电系统带来损坏。

(5) 并网光伏发电系统因单相供电而造成系统三相负载的欠相供电问题。

由此可见，作为一个安全可靠的并网逆变装置，必须能及时检测出孤岛效应并避免其带来的危害。

2. 完善的并网保护功能及防护措施

逆变器是光伏发电并网系统的核心。因此，需要各种完善的保护措施，应具有基本的保护功能（如短路、过压、过流、欠频、过频、过热等）。光伏并网保护装置一方面对光伏发电系统进行保护，防止孤岛效应等发生；另一方面防止线路事故或功率失稳，以保证在光伏逆变系统发生故障时，不对电网产生不良影响，以及在发生电网故障时，其不对光伏发电系统产生损害。

除并网保护功能外，还要采取可靠的防震、防雷击、对地短路等防护措施。

3. 优质的正弦波输出性能

优质的正弦波输出性能是指逆变器能输出纯净的正弦波，尽量少含高次谐波。

4. 最大功率追踪功能

最大功率追踪功能（MPPT，Maximum Power Point Tracking）控制器能够实时侦测太阳能板的发电电压，并追踪最高功率输出点（Ⅵ），使系统以最大功率输出对蓄电池充电，相比非 MPPT 系统而言，其充电效率要高很多。

5. 额定输出功率

额定输出功率表示光伏逆变器向负载供电的能力。额定输出功率高的光伏逆变器可以带更多的用电负载。选用光伏逆变器时应首先考虑具有足够的额定功率，以满足最大负荷下设备对电功率的要求，以及系统的扩容和一些临时负载的接入。当用电设备以纯电阻性负载为主或功率因数大于 0.9 时，一般选取光伏逆变器的额定输出功率比用电设备总功率大 10%～15%。

6. 输出电压的调整性能

输出电压的调整性能表示光伏逆变器输出电压的稳压能力。一般光伏逆变器产品都给出了当直流输入电压在允许波动范围变动时，该光伏逆变器输出电压的波动偏差百分率，通常称为电压调整率。高性能的光伏逆变器应同时给出当负载由 0 向 100% 变化时，该光伏逆变器输出电压的偏差百分率，通常称为负载调整率。性能优良的光伏逆变器的电压调整率应不大于±3%，负载调整率就不大于±6%。

7. 整机效率

整机效率表示光伏逆变器自身功率损耗的大小。容量较大的光伏逆变器还要给出满负荷工作和低负荷工作下的效率值。一般千瓦级以下的逆变器的效率应为 80%～85%；10kW 级的效率应为 85%～90%；更大功率的效率必须在 90% 以上。逆变器效率的高低对光伏发电系统提高有效发电量和降低发电成本有重要影响，因此选用光伏逆变器时要尽量进行比较，选择整机效率高一些的产品。

8. 启动性能

光伏逆变器应保证在额定负载下可靠启动。高性能的光伏逆变器可以做到连续多次满负荷启动而不损坏功率开关器件及其他电路。小型逆变器为了自身安全，有时采用软启动或限流启动措施或电路。

3.2.4 光伏逆变器的 RS485 通信

光伏逆变器一般采用 RS485 通信方式。RS485 通信是典型的串行通信标准，RS485 总线标准规定了总线接口的电气特性标准即对于 2 个逻辑状态的定义：正电平在＋2～＋6V 之间，表示一个逻辑状态；负电平在－2～－6V 之间，则表示另一个逻辑状态。数字信号采用差分传输方式，能够有效减少噪声信号的干扰。RS485 接口的最大传输距离标准值为 4000 英尺，实际上可达 3000m（理论上的数据，在实际操作中，极限距离仅达 1200m 左右），RS485 接口在总线上允许连接多达 128 个收发器，即具有多站能力，这样用户可以利用单一的 RS485 接口方便地建立起设备网络。

RS485 接口组成的半双工网络一般只需 2 根连线，所以 RS485 接口均采用屏蔽双绞线传输。RS485 控制器通信只需 2 个接线端子，通常两个接线端子分别用"A"和"B"表示，如图 3.5 所示。

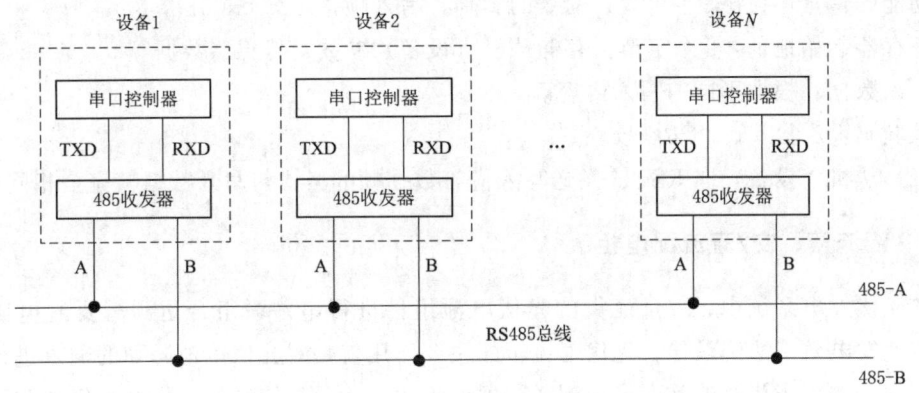

图 3.5　RS485 通信网络连接图

RS485 的通信参数有：波特率 2400～115200bps，一般默认 9600bps；数据位 7～9 位，默认 8 位；停止位 1～2 位，默认 1 位；奇偶校验包括无校验、奇校验、偶校验。

在用 RS485 进行通信时，有主机和从机之分，主机向从机发送指令，从机回应主机的指定，它们按照统一数据格式进行通信。

1. 问询数据格式

（1）主机向 RS485 总线发送问询数据帧格式如下：

地址码	功能码	寄存器起始地址	寄存器长度	校验码

地址码：1 个字节，设备在 RS485 总线中的唯一地址，可设置。

功能码：1 个字节，主机发送命令的类别，问询帧指定为 0x03。

寄存器起始地址：2 个字节，存储从机（设备）参数、传感器数据等。

寄存器长度：2个字节，获取寄存器的个数。

校验码：2个字节，CRC校验。

（2）从机（设备）向RS485发送问询应答数据帧格式如下：

地址码	功能码	数据字节个数	数据1	数据1	…	数据n	校验码

地址码：1个字节，从机（设备）在RS485总线中的唯一地址。

功能码：1个字节，主机发送命令的类别，问询帧指定为0x03。

数据字节个数：1个字节，数据1至数据n的字节个数。

数据1～数据n：应答数据。

校验码：2个字节，CRC校验。

2. 写入数据格式

（1）主机向指定的从机（设备）发送写入数据帧格式如下：

地址码	功能码	寄存器起始地址	写入数据	校验码

地址码：1个字节，设备在RS485总线中的唯一地址，可设置。

功能码：1个字节，主机发送命令的类别，写入帧指定为0x06。

寄存器起始地址：2个字节，存储从机（设备）参数、传感器数据等。

写入数据：根据不同的写入内容确定。

校验码：2个字节，CRC校验。

（2）从机（设备）向RS485发送写入应答数据帧的格式与写入数据帧完全相同。

3.2.5 汇流箱、交/直流配电柜

在光伏发电系统中，数量庞大的光伏电池组件进行串并联组合达到需要的电压电流值，以使发电效率达到最佳。光伏汇流箱的主要作用就是对光伏电池阵列的输入进行一级汇流，用于减少光伏电池阵列接入到逆变器的连线，优化系统结构，提高可靠性和可维护性。在提供汇流防雷功能的同时，还可以监测光伏电池板运行状态；汇流后电流大小、电压大小、功率；防雷器状态、直流断路器状态采集；继电器接点输出等功能，并把测量和采集到的数据上传到监控系统。

在汇流箱选型时，主要考虑其输入路数、每路最大输入电流、防雷反应时间、防水性能等指标。

光伏直流（防雷）配电柜主要是将汇流箱输出的直流电缆接入后进行汇流，再接至并网逆变器。配电柜内含有直流输入断路器、漏电保护器、防反二极管、光伏防雷器等主要器件，在保证系统不受漏电、短路、过载与雷电冲击等损坏及有效保证负载设备运行的同时，方便客户操作和维护。

光伏交流（防雷）配电柜主要是通过配电给逆变器提供并网接丝、断路器、防雷器，选配有发电计量表、逆变器并网接口及交流电压电流表等装置。

【任务实施】

1. 任务准备

职业技能等级证书设备平台 1 个、电脑主机 1 套、万用表 1 个、上电检查记录表 1 份、并网光伏发电系统设计记录表 1 份。

任务 3.2 相关实施图表

2. 任务内容及步骤

任务 1：光伏电站规划设计方案

任务内容：光伏电站工程规划与工程部署设计方案。

任务步骤：

（1）根据功能要求及工艺要求，对光伏工程进行部署规划。

（2）完成设备的安装与线路连接，满足光伏电站及控制系统功能及工艺要求。

任务 2：并网光伏发电系统设计与接线

任务内容：完成并网光伏发电系统设计与接线。

任务步骤：

（1）完成并网主接线的设计与连接。

（2）完成并网逆变器 RS485 通信端子的安装与接线。

（3）完成并网通信地址设置并记录。

（4）使用串口调试软件完成通信测试并记录。

3. 技能要求

（1）能根据电气图要求、功能要求及工艺要求，选型关键器件。

（2）能够完成组件组串设计和逆变器参数选定。

（3）能够按照相关施工图纸，以及施工工艺要求，进行规范施工，完成智能微电网系统搭建。

（4）完成设备的安装与线路连接，满足光伏电站及控制系统功能及工艺要求。

（5）能够检查逆变器通信电源运行装调，风扇状态、各信号指示灯状态，是否存在异常，并能够分析排除故障。

（6）能够检查通信协议转换器、路由器、交换机、防火墙和各类服务器以及光传输设备的运行状态，是否有异常报警指示，并能够分析排除故障。

4. 任务成果及考核评价

（1）光伏电站规划设计方案、逆变器通信装调操作步骤正确、数据正确，占 90%。

（2）操作过程展现较好职业素养，做到 7S 管理，占 10%。

【练习】

1. 并网光伏发电系统的主要组成包含哪几部分？
2. 孤岛效应可能对整个配电系统设备及用户端的设备造成什么影响？
3. 并网发电系统和独立发电系统有什么区别？

Project 3　Designing Solar Photovoltaic Power Generation Systems

Task 3.1　Designing Stand-Alone Photovoltaic Power Generation Systems

【Learning objectives】

Knowledge objective: To master the design requirements of stand-alone photovoltaic power generation systems

Ability objective: To be able to design photovoltaic cell arrays, storage battery packs and load capacity of stand-alone photovoltaic power generation systems; to be able to complete the commissioning of monitoring systems and combiner box communication

Qualification objective: To cultivate a sense of pride and mission in China's photovoltaic industry.

Learning priority: Design essentials of stand-alone photovoltaic power generation systems

Learning challenge: Commissioning of the monitoring system and communication of stand-alone photovoltaic power generation systems

【Task analysis】

The composition of stand-alone photovoltaic power generation systems varies depending on the load, with photovoltaic cells being an indispensable part and storage batteries being a common component. The capacity and series-parallel connection schemes of photovoltaic systems must be designed based on the demand of the load for electrical energy.

This task relies on the equipment platform of the National Vocational College Skills Competition. It corresponds to various tasks of the design positions at photovoltaic power generation systems, and involves the task of partially designed installation and commissioning. It also includes learning of various designs of photovoltaic power generation systems using hands-on activities, including touch screen interface design of intelligent off-grid micro inverter systems, and installation and commissioning of combiner box communication.

【Knowledge learning】

3.1.1 Design overview

The design of photovoltaic systems concerns two aspects: capacity design and hardware design.

The main purpose of photovoltaic system capacity design is to calculate the number of solar cell modules and storage batteries required for photovoltaic systems to operate robustly throughout the year. Meanwhile, attention should be paid to coordinating the relationship between maximum robustness of the systems and system costs, so as to realize maximum robustness of system operation while minimizing system costs.

The main purpose of the hardware design of photovoltaic systems is to select appropriate hardware equipment according to the actual situation, including the selection of solar cell modules, the design of racks, the selection of inverters, the selection of cables, the design of control and measurement systems, the design of lightning protection, and the design of power distribution systems. System design requires taking into account both the software and hardware of the systems.

Before designing photovoltaic systems, it is necessary to understand and obtain some basic data essential for calculation and selection: the geographical location of the photovoltaic system site (including the location, latitude, longitude and altitude) and the meteorological data of the region (including total monthly solar radiation, monthly direct radiant exposure, monthly scattered radiant exposure, annual average temperature, the highest and lowest temperatures, the maximum number of consecutive cloudy and rainy days, the maximum wind speed, and special meteorological conditions such as hail and snow).

Stand-alone photovoltaic power generation systems are systems where solar photovoltaic power generation is not connected to the grid, typically characterized by the need for storage batteries to store energy. Stand-alone photovoltaic power generation systems are mainly applied to household and village-level solar photovoltaic power stations, photovoltaic lighting systems, communication base stations, solar water pumps, etc. In regions where wind power generation and small hydropower are available, hybrid power generation systems (e.g., wind/solar power generation complementary systems) can also be constructed.

As shown in Figure 3.1, a stand-alone photovoltaic power generation system consists of the following parts: photovoltaic cell arrays, the controller, the inverter, storage batteries, the AC load, and the DC load.

Functions of each part of the system are as follows:

(1) Photovoltaic cell module: Photovoltaic cells are the basic units of solar photovoltaic power generation systems. However, single photovoltaic cells only generate a small

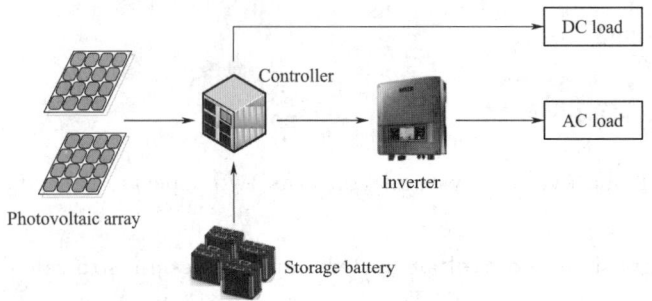

Figure 3.1 Stand-alone photovoltaic power generation system

amount of electrical energy, with the operating voltage of about 0.45 – 0.50V and the operating current of $20 - 25\text{mA/cm}^2$. In most cases, it is difficult to meet the needs of practical applications. Generally, battery packs are connected in series or parallel to form a solar cell module, so as to increase the output voltage and current to meet the load operating requirements.

(2) Controller: As one of the core components of photovoltaic power generation systems, the controller is mainly used to realize the charging and discharging management of the whole system and prevent storage batteries from overcharging and overdischarging. The DC electrical energy generated by solar photovoltaic arrays is used for storage battery charging via the controller. When storage batteries are not fully charged, the controller's role is to maximize the charging; when the batteries are fully charged, the controller's role is to control solar charging, so that the batteries are in the state of floating charge. When storage batteries are discharged too close to their over-discharge voltage, the controller will sound an alarm for insufficient power of storage batteries and cut off the discharge circuit of storage batteries to protect the batteries. With the development of the photovoltaic industry, functions of controllers are increasingly powerful. There is a trend of integrating traditional controllers and inverters with monitoring systems.

(3) Inverter: A device that converts direct current (DC) to alternating current (AC). Basic requirements for inverters are as follows.

1) To be able to output alternating current with stable voltage and frequency; to be able to realize certain voltage accuracy, regardless of input voltage fluctuation or load shift.

2) Have a certain overload capacity, generally 125%– 150%.

3) Harmonic waves contained in output voltage waveforms should be as few as possible.

4) Have short-circuit, overload, overheating, overvoltage, undervoltage and other protection functions and alarm functions, as well as quick dynamic responses.

(4) Storage battery: Solar power generation systems can only generate electricity in the daytime when there is sunlight. Yet, a large amount of electricity is consumed during

the night time. Therefore, electrical energy generated by solar cell arrays needs to be stored and supplied to the load for the sustenance of lead-acid storage batteries used as energy storage devices. Basic requirements for storage batteries are: low self-discharge rate, long service life, high deep charging efficiency, minimal maintenance or maintenance-free, wide operating temperature range, and low price.

(5) AC/DC load: Main energy-consuming components in the system, including various electrical appliances.

3.1.2 Basic design principles

One of the main principles of solar cell module design is to meet the daily electricity demand of the load under average weather conditions. Since actual weather conditions may be below or above average, it is important to ensure that solar cell modules and storage batteries operate in harmony under weather conditions different from average. The state of charge (SOC) of storage batteries will be much lower under several days of bad weather conditions. In the size design of solar cell modules, full charging of storage batteries as quickly as possible should not be expected, as this would result in a large-sized solar cell module (leading to excessively high system costs) and a power generation capacity of solar cell modules much larger than the load usage for most of the year (resulting in unnecessary wastage of solar cell modules). The main function of storage batteries is to supply power to the load when solar radiation is below average; in subsequent weather conditions when solar radiation is above average, solar cell modules will charge storage batteries.

Solar cell modules are designed to meet electricity demand in seasons with the worst light conditions. The priority when designing solar cell modules is to ensure their output meets the average yearly load demand. In that case, solar cell modules will provide all the energy needed by the load. But this also means that storage batteries will be insufficiently charged for nearly half of the year. Insufficient charging of storage batteries for a long period of time will cause the plates of storage batteries to sulphate. On the other hand, there is no standby power supply in stand-alone photovoltaic systems. If storage batteries are charged under poor weather conditions, the service life and performance of storage batteries will be greatly affected, and the operating costs of the entire system will also increase significantly. A better approach is to design solar cell modules to meet the load demand in seasons with the worst light conditions, that is, to ensure full charging of storage batteries even in the worst light conditions. In this way, storage batteries can be fully charged throughout the year, thereby extending the service life of storage batteries and reducing maintenance costs.

Designing solar cell modules for the worst-case scenario ensures efficiency during low light periods but results in higher costs due to overcapacity for most of the year. In such case, hybrid systems with a standby power supply can be considered. However, for small systems, installation costs of hybrid systems can be prohibitive, and operation and maintenance costs of using a standby power supply can be excessively high in remote areas. Thus, the key to designing stand-alone photovoltaic systems is to choose the most cost-effective option.

3.1.3 Design of storage batteries

The design idea of storage batteries is to ensure that the load can still operate normally when solar exposure is continuously below the average. Please imagine that storage batteries are fully charged, and that light levels are lower than the average. In such case, electrical energy generated by solar cell modules cannot completely replenish energy consumed by the load from storage batteries. In this way, storage batteries will not be fully charged at the end of the first day. If the light levels are still lower than the average on the second day, storage batteries will still have to be discharged to meet load demand, and the SOC of storage batteries will continue to decrease. This situation may continue on the third and fourth days. However, to avoid damage to storage batteries, such a discharge process can only be allowed to continue for a certain period of time until the SOC of storage batteries reaches a specified critical value. To quantitatively assess the effect of such scenario where solar exposure is continuously below the average, an important parameter needs to be introduced into the design of storage batteries: the number of self-sustaining days, i.e. the number of days that the system load can operate without any external energy source. This parameter allows system designers to choose the desired storage battery capacity. In general, determining the number of self-sustaining days involves two factors: the degree of power supply requirements of the load and the meteorological conditions of the location where photovoltaic systems are installed, i.e., the maximum number of consecutive cloudy and rainy days. The maximum number of consecutive cloudy and rainy days at the location where photovoltaic systems are installed can generally be used as the number of self-sustaining days to be used in system design. However, the power supply requirements of the load should also be taken into account. For photovoltaic applications where power supply requirements of the load are not stringent, 3 – 5 days is generally used as the number of self-sustaining days in design. For photovoltaic applications with stringent load requirements, 7 – 14 days is generally used as the number of self-sustaining days in design. A system with less stringent load requirements means users can adjust demand during bad weather, whereas a stringent system means that electricity load (e.g., commonly used for communication, navigation, or important health facilities such as hospitals and clinics) is critical. Moreover, the location where photovoltaic systems are installed should be taken into account. For a very remote region, it is necessary to design storage batteries with larger capacity, as it takes a long time for maintenance personnel to reach the site.

Storage batteries used in photovoltaic systems are nickel-metal hydride (Ni-MH), nickel-cadmium, and lead-acid storage batteries, whereas in larger systems, lead-acid storage batteries are generally used due to factors such as technological maturity and costs. Storage batteries mentioned below refer to lead-acid storage batteries unless otherwise specified.

The design of storage batteries involves calculation of storage battery capacity and the design of series-parallel connections of storage battery packs. Firstly, the basic method for calculating storage battery capacity is given below.

1. Basic formula

(1) Multiply the daily electricity consumption required by the load by the number of self-sustaining days to obtain the preliminary storage battery capacity.

(2) Divide the storage battery capacity obtained in the first step by the maximum permissible depth of discharge (DOD) of storage batteries. Since fully discharging storage batteries is not allowed during self-sustaining days, it is necessary to divide by the maximum DOD to obtain the desired storage battery capacity. For the selection of the maximum DOD, it is necessary to refer to performance parameters of storage batteries used in photovoltaic systems. Detailed information about the maximum DOD of storage batteries can be obtained from storage battery suppliers. Normally, if deep-cycle storage batteries are used, 80% DOD is recommended; if shallow-cycle storage batteries are used, 50% DOD is recommended. The basic formula for designing storage battery capacity is

$$\text{Storage battery capacity} = \frac{\text{Self-sustaining days} \times \text{Daily average load}}{\text{The maximum permissible depth of discharge}} \quad (3.1)$$

The method for determining the series-parallel connection of storage batteries is described below. Each storage battery has its nominal voltage. To obtain the nominal voltage at which the load operates, storage batteries are connected in series to supply power to the load, and the number of storage batteries to be connected in series is equal to the nominal voltage of the load divided by the nominal voltage of storage batteries.

$$\text{Storage batteries in series} = \frac{\text{Nominal voltage of a load}}{\text{Nominal voltage of a battery}} \quad (3.2)$$

To illustrate the application of the above basic formula, a small AC photovoltaic application system is used here as an example. Assuming that the electricity consumption of the AC load of this photovoltaic system is 10 kW·h/day, and that the efficiency of the inverter used in this system is 90%, and that input voltage is 24 V, then the desired DC load demand is 462.96 A·h/day (10,000 W·h ÷ 0.9 ÷ 24 V = 462.96 A·h). Assuming that this is a system where load requirements for power supply are not very stringent, and that users can flexibly adjust electricity consumption according to weather conditions. Assuming that 5 days is used as the number of self-sustaining days and that deep-cycle batteries with 80% DOD are used. Then

Storage battery capacity = 5 days × 462.96 A·h/0.8 = 2,893.51 A·h

If single storage batteries of 2 V/400 A·h are used, then the number of batteries to be connected in series are:

Number of storage batteries to be connected in series = 24 V/2V = 12 (pcs)

Number of storage battery packs to be connected in parallel:

Number of storage battery packs to be connected in parallel = 2893.51/400 = 7.23

The result is rounded to the integer of 8. So, the number of storage batteries needed for this system is: 12 in series × 8 in parallel = 96pcs.

An example of a pure DC system is given below: a photovoltaic power supply system for a rustic cottage. The cottage is only used on weekends, and low-cost shallow-cycle storage batteries can be used to reduce system costs. The load of the rustic cottage is 90A·h/day and the system voltage is 24 V. Assuming that 2 days is used as the number of self-sustaining days and that the maximum permissible DOD of storage batteries is 50%, then

Storage battery capacity = 2 days × 90 A·h/0.5 = 360 A·h

If storage batteries of 12 V/100A·h are used, then the number of storage batteries required is: 2 in series × 4 in parallel = 8

2. Design correction

The example given above only describes the basic estimation method of storage battery capacity. In the actual situation, many performance parameters have a great impact on the capacity and service life of storage batteries. To obtaina correct design for storage battery capacity, the above basic formula must be corrected.

The capacity of storage batteries is not static, but related to two important factors: the discharge rate of storage batteries and the ambient temperature.

The discharge rate can be expressed in two ways: the discharge time rate and the discharge rate.

The discharge time rate is the discharge rate expressed in terms of discharge time, i.e., the time taken to discharge at a certain current to the specified cut-off discharge voltage. For example, assuming that the rated capacity of a battery is 20A·h and that the discharge time is 12h, i.e., then the battery should be discharged at a current of 12÷20=0.6 A, and the battery is qualified if it is discharged continuously for 20 h.

The discharge rate refers to the value of battery discharge current as a multiple of the rated value. If the discharge current is expressed as $0.1\ C_{20}$, for a 12 A·h (C_{20}) battery, the battery is discharged at a current of 0.1 × 12 = 1.2 A. In this way, $3\ C_{20}$ means the battery is discharged at a current of 36 A. The subscript of C denotes the discharge time rate.

3. Parallel connection design of storage battery packs

Following the calculation of desired storage battery capacity, the next step is to decide how many single storage batteries should be connected in parallel to obtain the

Project 3 Designing Solar Photovoltaic Power Generation Systems

desired storage battery capacity. Various options are available. For example, if the calculated storage battery capacity is 500 A · h, you can choose one 500 A · h single storage battery, or two 250 A · h storage batteries to be connected in parallel, or five 100 A · h storage batteries to be connected in parallel. Theoretically, all these options can meet the requirements, but in practical applications, the number of parallel connections should be minimized. In other words, it is preferable to choose large-capacity storage batteries to reduce the number of parallel connections required. The purpose is to minimize the impact of imbalance between storage batteries, which means that storage batteries charge and discharge each other. The greater the number of parallel connections, the greater the possibility of storage battery imbalance. Generally speaking, it is recommended that the number of parallel connections should not exceed four groups.

Currently, many photovoltaic systems adopt the mode of two groups connected in parallel. In this mode, if one group of storage batteries fails and cannot operate properly, the group can be disconnected for repair, while the other group (normal storage batteries) is used. In this way, although the current decreases, the system can still maintain normal operation at the nominal voltage. In conclusion, in the parallel connection design of storage battery packs, various practical situations should be taken into account, and different choices should be made according to different needs.

3.1.4 Design of photovoltaic module arrays

Size design and array connection of photovoltaic modules is one of the most important parts of photovoltaic system design. This step determines whether 60% of the user's investment is wasted or insufficient.

1. Basic formula

The basic idea behind the design of solar cell modules is to meet the annual average daily electricity demand of the load. For solar cell modules, the basic method is to divide the average daily energy required by the load (number of ampere-hours) by the amount of energy that can be generated by one solar cell module in a day (number of ampere-hours). In this way, the number of solar cell modules that need to be connected in parallel by the system can be calculated, and the current required by the system load can be generated by using these modules connected in parallel. Divide the nominal voltage of the system by the nominal voltage of solar cell modules, so that you can obtain the number of solar cell modules that need to be connected in series to generate the voltage required by the system load. The basic calculation formula is as follows:

$$\text{Number of Parallel Components} = \frac{\text{Daily Average Load}(A \cdot h)}{\text{Daily Output of Components}(A \cdot h)} \qquad (3.3)$$

$$\text{Number of Components in Series} = \frac{\text{System Voltage}(V)}{\text{Component Voltage}(V)} \qquad (3.4)$$

2. Design correction

The output of solar cell modules is reduced by some external factors. Thus, solar cell modules calculated by the above basic formula are generally unable to meet the electricity demand of photovoltaic systems in the actual situation. To obtain more accurate results, it is necessary to correct the above basic formula.

(1) Reducing the output of solar cell modules by 10%. In practice, the output of solar cell modules is reduced by the external environment. Coverage by dirt and dust and the slow decay of module performance reduce the output of solar cell modules. The common practice is to address these unpredictable and unquantifiable factors by reducing the output of solar cell modules by 10% at the time of calculation. You can think of this as an engineering safety factor to be considered when designing photovoltaic systems. Since the operation of photovoltaic power supply systems is also dependent on weather conditions, it is necessary to evaluate and technically estimate these factors, so that a margin in the design will allow the system to function properly for a long period of time year after year.

(2) Increasing the load by 10% to cope with the coulombic efficiency of storage batteries. During the charging and discharging process of storage batteries, lead-acid storage batteries electrolyze water and generate gas that escapes, which means that part of the current generated by solar cell modules cannot be converted and stored but is dissipated. So, it can be assumed that a small portion of the current must be used to compensate for the loss, and we use the coulombic efficiency of storage batteries to evaluate this current loss. Different storage batteries have different coulombic efficiencies, and it can generally be assumed that there is a loss of 5%-10%. Thus, it is necessary to increase the power of solar cell modules by 10% in conservative design to offset the dissipation loss of storage batteries.

3. Complete photovoltaic module design

In view of the above factors, it is necessary to modify the simple photovoltaic module design formula by, firstly, dividing the daily load by the coulombic efficiency of storage batteries (in this way, the daily load is increased, and, as a matter of fact, the true load that photovoltaic modules need to bear is determined), and secondly, multiplying the attenuation factor by the daily output of photovoltaic modules (in this way, both environmental factors and the reduction of the daily output of photovoltaic modules due to its own attenuation are taken into account, and a conservative estimate of the output of photovoltaic modules in the actual situation is obtained). Taking the above factors into account, the following formula can be obtained:

$$\text{Number of Parallel Components} = \frac{\text{Daily Average Load}(A \cdot h)}{\text{Coulombic Efficiency} \times \text{Daily Output of Components}(A \cdot h) \times \text{Attenuation Factor}}$$

(3.5)

The method is to convert the actual solar radiation on the inclined plane into an equivalent number of hours of solar exposure using standard solar radiation of $1,000 \text{ W/m}^2$. This number of hours is multiplied by the peak output of photovoltaic modules to estimate the number of ampere-hours per day output from photovoltaic modules. The output of photovoltaic modules is the number of peak hours × peak power.

For example, if the monthly average solar radiation is $5.0 \text{ kW} \cdot \text{h/m}^2$ (it can be expressed as $5.0 \text{ h} \times 1000 \text{ W/m}^2$) and 1000 W/m^2 is exactly the same amount of standard solar radiation used to calibrate the power of photovoltaic modules, then the average solar radiation of $5.0 \text{ kW} \cdot \text{h/m}^2$ is basically equivalent to a 5.0 h of solar radiation received by photovoltaic modules under standard solar radiation. While this may not reflect the exact situation, but it can be used to simplify the calculation.

Since 1000 W/m^2 is the radiation used by manufacturers to calibrate the power of photovoltaic modules, the value of the module output in this radiation case can be easily obtained from manufacturers. To calculate the number of ampere-hours per day produced by photovoltaic modules, peak hours × I_{mp} of photovoltaic modules can be used.

For example, assuming a monthly average daily radiation of $5.0 \text{kW} \cdot \text{h/m}^2$ on a sloping surface with an inclination of 30° in a given region, this can be expressed as $5.0 \text{ h} \times 1000 \text{ W} \cdot \text{h/m}^2$. For a typical 75 W photovoltaic module with an I_{mp} of 75 W/17 V=4.4 A, the number of ampere-hours of electricity generated per day can be calculated as $5.0 \text{ h} \times 4.4 \text{ A} = 22.0 \text{ A} \cdot \text{h}$.

Overall, the method of peak sunshine hours estimation is an effective method for quick estimation of the output of photovoltaic modules when photovoltaic radiation data on local tilted slopes are known.

An example of how to calculate the number of photovoltaic modules required for a photovoltaic power generation system using the above method is given below.

Assume a photovoltaic power supply system constructed in a remote area, with a DC voltage of 24 V and a load of $400 \text{A} \cdot \text{h/day}$. The lowest solar radiation in the area is found in January. If a 30° inclination is adopted, the average daily solar radiation on the slope is 3.0 kWh/m^2, or the equivalent of 3 standard peak hours. For a typical 75 W photovoltaic module, the daily output is:

Module daily output = 3.0 peak hours × 4.4 A = $13.2 \text{ A} \cdot \text{h/day}$

Assume that the coulombic efficiency of storage batteries is 90% and the output attenuation of the photovoltaic module is 10%. According to formulas (3.5) and (3.4), the following formula can be obtained:

$$\frac{\text{Number of Parallel}}{\text{Components}} = \frac{\text{Daily Average Load}(\text{A} \cdot \text{h})}{\text{Coulombic Efficiency} \times \text{Daily Output of Components}(\text{A} \cdot \text{h}) \times \text{Attenuation Factor}}$$

$$= \frac{400}{0.9 \times 13.2 \times 0.9} = 37.4 \text{ (Rounded to the integer of 38)}$$

$$\text{Number of Components in Series} = \frac{\text{System Voltage(V)}}{\text{Component Voltage(V)}} = \frac{24}{17} = 1.4 \text{(Rounded to the integer of 2)}$$

Based on the above calculated data, the number of modules in parallel can be selected as 38, the number of modules in series can be selected as 2, and the number of photovoltaic modules required is 2 in series × 38 in parallel = 76.

3.1.5 Calculation of the load of stand-alone photovoltaic power generation systems

Load is the main design basis for stand-alone photovoltaic systems, as well as one of the key factors in the design and pricing of stand-alone photovoltaic power generation systems. It is generally determined by users, but sometimes designers can modify it or propose a more reasonable solution according to the specific situation. In terms of load, the most important thing to consider is whether to use DC or AC loads. The following considerations are included in the adoption of AC loads: which are resistive loads, which are inductive loads impacted by surge currents, which important loads must have guaranteed power supply, and which are general loads. Resistive AC loads (e.g., incandescent lamps, electronic energy-saving lamps, and electric heaters) have no surge current. Inductive AC loads (e.g., electric motors, refrigerators, water pumps, televisions, and fluorescent lamps with electronic ballasts) have surge currents. Generally, the surge current of electric motors and refrigerators is 5 to 8 times of the rated current, and the surge current of televisions is 2 to 5 times of the rated current. This should be given full attention when configuring inverters. In addition, to reduce the configuration and cost of photovoltaic systems, loads should be reasonably scheduled according to the time of electricity consumption, and the loads of larger power are preferably used at different times and zones.

It is common practice to list the names of all loads, their power requirements, rated operating voltages, and the time of daily electricity consumption. Both AC and DC loads should be listed, and the power factor should not be considered in AC power calculations. Then, categorize the loads and group them by operating voltage, and calculate the total power requirements for each group. Next, select the system operating voltage and calculate the average number of ampere-hours (A·h) required for the entire system at this voltage, that is, calculate the sum of the average daily electricity consumption for all loads. In terms of the selection of the system operating voltage, the voltage required by the maximum power load is often selected. In systems where AC loads are dominant, the DC system voltage should be compatible with the selected inverter input voltage. Generally, for independently operated solar photovoltaic power generation systems, the AC load is operating at 220 V, and the DC load is operating at 12 V or multiples of 12 V (i.e., 24 V or 48 V, etc.). In theory, determining the loads is straightforward, whereas in practice, load requirements are often not defined. For example, the power required by household appliances can be obtained from specifications provided by manufacturers, but not their operating hours. Daily, weekly and monthly usage hours are likely to be overestimated, with the cumulative effect leading to an increase in the design capacity and cost of photovoltaic power generation systems. In practice, certain higher power loads can be scheduled for use at different times. In strict design, it is necessary to understand load characteristics of stand-alone photovoltaic power generation systems, i.e., the load power at different times of the 24h in a day, especially for centralized power supply systems. These characteristics can be controlled appropriately after understanding the pattern of electricity consumption.

In addition, when designing photovoltaic power generation systems, the impact of feeders used on the entire system is also significant. Here, feeders can be considered as part of the load for calculation. For example, assume the DC load power is P_0, the rated operating voltage is U_0, the operating current is I_0, and the resistance, length, cross-sectional area, and material resistivity of the electricity transmission line are R, L, S, and ρ, respectively, then the voltage drop ΔU and power loss ΔP on the transmission line are as follows, respectively

$$\Delta U = I_0 R = \frac{P_0}{U_0} \cdot \frac{\rho L}{S} \tag{3.6}$$

$$\Delta P = I_0 \Delta U = \left(\frac{P_0}{U_0}\right)^2 \cdot \frac{\rho L}{S} \tag{3.7}$$

The voltage drop ΔU on the transmission line is determined by the output voltage of storage batteries and the minimum start-up operating voltage of the load, which should generally not exceed 2 V, and the power loss ΔP on the transmission line should generally not exceed 2%-5% of the rated output power of photovoltaic arrays. These parameters can be used to determine the wire diameter or cross-sectional area of the system transmission conductor. The resistivity of copper and aluminium conducting wires is 1.75×10^{-8} $\Omega \cdot m$ and 2.90×10^{-8} $\Omega \cdot m$, respectively. A copper conducting wire with a diameter of 1 mm and a length of 10 m has a resistance of 0.223 Ω. So, the voltage drop for a 10 A DC current is 2.23 V, and the power loss can be as high as 22.3 W. A copper conducting wire with a diameter of 2 mm and the same length of 10 m has a resistance of 0.0557 Ω. So, the voltage drop for a 10 A DC current is 0.557 V, and the power loss is 5.57 W. It can be seen that power loss related to conductors is considerable for larger DC currents. While the use of conductors with a larger cross-sectional area reduces the loss, it also leads to an increase in the cost of the entire system. Moreover, the length of feeders needs to be carefully calculated and integrated, with or without the placement of photovoltaic arrays.

【Task implementation】

I. Task preparations

1 competition equipment platform, 1 slotted screwdriver, 1 philips screwdriver, 1 RS485-USB connector, 1 communication schematic diagram, 1 set of string inverter and its accessories, 1 set of computer mainframe, 1 copy of record sheet for power-up inspection, and 1 copy of record sheet for off-grid photovoltaic system design and commissioning.

II. Task content and procedures

Task 3.1 Related implementation charts

(i) Task 1: Touch screen interface design of intelligent off-grid micro inverter systems

Task content: Touch screen interface design of the monitoring system of intelligent off-grid micro inverter systems

Task procedures:

(1) Complete the function of the "Settings" screen.

(2) Complete the design of the "Data Monitoring" screen.

(3) Complete the design of the "Inversion Control" screen.

(ii) Task 2: Installation and commissioning of combiner box communication

Task procedures: Installation and commissioning of combiner box communication of off-grid micro inverter systems.

Task procedures:

(1) Carry out communication wiring of the intelligent monitoring unit of the photovoltaic combiner box.

(2) Inspect the operating status of the intelligent monitoring unit.

(3) Complete the commissioning and recording of the station number, COM port number, equipment address code, hexadecimal address code, baud rate, parity bit, sending address code, and feedback code of the intelligent monitoring unit.

III. Skill requirements

(1) To be able to construct four monitoring screens: one main screen and three sub-screens (three button controls are needed in the main screen for switching to the three sub-screens).

(2) The three sub-screens are named "Settings", "Data Monitoring" and "Inversion Control", respectively, and in each sub-screen, a button control is needed in the lower left corner, named "Back" (this button is used to return to the main screen).

(3) To be able to complete the installation and wiring of the communication module of the combiner box, including the installation of the main control module and the current sensor module, FMB wiring connection of the current sensor, wiring of the DC busbar power supply terminal, wiring of the RS485 communication terminal, and wiring of the

Project 3 Designing Solar Photovoltaic Power Generation Systems

24 V DC power supply terminal.

(4) To be able to complete the commissioning of the communication module of the combiner box, and analyze commissioning methods of other components of stand-alone photovoltaic power generation systems.

Ⅳ. **Task results, appraisal and evaluation**

(1) Both procedures and data of touch screen interface design of intelligent off-grid micro inverter systems are correct, and both procedures and data of the installation and commissioning of combiner box communication are correct (accounting for 90%).

(2) The operator exhibits good professional quality during the operation process and follows 7S management model (accounting for 10%).

【Exercises】

1. What are the general components of stand-alone photovoltaic power generation systems?

2. What is the method for calculating the number of series-connected and parallel-connected solar cell modules, respectively, during the calculation of photovoltaic module arrays?

3. Assume a photovoltaic power supply system uses 100 solar cell modules of 255 W (25 in parallel × 4 in series), with an operating voltage of 24 V and 4500 A·h storage batteries. What is the maximum charging rate?

Task 3.2   Designing Grid-Connected Photovoltaic Power Generation Systems

【Learning objectives】

Knowledge objective: To master design requirements of grid-connected photovoltaic power generation systems

Ability objective: To be able to design photovoltaic cell series-parallel connection schemes, grid access schemes, and grid connection modes for grid-connected photovoltaic power generation systems

Qualification objective: To cultivate the professional spirit of pursuing meticulousness and striving for perfection

Learning priority: Design essentials of grid-connected photovoltaic power generation systems

Learning challenge: Design and commissioning of the communication systems of grid-connected photovoltaic power generation systems

【Task analysis】

The composition of grid-connected photovoltaic power generation systems varies depending on the capacity of power stations. A variety of grid connection schemes are available. Thus, the capacity of photovoltaic cells, as well as the series-parallel connection schemes, and grid access schemes must be designed according to the actual situation.

This task relies on the equipment plat form of the vocational skills certificate, and corresponds to various maintenance tasks related to the communication systems of photovoltaic power stations. It involves partially designing, installing and commissioning of the communication system, learning various design related hands-on activities of photovoltaic power generation systems, and completing tasks such as planning and design schemes of photovoltaic power stations, and inverter communication installation and commissioning.

【Knowledge learning】

3.2.1 Composition of photovoltaic grid-connected power generation systems

As shown in Figure 3.2, the main components of a photovoltaic grid-connected power generation system are as follows:

(1) Photovoltaic cell module and its rack.
(2) Photovoltaic array combiner box.
(3) DC power distribution cabinet.
(4) Photovoltaic grid-connected inverter.
(5) Grid access device.
(6) Communication and monitoring device of the system.
(7) Lightning protection and grounding device of the system.
(8) Infrastructure such as civil construction and power distribution rooms.
(9) Connecting cables and protective materials of the system.

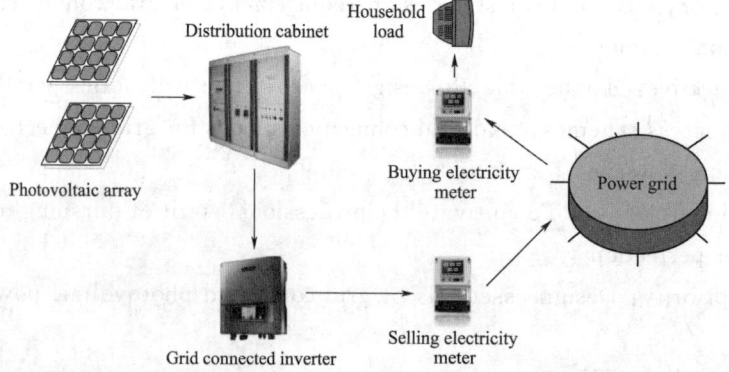

Figure 3.2 Grid-connected photovoltaic power generation system

3.2.2 Classification of photovoltaic grid-connected power generation systems

According to the mode of combination of photovoltaic power stations and buildings, grid-connected power generation can be divided into two types: centralized grid-connected power generation (as shown in Figure 3.3) and string grid-connected power generation (as shown in Figure 3.4).

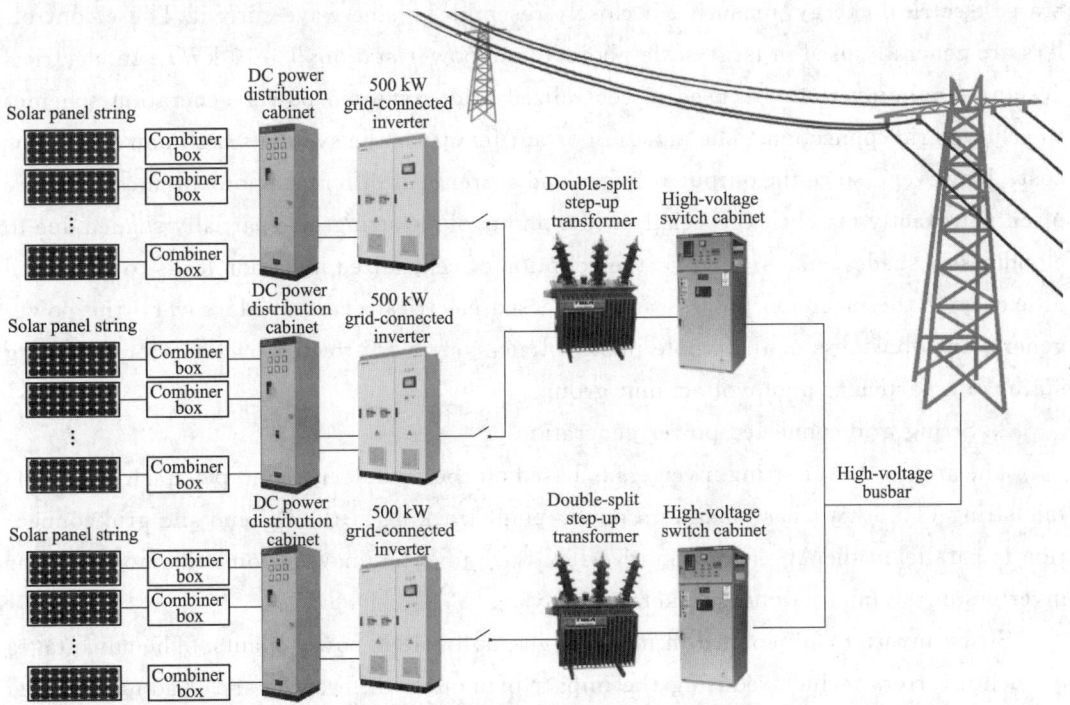

Figure 3.3 Centralized grid-connected photovoltaic power generation system

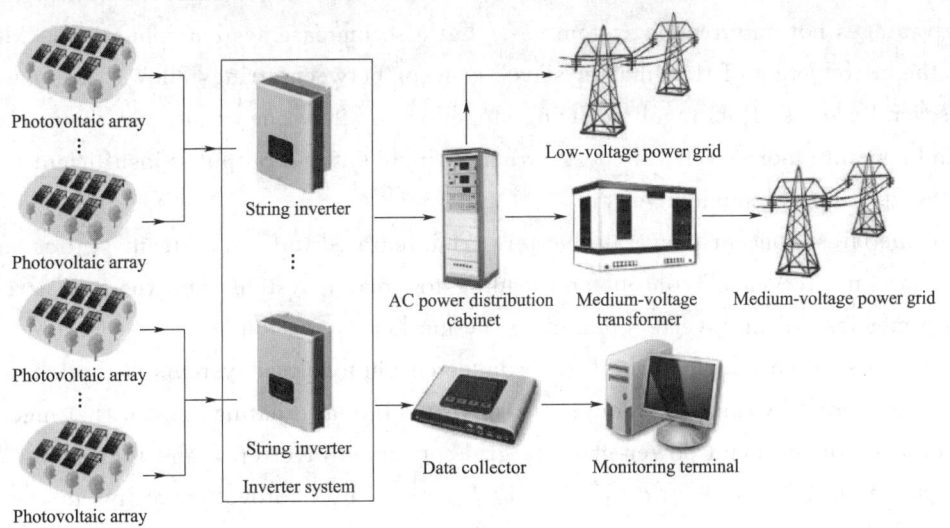

Figure 3.4 String grid-connected photovoltaic power generation system

1. Centralized grid-connected power generation

In centralized inversion technology, several parallel photovoltaic strings are connected to the DC input terminal of the same centralized inverter. Generally, three-phase IGBT power modules are used for larger power, and field effect transistors are adopted for smaller power. Meanwhile, DSP conversion controllers are used to improve the quality of generated electrical energy, ensuring it closely resembles a sine-wave current. These controllers are generally used in large-scale photovoltaic power stations (>10 kW). In electrical design, single inverters are used in centralized grid-connected power generation schemes to achieve grid connection. The most important feature is the system's high power and low cost. However, since the output voltages and currents of different photovoltaic strings are often not exactly matched (especially when photovoltaic strings are partially shaded due to cloudiness, shade, stains, etc.), the adoption of centralized inversion leads to decreased efficiency of the inversion process and decreased electrical energy. Moreover, the power generation robustness of the whole photovoltaic system is affected by the poor operating status of a particular photovoltaic unit group.

2. String grid-connected power generation

The application of string inverters is based on the modularity concept. Each photovoltaic string (1 – 5 kW) has maximum power point tracking at the DC end and grid connection in parallel at the AC end via an inverter. Such inverters have become the most popular inverters in the international market nowadays.

String inverters are applied in many large photovoltaic power plants. The advantages of such inverters include reducing the impact of module differences and shading between strings, and decreasing the mismatch between optimal operating points of photovoltaic modules and inverters, thus increasing the amount of electricity generated. These technical advantages not only reduce system costs but also increase system robustness. Moreover, the introduction of the "master-slave" concept between strings allows the system to link several groups of photovoltaic strings together to allow one or more of them to operate and generate more electrical energy when a single string's output is insufficient to sustain the operation of single inverters.

In the latest concept, several inverters are integrated to form a "team", thus substituting the "master-slave" concept and leading to greater system robustness. Currently, transformer less string inverters dominate the market.

The most important feature of grid-connected photovoltaic systems is that the direct current generated by solar cell modules is converted into alternating current that meets the requirements of the main power grid via grid-connected inverters, and then gains direct access to the public power grid. Electricity generated by photovoltaic arrays in the grid-connected system is not only supplied to AC loads, but also fed to the grid. On cloudy and rainy days or at night, when solar cell modules do not generate electrical energy or generated electrical energy does not meet load demand, the grid is used to supply power. Because of the direct input of electrical energy into the grid, which eliminates the need for storage batteries and the energy storage and release process, solar cell arrays should be installed at a specific angle so that maximum solar radiation can be received throughout the year. In this way, electricity generated by photovoltaic arrays can be fully utilized, thereby reducing energy loss and lowering system cost. However, dedicated grid-connected inverters are required in the system to ensure that the output electricity meets the requirements of grid power for voltage, frequency and other electrical performance indicators. Due to the efficiency of inverters, some energy loss is inevitable. Such systems are generally able to use mains power and solar cell module arrays in parallel as the power source for local AC loads. This not only reduces the loss-of-load probability of the whole system, but enables grid-connected photovoltaic systems to play a peak-shaving role in the utility power grid.

3.2.3 Design and selection of grid-connected inverters

1. Robust protection against the "islanding effect"

The so-called "islanding effect" refers to the fact that a power generating device connected to the public power grid does not have corresponding detection means to detect the power grid is disconnected, and continues to feed power to the public power grid.

In general, the islanding effect may adversely affect the entire power distribution system equipment and also the equipment at the user end, including:

(1) Endangering the lives of power maintenance personnel.

(2) Affecting protective switching action procedures in the power distribution system.

(3) Unstable supply voltage and frequency in the islanded area can cause damage to electrical equipment.

(4) When power supply is restored, the resulting voltage phase non-synchronization will generate surge currents that may cause re-tripping or damage to photovoltaic systems, loads and power supply systems.

(5) Grid-connected photovoltaic power generation systems cause under-phase power supply problems for three-phase loads due to single-phase power supply.

It can be seen that a safe and robust grid-connected inversion device must be able to timely detect the islanding effect and avoid the resulting hazards.

2. Complete grid-connected protection functions and protection measures

Inverters are the core of photovoltaic grid-connected power generation systems. Therefore, a variety of complete protection measures are needed, which should have basic protection functions (such as short circuit, over-voltage, over-current, under-frequency, over-frequency, and overheating). Photovoltaic grid-connected protection devices protect photovoltaic power generation systems against the islanding effect on the one hand, and prevent line accidents or power instability on the other hand. This ensures that in the event of failure of photovoltaic inverter systems, the grid is not adversely affected and photovoltaic systems are not damaged.

In addition to grid-connected protection functions, other protective measures are also needed, e. g. , anti-vibration, lightning protection, and short-circuit grounding protection.

3. Superior sine wave output performance

Superior sine wave output performance refers to the fact that inverters can output pure sine waves, with minimal high order harmonics.

4. Maximum power point tracking

Maximum Power Point Tracking (MPPT) controllers are able to detect the generation voltage of solar panels in real time and track the maximum power output point ($Ⅵ$), so that the system can charge storage batteries at the maximum power output, which is much more efficient as compared to non-MPPT systems.

5. Rated output power

Rated output power refers to the ability of photovoltaic inverters to supply power to loads. Photovoltaic inverters with high rated output power can carry more electrical loads. When selecting photovoltaic inverters, the first consideration should be to have adequate rated power to meet the requirements of the equipment for electric power at the maximum load, as well as the expansion of the system and the access of some temporary loads. When electrical equipment is dominated by purely resistive loads or when the power factor is greater than 0.9, it is common practice to choose photovoltaic inverters whose rated output power is 10%–15% higher than the total power of the equipment.

6. Regulation performance of output voltage

The regulation performance of output voltage refers to the ability of photovoltaic inverters to regulate output voltage. For general photovoltaic inverter products, the percentage of fluctuation deviations in photovoltaic inverter output voltage when the DC input voltage varies within the allowable fluctuation range (generally referred to as the voltage regulation rate) is provided. For high-performance photovoltaic inverters, the percentage of fluctuation deviations in photovoltaic inverter output voltage when the load varies from 0 to 100% (generally referred to as the load regulation rate) should also be provided. High-performance photovoltaic inverters should have a voltage regulation rate of less than or equal to $\pm 3\%$ and a load regulation rate of less than or equal to $\pm 6\%$.

7. Efficiency of the whole machine

The efficiency of the whole machine refers to the magnitude of self-power loss of photovoltaic inverters. For photovoltaic inverters with larger capacity, the efficiency value under full-load operation and low-load operation should also be provided. Generally, the efficiency of inverters below the kW level should be 80%–85% and that of inverters below the 10 kW level should be 85%–90%; the efficiency of inverters with higher power must be above 90%. Inverter efficiency has a significant impact on photovoltaic power generation systems to increase effective power generation and reduce power generation cost. Therefore, comparison should be made as far as possible when selecting photovoltaic inverters, and products with higher whole-machine efficiency should be chosen.

8. Start-up performance

Make sure that photovoltaic inverters are properly started at the rated load. Multiple consecutive full-load start-ups are possible for high-performance photovoltaic inverters, without damaging power switching devices and other circuits. Small inverters, for their own safety, sometimes adopt soft start-up or current-limiting start-up measures or circuits.

3.2.4 RS485 communication of photovoltaic inverters

Photovoltaic inverters generally adopt RS485 communication, a typical serial communication standard. RS485 bus standard specifies standards for electrical characteristics of the bus interface, that is, for the definition of the two logical states: positive electrical level between $+2$ V and $+6$ V stands for a logical state; negative electrical level between -2V and -6V stands for the other logical state; digital signals adopt differential transmission modes, which can effectively reduce the interference of noise signals. For RS485 interfaces, the standard value of the maximum transmission distance is 4000 feet, in fact, up to 3000 meters (theoretical data; in practice, the limit distance is only about 1200 meters). For RS485 interfaces, up to 128 transceivers are allowed to be connected to the bus to support multi-station ability. For this reason, users can use a single RS485 interface to conveniently construct a network of equipment.

Half-duplex network composed of RS485 interfaces generally requires only two wires, so all RS485 interfaces adopt shielded twisted pairs for transmission. RS485 controller communication requires only two terminals, generally denoted by "A" and "B" (as shown in Figure 3.5).

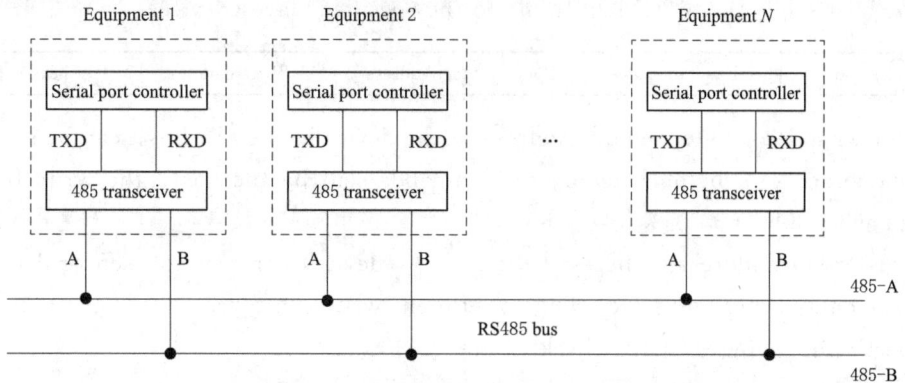

Figure 3.5 Diagram of RS485 communication network connection

RS485 communication parameters include: baud rate: 2400 – 115200 bps (the general default is 9600 bps); data bits: 7 – 9 bits (default: 8 bits); stop bit: 1 – 2 bits (default: 1 bit); parity: no parity, odd parity, and even parity.

Communication via RS485 involves the host and the slave. The host sends commands to the slave; the slave responds to the host's commands; they communicate following a uniform data format.

1. Inquiry data format

The format of the inquiry data frame sent by the host to the 485 bus is:

Address code	Function code	Register start address	Register length	Check code

Address code: 1 byte; unique address of the device in the 485 bus; can be set.

Function code: 1 byte; category of commands sent by the host; the inquiry frame is specified as 0x03.

Register start address: 2 bytes; stores slave (device) parameters, sensor data, etc.

Register length: 2 bytes; number of registers obtained.

Check code: 2 bytes; CRC check.

The slave (device) sends the inquiry response data frame to 485:

Address code	Function code	Number of data bytes	Data 1	Data 1	...	Data n	Check code

Address code: 1 byte; unique address of the slave (device) in the 485 bus.

Function code: 1 byte; category of commands sent by the host; the inquiry frame is specified as 0x03.

Number of data bytes: 1 byte; number of bytes from Data 1 to Data n.

Data 1 to Data n: Response data.

Check code: 2 bytes, CRC check.

2. Write data format

The host sends the write data frame to the specified slave (device):

Address code	Function code	Register start address	Write data	Check code

Address code: 1 byte; unique address of the device in the 485 bus; can be set.

Function code: 1 byte; category of commands sent by the host; the write frame is specified as 0x06.

Register start address: 2 bytes; stores slave (device) parameters, sensor data, etc.

Write data: Determined according to different write contents.

Check code: 2 bytes, CRC check.

The slave (device) sends the write response data frame to 485.

The content of the write response data frame is identical to the write data frame.

3.2.5 Combiner box and AC/DC power distribution cabinet

In photovoltaic power generation systems, a large number of photovoltaic cell modules are connected in series and parallel to obtain the required voltage and current values, so as to realize the optimal power generation efficiency. The main role of photovoltaic combiner boxes is to perform primary convergence of the input of photovoltaic cell arrays. They are used to reduce the number of connections between the photovoltaic cell array and the inverters, optimize system structure, and improve robustness and maintainability. Photovoltaic combiner boxes can not only provide convergence lightning protection function, but also monitor the operation status of photovoltaic cell panels, the magnitude of the current, voltage and power after convergence, as well as status collection of the lightning protector and DC breaker. In addition to relay contact output and other functions, they can also upload the measured and collected data to the monitoring system.

When selecting combiner boxes, the main consideration is the number of input channels, the maximum input current of each channel, the lightning protection reaction time, waterproof performance and other indicators.

The main role of photovoltaic DC (lightning protection) power distribution cabinets is to connect the DC cable output from the combiner box to grid-connected inverters. These cabinets consist of the DC input circuit breaker, leakage protector, anti-reverse diode, photovoltaic lightning protector, and other major devices. They are designed to ensure that the system is not subjected to electric leakage, short-circuit, overload, lightning impulse and other damages, and effectively ensuring load equipment operation and facilitating user operation and maintenance.

The main role of photovoltaic AC (lightning protection) power distribution cabinets is to provide grid-connected wires, circuit breakers, and lightning protectors for inverters via power distribution. Optional devices include power generation meters, inverter grid-connected interfaces, AC voltage and current meters, and other devices.

【Task implementation】

Ⅰ. Task preparations

1 equipment platform of the vocational skills certificate, 1 set of computer mainframe, 1 multimeter, 1 copy of record sheet for power-up inspection, and 1 copy of record sheet for grid-connected photovoltaic systems.

Task 3.2 Related implementation charts

Ⅱ. Task content and procedures

(ⅰ) Task 1: Photovoltaic power station planning and design scheme

Task content: Engineering planning and design scheme for the photovoltaic power station

Task procedures:

(1) Plan the deployment of the photovoltaic project according to functional requirements and process requirements.

(2) Complete equipment installation and wiring to meet the functional and process requirements of the photovoltaic power station and the control system.

(ⅱ) Task 2: Design and wiring of the grid-connected photovoltaic power generation system

Task content: Complete the design and wiring of the grid-connected photovoltaic power generation system

Task procedures:

(1) Complete the design and wiring of the grid-connected main electrical connection.

(2) Complete the installation and wiring of RS485 communication terminals of the grid-connected inverter.

(3) Set and record the grid-connected communication addresses.

(4) Use serial port debugging software for communication testing, and making relevant records.

Ⅲ. Skill requirements

(1) To be able to select key devices according to the requirements of electrical diagrams, functional and process requirements.

(2) To be able to complete component string design and inverter parameter selection.

(3) To be able to carry out standard construction to construct the intelligent microgrid system according to construction drawings and construction process requirements.

(4) Complete equipment installation and wiring to meet the functional and process requirements of the photovoltaic power station and the control system.

(5) To be able to inspect the operation, installation and commissioning of inverter communication power supply, as well as the fan and signal indicator status, for any abnormality and perform analysis and troubleshooting.

(6) To be able to inspect the operation status of the communication protocol converter, router, switch, firewall, as well as all types of servers and optical transmission equipment, for any abnormal alarm message and perform analysis and troubleshooting.

Ⅳ. Task results, appraisal and evaluation

(1) Both procedures and data of planning and design schemes for the photovoltaic power station are correct, and both procedures and data of inverter communication installation and commissioning are correct (accounting for 90%).

(2) The operator exhibits good professional quality during the operation process and follows 7S management model (accounting for 10%).

Project 3 Designing Solar Photovoltaic Power Generation Systems

【Exercises】

1. What are the main components of photovoltaic grid-connected power generation systems?

2. What is the possible impact of the islanding effect on the entire power distribution system equipment and the equipment at the user end?

3. What are the differences between grid-connected power generation systems and stand-alone power generation systems?

项目 4　安装与运维太阳能光伏发电系统

任务 4.1　安装太阳能光伏发电系统

【学习目标】

知识目标：掌握太阳能光伏发电系统安装内容。

能力目标：能安装太阳能光伏电池基础及组件；能安装太阳能光伏发电系统的蓄电池和逆变器。

素质目标：培养吃苦耐劳、扎根基层的职业品质。

重点：光伏发电系统的安装要点。

难点：光伏发电系统的电气测试。

【任务分析】

太阳能光伏发电系统包含的设备、部件较多，其中光伏电池组件的安装是该系统特有部分，能正确安装系统设备和部件对系统整体效率具有重要的影响。

【知识学习】

4.1.1　桩基础施工

1. 钻孔施工

钻机就位：就位时，钻头尖对准桩位，对位误差不大于 2.0cm，调整钻机平整稳固，保证主钻杆垂直地面，主杆垂直度不大于 20mm。

成孔采用机械成孔，钻杆直径 250mm，钻孔机就位时，保持平稳，不发生倾斜、位移，保持钻杆垂直，在钻杆上标注 1800mm 刻度线，以便控制钻孔深度不低于 1800mm。

成孔质量要求：桩孔的中心位置偏差±10mm，桩孔深度允许偏差+10mm（只能深不能浅），钻孔垂直度偏差不大于 20mm 桩长，孔低虚土须清理干净。

2. 混凝土工程施工

(1) 混凝土浇筑混凝土浇筑前的具体准备工作如下：

1) 混凝土浇筑前的模板、钢筋、预埋件等全部安装完毕，经检验符合设计规范要求，并办完隐检手续。

2) 模板内的杂物及钢筋上的污物等清理干净。模板的缝隙及孔洞已堵严，并办完隐检手续。

3）混凝土原材料的各项指标已经过检验。

4）技术交底全面完成，各专业负责人已在浇筑申请书上签字。

5）混凝土施工工艺流程中，自拌混凝土人力拉车沿施工便道运至离浇筑地点最近点，运至浇筑地点后，挂好料斗，倒入桩基内，快到顶部时停止倒料，工人用铁锹装混凝土至模板上平面，用铁抹子压实抹光。

（2）混凝土浇筑与振捣的要求如下：

1）混凝土自吊斗口或人工布料管口下落得自由倾落高度不得超过 2.5m，浇筑高度如超过 2.5m 时必须用溜管伸到桩的下部，浇筑混凝土。

2）浇筑混凝土时要分层连续进行。

3）使用插入式振捣器应快插慢拔，插点要均应排列，逐点移动，顺序进行，不得遗漏，做到均匀振实。移动间距不大于振捣作用半径的 1.5 倍（一般为 45cm）。振捣上一层时应插入下层 5cm，以消除两层间的接缝。

4）浇筑混凝土时应派木工、钢筋工随时观察模板、钢筋、预埋件等有无移动，变形或堵塞情况，发生问题应立即处理并应在已浇筑的混凝土初凝结前修正完好。

（3）混凝土养护要求如下：

1）基础要在浇筑混凝土强度达 1.2MPa 后拆模，拆模后立即采用塑料薄膜覆盖进行养护，养护过程中保证塑料薄膜内应有凝结水。

2）养护时间不少于 3 天。

3）混凝土浇筑完，在混凝土强度未达到 1.2MPa 之前不得进行下一步施工。

（4）混凝土试验。混凝土如模前，在现场随机取样制作混凝土试件，取样的试件不少于 30%，试件的留置应符合如下规定：强度试块为 200m^3，同一强度等级、同配合比、同班组混凝土取样不少于 9 次，同批同配合比混凝土少于 200m^3时，取样不少于 1 次。试块留置组数按照规范要求留置。

3. 混凝土质量标准

混凝土技术资料要齐全并符合规范及设计要求，包括水泥、骨料、外加剂的材质证明和复试报告，配合比通知单等；混凝土的配合比、养护处理，必须合乎前文规定；混凝土的试件取样、制作、养护和试验符合《混凝土结构工程施工质量验收规范》（GB 50204—2015）要求。

4. 模板工程施工

（1）材料规格：波纹管内径 350mm，环形箍用铁丝制作。

（2）施工准备：混凝土桩模板按设计图纸尺寸裁断波纹管，按设计图纸统计每种类型波纹管用量，按比例下料，分类堆放备用。

（3）模板安装的一般要求如下：

1）模板安装前应挂出模板就位线及检查线，以保证模板安装的准确性。

2）模板成型后截面尺寸偏差应控制在±2mm。

3）安装模板后，应拉通线调整模板，检查模板标高、截面尺寸、平整度、垂直度、确认合格后方可进行下道工序。

(4) 模板安装工艺如下：

1) 将波纹管埋深地下 10cm，波纹管均分三点外 50cm 砸 3 根钢筋桩，钢筋桩与波纹管之间用一平顶底部，一斜顶上部加固波纹管，保持上部波纹管在施工过程中不发生偏移，然后安装好螺栓固定支架，将预埋螺栓按外露尺寸固定。

2) 校验柱子位置。

3) 模板安装工序完成，准备下道工序施工。

(5) 模板成品保护措施如下：

1) 安装模板时应轻起轻放，不准碰撞，防止模板变形。

2) 模板安好后一定要刷脱模剂，防止沾模。

3) 拆下的模板如发现表面不平或损坏时，应及时修理或更换。

4) 模板在使用过程中应加强管理，码放整齐。

5) 模板应注意防雨保存，避免受潮生锈及变形。

6) 在浇铸混凝土过程中派专人看模，检查紧固情况，发现变形、松动等现象及时修整加固。

(6) 模板拆除要求如下：

1) 波纹管模型的拆除，应符合《混凝土结构工程施工验收规范》（GB 50204—2015）所要求的混凝土强度。

2) 拆模时严禁使用大锤或硬撬；人员不得站在正在拆除的横板上操作；一定要等到混凝土初凝后方可拆模，并且轻拿轻放，防止预埋螺栓松动移位。

3) 拆除下来的波纹管一定要分类堆放，设立尺寸标牌，码放整齐，以备下次使用。

(7) 对于部分已经浇筑至地面的桩，施工步骤如下：

1) 先将上的土清理干净，将桩头周围的土下降 10cm。

2) 把桩头上的石子清理，用吹风机将桩头上的浮土清理干净。

3) 波纹管模具的安装时必须埋入地 10cm。

4) 定模固定后报监理单位进行验收，合格后进行混凝土浇筑施工。

5) 浇筑混凝土时用震动棒振捣密实，抹面压光。

6) 浇筑完成 24h 后拆除模板，并养护。

(8) 原材料进场检验要求如下：

1) 所有运至现场的钢筋，其品种、规格、牌号、质量等级均应符合设计要求，进厂时资料员负责收集出厂质量证明或厂家的试验报告单，钢筋表面或每捆钢筋均应有标志，且与报告单中批号吻合，否则不得进场。

2) 所有运至现场的钢筋，均应进行外观检查。钢筋应平直，无损伤，表面不得有裂纹、油污、颗粒状或片状老锈，不符合要求的钢筋禁止使用。

3) 钢筋的取样：钢筋进场时，应按批进行检查和验收。每批由同牌号、同规格、同交货状态的钢筋组成，重量不大于 60t。

(9) 钢筋加工机械设备有切割机、调直机、电焊机、切断机、钢筋弯折机。钢筋、加工及储存要求如下：

1)建立严格的钢筋生产、安全、文明、环保管理制度,并制定节约措施,降低材料损耗。下料前要熟悉图纸,依据图纸审核材料单。下料过程中,注意设计和规范的各项要求。钢筋的弯折长度、弯折角度、搭接长度、平直长度以及高度等都需注意,发现问题及时与技术人员联系,防止下料中尺寸出现偏差。钢筋加工前由技术部门做出钢筋配料单,由项目技术负责人审批后进行下料加工。

2)钢筋切断应根据钢筋号、直径、长度和数量,长短搭配,先断长料后断短料,尽量减少和缩短钢筋的短头,以节约钢材。

3)制作的半成品钢筋,应在制作场内预检,合格后方可用于现场,并做好记录。

4)垂直运输采用汽车吊进行根据需要吊运至指定部位。长钢筋吊运时,应进行试吊以确定吊点,防止吊点距离过大,钢筋产生变形。水平运输采用板车运输,运输过程中要捆绑牢靠,防止挤压变形。

5)成型钢筋按规格、使用部位等整齐码放,挂标志牌,做到整洁清楚,一目了然。

6)钢筋加工质量要求:①钢筋拉直应平直,无局部曲折;②钢筋切断端口不得有马蹄形或起弯等现象,钢筋的长度应力求准确;③钢筋弯曲成型形状正确,平面上没有翘曲不平现象。

(10)钢筋电焊准备工作如下:

1)核对半成品钢筋的钢号、直径、形状、尺寸和数量等是否与料单牌符合,如有错漏应纠正增补。

2)钢筋电焊,先按施工图纸要求,标出尺寸线,电焊时按放线尺寸确定钢筋位置。

3)钢筋的接头位置,搭接长度,抗震构造钢筋及钢筋锚固长度要符合施工规范和设计要求。

4)准备电焊机及电焊条,搭设操作架。电焊条采用2.5号电焊丝,电焊必须保证受力钢筋不移位,双向受力钢筋必须全部电焊。

桩基础施工如图4.1所示。

图4.1 桩基础施工

4.1.2 支架安装

1. 场地勘查与准备

（1）确认安装地点的地质条件、承载能力、风荷载、雪荷载等环境因素，符合支架设计要求。

（2）清理场地，确保地面平整，无尖锐物、杂物等影响支架安装的障碍物。

（3）按照设计图纸进行测量放线，标出支架基础位置。

光伏支架安装如图4.2所示。

图4.2　光伏支架安装

2. 支架基础施工

（1）根据地质条件和设计要求，进行混凝土基础浇筑或螺旋地桩打入。

（2）对于混凝土基础，确保混凝土强度达标，预埋件位置准确；对于螺旋地桩，确保打入深度和垂直度符合要求。

3. 支架组装与安装

（1）按照支架图纸和组件排布图，进行支架组件的组装，确保连接件紧固、无松动。

（2）使用水平尺、吊线等工具，确保支架安装的水平度和垂直度在允许范围内。

（3）将组装好的支架安装到预定位置，与基础连接牢固，如有必要，进行防锈处理。

4. 支架接地

按照设计要求，进行支架接地系统的安装，包括接地体埋设、接地扁钢连接、接地电阻测试等，确保接地电阻符合标准。

4.1.3 光伏组件安装

1. 组件检查与准备

（1）检查光伏组件外观无破损、划痕，接线盒、边框等无变形或破损。

（2）核对组件型号、功率等信息与设计图纸一致，检查接线盒内二极管、连接线等无损坏。

2. 组件安装

（1）将组件按照设计图纸的排布顺序，平稳放置在支架上，使用专用夹具或螺栓固定，确保组件与支架接触面平整，无应力集中。

（2）连接组件间的串联或并联电缆，使用专用接线盒或连接器，确保接线紧固、防水密封良好。

3. 组件接线与防护

（1）按照系统电气图纸，进行组件串的并联、汇流箱接入等接线工作，确保接线正确，线径、压接等符合规范。

（2）对接线部位进行必要的防护处理，如使用线槽、热缩管、防水盒等，防止磨损、腐蚀、短路等风险。

4. 组件测试与标识

（1）完成安装后，进行组件串的 I-V 曲线测试，确保其性能符合出厂标准，无热斑、隐裂等问题。

（2）在明显位置标注组件串编号、功率等信息，便于后期运维识别。

光伏组件安装如图 4.3 所示。

图 4.3　光伏组件安装

4.1.4　逆变器及变压器安装

设备进场由施工单位、建设单位（或其代表）、监理单位、供货单位共同对其进行外观检查，是否变形，有无锈蚀损伤，有无碰撞现象，还应检查有无渗漏油，并做记录。按产品装箱单查对货箱数是否齐全。有无漏发、错发现象，检查外包装箱有无破损、丢失现象，并做记录。绝缘件应无裂纹、缺损，外表清洁，测温仪指示正确。

1. 吊装规程

（1）吊装准备。施工方案已经批准，并进行技术交底，做到施工人员熟悉施工程序和施工要求；施工场地平整，吊车作业范围应进行压实；吊装用机具和材料必须具有合格证并经检验合格；检查设备吊耳是否合格，必要时另行设置吊耳或捆绑设备；吊装准备工作完善后，由负责人统一指挥起吊设备安装就位。

(2) 吊装方案及注意事项。起吊时,将两根柔性吊带分别通过起吊标识拴在外包装箱上,吊钩垂直通过设备重心进行起吊,严禁倾斜运输。在使用吊车对逆变器进行吊起、放下及移动过程中,要保证缓慢、平稳。过程中必须严格遵守吊车安全操作规程,如遇恶劣天气条件,应停止起吊工作。

2. 逆变器及变压器就位安装

逆变器及变压器的安装采用整体式安装,就位应严格按照设计文件和厂家图纸进行,安装前由技术负责人对施工人员进行技术交底。

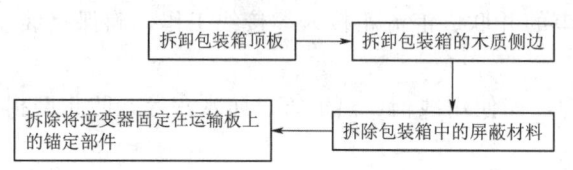

图 4.4 逆变器及变压器拆卸包装步骤

(1) 拆卸包装。应按图 4.4 所示步骤拆卸包装。

(2) 固定前检查。确保线缆地沟的铺设符合逆变器安装要求;确保槽钢的安装及开孔符合逆变器安装要求。

(3) 固定逆变器。采用吊装将逆变器运送至安装位置,并对准安装孔。使用 M12 螺栓通过底座上的腰孔将逆变器固定在槽钢或地基上。将逆变器底座的前后挡板安装好,完成逆变器的固定安装。

(4) 注意事项。变压器就位时应使高压侧朝线路侧,低压侧超逆变器室箱变重心轴线应与箱变基础纵向、横向几何中心线重合,误差应在 5mm 以内。箱式逆变器就位时应严格按照施工图纸,确保变压器与逆变器的安装接线。

(5) 清洁、喷漆。箱式逆变器及变压器安装全部结束应把所有部位清擦干净,局部可补刷同色漆,用户有要求时应按对方同意的色调重新喷漆,漆膜一般应为 0.02~0.05mm。

3. 电缆敷设施工

(1) 工艺流程如图 4.5 所示。

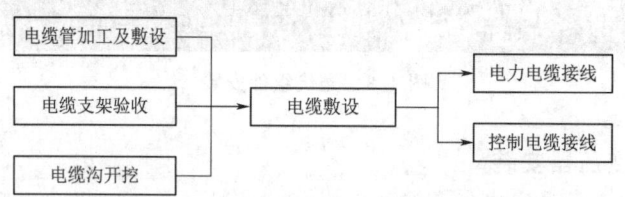

图 4.5 电缆敷设施工工艺流程图

(2) 施工方法及步骤。

1) 电缆套管的加工及敷设。按实际尺寸确定电缆管的长度、带有弯头的电缆管、先用弯管机弯出弯头部分,按电缆管的实际长度和高度切掉多余部分、清除毛刺、并除锈刷防腐漆。

若电缆管长度不够长,按所需长度再切一根钢管,打磨管口毛刺,将两段管口对齐一周满焊并打磨处理后补刷防腐漆。

明敷电缆管使用角钢固定在墙面或钢结构上(作为固定件用)、再把电缆管焊接在角钢上，管口用钢板点焊封堵、如管子较长应适当增加固定点。电缆管敷设完毕后、电缆管用－40×4 的扁钢将电缆管与接地网可靠焊接，电缆管地埋部分应刷防腐漆、露出地面部分刷银粉漆。电缆管口应安装喇叭口。

2）电缆支架配制及安装。土建施工完后与安装单位土建办理中间交接手续。合格后方可进行电缆敷设。

直埋电缆敷设安装：电缆线路有可能受到机械损伤、化学作用，同时有可能经过包含有地下电流、振动、热影响、虫鼠等危险因素的地段，应采取保护措施。直埋电缆敷设应符合设计要求：电缆敷设前检查电缆通道是否畅通、排水是否良好，照明、通风是否正常，检查电缆外观、型号、规格是否符合要求。在电缆放设时应根据现场实际情况安装电缆拖轨。

检查电缆管的敷设、电缆支架和吊架的安装情况。根据电缆清册和设计图纸、仔细观察电缆的敷设路径、顺序及实际长度，若设计有误及时与各部门联系。准备工作完毕后将电缆倒运到施工现场。电缆放线架放置牢固后电缆敷设在放线架上，电缆从电缆盘的上端引出敷设。高低压电力电缆、强电、弱电控制电缆按顺序由上而下敷设并排列整齐、固定牢固，电缆两端留够余度、将电缆两端处装设电缆标志牌。

（3）低压动力电缆和控制电缆头制作及接线。

1）低压动力电缆、控制电缆采用黏胶带包缠工艺；动力电缆采用专用液压压线钳压接接线鼻子；控制电缆、计算机电缆如为多股芯线，根据接线端子情况选择相应的压线钳及接线端子压接，如为单股芯线，则可直接压接；动力电缆相色标识采用包缠不同相色带形式，控制电缆相色标识可使用购买的芯线号头成品；电缆试验、对线合格后，对各电缆进行一一对应接线，电缆外护层及屏蔽层按要求进行接地。

2）尽可能做到动力电缆和控制电缆无中间接头；如不得已有中间接头时，要将接头处拉出，使其离开其他平行电缆，在其接头范围内加装一定强度的槽盒捆紧；对接头的位置等要做好标识、记录，并会同监理方对其进行验收，有关资料也要移交。

3）在电缆做头之前的电缆运输、存放、敷设时，确保所有的电缆头始终用塑料薄膜清水混凝土的配合比设计中，要针对当地水泥、砂石外掺料及加剂等原材影响混凝土质量的多种因素进行分析，确定主要控制因素，并从经济性和使用要求综合考虑，优选出符合生产条件的最优方案组合。及密封带密封，对敷设时切出的新电缆头要及时密封。

（4）电缆试验。电缆头制作完成后根据电缆的绝缘等级及规范的要求对每根电缆进行绝缘试验和校验，以检验电缆的完好程度。

（5）防火封堵。全部电缆敷设完后，按设计及规程进行防火封堵施工。对电缆穿越电缆沟、竖井、建筑物、楼板、墙体、设备、盘柜以及电缆管口均进行防火封堵，防火涂料的粉刷及防火盖板的安装要符合规范和设计要求，做到密实、平整、美观。

1）高低压开关柜底部孔洞及穿楼板孔洞防火封堵：屏柜底部孔洞采用 10mm 厚的防火隔板用膨胀螺栓安装在地面下；电缆穿隔板的孔隙用有机堵料包裹电缆；用 10mm 厚的隔板按屏柜大小切割后安装在屏板底部；电缆穿封堵墙隔板的孔隙用有机堵料严密封堵成形。

2）开关柜上进线防火封堵：清洁安装阻火墙处的电缆、桥架及开关柜壁，使之干燥、无灰尘与杂物；在电缆间涂有机堵料。

3）电缆竖井阻火段封堵：选用角钢做支撑安装好防火隔板作底板；用有机堵料包裹电缆封堵处；再采用防火膨胀模块交错堆砌与楼板相平，然后安装顶面隔板；电缆穿隔板的孔隙用有机堵料严密封堵成形。

4. 箱式逆变器及变压器箱体应接地

接地通过设备箱体上的接地孔，利用 40mm×4mm 热镀锌扁铁与厂区接地网连接，扁铁与设备箱体的连接采用螺栓连接，扁铁与箱体的接触面应除去镀锌层。

低压电缆运输与敷设。在运输装卸过程中，不应使电缆及电缆盘受到损伤。严禁将电缆盘直接由车上推下。电缆盘不应平放运输，平放储存。运输或滚动电缆盘前，必须保证电缆盘牢固，电缆绕紧，滚时必须顺着电缆的缠紧方向。

电缆及其附件到达现场后，应按要求及时进行检查，产品的技术文件应齐全；电缆型号、规格、长度应符合设计要求，附件应齐全，电缆外观不应受损，电缆封端应严密。电缆桥架应分类保管，不得因受力变形。

电缆敷设前应按下列要求进行检查：电缆通道畅通，排水良好，金属部分的防腐层完整。电缆型号、电压规格应符合设计，电缆外观无损伤，绝缘良好。电缆放线架应放置稳妥，钢轴的强度和长度应与电缆盘重量和宽度相配合。敷设前应按设计和实际路径计算每根电缆的长度，合理安排每盘电缆，减少电缆接头在带电区域敷设电缆，应有安全措施。

电力电缆在终端头与接头附近宜留有备用长度；电缆支架各支持点的水平距离不得大于 0.8m，电缆井架间距为 1m，电缆桥架支吊架间距 1.5m 左右，最大不超过 2m。电缆的最小弯曲半径应符合表 4.1 的规定。

表 4.1　　　　　　　　　　　电缆的最小弯曲半径

电缆型号		多芯	单芯
控制电缆		10D	
橡皮电力电缆	无铝包钢铠防护套	10D	
	钢铠护套	20D	
聚氯乙烯绝缘电力电缆		10D	
交联聚乙烯绝缘电力电缆		15D	20D

注　D 为电缆外径。

5. 电力电缆终端制作及安装

电缆头制作应由经过培训的熟悉工艺的人员进行，并严格遵守制作工艺规程。

制作电缆终端和接头前，符合下列要求：电缆绝缘良好，无受潮，塑料电缆内不得进水；附件规格应与电缆一致，零部件应齐全无损伤，绝缘材料不得受潮，密封材料不得失效；施工用具齐全，便于操作，消材齐备；制作电缆头，从剥切电缆开始应连续操作直至完成，缩短绝缘暴露时间；剥切电缆时不应损伤线芯和保留的绝缘层，附加绝缘的系统装配热缩要清洁；电缆终端头应采取加强绝缘，密封防潮，机械保护等措施，并确保外绝缘相同和对地距离；高压交联电缆在制作终端和接头时，应彻底清除半导电屏蔽层；电力电缆的热缩头制作时，喷灯烤制时火焰均匀，热缩管中无气泡；线鼻子与芯线连接时，线鼻子规格应与芯线相符，线鼻子与芯线表面接触良好，无裂纹、断线，铜线鼻子表面应光滑，清除线芯和连接管内壁油污及氧化层，压接模具与金具配合恰当压接牢固，压接后将端子或连接管上的凸痕修理光滑，不得残留毛刺；电力电缆终端处的金属护层必须接地良好，电缆每根铜屏蔽层和钢铠锡焊接地线；电缆通过零序电流互感器时，电缆金属护层和接地线应对地绝缘、接地点在互感器以上时，接地线应穿过互感器接地，接地点在互感器以下时，接地线应直接接地；装配组合电缆终端头时，各部件间配合或搭接处必须采取堵漏、防潮和密封措施，塑料电缆粘胶带、胶粘剂等方式密封，粘接要良好；电缆终端上应有明显的相色标志，且与系统的相互一致。

4.1.5 试验、调试

1. 启动调试

（1）启动应具备条件。电池组件、汇流箱、逆变器、直流柜、配电柜、升压变压器、高压配电柜、计算机监控系统、电能计费系统及电能监测装置、火灾报警系统等设备安装调试完毕，电缆孔洞的防火封堵已全部完成，并已进行全面检查验收，确定各设备处于正常工作状态后，进行启动调试。

（2）启动调试前的检查。完成汇流箱、逆变器室内系统、10kV配电部分、太阳能光伏电池组件、计算机监控系统、电量计费系统、电能质量监测装置、火灾报警系统等电气设备的检查和清理，包括电气设备和计算机监控系统、电气控制、保护系统设备之间的通信。投运设备与未投运部分设备连接部位必须进行可靠隔离，并做好相应的防护措施。

2. 试验

（1）计算机监控试验。光伏电站所有设备安装、调试结束后，检查与电量计费系统、电能质量监测装置、逆变器、直流防雷汇流箱、直流柜、低压配电柜、高压开关柜、箱式变电站、直流电源控制系统之间的通信畅通。计算机监控系统远方对逆变器限负荷、启停试验、断路器、隔离开关远方操作试验、断路器、隔离开关位置接点反馈信号、保护动作信号及故障信号试验，以上试验均符合相关设计要求。

（2）光伏发电站反送电试验。光伏电站所有设备安装、调试结束后，进行光伏电站反送电试验。线路带电，合上出线开关、出线隔离开关、相应进线开关、升压变压器高压侧隔离开关，反送电至逆变器交流侧。全面检查升压变压器、逆变器、交流配电柜、PT柜工作正常，断路器及隔离刀闸动作正常、位置接点反馈正确，计算机监控能够正确采集各设备的数据量。

（3）光伏电站正充电试验。光伏电站所有设备安装、调试结束后，进行光伏电站正充电试验。合上汇流箱出口开关、直流柜开关，正充电至逆变器直流侧。全面检查汇流箱、直流防雷配电柜、逆变器工作正常，计算机监控能够正确采集各设备的数据量。

（4）光伏电站正核相试验。完成光伏发电站反送电试验、正充电试验后，进行电站核相试验，光伏电站离网运行，检查电站侧电压互感器与线路测电压互感器相序正确无误。

（5）逆变器试验。光伏电站核相试验结束后，进行现地逆变器限负荷、启停试验及保护试验，各试验符合设计要求。

（6）光伏发电单元带负荷24小时试运行 在所有上述试验完成之后，每个光伏发电单元应进行试运行。试运行应在自动控制方式下进行,试运行应为 24 小时。如果由于故障引起试运行中断,试验将按规程要求重新进行。试运行结束后,应对设备进行全面检查,消除并处理 24 小时试运行中所发现的所有缺陷。

(7) 30 天试运行天考核试运行。在通过 24 小时试运行并经检查处理所有缺陷后,立即进行 30 天考核试运行。光伏电站 30 天考核试运行期间,由于光伏发电单元及其附属设备故障或因设备安装质量原因引起中断,应及时加以处理,合格后继续进行 30 天运行。

(8) 其他试验。规程规范规定的其他试验及制造厂、发包人要求的其他试验。

4.1.6 环境适应性

(1) 环境温度:根据项目所在地的气候条件,选择适应高温、低温、盐雾、沙尘等环境的支架和组件材料,确保其长期稳定运行。对于极端环境,应采取必要的隔热、保温、防腐等措施。

(2) 防尘防水:支架设计应考虑防尘、排水需求,避免雨水、灰尘在支架内积聚。组件安装时,确保接线盒、边框等密封良好,防止水分进入。

(3) 防雷保护:根据项目所在地的雷电活动情况,按照相关标准设置合适的防雷保护措施,如安装避雷针、浪涌保护器等,并确保接地系统可靠。

4.1.7 后期运维便利性

(1) 设备布局:安装支架、组件时,充分考虑后期运维的便利性,如预留足够的检修空间,设置易于接近的检修门,确保运维人员可以方便地进行设备检查、故障排查、定期维护等工作。

(2) 标识清晰:对所有设备、电缆、接线端子等进行清晰、持久的标识,包括设备名称、编号、接线图、相序等信息,便于运维人员快速识别系统结构和运行状态。

(3) 文档归档:完成安装后,整理并妥善保管所有设备手册、接线图、测试报告、验收资料等,为后期运维、故障排查、设备更换等提供依据。

4.1.8 法规与标准

(1) 并网手续:完成安装调试后,及时办理并网申请手续,配合电力公司进行并网验收,确保项目合法合规运营。

(2) 安全法规:严格遵守国家及地方关于电力设施安装、运行、维护的相关法律法规,如《中华人民共和国电力法》《中华人民共和国安全生产法》《光伏发电接入电力系统技术规定》等,确保项目安全、规范运行。

(3) 环保要求:遵守项目所在地的环保法规,如噪声控制、废弃物处理等要求,确保项目建设与运营不对环境造成负面影响。

【任务实施】

1. 任务准备

竞赛设备平台 1 个、一字螺丝刀 1 把、十字螺丝刀 1 把、万用表 2 把、六角螺丝刀 1

把、剥线钳 1 把、直流电缆（红色和黑色各 10m）、MC4 接头套件若干、电烙铁 1 把、焊锡 1 卷、电站原理图 1 张、汇流箱及其配件 1 套、并网配电箱及其配件开关 1 个、上电检查记录表 1 份、光伏电站搭建记录表 1 份。

2. 任务内容及步骤

任务 1：光伏电站的搭建

任务内容：绘制光伏电站接线图，完成光伏电站的搭建。

任务步骤：

（1）完成电站原理图的识图。

（2）根据原理图绘制光伏电站接线图。

（3）在光伏电池组件接线盒的完成线路焊接。

（4）在光伏支架平台完成光伏组件安装。

（5）在汇流箱完成光伏电站的串并联接线。

任务 4.1 相关实施图表

任务 2：汇流箱的安装与检查

任务内容：完成 4 进 1 出汇流箱的安装与检查。

任务步骤：

（1）完成汇流箱的安装固定。

（2）完成汇流箱直流侧接线与布线。

（3）完成汇流箱交流侧接线与布线。

（4）完成汇流箱上电前检查。

任务 3：并网配电箱的安装与检查

任务内容：完成并网配电箱的安装与检查。

任务步骤：

（1）完成并网配电箱的安装固定。

（2）完成并网配电箱输入侧接线与布线。

（3）完成并网配电箱输出侧接线与布线。

（4）完成汇流箱上电前检查。

3. 技能要求

（1）组件安装不能缺少螺栓、弹簧垫圈、螺母等，螺母要拧紧。连线及组件的输出电缆安装也要牢固，检查连线是否正确。

（2）用万用表测试每路方阵的开路电压和测短路电流。根据开路电压、短路电流来判断每路组件方阵电气连接是否正常。

（3）布线要耐短路电流。太阳能光伏电池组件间的布线，若使用 $2mm^2$ 的导线，则可耐短路电流。

（4）为了减少接线的线压和降低成本，接线箱的位置应该离阵列尽可能近一些，但不要影响建筑物的构造、美观和日后的检查及部件更换。

4. 任务成果及考核评价

（1）光伏电站、汇流箱、并网配电箱安装正确且接线正确，占 90%。

(2) 操作过程展现较好职业素养,做到 7S 管理,占 10%。

【练习】

1. 控制器的安装、逆变器的安装、蓄电池的安装各要注意什么?
2. 布线工程中,为什么要特别注意部件的极性?在什么情况下,各个支路要相互断开?在有端子箱的条件下,为什么要确认接线的极性?
3. 太阳能光伏发电系统对接地有什么要求?说明一下控制器的安装顺序是怎样的?
4. 太阳能光伏电池组件和逆变器之间的布线应注意哪些内容?

任务 4.2　太阳能光伏发电系统的运维

【学习目标】

知识目标:掌握太阳能光伏发电系统调试前需检查的内容。
能力目标:能调试太阳能光伏发电系统;能维护太阳能光伏发电系统正常运行。
素养目标:培养团队协作、精益求精、刻苦钻研的职业品质。
重点:太阳能光伏发电系统的调试。
难点:太能光伏发电系统的维护。

【任务分析】

太阳能光伏电池方阵和相关设备安装完成之后,整个系统就已经做好了检查及投运的准备,在调试之前需要进行系统检查,检查合格后才能开始调试。系统在整体联调通过后投运,之后进行日常运行维护。

依托全国职业院校技能大赛设备平台或职业技能等级证书设备平台,完成上电前系统的调试、系统并网操作、光伏发电系统监控界面组态与运行。

【知识学习】

4.2.1　太阳能光伏发电系统的调试

太阳能光伏电池方阵和相关设备安装完成之后,整个光伏发电系统的电气部分就已经做好了检查及投运的准备,但为了保证光伏电站安全可靠运行,需要对太阳能光伏发电系统进行系统调试。

光伏发电系统的系统调试包括光伏组串、直流系统、电能变换装置、交流系统的调试,并网型光伏电站还需要完成并网与监控系统调试。按照光伏电站的类型,结合光伏电站运维规范与行业证书的要求,调试内容见表 4.2。

调试太阳能光伏发电系统,进行作业时,一定要保证使用正确的工具。系统调试使用的工具与安装使用的工具相似,需要带好表 4.3 中的工具。

表 4.2　太阳能光伏发电系统调试

调试项目＼光伏发电系统类型	离网型光伏发电系统	分布式并网光伏电站	集中型光伏发电站
光伏组串调试	光伏组串调试	并网光伏电池组串的调试	光伏方阵调试
直流系统调试	直流汇流箱调试、蓄电池调试	光伏汇流箱的调试	直流汇流箱调试、直流配电柜调试
电能变换装置调试	光伏控制器调试、微逆变器调试	组串型光伏逆变器的调试	集中型逆变器调试
交流系统调试	交流负载装调	光伏并网箱装调	变压器调试、交流配电柜调试
通信调试	光伏发电系统通信装调	光伏发电系统通信装调	光伏发电系统通信装调
系统启动调试	启动检验与离网测试	启动检验与并网测试	启动检验与并网测试

表 4.3　太阳能光伏发电系统调试工具

序号	工具	说　明
1	调试表格、钢笔和记事板	为便于直观，应将调试表格做成统一格式
2	十合一螺丝刀	这种方便工具有系统启动需要的每一种螺丝刀
3	数字万用表（DMM）	最理想的情况是 DMM 带一个钳形直流电流表
4	高压绝缘手套和防电弧护目镜	只要测量电压和电流值都要戴好这些保护装备
5	红外温度计	在进行组件性能测试时，用这种仪器来测量组件温度
6	辐照感应器	用于直接测量方阵辐照值时，辐照值可用来确定方阵的输出功率
7	可靠的跌落防护工具	防止可能的跌落危险；这种跌落防护工具与系统安装时使用的相同——安全带和安全绳

太阳能光伏发电系统调试内容如下：

（1）光伏电池组串的调试。光伏电站无论并网还是离网，组串的构成类似，光伏组串调试方法与步骤可通用。其中包括检查机械元件、光伏危险源排查、排除断线等故障、光伏组串投入与正常运行检测。

1）检查机械元件。要保证系统的机械部分符合原来预期，能使方阵固定在合适位置。下面介绍在检查整个固定系统时要关注的问题。

a. 光伏组串底脚。在整个方阵安装完成前，应对底脚（把方阵固定在合适位置的方法）进行调试前的检查，以便及早发现问题，解决问题，避免增加安装成本。参考以下问题进行检查提问，可以省去安装成本。

（a）对于屋顶方阵，底脚安装位置是否合适？间隔是否合理？

（b）安装底脚使用的硬件是否正确？

（c）对于固定在地面和杆顶的方阵，挖的坑尺寸是否合适？浇注的混凝土是否足够厚？杆子的间距是否正确？

b. 光伏组串支架。应该把检查支架系统（由轨道和线夹组成）作为检查系统机械部分的一部分，但这可能是一项挑战，尤其是对于屋顶安装的方阵，而且在所有爬梯和脚手架都撤掉之后，接近地面安装及杆顶安装的方阵可能相当不便。要关注以下问题。

（a）组件是否使用正确硬件与支架系统正确连接？

（b）组件是否以恰当方法接地到支架系统（用接地夹或设备接地导线可靠连接到每个组件）？

（c）支架系统是否可靠固定到底脚系统？

2）光伏危险源排查。若光伏发电系统的设计合理、施工规范、设施设备质量合格，则在其正常的运行过程中安全风险比较小，但正常运行的光伏电站也有存在的危险源。排查光伏电站危险源在光伏电站运维过程中极为重要，是掌握以下技能的前提：熟悉光伏组件清理维护方法、能够清理光伏组件表面污染物、能够进行光伏组件外观检查并根据现象确定后续处理方法。

a. 光伏组件钢化玻璃自爆。晶体硅光伏组件的正面一般使用钢化玻璃（部分组件双面都是钢化玻璃），钢化玻璃在储存、运输、使用过程中无直接外力作用下可能发生自动炸裂，即自爆现象，大部分钢化玻璃产品的自爆率在 0.3%～3%。光伏组件使用的钢化玻璃在运行中自爆会导致组件丧失机械完整性和密封性，水汽一旦侵入组件内部，很容易造成组件漏电，自爆的组件遇到下雨或者潮湿天气则更危险，存在很大的安全隐患，必须更换。

b. 光伏组件的"热斑效应"及自燃现象。在一定的条件下，光伏组件中缺陷区域成为负载，消耗其他区域所产生的能量，导致局部过热，这种现象称为"热斑效应"。高温下严重的热斑会导致电池局部烧毁、焊点熔化、栅线毁坏、封装材料老化等永久性损坏，局部过热还可能导致玻璃破裂、背板烧穿，甚至发生组件自燃，导致火灾等。"热斑效应"及自燃现象可使用热成像仪发现并排查，可有效避免"热斑效应"造成自燃。

c. 线缆的虚接和老化。线缆是光伏发电系统的重要组成部分，也是容易破损的材料，不规范的施工可能带来很大的安全隐患。常见的问题如下：

（a）电缆接头连接不牢，虚接将导致设备运行时接触点的电阻增加，设备异常发热，存在自燃危险。

（b）电缆在施工过程中不慎扎破，如果破损部位与金属部件接触，将导致正极或者负极接地。

（c）组件的电缆未收纳进背板下或者未走线槽，直接在阳光下曝晒，使电缆表面绝缘材料很容易老化，绝缘等级降低。

（d）电缆泡在水中或者潮湿的环境下，绝缘等级也容易降低。

线缆的虚接和老化可使用万用表、热成像仪等设备排查。

d. 电气设备进水或者异物。室外使用的电气设备必须具有良好的密封性和 IP 防护等级，但部分设备由于本身质量不合格或者安装方式不合理，容易进入水汽或者异物。比如早年建设的极个别项目使用了无边框的组件，边缘的密封性极差，水汽直接进入了组件内部；部分彩钢瓦屋顶的电站将汇流箱沿着屋顶坡面安装，下雨时水很容易进入箱体内；有些汇流箱甚至由于密封性不好，进入青蛙等小动物。这些都很容易造成组件、汇流箱内部短路。为了避免认为因素造成进水，清洗光伏方阵时需要按规范进行。

e. 其他危险源包括登高、天气、夜间巡检等。

3) 排除断线等故障。排除短线故障包含光伏组串链接电气检查和光伏汇流箱检测两部分。这里先介绍光伏组串链接电气检查，主要包括：连接次序检查、电缆状态检查、光伏特性曲线检查等。

a. 光伏连接次序检查：电气检查应该从太阳能光伏电池组件开始，关注以下问题来确保已安装的方阵与单线图相符。

(a) 安装的组件数量是否正确？

(b) 厂家及型号是否与申请许可过程提交的图纸相符？

(c) 组件连线是否符合组件串正确配置？这种配置可能是串联、并联或串并联。

检查太阳能光伏发电系统时要检查所有电气元件，以确认所有元件都安装正确。彻底检查每个电气元件是否正常。对照所有电气元件的清单，在调试程序开始前进行检查。如果工作中发现了错误，要停下来仔细考虑。在做出变动之前，一定要确认系统状态对使用工具来说是安全的。

b. 电缆状态检查，主要使用目测、万用表、热成像仪、绝缘电阻表、I-V曲线测试仪、EL检测仪分别检查排除以下故障：

(a) 目测、万用表与热成像仪等工具，检查和识别光伏直流电缆，确保电缆无短路和破损等情况。

(b) 使用绝缘电阻表排除光伏组件/串接地故障等。

c. 光伏特性曲线检查

(a) 使用I-V曲线测试仪对光伏组件或组串I-V曲线特性测试，并能够识别故障光伏组件或组串故障和分析组件/组串故障原因。

(b) 使用EL检测仪，对光伏组件进行电致发光测试，并能够识别故障组件和分析组件故障原因。

(c) 能够使用红外热成像仪，对光伏组件的表明温度进行测试，并能够识别故障组件和分析组件故障原因。

4) 光伏组串投入与正常运行检测。当确认光伏电站机械结构完好、光伏电站危险源已排除、电气连接正确，可对光伏组串进行投入与正常运行检测。可使用监控计算机，监控光伏组串运行状态，利用监控系统，结合现场工况判断光伏组串是否存在故障，定位问题。并编写光伏组件/组串检测分析报告。

(2) 直流系统调试。光伏发电系统的直流系统调试包括直流汇流箱调试、蓄电池调试等。

1) 直流汇流箱调试。光伏直流汇流箱调试包括规格检查、内外观检查、电器性能测试和电器性能测试。

2) 蓄电池。如果安装了蓄电池，要对它们特别注意。关注以下问题来评估蓄电池的安装及将来的维护。

a. 蓄电池是否与外部可靠通风？所有蓄电池都会释放氢气，尽管密封式蓄电池释放的氢气很少。

b. 蓄电池是否安装在适当的外壳里？蓄电池应加以保护以免受损，而且蓄电池可能对人员造成伤害。

c. 蓄电池的安装及连线是否正确？太阳能光伏发电系统对蓄电池电压有严格要求，如果蓄电池连线错误，系统就不能正确运行。

（3）电能变换装置调试。光伏发电系统中的电能变换装置主要包括太阳能充放电控制器、光伏逆变器。

1）太阳能充放电控制器调试。在与带蓄电池的系统打交道时，无论是与电网交互系统还是电力系统，都需要使用充电控制器来保证太阳能光伏电池方阵对蓄电池正确充电。给充电控制器通电之前一定要关注以下问题。

a. 充电控制器安装位置是否适当？它通常的安装位置是紧靠逆变器和蓄电池。

b. 控制器的输入侧和输出侧是否都有隔离开关和过电流保护装置？

c. 与控制器连接的导线使用的线规是否正确？

2）光伏逆变器调试。因为逆变器是太阳能光伏发电系统太重要的部件，所以如果逆变器存在问题，它会完全打断光伏发电系统的运行。在调试前检查逆变器时要提出以下问题。

结合相关国家标准，以及户用光伏电站的实际情况，逆变器的参数测试可包括保护功能检测、转换效率、电能质量检测几个方面。

a. 保护功能检测。防反放电保护是指逆变器直流侧电压低于允许工作范围或逆变器处于关机状态时，逆变器的直流侧没有反方向电流流过。也就是说，当逆变器处于待机或关机状态时，检测直流侧，不会出现逆变器的电流往直流源（太阳能光伏电池板）流动。

根据相关国家标准，防孤岛效应保护的动作时间不大于 2s。可根据场地情况进行测试，检查逆变器的防孤岛保护是否正常工作。

b. 转换效率。对于光伏电站的运维而言，转换效率是逆变器最重要的性能指标。选择一个典型工作日，从早到晚利用逆变器显示参数在不同负载率时读取逆变器的输入/输出功率，并根据逆变器加权效率公式计算逆变器的加权转换效率。

如有必要，在进行读数的同时，可同时测量太阳辐照度、环境温度和组件温度，并记录备用。为了提高工作效率，可综合使用运维平台监控数据和现场实际测量相结合。

（4）交流系统调试。交流系统调试包括光伏并网箱调试、开关设备调试、保护装置调试、变压器及接入箱调试、交流配电柜调试、交流负载装调等。下面主要介绍光伏并网箱调试、隔离开关设备调试、过电流保护装置调试。

1）光伏并网箱调试。包括并网箱调试与安全隐患排除，主要包括：

a. 判断并网箱内保护器件是否符合电气安全及电力部门要求。

b. 根据电气图，检查并进行并网箱内的电气连接。

c. 检查并网箱内各开关器件是否可以正常操作。

d. 能够检查输入电缆、输出电缆线序是否正确。

e. 能够检查金属机壳接地及内部元器件是否漏接或虚接。

f. 并网箱调试与安全隐患排除要求能够开展并网箱的基本维护，如锈蚀、积灰等；能够观察到变形、漏水等问题，能够更换并网箱。

g. 检测并网箱内电气设备状态，更换并网箱内断路器、隔离刀闸等故障元器件。

h. 检测并网箱的保护接地、外壳防护、电气隔离、故障保护等保护措施，不符合要求应及时更换。

i. 检查交流汇流箱基本情况，处理锈蚀、积灰、设备标识脱落等工作。

j. 能够更换变形、漏水等状态的汇流箱；能够更换交流汇流箱断路器、防雷模块等元器件。

k. 能够使用红外热探测仪检查交流汇流箱的端子温度，处理局部异常高温等隐藏缺陷。

2）隔离开关调试。太阳能光伏发电系统的交流侧和直流侧都有隔离开关。很多直接联网系统的逆变器至少有一台光伏隔离开关。在进行系统调试准备、全面进行系统检查时，要提出以下问题。

a. 安装的隔离开关是否符合要求？太阳能光伏电池方阵和逆变器的交流电源是否能切断，而且这两台隔离开关是否集合为一组？

b. 如果电力部门要求有可见、可闭锁的隔离开关，那么它是否按照电力部门的要求正确安装了？

c. 每个隔离开关切断的导线是否正确？因为不应切断接地载流导线。

d. 安装的隔离开关是否适用于它们的环境及承载电压、电流值？

e. 隔离开关是否配置了适当的标识？如果你对隔离开关是做什么的有疑问，就更不能指望对系统完全不熟悉的人了解他在与什么打交道。

3）过电流保护装置调试。逆变器的交流侧和直流侧通常都可能安装过电流保护装置（OCPD）。闭合开关之前，不仅需要检查安装的 OCPD 是否正确，而且要检查它们是否能正确保护系统。花一点时间来考虑以下问题。

a. 电流额定值是否与电路匹配？OCPD 容量错误（无论是过大还是过小）会导致问题。

b. OCPD 的电压额定值是否正确？这一点很关键，尤其是对于太阳能光伏发电系统电源电路。OCPD 的直流额定值必须正确，否则它就不能在真正需要时正确保护系统。

c. OCPD 状态是否良好？有故障的熔断器或断路器第一天就会导致花费数小时消除缺陷。为确认系统投入时电流是否能通过 OCPD，要进行连续性试验。

（5）光伏发电系统通信装调。光伏发电系统通信装调包括汇流箱通信装调、逆变器通信装调、并网箱通信装调等。

1）汇流箱通信装调。需要完成通信模块安装与接线，主要包括如下内容：

a. 完成主控模块与电流传感器模块的安装。

b. 完成主控模块与电流传感器 FMB 排线连接。

c. 完成主控模块直流母线供电端子接线。

d. 完成主控模块 RS485 通信端子接线。

e. 完成主控模块直流 24V 供电端子接线。

f. 完成主控模块通信地址设置并记录。

g. 使用串口调试软件完成通信测试并记录。

2）逆变器通信装调。主要包括如下内容：

a. 完成逆变器 RS485 通信线的连接。

b. 完成逆变器 RS485 通信端子的安装。

c. 完成逆变器通讯地址设置并记录。

d. 使用串口调试软件完成逆变器通讯测试并记录。

3）电表通信装调。主要包括如下内容，包括电表通讯接线和电表通信调试：

a. 完成电表 RS485 通信线的连接。

b. 读取电表通信地址设置并记录。

c. 使用串口调试软件完成逆变器通信测试并记录。

（6）光伏发电系统启动调试。检查系统，确认机械元件和电气元件都安全正确安装之后，就可以实际获得系统调试（投入）的乐趣。进行这一过程时要一次一步，这样就不会漏掉任何关键部分。以下将介绍调试过程的主要方面。

经过系统调试并确认一切正常之后，必须把系统关闭，直至系统通过当地建设部门的检查。

进行系统调试的第一步是保证自己和整个系统是安全的。如何做到这一点呢？要谨记在安装过程中保证安全的太阳能光伏发电系统接入顺序。在调试过程中，为保证自己和安装队伍成员的安全，也要遵循这些简单规则。首要的策略是永远在不带电电路上作业，遵循正确的连线顺序，以保证所有电路都不带电。还需要确认所有隔离开关都在开断位置并加以闭锁。

对于直接联网系统，不要把太阳能光伏发电系统电源电路接到并线盒、接线盒或与公用电网进行交流互连。

对于带蓄电池的系统，它与太阳能光伏发电系统和电网（如果可用的话）的互连也适用直接联网系统同样的规则。无论如何，蓄电池组是需要以正确顺序连线的另一个电源，以避免发生可能的电击。蓄电池组到逆变器的连接应该在逆变器处进行，在逆变器写蓄电池组连接之前要首先断开逆变器的隔离开关。这样做可以保证手中不会有带电导线，不致发生问题。

4.2.2 并网光伏发电系统的投运

对于并网光伏发电系统，根据光伏发电系统是否允许通过供电区的变压器向高压电网送电，分为可逆流和不可逆流的并网方式。

1. 并网启动必须具备的条件

（1）与并网整套启动有关的一次、二次电气设备静态调试、实验工作均已全部结束，并符合相关标准。

（2）与并网整套启动有关的电气设备整定值均已完毕，并可投入运行。

（3）与并网整套启动有关的带电房间均已悬挂警示牌，设有遮拦。

（4）消防设施完善，逆变器室、变压器室等处应有足够的灭火器等。

（5）通信设备应畅通，照明充足，事故照明实验正常，通风良好。

（6）所有参加应持证入场，无关人员一律禁止入场。

2. 并网启动步骤

（1）检查逆变器、逆变器直流侧开关、逆变器交流侧开关、直流柜去逆变器的直流开关、升压变压器、升压变压器高压侧开关及其回路均符合送电条件。

（2）检查逆变器直流侧开关、逆变器交流侧开关、直流柜去逆变器的直流开关、升压变压器高压侧开关均在断开状态。

（3）使用专用摇把将净化站高压配电房光伏进线高压柜开关由"实验"位置移到"工作"位置。

（4）使用子站的监控系统在远方合上进线高压柜断路器，由"分闸"移到"合闸"位置，检查升压变压器和升压变压器高压侧开关空载运行无异常。没有公司分管领导批准并做好安全措施，禁止用高压柜上的合闸按钮合上升压变压器高压侧开关。

（5）合上逆变器交流侧开关，并再次确认开关已合闸。（逆变器控制板使用采用交流供电）

（6）合上汇流箱内的直流断路器，并再次确认断路器已合闸。观测监控系统，查看各线路是否正常，如有异常，断开开关，重新检查设备及接线，直到正常为止。

（7）再合上直流配电柜去逆变器的直流开关，并再次确认断路器已合闸，查看电压电流大小是否偏高或偏低。

（8）合上逆变器直流侧开关，并再次确认开关已合闸。

（9）检查逆变器能否在并网前完成自检，并在直流侧电压高于并网规定电压值时完成并网发电。

（10）检查逆变器并网运行后参数有无异常。

（11）检查逆变器直流侧开关、逆变器交流侧开关、直流柜去逆变器的直流开关及其回路均无异常。

3. 注意事项

（1）在并网发电过程中，出现异常情况，应立即停止操作并查明原因和排除，否则严禁继续下一步操作，并做好数据记录准备。

（2）如果逆变器在运行过程中听到异响或发现逆变器参数发生异常，可通过控制屏停机按钮或紧急停机按钮停止机器运行。

4. 并网规程要求

电压偏差：为了使当地交流负载正常工作，光伏发电系统中逆变器的输出电压应与电网相匹配。正常运行时，光伏发电系统和电网接口处的电压允许偏差应符合《电能质量供电电压偏差》（GB/T 12325—2008）的规定。三相电压的允许偏差为额定电压的±7%，单相电压的允许偏差为额定电压的+7%、-10%。

频率：光伏发电系统并网时应与电网同步运行。电网额定频率为50Hz，光伏发电系统并网后的频率允许偏差应符合《电能质量电力系统频率偏差》（GB/T 15945—2008）的规定，即偏差值允许±0.5Hz。

光伏系统并网技术要求规程

谐波和波形畸变：低的电流和电压的谐波水平是所希望的；较高的谐波增加了对所连接的设备产生有害影响的可能性。谐波电压和电流的允许水平取决于配电系统的特性、供电类型、所连接的负载/设备，以及电网的现行规定。光伏发电系统的输出应有较低的电流畸变，以确保对连接到电网的其他设备不造成不利影响。总谐波电流应小于逆变器额定输出的5%。

更多规程要求详见《光伏系统并网技术要求》(GB/T 19939—2005)。

4.2.3 太阳能光伏发电系统的维护

太阳能光伏发电系统突出的一个特点是需要的维护量很小。因为太阳能光伏发电系统没有运动部件,所以不需要定期维护最终会磨损或失效的部件。逆变器很可能需要在系统寿命期间更换一次,而且如果安装了蓄电池,在系统寿命期间,蓄电池组也需要更换一两次。除此之外,太阳能光伏方阵可以年复一年运行而极少需要维护。

注意,这里说的是极少维护而非免维护。以下简要介绍几项需要定期进行的维护任务。

1. 组件和支架的维护

(1) 光伏组件表面应保持清洁,应使用干燥或潮湿的柔软洁净的布料擦拭光伏组件,严禁使用腐蚀性溶剂或硬物擦拭光伏组件。应在辐照度低于 $200W/m^2$ 的情况下清洁光伏组件,不宜使用与组件温差较大的液体清洗组件。

(2) 光伏组件应定期检查。若发现下列问题立即调整或更换光伏组件:①光伏组件存在玻璃粉碎、背板灼焦、明显的颜色变化;②光伏组件中存在与组件边缘或任何电路之间形成连通通道的气泡;③光伏组件接线盒变形、扭曲、开裂或烧毁,接线端子无法良好接触。

(3) 光伏组件上的带电警告标识不得丢失。

(4) 使用金属边框的光伏组件,边框和支架应结合良好,两者之间接触电阻不大于 4Ω,边框必须牢固接地。

(5) 在无阴影遮挡条件下工作时,在太阳辐照度为 $500W/m^2$ 以上,风速不大于 2m/s 的条件下,同一光伏组件外表面(电池正上方区域)温度差异应小于 20℃。装机容量大于 50kW 的光伏电站,应配备红外线热像仪,检测光伏组件外表面温度差异。

(6) 使用直流钳型电流表在太阳辐射强度基本一致的条件下测量接入同一个直流汇流箱的各光伏组件串的输入电流,其偏差应不超过 5%。

(7) 支架的所有螺栓、焊缝和支架连接应牢固可靠,表面的防腐涂层不应出现开裂和脱落现象,否则应及时补刷。

2. 汇流箱的维护

(1) 直流汇流箱不得存在变形、锈蚀、漏水、积灰现象,箱体外表面的安全警示标识应完整无破损,箱体上的防水锁启闭应灵活。

(2) 直流汇流箱内各个接线端子不应出现松动、锈蚀现象。

(3) 直流汇流箱内的高压直流熔丝的规格应符合设计规定。

(4) 直流输出母线的正极对地、负极对地的绝缘电阻应大于 $2M\Omega$。

(5) 直流输出母线端配备的直流断路器,其分断功能应灵活、可靠。

(6) 直流汇流箱内防雷器应有效。

3. 直流配电柜的维护

(1) 直流配电柜不得存在变形、锈蚀、漏水、积灰现象,箱体外表面的安全警示标识应完整无破损,箱体上的防水锁开启应灵活。

(2) 直流配电柜内各个接线端子不应出现松动、锈蚀现象。

(3) 直流输出母线的正极对地、负极对地的绝缘电阻应大于 $2M\Omega$。

(4) 直流配电柜的直流输入接口与汇流箱的连接应稳定可靠。

(5) 直流配电柜的直流输出与并网主机直流输入处的连接应稳定可靠。

(6) 直流配电柜的直流断路器动作应灵活，性能应稳定可靠。

(7) 直流母线输出侧配置的防雷器应有效。

4. 逆变器的维护

(1) 逆变器结构和电气连接应保持完整，不应存在锈蚀、积灰等现象，散热环境应良好，逆变器运行时不应有较大振动和异常噪声。

(2) 逆变器上的警示标识应完整无破损。

(3) 逆变器中模块、电抗器、变压器的散热风扇根据温度自行启动和停止的功能应正常，散热风扇运行时不应有较大振动及异常噪声，如有异常情况应断电检查。

(4) 定期将交流输出侧（网侧）断路器断开，若断开器断开逆变器应立即停止向电网馈电。

(5) 逆变器中直流母线电容温度过高或超过使用年限，应及时更换。

5. 交流配电柜的维护

(1) 确保配电柜的金属架与基础型钢应用镀锌螺栓完好连接，且防松零件齐全。

(2) 配电柜标明被控设备编号、名称或操作位置的标识器件应完整，编号应清晰、工整。

(3) 母线接头应连接紧密，无变形，无放电变黑痕迹，绝缘无松动和损坏，紧固联接螺栓无生锈。

(4) 手车、抽出式成套配电柜推拉应灵活，无卡阻碰撞现象，动静头与静触头的中心线应一致，且触头接触紧密。

(5) 配电柜中开关、主触点无烧熔痕迹，灭弧罩无烧黑和损坏。紧固各接线螺丝，清洁柜内灰尘。

(6) 把各分开关柜从抽屉中取出，紧固各接线端子。检查电流互感器、电流表、电度表的安装和接线，手柄操作机构应灵活可靠性，紧固断路器进出线，清洁开关柜内和配电柜后面引出线处的灰尘。

(7) 低压电器发热物件散热应良好，切换压板应解除良好，信号回路的信号灯、按钮、光字牌、电铃、电筒、事故电钟等动作和信号显示应准确。

(8) 检验柜、屏、台、箱、盘间线路的线间和线对地间绝缘电阻值，馈电线路必须大于 $0.5M\Omega$，二次回路必须大于 $1M\Omega$。

6. 变压器维护

(1) 变压器的温度计应完好，油温应正常，储油柜的油位应与环境温度相对应，各部位无渗、漏油。每台变压器负荷大小、冷却条件及季节可能不同，运行中的变压器不能单纯以上层油温不超过允许值为依据，还应根据以往运行经验在上述情况下与上次的油温比较。

(2) 套管油位应正常，套管外部无破损裂纹、无严重油污、无放电痕迹及其他异常现象。油质应为透明、微带黄色，由此可判断油质的好坏。油面应符合周围温度的标准线，如油面过低应检查变压器是否漏油等。油面过高应检查冷却装置的使用情况，是否有内部故障。

(3) 变压器声响应正常，正常运行时一般有均匀的嗡嗡电磁声。如声音有所异常，应细心检查，作出正确判断，并立即进行处理。

(4) 变压器引线应无断股，接头应无过热变色或示温片熔化（变色）现象，呼吸器应完好，硅胶变色程度不应超过 3/4。

(5) 有励磁调压分接开关的分接位置及电源指示应正常，瓦斯继电器内应无气体，变压器外壳接地、铁芯接地应完好等。

(6) 恶劣天气时，应重点进行特殊检查。大风时检查引线有无剧烈摆动；弧垂是否足够；变压器顶盖、套管引线处是否有杂物。各部触点在落雪后，不应立即熔化或有放电现象。大雾天各部有无火花放电现象等。

7. 电缆的维护

(1) 电缆不应在过负荷的状态下运行，电缆的铅包不应出现膨胀、龟裂现象。

(2) 电缆在进出设备处的部位应封堵完好，不应存在直径大于 10mm 的孔洞，否则用防火堵泥墙封堵。

(3) 在电缆对设备外壳压力、拉力过大部位，电缆的支撑点应完好。

(4) 电缆保护钢管口不应有穿孔、裂缝和显著的凹凸不平，内壁应光滑，金属电缆管不应有严重锈蚀，不应有毛刺、硬物、垃圾，如有毛刺，锉光后用电缆外套包裹并扎紧。

(5) 应及时清理室外电缆井内的堆积物、垃圾，如电缆外皮损坏，应进行处理。

(6) 检查室内电缆明沟时，要防止损坏电缆，确保支架接地与沟内散热良好。

(7) 直埋电缆线路沿线的标桩应完好无损，路径附近地面无挖掘，确保沿路径地面上无堆放重物、建材及临时设施，无腐蚀性物质排泄，确保室外露地面电缆保护设施完好。

(8) 确保电缆沟或电缆井的盖板完好无缺，沟道中不应有积水或杂物，确保沟内支架应牢固、有无锈蚀、松动现象，铠装电缆外皮及铠装不应有严重锈蚀。

(9) 多根并列敷设的电缆，应检查电流分配和电缆外皮的温度，防止因接触不良而引起电缆烧坏连接点。

(10) 确保电缆终端头接地良好，绝缘套管完好、清洁、无闪络放电痕迹，确保电缆相色明显。

8. 极端天气维护

(1) 如碰到下雨跳闸，有可能是接线头不紧，如出现这类情况，必须在雨过晴天后处理，可用绝缘胶带缠绕接线头，再观察是否跳闸，如继续出现跳闸现象，应向维修中心或当地电管站报告。

(2) 雷雨天，应将电表下方空气开关关闭，防止电气设备受损。待雷雨天过后，再将开关合上。

【任务实施】

1. 任务准备

竞赛设备平台 1 个、"光伏电站运维"设备平台 1 个、一字螺丝刀 1 把、十字螺丝刀

1把、万用表1把、上电检查记录表1份、光伏阵列调试记录表1份、直流汇流箱调试记录表1份、并网逆变器调试记录表1份、并网配电箱调试记录表1份、电脑主机1套。

2. 任务内容及步骤

任务1：系统调试与并网

任务内容：完成光伏发电系统调试与并网。

任务步骤：

(1) 完成系统上电前的检查，并填写上电检查记录表。

(2) 完成光伏阵列调试，并填写光伏阵列调试记录表。

(3) 完成直流汇流箱调试，并填写直流汇流箱调试记录表。

任务4.2 相关实施表格

(4) 完成并网逆变器调试，并填写并网逆变器调试记录表。

(5) 完成并网配电箱调试，并填写并网配电箱调试记录表。

任务2：监控系统组态与运行

任务内容：完成光伏发电系统监控系统的组态与运行。

任务步骤：

(1) 完成光伏发电系统与监控主机的通信检查。

(2) 完成光伏发电系统登录界面、导航条的组态。

(3) 完成光伏发电系统操作界面的组态。

(4) 完成光伏发电系统数据界面的组态。

(5) 完成光伏发电监控系统的设备组态。

(6) 完成光伏发电监控系统的运行，实现运行数据的实时显示与记录。

3. 技能要求

(1) 正确使用万用表挡位进行不同参数的测量，操作规范，无短路、无错挡测量。

(2) 正确测量太阳能光伏电池串联输入开路电压和工作电流。

(3) 按照规范逐一完成设备安装固定、连接线情况检查、接地线检查等步骤检查，标准严格、无漏项、无错项。

(4) 对设备运行数据观察到位，记录正确，记录参数数据包含数值和单位。

(5) 监控界面布局美观，元件尺寸大小适当，颜色配置协调，功能控件齐全，元件标注和名称正确，无漏项。

4. 任务成果及考核评价

(1) 系统调试正确且成功并网、数据界面运行数据正确，能记录运行数据，占90%。

(2) 操作过程展现较好职业素养，做到7S管理，占10%。

【练习】

1. 调试时对电气元件检查包含哪些内容？

2. 必须安装的常用表示包括哪几类？

3. 光伏发电系统需要定期维护的任务有哪几项？

Project 4 Installing, Operating and Maintaining Solar Photovoltaic Power Generation Systems

Task 4.1 Installing Solar Photovoltaic Power Generation Systems

【Learning objectives】

Knowledge objective: To master the installation contents of solar photovoltaic power generation systems

Ability objective: To be able to install solar photovoltaic cell foundation and modules; to be able to install storage batteries and inverters of solar photovoltaic power generation systems

Qualification objective: To cultivate the professional quality of willingness to work hard at the grass-roots level

Learning priority: Installation essentials of photovoltaic power generation systems

Learning challenge: Electrical testing of photovoltaic power generation systems

【Task analysis】

A solar photovoltaic power generation system consists of many devices and components, of which the installation of photovoltaic cell modules is a unique part of the system. The ability to properly install system devices and components has an important impact on the overall efficiency of the system.

【Knowledge learning】

4.1.1 Pile foundation construction

1. Drilling construction plan

Drill in place: When the drill is in place, the tip of the drill bit is aligned with the pile position, with an alignment error of $\leqslant 2.0$ cm. Adjust the drill to make it stable and to ensure that the main drill rod is perpendicular to the ground, with the perpendicularity of $\leqslant 20$ mm.

Mechanical hole drilling is adopted. The diameter of the drill rod is 250 mm. When the drill is in place, keep it stable without tilting or displacing; keep the drill rod vertical; mark a scale line of 1800 mm on the drill rod, so as to control the depth of the hole (not less than 1800 mm). Quality requirements for hole drilling: Deviation of center position of pile hole: ± 10 mm; permissible deviation of pile hole depth: + 10 mm (deeper depth is permissible, but not shallower depth); deviation of hole drilling perpendicularity: ≤ 20 mm pile length; loosened soil at the bottom of the hole must be cleaned up.

2. Concrete construction plan

(1) Specific preparations before concrete pouring are as follows:

1) Prior to concrete pouring, all the formworks, reinforcing bars, embedded parts, etc., are installed and inspected to meet design specification requirements, and acceptance procedures for concealed work are completed.

2) Sundries in formworks and dirt on reinforcing bars are cleaned up. Gaps and holes of formworks are blocked, and acceptance procedures for concealed work are completed.

3) Indicators of concrete raw materials are inspected.

4) Technical briefing is completed, and professional leaders sign the application form for pouring.

5) In the concrete construction process, self-mixed concrete is transported to the nearest point of the pouring site along the construction road using hand trucks; then, the hopper is raised, and the concrete is poured into the pile foundation; pouring is stopped when the top of the pile is nearly reached, then workers use shovels to load the concrete to the upper plane of the formwork, and use iron trowels to compact and smooth the concrete.

(2) Requirements for concrete pouring and vibrating:

1) The free falling height of the concrete from the mouth of the bucket or the mouth of the artificial fabric pipe should not exceed 2.5 m; if the pouring height is more than 2.5 m, a chute must be used to reach the lower part of the pile for concrete pouring.

2) Concrete pouring should be carried out continuously in layers.

3) When using an immersion vibrator, it should be immersed quickly and pulled out slowly; immersion points should be evenly spaced; immersion actions should be carried out point by point in sequence without missing any spaces, to achieve uniform and solid vibration. The distance between the displacement of the vibrator should not be greater than 1.5 times the radius of the vibration action (generally 45 cm). When vibrating in the upper layer, the vibrator should be immersed 5 cm into the lower layer to eliminate the joints between the two layers.

4) During concrete pouring, carpenters and reinforcing bar workers should be dispatched to observe whether there is any movement, deformation or blockage of formworks, reinforcing bars and embedded parts. In case of any problem, proper handling must be carried out immediately, and correction must be completed before the initial set-

ting of the poured concrete.

(3) Concrete maintenance:

1) When the strength of the poured concrete reaches 1.2 MPa, remove the formwork. After that, use a plastic film for coverage and maintenance. During the maintenance process, make sure that the plastic film has condensation.

2) The maintenance time is not less than 3 days.

3) After concrete pouring is completed and before the strength of the concrete reaches 1.2 MPa, no further construction should be carried out.

(4) Concrete test. Before concrete is poured into the formwork, randomly take concrete samples at the site and make concrete specimens. The number of specimens should not be less than 30% of the samples. Specimen retention should meet the following specifications: every 200 m^3 is adopted for test block strength testing; for concrete of the same strength class, same proportion of concrete mix, and same working group, the number of sampling should not be less than 9; for concrete less than 200 m^3 of the same batch and same proportion of concrete mix, the number of sampling should not be less than 1. The number of test blocks retained should meet specification requirements.

3. Concrete quality standards

Technical data of concrete should be complete and compliant with specifications and design requirements, including material certificates and retest reports of cement, aggregate and concrete admixtures, as well as notification sheets of proportion of concrete mix; the proportion of concrete mix and maintenance of concrete should meet the above specifications; the sampling, production, maintenance and testing of concrete specimens should meet the requirements of *the Code for Acceptance of Construction Quality of Concrete Structural Engineering* (GB 50204 - 2015).

4. Formwork construction plan

(1) Material specifications: The inner diameter of corrugated pipes is 350 mm; the hoop is made of iron wire.

(2) Construction preparations: Cut corrugated pipes according to dimensions specified in the design drawings of concrete pile formworks; determine the quantity of each type of corrugated pipes to be used according to the design drawings; cut corrugated pipes according to specified proportions and sort the pipes into piles for later use.

(3) General requirements for formwork installation:

1) Before formwork installation, formwork positioning and inspection lines should be set up to ensure the accuracy of formwork installation.

2) The deviation of sectional dimensions after formwork molding should be controlled at ± 2 mm.

3) After formwork installation, the formwork should be adjusted by pulling the calibration line to inspect the formwork elevation, sectional dimensions, smoothness and

perpendicularity. This ensures qualification validation before proceeding to the next process.

(4) Formwork installation process:

1) Embed corrugated pipes underground (10 cm); divide the corrugated pipes equally into three parts, and drive three rebar piles into the ground at a distance of 50 cm from the pipes; use a flat bottom and a sloping top between the rebar piles and the corrugated pipes to reinforce the corrugate pipes, so as to prevent the upper part of the corrugated pipes from deflection during construction; properly install bolt fixing racks and fix embedded bolts in accordance with external dimensions.

2) Calibrate the positions of the piles.

3) Prepare for the next construction process after the completion of formwork installation.

(5) Protection measures for finished formworks:

1) During installation, formworks should be lifted up and put down with care, and collision should be avoided to prevent formwork deformation.

2) Installed formworks must be brushed with formwork releasing agents to prevent from sticking.

3) Removed formworks should be timely repaired or replaced if any uneven or damaged surface is found.

4) Formworks should be properly used and neatly stacked.

5) Formworks should be kept in rainproof conditions to prevent rust and deformation by dampness.

6) During concrete pouring, specific personnel should be dispatched to observe formwork fastening; if any formwork is deformed or comes loose, it should be timely repaired or fastened.

(6) Formwork removal requirements:

1) During the removal of corrugated pipe models, the concrete strength required by *the Code for Acceptance of Construction Quality of Concrete Structural Engineering* (GB 50204 – 2015) should be adopted.

2) During formwork removal, it is strictly prohibited to use sledgehammers or crowbars; personnel should not stand on the crosspieces being removed to carry out operations; no formwork removal can be carried out until concrete initial setting; during formwork removal, formworks should be handled gently to prevent embedded bolts from displacement or coming loose.

3) Removed corrugated pipes must be properly sorted with dimension identifiers and neatly stacked for later use.

(7) For some piles that have been driven into the ground, construction procedures are as follows:

1) Clean up the soil on the pile first, and lower the soil around the pile head by 10 cm.

2) Clean up the stones and floating soil on the pile head using a blower.

3) Corrugated pipe molds must be embedded into the ground by 10 cm at the time of installation.

4) Report to the supervision unit for acceptance after fixing the molds, and carry out concrete pouring after acceptance.

5) When pouring concrete, vibrate and compact the concrete using a vibrating rod, and smooth the surface.

6) Remove the formwork 24 hours after the completion of pouring, and carry out maintenance.

(8) Incoming inspection of raw materials:

1) For all reinforcing bars transported to the site, varieties, specifications, grades, and quality levels should meet the design requirements; when reinforcing bars enter the factory, the person in charge of data management is responsible for collecting factory quality certificates or manufacturers' test report forms; reinforcing bar surfaces or each bundle of reinforcing bars should be marked with batch numbers that are consistent with the batch numbers in the report forms; otherwise, reinforcing bars are not allowed to enter the site.

2) All reinforcing bars transported to the site should be inspected for appearance. Reinforcing bars should be straight and free of damage, without any crack, oil, granular or flaky old rust on the surface; reinforcing bars not meeting these requirements are prohibited from use.

3) Reinforcing bar sampling: when reinforcing bars enter the site, they should be inspected and accepted by batch. Each batch is composed of reinforcing bars of the same grade, same specifications, same delivery state, with the weight not more than 60 t.

(9) Mechanical equipment for reinforcing bar processing includes cutting machines, straightening machines, welding machines, shearing machines, and reinforcing bar bending machines. Processing and storage of reinforcing bars:

1) A strict management system for reinforcing bars should be established in terms of production, safety, civilization, and environmental protection; conservation measures should be taken to reduce material loss. Before cutting reinforcing bars, relevant personnel should familiarize themselves with drawings and review material lists according to drawings. In the process of cutting reinforcing bars, design and specification requirements should be observed. Requirements for bending lengths, bending angles, lap lengths, straight lengths and heights of reinforcing bars should be observed. In case of any problem, technicians should be timely contacted to prevent any dimension deviations. Prior to reinforcing bar processing, the technical department develops reinforcing bar ingredient lists, and the technical project manager reviews and approves the lists for later processing.

2) Reinforcing bar cutting should meet specifications of types, diameters, lengths and quantities of reinforcing bars; long bars should be cut first, followed by short bars, to minimize waste and save steel.

3) Semi-finished reinforcing bars should be pre-inspected at the production site and can only be used on site after qualification validation; proper records should be made as specified.

4) Auto cranes are used for vertical transport to lift reinforcing bars to designated locations as needed. When lifting long reinforcing bars, trial lifting should be carried out to determine the lifting point, so as to prevent deformation of reinforcing bars caused by too large a distance from the lifting point. Hand pallet trucks are used for horizontal transport; reinforcing bars should be tied securely during transport to prevent extrusion and deformation.

5) Molding reinforcing bars should be neatly stacked by specifications and use of parts and labeled with clear identifiers.

6) Quality requirements for reinforcing bar processing: ① Reinforcing bars should be straight and free of local zigzags. ② Cutting ports of reinforcing bars should be free of horseshoe-shaped or bending cut-outs; the length of reinforcing bars should be as accurate as possible. ③ Reinforcing bars should be properly bent and molded, without any warping or unevenness on the plane.

(10) Preparations for reinforcing bar welding:

1) Check whether the steel grade, diameter, shape, dimension and quantity, etc., of semi-finished reinforcing bars are consistent with material lists; in case of any error or omission, correction or addition should be made.

2) For reinforcing bar welding, firstly mark dimension lines according to requirements of construction drawings, and determine positions of reinforcing bars according to dimension lines during welding.

3) Joint locations, lap lengths, seismic reinforcement and anchorage lengths of reinforcing bars should meet construction specifications and design requirements.

4) Prepare welding machines and welding rods; set up the operating rack. Welding rods adopt No. 2.5 welding wire; during welding it should be made sure that the stressed reinforcing bars are not displaced, and that two-way stressed reinforcing bars are fully welded.

The construction of the pile foundation is shown in Figure 4.1.

4.1.2 Rack installation

1. Site inspection and preparation

(1) Confirm that the geological conditions, bearing capacity, wind load, snow load and other environmental factors of the installation site meet design requirements of racks.

Figure 4.1 Pile foundation construction

(2) Clean up the site to ensure that the ground is even and free of sharp objects, sundries and other obstacles that may affect rack installation.

(3) Carry out measurement and construction setting according to design drawings; mark the position of the rack foundation.

The installation of the photovoltatic bracket is shown in Figure 4.2.

Figure 4.2 Photovoltaic rack installation

2. Rack foundation construction

(1) Carry out concrete foundation pouring or screw pile driving according to geological conditions and design requirements.

(2) For concrete foundation, make sure the concrete strength is up to specification and the locations of pre-embedded parts are accurate; for screw piles, make sure driving depth and perpendicularity meet requirements.

3. Rack assembly and installation

(1) Assemble racks and modules according to rack drawings and module layout diagrams to ensure that connectors are securely tightened and do not come loose.

(2) Use tools such as leveling instruments and suspension wires to ensure that the levelness and perpendicularity of rack installation are within permissible ranges.

(3) Install assembled racks to predetermined positions, connect them securely with the foundation and, if necessary, carry out anti-rust treatment.

4. Rack grounding

Carry out the installation of the rack grounding system according to design requirements, including grounding electrode embedding, grounding flat steel connection, grounding resistance testing, etc., to ensure that grounding resistance meets relevant standards.

4.1.3 Photovoltaic module installation

1. Module inspection and preparation:

(1) Inspect the appearance of photovoltaic modules for any damage or scratches; inspect junction boxes, borders, etc., for any deformation or damage.

(2) Check that the model, power and other information of the modules are consistent with design drawings; inspect the diodes, connecting wires, etc., in junction boxes for any damage.

2. Module installation:

(1) Place modules stably on racks in accordance with the layout order in design drawings; use special jigs or bolts to fix the modules; make sure that the contact surface between modules and their racks is flat without stress concentration.

(2) Connect series or parallel cables between modules; use special junction boxes or connectors to ensure tight wiring and good waterproof sealing.

3. Module wiring and protection:

(1) Carry out parallel connection of module strings, combiner box access and other wiring tasks according to system electrical drawings to ensure that wiring is correct and that wire diameter, crimping, etc., are up to specification.

(2) Carry out necessary protection treatment for wiring parts, for example, using cable trunking, heat-shrinkable tubes, waterproof cases, etc., to prevent risks of wear and tear, corrosion, and short circuit.

4. Module testing and identification:

(1) After the completion of installation, carry out IV curve testing of module strings to ensure that the performance meets the factory standard and that no hot spots, hidden cracks or other problems are found.

(2) Label the module string number, it's power and other information in prominent

positions for easy identification during later operation and maintenance.

The installation of photovoltaic modules is shown in Figure 4.3.

Figure 4.3　Photovoltaic module installation

4.1.4　Installation of inverters and transformers

When devices enter the site, the construction unit, the development unit (or its representative), the supervision unit, and the supply unit jointly carries out an appearance inspection for any deformation, corrosion damage, collision, or oil leakage; proper records should be made as specified. Check whether the number of cases is correct according to the product packing lists. Inspect for any missing or wrong cases; inspect outer packaging cases for any damage or loss; make proper records as specified. Insulating components should be free of cracks and defects, with a clean appearance; thermometers should indicate correctly.

1. Hoisting specifications are as follows

(1) Hoisting preparations. The construction plan has been approved; technical briefing is completed; construction personnel are familiar with construction procedures and construction requirements; the construction site is even; the crane operating range should be compacted; lifting tools and materials must have a certificate of conformity and have passed inspection; lifting lugs should be inspected for qualification validation, and additional lifting lugs or bundling devices should be provided if necessary; after the completion of hoisting preparations, the person in charge gives unified directions for lifting and installation.

(2) Hoisting plan and cautions. During lifting, the two flexible slings are tied to the outer packing case through the lifting sign respectively. The lifting hook passes vertically through the center of gravity of devices for lifting. Tilting transport is strictly prohibited! When lifting, lowering and moving inverters with cranes, make sure the operating process is slow and smooth. During the process, crane safety operating procedures must

be strictly observed. In the event of adverse weather conditions, lifting work should be stopped.

2. Placement and installation of inverters and transformers

The installation of inverters and transformers adopts integral installation; placement should be performed in strict accordance with design documents and manufacturers' drawings; prior to installation, the technical leader provides technical briefing to the construction personnel.

(1) Unpacking. Unpacking procedures should be performed as follows (Figure 4.4):

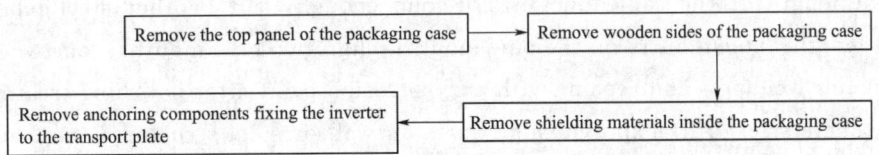

Figure 4.4 Unpacking procedures for inverters and transformers

(2) Inspection before fixing. Ensure that the laying of cable trenches meets inverter installation requirements; ensure that the installation and openings of channel steel meet inverter installation requirements.

(3) Fix inverters. Use lifting devices to transport inverters to the installation location and align mounting holes. Use M12 bolts to secure inverters to channel steel or foundation through waist holes in the base. Install front and rear baffles of inverter bases to complete the fixed installation of inverters.

(4) Cautions. When the transformer is in place, the high-voltage side should face the line side and the low-voltage side should face the inverter room; the axis of the center of gravity of the compact transformer should coincide with the longitudinal and transverse geometrical center lines of the compact transformer foundation, and the error should be within 5 mm. When compact inverters are in place, installation and wiring of transformers and inverters should be carried out in strict accordance with construction drawings.

(5) Cleaning and painting. After completing the installation of compact inverters and transformers, all parts should be wiped and cleaned; local parts can be repainted with paint of the same color; if required by the user, the shade of the paint agreed by the user should be used for repainting; the thickness of the paint film should generally be 0.02~0.05 mm.

3. Cable laying construction

(1) The process flowchart is shown in the Figure 4.5.

(2) Construction methods and procedures.

1) Processing and laying of cable sleeves. Determine lengths of the cable ducts according to the actual dimensions; for cable ducts with elbows, first bend the elbow part with a pipe bender, then cut off the excess part according to the actual length and height of the

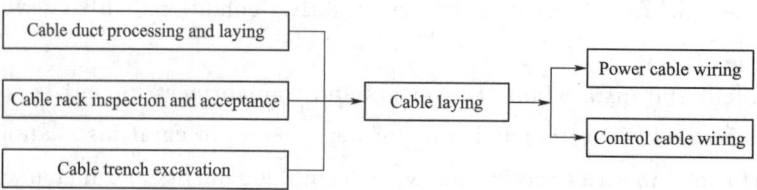

Figure 4.5　Process flowchart for cable laying construction

cable duct, and finally remove burrs and rust, and paint with anti-corrosion paint.

If the length of the cable duct is not long enough, cut another steel pipe to the required length; polish burrs on the pipe mouth; align two pipe mouths; one week later, carry out full welding, and repaint with anti-corrosion paint after polishing treatment.

Use angle steel to fix exposed cable ducts on wall or steel structures (as fasteners); weld cable ducts on the angle steel; spot weld pipe openings using a steel plate for blocking; for longer pipes, the number of fixing points should be increased as appropriate. After the completion of cable duct laying, carry out reliable welding between cable ducts and grounding grid with -40×4 flat steel; embedded parts of cable ducts should be painted with anti-corrosion paint, and exposed parts should be painted with silver paint. A bell mouth should be installed at the opening end of cable ducts.

2) Cable rack preparation and installation. After the completion of civil construction, go through intermediate handover procedures with the head of civil construction of the installation unit. Cable laying can be carried out only after acceptance inspection has been done.

Laying installation of directly embedded cables: In cable lines, cables are susceptible to mechanical damage and chemical effects. In dangerous areas with underground current, vibration, thermal effects, insects and rats, etc., protection measures should be taken. Directly embedded cable laying should meet design requirements: Prior to cable laying, inspect cable trunks for smoothness, proper drainage, and normal lighting and ventilation; check whether the appearance, model and specifications of cables meet requirements. When laying cables, cable sliding rails should be installed according to the site conditions.

Inspect the laying of cable ducts and the installation of cable racks and hangers. Carefully observe the path, sequence and actual length of cable laying according to the cable inventory and design drawings. Timely contact relevant departments in case of any design error. Transport cables to the construction site after completing all necessary preparations. After secure placement of the cable laying rack, lay the cable on the rack and lead it from the top end of the cable reel for laying. High- and low-voltage power cables and strong- and weak-power control cables should be laid in sequence from top to bottom, neatly arranged and securely fixed; enough margin should be reserved at both cable ends; cable signs should be attached to both ends.

(3) Production and wiring of low-voltage power cables and control cable heads.

1) For low-voltage power cables and control cables, use adhesive tapes for wrapping; for power cables, use special hydraulic crimping pliers to crimp cable lugs; for control cables and computer cables, if they are multi-stranded core wires, choose appropriate crimping pliers according to the terminals used to crimp the terminals, and if the cables are single-stranded core wires, carry out direct crimping; for phase color identification of power cables, use different phase color tapes for wrapping; for phase color identification of control cables, use purchased finished products of core wire heads; after qualification validation of cable testing and pairing, carry out one-to-one cable wiring; ground cable outer sheaths and shielding layers as required.

2) There should be no intermediate joints between power cables and control cables whenever possible; if there is no choice but to have intermediate joints, the joints should be pulled out, so that they are away from other parallel cables, and joint trays of a certain strength should be installed around the joints to tightly bundle the joints; locations of the joints should be properly marked and recorded, and should be subjected to joint acceptance with the supervision unit, and relevant materials should be handed over.

3) During cable transport, storage and laying prior to cable connector production, make sure that all cable heads are wrapped with plastic films all the time. In the design of the proportion of concrete mix of fair-faced concrete, analyze various factors affecting concrete quality, including raw materials like local cement, sand and gravel admixtures, and concrete admixtures, to determine major control factors, and choose optimal schemes meeting production conditions considering both the economic and user requirements. Use sealing tapes for sealing; newly cut cable heads during laying should be timely sealed.

(4) Cable test. After completing cable head production, carry out insulation testing and calibration for each cable according to cable insulation levels and specification requirements to inspect cable integrity.

(5) Fireproof blocking. After completing all cable laying, carry out fireproof blocking construction according to design and specifications. Fireproof blocking should be implemented for cables through cable trenches, shafts, buildings, floor slabs, walls, equipment, panels and cabinets, and cable duct openings. Fire-retardant coating and fireproof board installation should comply with specifications and design requirements, and achieve a compact, flat and aesthetic effect.

1) Fireproof blocking should be carried out for bottom holes of high- and low-voltage switch cabinets and holes through floor slabs: Embed the bottom holes of screen cabinets under the ground using fireproof partitions with a thickness of 10 mm and expansion bolts; for apertures due to cables passing through partitions, wrap cables using organic blocking materials; cut partitions with a thickness of 10 mm according to the dimensions

of the screen cabinet, and install them at the bottom of the screen board; for apertures due to cables passing through blocking wall partitions, use organic blocking materials for tight blocking and shaping.

2) Fireproof blocking for incoming wires through switch cabinets: Clean the cables, trays and switch cabinets where fireproof blocking walls are mounted, ensuring they are dry and free from dust and sundries; apply organic blocking materials between cables.

3) Fireproof blocking for fireproof blocking sections of cable shafts: Choose angle steel to support proper mounting of fire partitions as base plates; wrap cable blocking parts with organic blocking materials; stagger fireproof expansion modules so that they are in level with floor slabs, and then mount top partitions; for apertures due to cables passing through partitions, use organic blocking materials for tight blocking and shaping.

4. Compact inverters and transformer boxes should be grounded

Grounding is carried out through grounding holes on equipment boxes; use 40mm×4mm hot-dip galvanized flat iron to connect with the factory grounding grid; connect flat iron with equipment boxes using bolts; galvanized layers on contact surfaces of flat iron and equipment boxes should be removed.

Transportation and laying of low-voltage cables. In the process of transport, loading and unloading, cables and cable reels should not be damaged. It is strictly prohibited to push down cable reels directly from the transporting truck. Cable reels should not be transported and stored flat. Before transporting or rolling cable reels, make sure that cable reels are firm, cables are wound tightly, and the direction of cable winding is followed when rolling.

After cables and their accessories are transported to the site, timely inspection should be carried out as required: Technical documents of products should be complete; cable models, specifications and lengths should meet design requirements; accessories should be complete; the cables should not be damaged; cable blocking ends should be tight. Cable trays should be sorted, and should be free of deformation by force.

Before cable laying, inspection should be carried out to ensure the following requirements: Cable trunks are smooth; drainage is good; the anti-corrosion layer of the metal part is complete; cable models and voltage specifications meet design requirements; the appearance of cables is free of damage; insulation is good. The cable laying rack should be placed securely, and the strength and length of the steel shaft should be matched with the weight and width of the cable reel. Before laying, the length of each cable should be calculated according to design and the actual laying path; each reel of cable should be reasonably arranged to reduce the number of cable connectors; safety measures should be taken when laying cables in live working zones.

For power cables, spare lengths should be reserved in the vicinity of terminal heads and joints: The horizontal distance between support points of cable racks should not be greater than 0.8 m; cable derricks are spaced 1 m apart; supports and hangers of cable trays are spaced approximately 1.5 m apart (not greater than 2 m). The minimum bending radius of cables should meet specifications in Table 4.1.

Table 4.1　　　　　　　　　　**Minimum bending radius of cables**

Cable type		Multi-core	Single-core
Control cable		10D	
Rubber power cable	Without aluminum-sheathed steel armored protection	10D	
	Steel armored sheath	20D	
PVC insulated power cable		10D	
XLPE insulated power cable		15D	20D

Note: D refers to the cable's outer diameter.

5. Production and installation of power cable terminals

Cable head production should be carried out by trained personnel familiar with the process, in strict compliance with production process specifications.

The following requirements should be met before the production of cable terminals and connectors: Cables are well insulated and free of moisture, with no ingress of water in plastic cables; accessory specifications should be in line with cable specifications; parts should be complete without damage; insulating materials should be free of moisture; sealing materials should not fail; construction tools should be complete to facilitate operation; firefighting equipment should be complete; production of cable heads should start from peeling and cutting cables and should be operated continuously until the completion of operation to shorten insulation exposure time; when peeling and cutting cables, wire cores and retained insulating layers should not be damaged; additional insulation system assembly: heat-shrinkable parts should be cleaned; for cable terminal heads, protection measures, e.g., strengthening insulation, moisture-proof sealing, and mechanical protection, should be adopted, and same external insulation and distance to ground should be ensured; during the production of high-voltage cross-linked cable terminals and connectors, semi conductive shielding layers should be completely removed; during the production of heat-shrinkable heads of power cables, the flame should be uniform when a blowtorch is used for baking, and no air bubble should be present in the heat-shrinkable tube; when connecting cable lugs to core wires, cable lug specifications should be consistent with core wire specifications; the surface contact of cable lugs and core wires is good without crack or broken wire; the surface of copper cable lugs should be smooth; oil and oxidized layers should be removed from inner walls of wire cores and connecting tubes; crimping dies and armor clamps should be properly fitted and securely crimped; after crimping, protruding marks on terminals or connecting tubes should be repaired, so that the surface is smooth and no burrs remain; metal sheaths at power cable terminals must be properly grounded; each copper shielding layer and armored layer of cables should be soldered with earth wires; when the cable passes through the zero-sequence current transformer, the cable metal sheath and the earth wire should be insulated from the ground; when the grounding point is above the transformer, the earth wire should pass through the transformer and be grounded; when the grounding point is below the transformer, the earth wire should be directly grounded; when assembling combined cable terminals, leakage stoppage, moisture-proofing and sealing measures must be taken at the fit or lap joints between components; use plastic cable adhesive tapes, adhesives or other means for sealing, ensuring a proper bonding effect; there should be prominent phase color identifiers on cable terminals, and the identifiers should be consistent with those for the system.

4.1.5 Tests and commissioning

1. Start-up commissioning

(1) Start-up should be carried out under certain conditions. The installation and commissioning is completed for cell modules, combiner boxes, inverters, DC cabinets, power distribution cabinets, step-up transformers, high-voltage power distribution cabinets, computer monitoring systems, power charging systems, power monitoring devices, fire alarm systems and other devices; fireproof blocking of cable holes has been completed and gone through comprehensive inspection and acceptance; after the confirmation of proper operating status of each device, start-up commissioning can be carried out.

(2) Inspection prior to start-up commissioning. Complete the inspection and cleaning of electrical equipment such as combiner boxes, inverters indoor systems, 10 kV power distribution parts, solar photovoltaic cell modules, computer monitoring systems, electricity charging systems, power quality monitoring devices, fire alarm systems, etc., including the communication among electrical equipment, computer monitoring systems, and electrical control and protection system equipment. The connecting parts of commissioned equipment and non-commissioned equipment must be isolated reliably, and appropriate protection measures must be taken.

2. Tests

(1) Computer monitoring test. After the installation and commissioning of all devices for photovoltaic power stations, check for smooth communication between the devices and power charging systems, power quality monitoring devices, inverters, DC lightning protection combiner boxes, DC cabinets, low-voltage power distribution cabinets, high-voltage switch cabinets, compact substations, and DC power supply control systems. Results of the following tests should meet relevant design requirements: remote operation tests of inverter load limit, start/stop test, circuit breaker and isolating switches using a computer; tests of position contact feedback signals, protective action signals and fault

signals of circuit breakers and isolating switches.

(2) Reverse power transmission test of photovoltaic power stations. After completing the installation and commissioning of all devices for the photovoltaic power station, carry out the reverse power transmission test of the photovoltaic power station. Electrify the line; close the outlet switch, outlet isolating switch, corresponding inlet switch, and isolating switch on the high-voltage side of the step-up transformer; reverse power to the AC side of the inverter. Comprehensively check that the step-up transformer, the inverter, the AC power distribution cabinet and the PT cabinet are working properly, and that the circuit breaker and the isolating switch are operating normally with correct position contact feedback, and that the computer monitoring and control system can correctly collect data of each device.

(3) Positive charging test of photovoltaic power stations. After completing the installation and commissioning of all devices for the photovoltaic power station, carry out the positive charging test of the photovoltaic power station. Close the outlet switch of the combiner box and the DC cabinet switch; positively charge to the DC side of the inverter. Comprehensively check that the combiner box, the DC lightning protection distribution cabinet and the inverter are working properly, and that the computer monitoring and control system can correctly collect data of each device.

(4) Positive phasing verification test of photovoltaic power stations. After completing the reverse power transmission test and positive charging test of the photovoltaic power station, carry out the phase verification test of the power station, run the photovoltaic power station off the grid, and check that the potential transformer on the power station side and the potential transformer on the line test are in the correct phase sequence.

(5) Inverter test. After the completion of the phase verification test of the photovoltaic power station, carry out the inverter load limit test, start/stop test, and protection test; results of each test should meet design requirements.

(6) 24-hour test run of photovoltaic power generation units with load. After all the above tests are completed, a test run should be carried out for each photovoltaic power generation unit. The test run should be carried out in automatic control mode; the duration of the test run should be 24 h. If the test run is interrupted due to a fault, the test will be repeated according to specification requirements. After the completion of the test run, devices should be comprehensively inspected to eliminate and deal with all the defects found during the 24-hour test run.

(7) 30-day assessment test run. After the 24-hour test run and subsequent inspection and handling of all defects, the 30-day assessment test run is carried out without delay. During the 30-day assessment test run of the photovoltaic power station, interruptions due to malfunction of photovoltaic power generation units and their ancillary devices or due to equipment installation quality should be dealt with in a timely manner. Continue with

the 30-day test run after interruptions are resolved.

(8) Other tests. Other tests specified in the specifications and other tests required by the manufacturer and the developer should be performed.

4.1.6 Environmental adaptability

(1) Ambient temperature: According to climatic conditions in the region where the project is located, select rack and module materials adaptable to various environments, e.g., high temperature, low temperature, salt spray, and sand and dust, to ensure long-term stable operation. For extreme environments, necessary measures such as thermal insulation, heat preservation and anti-corrosion should be taken.

(2) Dustproof and waterproof: The design of racks should take into account the dustproof and drainage needs to prevent rainwater and dust from accumulating in racks. During module installation, make sure that junction boxes, borders, etc., are tightly sealed to prevent moisture from entering.

(3) Lightning protection: Appropriate lightning protection measures should be taken according to relevant standards and lightning activity in the project location, for example, installing lightning rods, surge protection devices, etc., and ensuring robust grounding systems.

4.1.7 Convenience of later operation and maintenance

(1) Equipment layout: When installing racks and modules, give full consideration to the convenience of later operation and maintenance, such as reserving enough space for inspection and maintenance and setting up easily accessible maintenance doors, to ensure that operation and maintenance personnel can conveniently carry out equipment inspection, fault troubleshooting, regular maintenance and other tasks.

(2) Clear identification: All devices, cables, terminals, etc., are clearly and permanently labeled, including the name, number, wiring diagram, phase sequence and other information of devices, so that operation and maintenance personnel can quickly identify system structures and operation statuses.

(3) Document archiving: After completing installation, collate and properly store all equipment manuals, wiring diagrams, test reports, acceptance data, etc., to provide a basis for later operation, maintenance, troubleshooting and equipment replacement.

4.1.8 Regulations and standards

(1) Grid connection procedures: After completing installation and commissioning, go through the grid connection application procedures timely, and cooperate with the power company for grid connection acceptance to ensure legal and compliant operation of the project.

(2) Safety regulations: Strictly comply with national and local laws and regulations

on installation, operation and maintenance of electric facilities, such as the Electricity Law, Work Safety Law, Technical Regulations on Connecting Photovoltaic Power Stations to Power Systems, etc., to ensure safe and standardized operation of the project.

(3) Environmental protection requirements: Comply with environmental protection laws and regulations of the region where the project is located, e. g., requirements for noise control and waste disposal, to ensure that project construction and operation does not adversely impact the environment.

【Task implementation】

I. Task preparations

1 competition equipment platform, 1 slotted screwdriver, 1 philips screw driver, 2 multimeters, a hex wrench screwdriver, 1 wire stripping plier, DC cables (10 meters for both red and black cables), a number of MC4 connector kits, 1 electric soldering iron, 1 roll of solder, 1 schematic diagram of the power station, 1 set of combiner box and its accessories, the grid-connected power distribution box and its fitting switch, 1 copy of record sheet for power-up inspection, and 1 copy of record sheet for photovoltaic power station construction.

II. Task content and procedures

(ⅰ) Task 1: Construction of a photovoltaic power station

Task content: Draw the wiring diagram of the photovoltaic power station; complete the construction of the photovoltaic power station.

Task 4.1 Related implementation charts

Task procedures:

(1) Understand the schematic diagram of the power station.

(2) Draw the wiring diagram of the photovoltaic power station according to the schematic diagram.

(3) Complete wire welding in the junction box of the photovoltaic cell module.

(4) Complete photovoltaic module installation on the photovoltaic rack platform.

(5) Complete series-parallel wiring of the photovoltaic power station in the combiner box.

(ⅱ) Task 2: Installation and inspection of the combiner box

Task content: Complete the installation and inspection of the 4-in-1-out combiner box.

Task procedures:

(1) Complete the installation and fixing of the combiner box.

(2) Complete wiring and cable routing on the DC side of the combiner box.

(3) Complete wiring and cable routing on the AC side of the combiner box.

(4) Complete pre-power-up inspection of the combiner box.

(ⅲ) Task 3: Installation and inspection of the grid-connected power distribution box

Task content: Complete the installation and inspection of the grid-connected power distribution box.

Task procedures:

(1) Complete the installation and fixing of the grid-connected power distribution box.

(2) Complete wiring and cable routing on the input side of the grid-connected power distribution box.

(3) Complete wiring and cable routing on the output side of the grid-connected power distribution box.

(4) Complete pre-power-up inspection of the combiner box.

III. Skill requirements

(1) Module installation requires bolts, spring washers, nuts, etc.; nuts should be tightened. Connecting wires and module output cables should also be installed securely; check whether the connections are correct.

(2) Use amultimeter to test the open-circuit voltage and short-circuit current of each array. Determine whether electrical connection of each module array is normal according to open-circuit voltage and short-circuit current.

(3) Cable routing should be resistant to short-circuit current. Cable routing between solar cell modules can withstand short-circuit current if 2 mm^2 wires are used.

(4) To reduce wiring line pressure and costs, the location of the junction box should beas close as possible to the array. However, it should not affect building structure, aesthetics, and future inspection and component replacement.

IV. Task results, appraisal and evaluation

(1) The photovoltaic power station, combiner box, and grid-connected power distribution box are correctly installed and wired (accounting for 90%).

(2) The operator exhibits good professional quality during the operation process and follows 7S management model (accounting for 10%).

【Exercises】

1. What considerations are involved in the installation of controllers, inverters, and storage batteries?

2. In cable routing projects, what is the common situation that requires special attention to the polarity of components? When measuring each branch circuit, what measure requires each branch circuit be disconnected from each other? Why is it necessary to check wiring polarity in the presence of a terminal box?

3. What are the grounding requirements for solar photovoltaic power generation systems? What is the order of controller installation? Please explain.

4. What should be noted about cable routing between solar cell modules and inverters?

Task 4.2 Operating and Maintaining Solar Photovoltaic Power Generation Systems

【Learning objectives】

Knowledge objective: To understand items to be inspected prior to the commissioning of solar photovoltaic power generation systems

Ability objective: To be able to commission solar photovoltaic power generation systems; to be able to maintain the proper operation of solar photovoltaic power generation systems

Qualification objective: To cultivate professional qualities of teamwork, assiduity, and striving for perfection

Learning priority: Commissioning of solar photovoltaic power generation systems

Learning challenge: Maintenance of solar photovoltaic power generation systems

【Task analysis】

After the completion of the installation of solar cell arrays and relevant devices, the whole photovoltaic system is ready for inspection and operation. System inspection is needed before commissioning. Commissioning can only be started after the system has passed the inspection. After passing integrated testing, the system begins initial operation. Then, daily operation and maintenance is carried out.

This task relies on the equipment platform of the National Vocational College Skills Competition or the equipment platform of the vocational skills certificate. It involves various tasks, including completing pre-power-up system commissioning, system grid connection operation, and configuration and operation of the monitoring screen of photovoltaic power generation systems.

【Knowledge learning】

4.2.1 Commissioning of solar photovoltaic power generation systems

After completing the installation of solar cell arrays and relevant devices, the electrical part of the whole photovoltaic system is ready for inspection and initial operation. However, to ensure the safe and robust operation of photovoltaic power stations, it is necessary to carry out the system commissioning of solar photovoltaic power generation systems.

System commissioning of photovoltaic power generation systems includes the commissioning of photovoltaic strings, DC systems, electrical energy conversion devices, and AC systems. For grid-connected photovoltaic power stations, the commissioning of grid connection and monitoring systems is also necessary. According to the types of photovoltaic power stations and the requirements of operation and maintenance specifications of photovoltaic power stations and industry certificates, the commissioning contents are listed in Table 4.2.

Table 4.2   Commissioning of solar photovoltaic power generation systems

Types of photovoltaic power generation systems / Debugging items	Off-grid photovoltaic power generation systems	Distributed grid-connected photovoltaic power stations	Centralized photovoltaic power stations
Commissioning of photovoltaic strings	Commissioning of photovoltaic strings	Commissioning of grid-connected photovoltaic cell strings	Commissioning of photovoltaic arrays
Commissioning of DC systems	Commissioning of DC combiner boxes; commissioning of storage batteries	Commissioning of photovoltaic combiner boxes	Commissioning of DC combiner boxes; commissioning of DC power distribution cabinets
Commissioning of electrical energy conversion devices	Commissioning of photovoltaic controllers; Commissioning of microinverters	Commissioning of string photovoltaic inverters	Commissioning of centralized inverters
Commissioning of AC systems	Installation and commissioning of AC loads	Installation and commissioning of photovoltaic grid-connected cabinets	Commissioning of transformers; commissioning of AC power distribution cabinets
Communication commissioning	Communication installation and commissioning of photovoltaic power generation systems	Communication installation and commissioning of photovoltaic power generation systems	Communication installation and commissioning of photovoltaic power generation systems
System start-up commissioning	Start-up inspection and off-grid testing	Start-up inspection and grid connection testing	Start-up inspection and grid connection testing

When carrying out the commissioning of solar photovoltaic power generation systems, it is important to ensure the use of correct tools. The tools used for system commissioning are similar to those used for installation. It is necessary to bring the tools listed in Table 4.3.

Table 4.3   Debugging Tools for Solar Photovoltaic Power Generation System

Number	Tools	Explanation
1	Commissioning form, pen and notepad	For visualization purposes, a sample commissioning form is provided in the next subsection
2	10-in-1 screwdriver	This handy tool has every type of screwdriver needed for system startup
3	Digital multimeter (DMM)	Ideally, the DMM comes with a clip-on DC ammeter

Continued Table

Number	Tools	Explanation
4	High-voltage insulating gloves and anti-arc goggles	Wear these protective equipment whenever measuring woltages and current values
5	Infrared thermometer	This instrument is used to measure module temperature during module performance testing
6	Irradiation sensor	It costs approximately RMB 1000 to buy an irradiation sensor. This may seem a bit expensive, but it is useful for directly measuring array irradiation values. Irradiation values can be used to determine the output power of arrays
7	Reliable fall protection tools against possible fall hazards	These fall protection tools are the same as those used for system installation-safety harnesses and safety ropes

Commissioning contents of solar photovoltaic power generation systems are as follows:

(1) Commissioning of photovoltaic cell strings. Whether the photovoltaic power stations are grid-connected or off-grid, the composition of strings is similar. Thus, commissioning methods and procedures are common for photovoltaic strings. To be specific, the commissioning includes inspection of mechanical components, identification of photovoltaic hazardous sources, troubleshooting of broken wires and other faults, and testing of initial and normal operation of photovoltaic strings.

1) Inspection of mechanical components. It is important to ensure that the mechanical part of the system meets original expectations and can hold arrays in place. Questions to be asked when inspecting the entiremounting system are described below.

a. Photovoltaic string footings. It is important to inspect the footings (the method for holding arrays in place). Ideally, this part of the pre-commissioning inspection should be carried out before installation of the entire arrays. If a problem is discovered too late, resolving it will be both difficult and expensive. Asking the following questions will relieve your worries and save costs.

(a) For roof arrays, are the footings mounted in the proper locations? Is the spacing reasonable?

(b) Is the correct hardware used to mount the footings?

(c) For arrays anchored in the ground and on top of the poles, are the pits dug with proper size requirements? Is concrete poured thick enough? Are the poles spaced correctly?

b. Photovoltaic string racks. Inspection of the rack system (consisting of rails and clamps) should be viewed as the mechanical part of the inspection. However, this can be a challenge, especially for roof-mounted arrays, and access to ground-mounted and pole-top-mounted arrays can be quite inconvenient after all climbing ladders and scaffolds are removed. Take extra care and remember to ask the following questions.

(a) Are the modules properly connected to the rack system using the correct hardware?

(b) Are the modules grounded to the rack system properly (reliably connected to each module using a grounding clamp or equipment grounding conductor)?

(c) Is the rack system reliably fixed to the footing system?

2) Identification of photovoltaic hazardous sources. If photovoltaic power generation systems are reasonably designed, constructed in compliance with relevant specifications, and equipped with facilities and devices of adequate quality, safety risk is relatively small during normal operation. Yet, normal operation of photovoltaic power stations also involves hazardous sources. The identification of hazardous sources in photovoltaic power stations is extremely important in the operation and maintenance of photovoltaic power stations. It is a prerequisite for mastering the following skills: being familiar with the methods of cleaning and maintaining photovoltaic modules, the ability to clean contaminants from the surface of photovoltaic modules, and the ability to conduct an inspection of the appearance of photovoltaic modules and determine subsequent handling methods based on observations.

a. Spontaneous explosion of tempered glass of photovoltaic modules. Crystalline silicon photovoltaic modules generally use tempered glass on the front side (some modules use tempered glass on both sides). Tempered glass may crack automatically during storage, transport and use without direct external force, this phenomenon is known as spontaneous explosion. For most tempered glass products, the rate of spontaneous explosion is $0.3\%-3\%$. Tempered glass used in photovoltaic modules can cause the modules to lose mechanical integrity and sealing. Once water vapor intrudes into the interior of modules, it tends to cause electrical leakage of modules. Self-exploding modules are even more hazardous in rainy or wet weather, presenting significant safety hazards. Thus, such modules must be replaced.

b. "Hot spot effect" and spontaneous combustion of photovoltaic modules. Under certain conditions, defective areas in photovoltaic modules become loads and consume energy generated in other areas, resulting in local overheating, this phenomenon is known as the "hot spot effect". Severe hot spots at high temperatures can lead to permanent damage such as partial burnout of cells, melting of solder joints, destruction of grid wires, and aging of encapsulation materials. Local overheating may also lead to glass rupture, backsheet burn-through, and even spontaneous combustion of modules, resulting in a fire. The "hot spot effect" and spontaneous combustion can be detected and identified using thermal imagers, thus effectively avoiding spontaneous combustion caused by the "hot spot effect".

c. Virtual connection and aging of cables. Cables are an essential part of photovoltaic power generation systems. However, cables are quick-wear materials, and out-of-specification construction may present significant safety hazards. Common problems are:

(a) Cable connectors are not securely connected, and virtual connections will lead to an increase in the resistance of contact points during equipment operation, equipment abnormal heating, and danger of spontaneous combustion.

(b) Cables are inadvertently punctured during construction. If the broken part is in contact with a metal component, it will result in positive or negative pole grounding.

(c) Cables of modules are not stowed under backsheets or routed in the cable trunking, but they are directly exposed to sunlight. Consequently, insulating materials on the surface of cables are susceptible to aging, resulting in lowered insulation levels.

(d) Cables are soaked in water or humid environment, causing insulation levels to reduce.

Virtual connection and aging of cables can be identified using multimeters, thermal imagers and other devices.

d. Ingress of water or foreign objects in electrical equipment. Electrical equipment for outdoor use must have good sealing and IP protection levels. However, some of the equipment is susceptible to ingress of water or foreign objects due to inadequate quality or improper installation. For example, some projects constructed in the early years used frameless modules, resulting in poor edge sealing and direct ingress of water vapor into the interior of the modules; in some power stations with color steel tile roofs, combiner boxes were installed along roof slopes, resulting in easy ingress of rainwater into the boxes; ingress of frogs and other small animals were even found in combiner boxes due to their poor sealing. All these intrusions can easily cause short circuit inside the modules and combiner boxes. To avoid water ingress caused by human factors, photovoltaic arrays should be cleaned in accordance with specifications.

e. Other hazardous sources include ascent, weather, and night inspection, etc.

3) Troubleshooting of broken wires and other faults. Troubleshooting of short-circuit faults involves two parts: photovoltaic string connection electrical inspection and photovoltaic combiner box testing. Let's first introduce photovoltaic string connection electrical inspection: connection sequence inspection, cable status inspection, and photovoltaic characteristic curve inspection.

a. Photovoltaic connection sequence inspection. The electrical inspection should start from solar cell modules. Take some time to ask the following questions to ensure that the installed arrays are consistent with the single-line diagrams.

(a) Is the number of modules installed correct?

(b) Are the manufacturers and model numbers consistent with the drawings submitted during the permit application process?

(c) Is module wiring consistent with the correct configuration of module strings? Such configuration may be series, parallel, or series-parallel.

When inspecting solar photovoltaic power generation systems, inspect all electrical components to verify that all components are properly installed. It is not necessary to touch the enclosure of electrical equipment by hand to verify proper voltage, but it is certainly necessary to thoroughly inspect each electrical component to see whether it is in order. All electrical components that need to be inspected before beginning the commissioning process are listed below. In case of any error found during operation, it is important to stop and consider it carefully. Always verify that the system status is safe for the tool being used before making changes.

b. Cable status inspection. The methods or devices generally used to inspect the faults include visual inspection, multimeter, thermal imager, insulation resistance meter, I-V curve tester, and EL detector.

(a) Use visual inspection, amultimeter, a thermal imager and other tools to inspect and identify photovoltaic DC cables to ensure that the cables are not short-circuited or broken.

(b) Use an insulation resistance meter to eliminate photovoltaic module/string ground faults, etc.

c. Photovoltaic characteristic curve inspection.

(a) Use an I-V curve tester to test I-V curve characteristics of photovoltaic modules or strings; to be able to identify faulty photovoltaic modules or string faults and analyze the causes of these faults.

(b) Use an EL tester to perform electroluminescence testing of photovoltaic modules; to be able to identify faulty modules and analyze the causes of these faults.

(c) To be able to use an infrared thermal imager to test the surface temperature of photovoltaic modules; to be able to identify faulty modules and analyze the causes of module faults.

4) Initial operation and normal operation testing of photovoltaic strings. When it is verified that the mechanical structure of the photovoltaic power station is intact, that the hazardous sources have been eliminated, and that the electrical connections are correct, initial operation and normal operation testing of photovoltaic strings can be performed. The monitoring computer can be used to monitor the operation status of photovoltaic strings. It can be used to determine whether there is any fault or positioning problem in photovoltaic strings by combining with on-site working conditions. Prepare photovoltaic module/string testing and analysis report.

(2) Commissioning of DC systems.

DC system commissioning of photovoltaic power generation systems includes commissioning of DC combiner boxes and storage batteries.

1) Commissioning of DC combiner boxes. Commissioning of photovoltaic DC combiner boxes includes specification inspection, internal and external appearance inspection, and electrical performance testing.

2) Storage batteries. If storage batteries are installed, pay special attention to them. Take some time to ask the following questions to evaluate the installation and future maintenance of storage batteries.

a. Are storage batteries reliably ventilated to the outside? All storage batteries emit hydrogen, although sealed storage batteries emit minimal hydrogen.

b. Are storage batteries installed in an appropriate enclosure? Storage batteries should be protected from damage, and they can cause personal injury.

c. Are storage batteries correctly installed and wired? Solar photovoltaic power generation systems have strict requirements for storage battery voltage. If storage batteries are incorrectly wired, the system will not operate properly.

(3) Commissioning of electrical energy conversion devices. Electrical energy conversion devices in photovoltaic power generation systems mainly include solar charge/discharge controllers and photovoltaic inverters.

1) Commissioning of solar charge/discharge controllers. When dealing with systems with storage batteries - whether it is a grid-tied system or an off-grid system- charge controllers are needed to ensure that solar photovoltaic cell arrays charge the storage batteries properly. Always ask the following questions before energizing a charge controller.

a. Is the charge controller mounted in the proper position? Its usual mounting position is immediately adjacent to the inverter and the storage battery.

b. Are there isolating switches and overcurrent protective devices on both input and output sides of the controller?

c. Is the wire gauge, used for the wires connected to the controller, correct?

2) Commissioning of photovoltaic inverters. Since inverters are extremely important components of solar photovoltaic power generation systems, it will completely interrupt the operation of photovoltaic power generation systems if there is a problem with inverters. Ask the following questions when inspecting inverters before commissioning.

Combined with relevant national standards and the actual situation of household photovoltaic power stations, parameter testing of inverters can include several aspects of protection function testing, conversion efficiency, and power quality testing:

a. Protection function testing. Anti-reverse discharge protection means that when the DC side voltage of the inverter is lower than the permissible working range or when the inverter is in the shutdown state, there is no current flowing in the opposite direction on the DC side of the inverter. In other words, when the inverter is in standby or shutdown state, if you detect the DC side, there should be no current flowing from the inverter towards the DC source (solar panel).

According to relevant national standards, the action time of anti-islanding protection is no more than 2 s. Tests can be carried out according to site conditions to check whether the anti-islanding protection of the inverter works properly.

b. Conversion efficiency. For the operation and maintenance of photovoltaic power stations, conversion efficiency is the most important performance indicator of inverters. Choose a typical working day, read the input/output power of the inverter from morning to evening at different load rates using inverter display parameters, and calculate the weighted conversion efficiency of the inverter using the inverter weighted efficiency formula.

If necessary, measure solar irradiance, ambient temperature, and module temperature during the reading process, and record the results for later use. To improve work efficiency, monitoring data obtained from the operation and maintenance platform can be combined with actual on-site measurements.

(4) Commissioning of AC systems. Commissioning of AC systems includes commissioning of photovoltaic grid-connected cabinets, commissioning of switchgears, commissioning of protective devices, commissioning of transformers and access boxes, commissioning of AC power distribution cabinets, installation and commissioning of AC loads, etc. The following mainly introduces the commissioning of photovoltaic grid-connected cabinets, switchgears, and protective devices.

1) Commissioning of photovoltaic grid-connected cabinets. This commissioning includes grid-connected cabinet commissioning and safety hazard elimination. The main requirements are as follows:

a. Determine whether the protective device in the grid-connected cabinet meets the requirements of electrical safety and the relevant power sector standards.

b. Inspect and perform electrical connections in the grid-connected cabinet according to the electrical diagram.

c. Check whether switching devices in the grid-connected cabinet can be operated normally.

d. To be able to check whether wire sequences of input and output cables are correct.

e. To be able to inspect metal chassis grounding and check internal components for missing or virtual connection.

f. To be able to carry out basic maintenance (e. g. , corrosion, accumulation of dust, etc.) of grid-connected cabinets according to the requirements for grid-connected cabinet commissioning and safety hazard elimination; to be able to observe deformation, leakage, and other problems; to be able to replace grid-connected cabinets.

g. Detect the status of electrical equipment in grid-connected cabinets; replace faulty components in grid-connected cabinets, such as circuit breakers and isolating switches.

h. Detect protective measures for grid-connected cabinets, e. g. , protective earthing, enclosure protection, electrical isolation, and fault protection; timely replacement should be carried out if they do not meet the requirements.

i. Inspect the basic condition of AC combiner boxes; handle corrosion, accumulation of dust, detachment of equipment identifiers, and other tasks.

　　j. To be able to replace combiner boxes that show deformation, water leakage, and other issues; to be able to replace circuit breakers, lightning protection modules and other components of AC combiner boxes.

　　k. To be able to measure the terminal temperature of AC combiner boxes using an infrared thermal detector; to be able to handle hidden defects such as local abnormal high temperature.

　　2) Commissioning of isolating switches. Solar photovoltaic power generation systems are equipped with isolating switches on both AC and DC sides. Many directly networked systems have at least one photovoltaic isolating switch in the inverter. Ask the following questions when carrying out system commissioning preparation and thorough system inspection.

　　a. Do the installed isolating switches meet requirements? Can the AC power supply to the solar photovoltaic cell array and the inverter be disconnected? Are the two isolating switches combined as a group?

　　b. If a visible, lockable isolating switch is required by the power sector, is it properly installed in accordance with the power sector's requirements?

　　c. Is the right conductor cut for each isolating switch? This is because the grounded current-carrying conductor should not be cut.

　　d. Are the installed isolating switches appropriate for their environment and rated for the appropriate voltage and current values?

　　e. Are isolating switches equipped with appropriate identifiers? If you are in doubt about the role of isolating switches, it is even less likely to expect someone who is completely unfamiliar with the system to understand what they are dealing with.

　　3) Commissioning of overcurrent protective devices. In general, overcurrent protective devices (OCPDs) may be installed on both AC and DC sides of inverters. Before closing the switch, it is important to check not only that the correct OCPDs are installed, but also that they protect the system properly. Take a moment to consider the following questions.

　　a. Does the rated current value match the circuit? Wrong OCPD capacity (either too large or too small) can cause problems.

　　b. Is the rated voltage value of the OCPD correct? This is critical, especially for power supply circuits of solar photovoltaic power generation systems. The rated DC value of the OCPD must be correct. Otherwise, it cannot protect the system properly when it is really needed.

　　c. Is the OCPD in good condition? Faulty fuses or circuit breakers can lead to wasting of hours in eliminating defects on the first day. Continuity tests should be performed to verify whether the current can pass through the OCPD during initial operation of the system.

(5) Communication installation and commissioning of photovoltaic power generation systems. Communication installation and commissioning of photovoltaic power generation systems include communication installation and commissioning of combiner boxes, inverters, and grid-connected cabinets.

1) Communication installation and commissioning of combiner boxes.

Installation and wiring of communication modules are required:

a. Complete the installation of the main control module and the current sensor module.

b. Complete FMB wiring connection of the main control module and the current sensor.

c. Complete wiring of the DC busbar power supply terminal of the main control module.

d. Complete wiring of the RS485 communication terminal of the main control module.

e. Complete wiring of the 24 V DC power supply terminal of the main control module.

f. Complete communication address setting and recording of the main control module.

g. Use serial port debugging software to complete communication testing, and make records.

2) Communication installation and commissioning of inverters.

a. Complete the connection of the RS485 communication cable of the inverter.

b. Complete the installation of the RS485 communication terminal of the inverter.

c. Complete communication address setting and recording of the inverter.

d. Use serial port debugging software to complete inverter communication testing, and make records.

3) Communication installation and commissioning of electric meters.

This includes communication wiring and commissioning of electric meters:

a. Complete the connection of the RS485 communication cable of the meter.

b. Read the communication address setting of the meter and make records.

c. Use serial port debugging software to complete inverter communication testing, and make records.

(6) Start-up commissioning of photovoltaic systems. After system inspection and verification of safe and proper installation of mechanical and electrical components, you can finally start with the system commissioning (initial operation). Perform this process by doing one procedure at a time so that no critical parts are missed. Main aspects of the commissioning process are described in the following subsections.

After commissioning the system and verifying that everything is in order, you must shut down the system until it passes inspection by the local construction authority.

The first step in performing system commissioning is to ensure that you and the entire system are safe. How can this be achieved? Keep in mind that a safe access sequence of the solar photovoltaic power generation system must be ensured during installation. In the commissioning process, these simple rules should also be followed to ensure your safety and safety of the members of installation team. The primary strategy is to always operate on uncharged circuits and follow the correct wiring sequence to ensure that all circuits are uncharged. It is also necessary to verify that all isolating switches are in the "Off" position and locked.

For directly networked systems, do not connect power circuits of solar photovoltaic power generation systems to combiner boxes, junction boxes, or the utility grid for AC interconnection.

In terms of interconnection of solar photovoltaic power generation systems and the grid (if available), the rules for directly networked systems apply equally for systems with storage batteries. In any case, storage battery packs are another power source that requires correct wiring sequence to avoid possible electric shocks. The connection of storage battery packs to the inverter should be performed at the inverter, but before the connection, the isolating switch of the inverter should be disconnected first. This ensures no live wires in hand and no resulting problems.

4.2.2 Initial operation of grid-connected photovoltaic power generation systems

Depending on whether photovoltaic systems are allowed to transmit power to the high-voltage grid through transformers in the power supply area, grid-connected photovoltaic power generation systems are divided into reversible and non-reversible grid connections.

1. Requirements for grid connection start-up

(1) The static commissioning and experimental work of the primary and secondary electrical equipment related to grid-connected complete start-up have been completed and are in compliance with relevant standards.

(2) Setting values of electrical equipment related to grid-connected complete start-up have been completed and are ready for initial operation.

(3) All the electrically charged rooms related to grid-connected complete start-up have been equipped with shelters and hanging warning signs.

(4) Fire-fighting facilities are complete; inverter rooms and transformer rooms should be equipped with adequate fire extinguishers.

(5) Communication equipment should be unimpeded, well ventilated, and equipped with adequate lighting; emergency lighting should be tested and in order.

(6) All participants should enter the site with a special permit; all irrelevant personnel are prohibited from entry.

2. Procedures for grid connection start-up

(1) Check that the inverter, the switch on the DC side of the inverter, the switch on the AC side of the inverter, the DC switch from the DC cabinet to the inverter, the step-up transformer, the switch on the high-voltage side of the step-up transformer and their

circuits meet power transmission conditions.

(2) Check that the switch on the DC side of the inverter, the switch on the AC side of the inverter, the DC switch from the DC cabinet to the inverter, and the switch on the high-voltage side of the step-up transformer, all are in the disconnected state.

(3) Move the switch of the photovoltaic inlet high-voltage cabinet in the high-voltage power distribution room of the purification station from the "Experiment" position to the "Work" position using a special crank.

(4) Use the monitoring system of the sub-station to remotely close the circuit breaker of the inlet high-voltage cabinet, and move it from the "Open" position to the "Close" position to check that the step-up transformer and the switch on the high-voltage side of the step-up transformer are performing no-load running without any abnormality. Without the approval of the company's supervisor and without safety measures, it is prohibited to close the switch on the high-voltage side of the step-up transformer with the "Close" button on the high-voltage cabinet.

(5) Close the switch on the AC side of the inverter and reconfirm that the switch is closed. (AC power supply is adopted for the control board of the inverter).

(6) Close the DC circuit breaker in the combiner box and reconfirm that the breaker is closed. Observe the monitoring system to check whether each line is in order. In case of any abnormality, disconnect the switch and recheck the devices and wiring until everything is in order.

(7) Close the DC switch from the DC power distribution cabinet to the inverter again and reconfirm that the circuit breaker is closed, so as to check whether the voltage and current levels are high or low.

(8) Close the switch on the DC side of the inverter and reconfirm that the switch is closed.

(9) Check whether the inverter can complete self-inspection before grid connection and complete grid-connected power generation when the DC side voltage is higher than the voltage value specified for grid connection.

(10) Check whether there is any abnormality in inverter parameters after grid-connected operation.

(11) Check that there is no abnormality in the switch on the DC side of the inverter, the switch on the AC side of the inverter, the DC switch from the DC cabinet to the inverter and their circuits.

3. Notes

(1) In case of any abnormality during the process of grid-connected power generation, operation should be stopped without delay and the cause should be ascertained and eliminated. Otherwise, it is strictly prohibited to continue with further operation. Moreover, data should be recorded properly.

(2) In case of any abnormal knocking or abnormal inverter parameters found during the operation of the inverter, the machine can be stopped using the "Stop" button on the control panel or the "Emergency Shutdown" button.

4. Requirements for grid connectionregulations

Voltage deviation: To make local AC loads work properly, the output voltage of the inverter in the photovoltaic system should match the grid. During normal operation, the permissible voltage deviation at the interface between the photovoltaic system and the power grid should meet specifications in *Power quality-Deviation of supply voltage* (GB/T 12325 - 2008). The permissible deviation of three-phase voltage is ±7% of the rated voltage, and that of single-phase voltage is + 7% and −10% of the rated voltage.

Technical requirements for grid connection of PV system

Frequency: Photovoltaic systems should run simultaneously with the grid during grid connection. The rated frequency of the grid is 50 Hz. The permissible frequency deviation for the photovoltaic system after grid connection should meet specifications in GB/T 15945, i.e., a permissible deviation value of ± 0.5 Hz.

Harmonic and waveform distortion: Low harmonic levels of current and voltage are desirable; higher harmonic waves increase the likelihood of harmful effects on connected devices. Permissible levels of harmonic voltages and currents depend on the characteristics of the power distribution system, the type of power supply, connected loads/devices, and current specifications of the grid. The output of photovoltaic systems should have low current distortion to ensure no detrimental effects on other devices connected to the grid. The total harmonic current should be less than 5% of the rated output of the inverter.

See the *Technical requirements for grid connection of PV systems* (GB/T 19939 - 2005) for more specification requirements.

4.2.3 Maintenance of solar photovoltaic power generation systems

One of the best features of solar photovoltaic power generation systems is that they require minimal maintenance. Since solar photovoltaic power generation systems have no moving parts, there is no need for regular maintenance of parts that would eventually wear out or fail. Of course, it is more than likely that the inverter needs to be replaced once during the service life of the system, and if storage batteries are installed, storage battery packs will need to be replaced once or twice during the service life of the system. But other than that, solar photovoltaic arrays can be expected to run year after year with minimal maintenance required.

Note that we are talking about minimal maintenance, not maintenance free. Several maintenance tasks need to be performed regularly. They are briefly described in the following subsections.

Project 4 Installing, Operating and Maintaining Solar Photovoltaic Power Generation Systems

1. Maintenance of modules and racks

(1) The surface of photovoltaic modules should be kept clean; photovoltaic modules should be wiped with dry or damp soft clean cloth. It is strictly prohibited to use corrosive solvents or hard objects to wipe photovoltaic modules. Photovoltaic modules should be cleaned under irradiance lower than 200 W/m^2. Liquids with a large temperature difference from the modules are not appropriate for module cleaning.

(2) Photovoltaic modules should be inspected periodically. In case of the following problems, photovoltaic modules should be adjusted or replaced without delay: ①Shattered glass, burnt backsheets, or visible color changes are found in photovoltaic modules; ②The presence of air bubbles in photovoltaic modules that form a communication channel with module edges or between any circuits; ③Junction boxes of photovoltaic modules are distorted, twisted, cracked, or burned, and the terminals cannot enable good contact.

(3) Electrical warning signs on photovoltaic modules must not be missing.

(4) For photovoltaic modules with metal frames, the frames and racks should be well bonded, with a contact resistance of no more than 4 Ω between them; the frames must be securely grounded.

(5) When working under conditions of no shadow, the temperature difference between the external surfaces of the same photovoltaic module (the area directly above the cell) should be less than 20℃ under the conditions that the solar irradiance is greater than 500 W/m^2 and the wind speed is not greater than 2 m/s. Photovoltaic power stations with an installed capacity of more than 50 kW should be equipped with infrared thermal imagers to detect the temperature difference between the external surfaces of photovoltaic modules.

(6) Measure the input current of each photovoltaic module string connected to the same DC combiner box using a clip-on DC ammeter under the condition that the intensity of solar radiation is basically the same; the deviation should not exceed 5%.

(7) All bolts, welding seams and rack connections should be firm and reliable. The anti-corrosion coating on the surfaces should not be cracked or peeled off. Otherwise, it should be timely repainted.

2. Maintenance of combiner boxes

(1) DC combiner boxes should be free of deformation, corrosion, water leakage, and dust accumulation; safety warning signs on the external surfaces of the boxes should be intact and unbroken; the opening and closing function of waterproof locks on the boxes should be flexible.

(2) Terminals in DC combiner boxes should not come loose or have signs of corrosion.

(3) Specifications of high-voltage DC fuses in DC combiner boxes should meet design specifications.

(4) The insulation resistance of the positive and negative terminals of the DC output

busbar to earth should be greater than 2 MΩ.

(5) The DC circuit breaker mounted on the DC output busbar terminal should have flexible and reliable breaking capacity.

(6) Lightning protectors in DC combiner boxes should be effective.

3. Maintenance of DC power distribution cabinets

(1) DC Power distribution cabinets should be free of deformation, corrosion, water leakage, and dust accumulation; safety warning signs on the external surfaces of the boxes should be intact and unbroken; the opening and closing function of waterproof locks on the boxes should be flexible.

(2) Terminals in DC power distribution cabinets should not come loose or have signs of corrosion.

(3) The insulation resistance of the positive and negative terminals of the DC output-busbar to earth should be greater than 2 MΩ.

(4) The connection between the DC input connector of the DC power distribution cabinet and the combiner box should be stable and reliable.

(5) The connection between the DC output of the DC power distribution cabinet and the DC input of the grid-connected host should be stable and reliable.

(6) The DC circuit breaker of the DC power distribution cabinet should be able to operate flexibly, with stable and reliable performance.

(7) The lightning protector mounted on the output side of the DC busbar should be effective.

4. Maintenance of inverters

(1) The structure and electrical connections of inverters should be kept intact, free of corrosion, accumulation of dust, etc. ; good heat dissipation conditions should be ensured; there should be no large vibration or abnormal noise during inverter operation.

(2) Warning signs on inverters should be intact and unbroken.

(3) The temperature-based self-start and self-stop functions of the cooling fan in the inverter module, as well as those of the inductor cooling fan and the transformer cooling fan, should be working properly; there should be no large vibration or abnormal noise during the operation of the cooling fans; in case of any abnormality, the fans should be disconnected from power supply for inspection.

(4) The circuit breaker on the AC output side (the grid side) should be periodically disconnected; once the breaker is disconnected, the inverter should immediately stop feeding power to the grid.

(5) The DC busbar capacitor in the inverter should be timely replaced if its temperature is too high or when it exceeds the service life.

5. Maintenance of AC power distribution cabinets

(1) Make sure that the metal frame of the power distribution cabinet is properly con-

nected to the foundation structural steel with galvanized bolts, and that anti-loosening parts are complete.

(2) Identifiers on the power distribution cabinet indicating the number, name or operation position of controlled equipment should be intact; the numbers should be clearly and neatly indicated.

(3) Busbar joints should be tightly connected, without deformation or discharge-related black signs; insulating components should not become loose or damaged; fastening connecting bolts should be free of rust.

(4) The push and pull functions of handcarts, and pull-out sets of power distribution cabinets should be flexible and free of any jam or collision; the center line of the dynamic contact and that of the static contact should be consistent, with tight contact.

(5) The switches and main contacts in the power distribution cabinet should be free of burnt traces; the arcing cover should be free of blackened marks and damage; wiring screws should be tightened; dust in the cabinet should be cleaned off.

(6) Remove each switch cabinet from the drawer and tighten each terminal. Check the installation and wiring of the current transformer, ammeter, and electric meter; the handle operating mechanism should be flexible and reliable; fasten the inlet and outlet wires of the circuit breaker; clean off the dust in the switch cabinet and the lead wires at the back of the power distribution cabinet.

(7) Low-voltage electrical heat generating components should have good heat dissipation function; switching pressure plates should be in good contact; the actions and signals of signal indicators, buttons, alarm windows, electric bells, electric torches, and accident clocks in signaling circuits should be displayed accurately.

(8) In terms of lines of test cabinets, screens, tables, boxes, and discs, line-to-line and line-to-earth insulation resistance values must be greater than 0.5MΩ for feeder lines, and greater than 1MΩ for secondary circuits.

6. Maintenance of transformers

(1) The thermometer of the transformer should be intact; the oil temperature should be normal; the oil level of the oil storage cabinet should correspond to the ambient temperature; there should be no oil seepage or leakage in any part. The load size, cooling conditions and seasons may vary from transformer to transformer. Therefore, the operation of the transformer cannot be based simply on the fact that the upper oil temperature does not exceed the permissible value, but it depends on the previous operating experience and comparison with the oil temperature in the last operation under the above conditions.

(2) The sleeve oil level should be normal; the external surface of the sleeve should be free of damages, cracks, heavy oil stains, discharge traces and other anomalies; the color of the oil should be transparent and slightly yellow, from which you can judge the quality of the oil. The oil level should correspond to the standard line of the ambient tempera-

ture. If the oil level is too low, the transformer should be inspected for oil leakage. If the oil level is too high, the cooling device should be inspected for its operational state and any internal failures.

(3) The transformer sound should be normal; a uniform buzzing electromagnetic sound is generally expected during normal operation. In case of abnormal sound, careful inspection should be conducted to make a correct judgment and prompt handling.

(4) Transformer leads should have no broken strands; joints should have no overheating discoloration; temperature indicating recorder labels should be free of melting (discoloration) signs; the respirator should be intact; the degree of discoloration of silicone should not exceed 3/4.

(5) Tap positions and power indicators of tap changers for excitation voltage regulation should be in order; there should be no gas in the gas relay; transformer enclosure grounding and iron core grounding should be intact.

(6) During bad weather, priority should be given to special inspection. In case of high winds, check whether leads are wiggling violently and whether the sag is adequate; there should be no debris on the transformer top cover and sleeve leads. In case of heavy snow, contacts of each component should not melt or discharge immediately after snowfall. In foggy days, inspect each component for spark discharge.

7. Maintenance of cables

(1) Cables should not operate under overload conditions; lead covering of cables should be free from signs of swelling and cracking.

(2) Positions where cables enter and exit equipment should be properly blocked; there should be no holes with a diameter greater than 10 mm; otherwise, fire clay should be used for blocking.

(3) Cable support points should be intact in positions where cables exert excessive strain or tension on the equipment enclosure.

(4) The openings of cable protective steel pipes should be free of perforations, cracks and significant unevenness; inner walls should be smooth; metal cable pipes should be free of serious corrosion, burrs, hard objects, and rubbish; in case of burrs, they should be filed and then wrapped and tied with cable jackets.

(5) Accumulations and rubbish in outdoor cable shafts should be cleared in a timely manner; in case of any damaged cable sheath, prompt handling should be carried out.

(6) When inspecting exposed indoor cable trenches, ensure prevention of damage to the cables, and ensure rack grounding and good heat dissipation between the rack and the trench.

(7) Stakes along directly embedded cable lines should be intact; the ground in the vicinity of cable paths should be free of excavation; make sure that the ground along the path is free of piles of heavy materials, building materials, temporary facilities, and dis-

charged corrosive substances; make sure that outdoor exposed cable protection facilities are intact.

(8) Make sure that the covers of cable trenches or cable shafts are intact; there should be no water or debris in the trenches; make sure that the racks in the trenches are firm and free of corrosion and looseness; cable sheaths and cable armoring of armored cables should be free of serious corrosion.

(9) Multiple cables laid side by side should be checked for current distribution and the temperature of cable sheaths, to prevent the cables from burning out from the connection points due to poor contact.

(10) Ensure that cable termination heads are well earthed, and that insulating sleeves are intact, clean and free from traces of flashover discharge, and that phase colors of cables are prominent.

8. Maintenance in extreme weather

(1) In rainy days, a loose terminal head may be responsible for the tripping of the system. In such cases, proper handling must be carried out in a sunny day after the rain. Use insulating tapes to wrap around the terminal head involved and then observe whether there is any sign of tripping. In case of re-tripping, report to the maintenance center or the local electric power management center.

(2) On thunderstorm days, the air circuit breaker below the electric meter should be turned off to prevent damage to electrical equipment. Wait until the thunderstorm has passed and then turn on the breaker.

【Task implementation】

Ⅰ. Task preparations

1 competition equipment platform, an equipment platform for "operation and maintenance of photovoltaic power stations", 1 slotted screwdriver, 1 philips screw driver, 1 multimeter, 1 copy of record sheet for power-up inspection, 1 copy of record sheet for photovoltaic array commissioning, 1 copy of record sheet for DC combiner box commissioning, 1 copy of record sheet for grid-connected inverter commissioning, 1 copy of record sheet for commissioning of grid-connected power distribution boxes, and 1 set of computer mainframe.

Task 4.2 Related implementation forms

Ⅱ. Task content and procedures

(ⅰ) Task 1: System commissioning and grid connection

Task content: Complete the commissioning and grid connection of photovoltaic power generation systems.

Task procedures:

(1) Complete system pre-power-up inspection and fill in the record sheet for power-up inspection.

(2) Complete photovoltaic array commissioning and fill in the record sheet for photovoltaic array commissioning.

(3) Complete DC combiner box commissioning and fill in the record sheet for DC combiner box commissioning.

(4) Complete grid-connected inverter commissioning and fill in the record sheet for grid-connected inverter commissioning.

(5) Complete the commissioning of grid-connected power distribution boxes and fill in the record sheet for commissioning of grid-connected power distribution boxes.

(ⅱ) Task 2: Configuration and operation of the monitoring system

Task content: Complete the configuration and operation of the monitoring system of the photovoltaic power generation system.

Task procedures:

(1) Complete communication inspection between the photovoltaic power generation system and the monitoring host.

(2) Complete the configuration of the login screen and navigation bar of the photovoltaic power generation system.

(3) Complete the configuration of the operation screen of the photovoltaic power generation system.

(4) Complete the configuration of the data screen of the photovoltaic power generation system.

(5) Complete the equipment configuration of the photovoltaic power generation monitoring system.

(6) Complete the operation of photovoltaic power generation monitoring system; complete real-time display and recording of operation data.

Ⅲ. Skill requirements

(1) Correctly use multimeter gears for the measurement of different parameters; observe operation specifications; avoid short circuit or wrong gear measurement.

(2) Correctly measure the open-circuit voltage and operating current of the solar cell series input.

(3) Complete the equipment installation and fixing, wiring condition inspection, earth wire inspection, and other procedure inspections in accordance with specifications; strict standards must be observed, and no missing or wrong items are allowed.

(4) Properly observe equipment operation data; make correct records; the recorded parameter data include numerical values and units.

(5) The monitoring interface layout is aesthetic; the dimensions of the components are appropriate; the color configuration is coordinated; the functional controls are complete; the components are correctly labeled and named; there are no missing items.

Ⅳ. Task results, appraisal and evaluation

(1) The system is correctly commissioned and successfully connected to the grid; the

data screen runs correctly; operation data are recorded (accounting for 90%).

(2) The operator exhibits good professional quality during the operation process and follows 7S management model (accounting for 10%).

【Exercises】

1. What is included in the inspection of electrical components during commissioning?
2. What common identifiers must be mounted?
3. What tasks require regular maintenance in photovoltaic power generation systems?

项目 5 勘察风资源与选址风电场

任务 5.1 勘察风资源

【学习目标】

知识目标:掌握风电场风速的预测计算方法。
能力目标:能评估风力资源。
素质目标:树立清洁低碳意识;培养严谨细致的职业品质。
重点:风的等级划分。
难点:风电场风资源测量。

【任务分析】

风电场的经济效益取决于风能资源、电网连接、交通运输、地质条件、地形地貌和社会经济等多方面因素。

【知识学习】

建设风电场是充分利用风能资源的有效途径,也是践行党的二十大关于推动能源清洁低碳高效利用的深刻体现。

表 5.1 列举了风的等级划分及能量特点。按照风力发电设计标准 IEC 61400-1,将风分为 Ⅰ、Ⅱ、Ⅲ 类风区,见表 5.2,也可以采用表 5.3 所示 IEC 风能分区。

表 5.1 风的等级划分及能量特点

台风的级别	风力/级	风速/(m/s)	风的能量特点
—	5	9~10	吹到物体表面的力达到 98Pa
热带低压	6~7	10.8~17.1	—
热带风暴	8~9	17.2~24.4	吹到物体表面的力达到 490Pa 左右
强热带风暴	10~11	24.5~32.6	—
台风	12~13	32.7~41.4	—
强台风	14~15	41.5~50.9	物体表面的压力 $1.96×10^5$ Pa 以上,被风激起的海浪对海岸的冲击力相当大,最大为 $5.88×10^5$ Pa
超强台风	16~17	>51.0	—

表 5.2　　　　　　　风力发电设计标准 IEC 61400-1 风区分类

风 区	年平均风速 V_{avg} /(m/s)	3s 平均极大风速 V_{avgm} /(m/s)	特　点
Ⅰ类风区	$8.5 < V_{avg} \leq 10$	$59.5 < V_{avgm} \leq 70$	在风力发电机组轮毂高度处
Ⅱ类风区	$7.5 < V_{avg} \leq 8.5$	$52.5 < V_{avgm} \leq 59.5$	在风力发电机组轮毂高度处
Ⅲ类风区	$V_{avg} \leq 7.5$	$V_{avgm} \leq 52.5$	在风力发电机组轮毂高度处

表 5.3　　　　　　　　　　　IEC 风能分区

IEC 标准	风速/(m/s)				
	平均风速	年最大风速	最大阵风	50 年最大风	50 年最大阵风
Ⅰ类风区	10	37.5	52.5	50	70
Ⅱ类风区	8.5	31.9	44.6	42.5	59.5
Ⅲ类风区	7.5	28.1	39.4	37.5	52.5
Ⅳ类风区	6	22.5	31.5	30	42

1. 风资源勘查

风资源初步评价主要借助气象站、石油钻井平台、卫星及船只的观测资料来估算发电量。我国风力资源分布集中在华北、西北和东北的草原、戈壁滩，以及东部沿海地带和岛屿。这些地区缺少煤炭和常规能源，并且冬春季节风速高，雨水少；夏季风速小，降雨多，风能和水能可季节互补。江西鄱阳湖地区、湖北省通山地区、新疆、甘肃、宁夏，特别是内蒙古自治区，有着丰富的风力资源；渤海、黄海和台湾海峡等漫长的海岸线上也有丰富的风资源。我国单靠风力发电就能将现有的电力生产能力翻一番。

2. 风资源勘测设备及测风塔位置选择

风力发电场设计规范

（1）风资源勘测设备。在风电场安装 50~100m 高的侧风塔，或 10m 高的浮标测风设备，通过综合浮标长期测得的数据与测风塔测得的短期数据，经相关分析，减少风能资源评估的不确定性。另外，还可以采用超声波雷达测风仪、激光雷达测风仪测风，仅仅安装在低平面和流动平台上就能够测量高空风资源。

以上海为例，早期安装的测风塔高度为 70m。2009 年 3 月，上海市气象局气候中心建成国内首个海上测风塔，该测风塔塔高为 100m，安装有 12 个 NRG 风速计，风速测量高度分为 100m、90m、80m、60m、40m 和 20m，并对 100m 和 20m 高度测量了风向、温度、气压及相对湿度。

传统测风仪主要分为机械式和电子式两大类。其中，机械式以风杯和风轮类为主，由于转轮是可动元件，机械摩擦、泥沙灰尘堆积等因素影响了该测风仪的可靠性，误差较大；电子式测风仪以热式（热线、热球）、超声波等为主，当在湍流中使用热敏式探头时，来自各个方向的气流同时冲击热元件，会影响测量的准确性，并且热式测风仪的长期稳定性差，输出特性具有非线性特征，超声波式测风仪价格比较昂贵。

（2）风翼式固态测风仪。

项目5　勘察风资源与选址风电场

1) 固态测风技术。固态测风技术中的测风装置没有旋转部件，避免了因设备磨损而引起的测量误差，可以长期使

图 5.1　风翼式固态测风仪系统框图

用且不影响精度，是当前世界气象组织（WMO）推荐的测风技术。图 5.1 为风翼式固态测风仪系统框图，由测风部件、数据采集系统和上位机监视系统三部分组成。

测风仪测风部件如图 5.2 所示。外部结构分为迎风体、连接套管和底座。其中，迎风体由 4 片相同的金属叶片呈 90°焊接而成，连接套管内装有电阻应变式压力传感器、温度传感器和湿度传感器。电阻应变式压力传感器通过连杆与迎风体相连，从而可以感受迎风体所承受的压力。传感器输出电压信号经放大后送到单片机。

2) 测量原理。自然风作用于迎风体产生作用力，风的大小决定了作用力的大小。该作用力可分解为作用在两个叶片上的力，通过求解两个叶片上的力的数值就可以得出风的作用力的大小，再利用风的作用力与风速的关系得出风速。同样，通过求解两个叶片上的力的比值就可以得出风向。

电阻应变式压力传感器利用弹性体在外力作用下产生弹性变形，使粘贴在其表面的电阻应变片（转换元件）也随之产生变形，引起阻值发生变化，再经相应的测量电路把电阻值变化转换为电信号（电压或电流）。

常用的电阻应变式传感器桥式电路如图 5.3 所示。当桥式电路中桥臂电阻发生变化时，桥式电路失去平衡，输出由初始化状态的零电位开始变化，这个变化量 ΔV 反映了压力的变化量。通过判断 ΔV 的正负即可确认作用力的方向。同理，两个垂直放置的电阻应变式传感器的电压输出，可分别用于判别东西方向和南北方向的力，并据此获得确切的风向。由于风作用在物体上通常为持续、微小的力，通过在固态测风仪上安装长杆及风翼，将风的作用效果转换为与其连接的金属的形变，从而改变传感器的输出电压值，提高测量灵敏度。

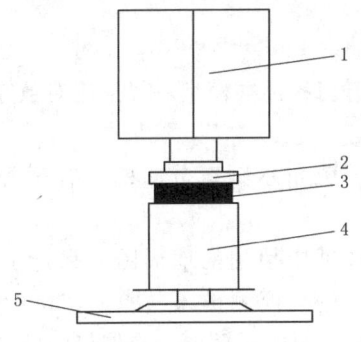

图 5.2　测风仪测风部件
1—迎风体；2—连接套管；3—软管；
4—保护套 3；5—底座

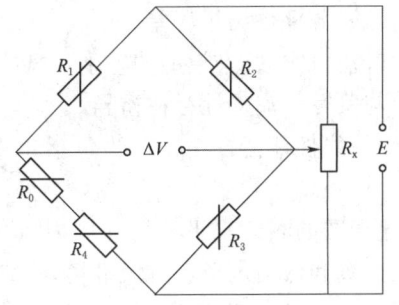

图 5.3　常用的电阻应变式传感器桥式电路
$R_1 \sim R_4$—应变片；R_x—多圈调零电位器；
R_0—温度补偿电阻；E—传感器桥；
ΔV—传感器输出电压

（3）测风塔位置选择。通常，根据现场地形再结合地形图，初步选定可供安装风电机组的机位。测风塔安装位置确定原则：树立在计划安装风电机组较多的地方，若遇到地形

较复杂情况，还要分片布置测风塔；测风塔不能立于风速分离区，测风塔附近应无高大建筑物、树木等障碍物，地形也不宜较陡，与单个障碍物距离应大于障碍物高度的3倍，与成排障碍物距离应保持在障碍物最大高度的10倍以上；测风塔在风电场主风向的上风向位置；测风高度应不低于风电机组轮毂高度的2/3，一般分3层以上测风。

3. 风资源评估

(1) 风资源特性。风资源的特性包括代表性、一致性和完整性。测风塔测风时间应保证至少1年以上，测风资料有效数据完整率应大于90%。然而，在实际风电场规划中，风电场场址测风设备设立较晚，缺乏足够的现场实测风速、风向等资料，往往采取引用邻近场址或地区的实测资料进行计算分析，误差较大。

风资源评估是风电场选址的关键步骤，其准确性对风电场以后运行的效益至关重要。传统的风资源评估是对气象观测资料内插或外推得到，以及在已建或待建风电场位置安装气象观测塔实施1~2年的观测。这样往往造成评估不准确或者太高。目前，人们已认识到应用中尺度数值模式模拟某一地区的风况是比较切实可行的方法，将模拟结果作为风资源普查的辅助资料，不仅可以填补对无风记录地区风资源状况不清的空白，而且对风电场宏观和微观选址也有一定的指导作用。因该方法仅利用计算机模拟，投资少，切实可行，现已被业界采用。

(2) 风资源评估软件应用。风资源评估是整个风电场建设、运行的重要环节，是风电场建设取得良好经济效益的关键。目前，我国常用风资源分布计算软件包括WAsP、WindFarm、MS-MICRO、WindFarmer和WindPro等。这些软件实际应用有局限性，如果坡度大于5°时，计算误差大。针对计算误差大的情形，可以采用CFD（Computational Fluid Dynamics，计算流体力学）技术对各种典型地形进行数值模拟，与实际结果进行比对和分析，确认数值模拟的可信度，并分析得出各种地形的风能分布情况，根据现有风资源评估结果由于模型建立原因造成的误差，提出相适应的风资源评估量化修正方法。

(3) 风资源评估结果误差。

1) 气流特性与标准模型的差别。风速廓线/风剪切的标准模型一般采用对数律或指数律分布，与实际气流特性存在差异。

2) 传统线性评估方法。主要包括年平均风速、威布尔频率分布的吻合度等参数化方法。

3) 地形图的测绘水平。目前国内风电场微观选址中使用的地形图大都是1:10000的，而在丘陵和低山地形进行风电场的微观选址时，一般应测量风电场1:5000地形图。为提高风电场的微观选址的准确性，在计算风资源分布时，风资源分布网格图的分辨率应尽量大，一般为10~50m。

4) 噪声、阴影闪烁等环保因素。目前在布置风电机组时，环保部门为防止噪声、阴影闪烁等影响居民，一般要求风电机组距离居民区的距离应大于500m。根据实际情况，一般村庄在上风向的，风电机组距离村庄的距离应大于300m；如果村庄在风电机组的下风向的，风电机组距离村庄的距离应大于500m。考虑阴影闪烁时，风电机组在村庄的南侧时，风电机组距离村庄的距离应大于500m；风电机组在村庄的北侧时，风电机组距离村庄的距离应大于300m。

(4) 风资源评估结果误差修正。

坡度、粗糙度及边界层厚度对复杂地形周围流场的影响。一般来说，风能密度随坡度的增加而增大；背风面受到旋涡及尾流的影响，在近地面处的风能分布较平坦地形差；粗糙度越小，风能分布越好，粗糙度在很小范围内变化时对风能影响不大，可以忽略，但当变化很大时，在安装风电机组时就应该尽量避开摩擦系数较大的区域；边界层厚度的选取对风速的捕获及湍流强度的分布都有影响，对速度分布的影响更大一些。

采用CFD数值模拟的方法分析各典型地形几何形状（坡度）、大气边界层特征（地表粗糙度及边界层厚度）对风能分布、风速捕获和湍流强度的影响，经与工程方法评估结果进行比较，分析评估工程方法存在误差的原因。

(5) 风电场数值模拟方法的修正。目前多数的风资源评估软件，如WAsP、WindFarm、MS-MICRO、WindFarmer和WindPro等采用风流体线性化模型（假定只存在小的风扰动），计算量小，但不适用于复杂地形（高山、森林、滩涂等）的风资源评估。WAsP软件已经有二十多年的历史，是风能资源评估与风电场设计软件，对于平坦地形的风能资源分析功能得到普遍认可，是世界上应用最广泛的风能资源分析软件。但是，WAsP软件采用标准线性模型去模拟风场，用于复杂地形时，对风资源的预测评估会出现较大偏差。CFD模拟是一个可替代常规工具且很有前途的方法，它把地形、粗糙度和障碍物等影响用参数表示，直接用数值求解流力方程，计算出在树林等复杂环境下气流在三维方向上的变化、三维粗糙度效应、三维湍流、风切变等。与现有软件WAsP相比，CFD能计算出三维的风场绕流，具有较高的计算精度，从而减少风资源评估的不确定性。

【任务实施】

1. 任务准备

智慧新能源仿真规划软件平台1个、电脑主机和显示器1套。

2. 任务内容及步骤

任务：仿真能源分析与系统设计。

任务内容：完成仿真能源分析与系统设计。

任务步骤：

(1) 分析耗能需求，合理设计能源种类和容量。

(2) 调试系统在供电不足天数、风能偏差等相关参数上综合设计方案最优，风机发电机参数扫一扫二维码表格。

(3) 完成包括风力发电产能在内的四个能源产出分析。

任务5.1 相关任务实施图表

(4) 完成单位面积风机容量选型、单位面积风力发电系统输出功率分析设计。

(5) 完成区域能源综合规划与优化，导出结果表格。

3. 技能要求

(1) 各种类型能源布局设计合理。

(2) 光伏发电容量与风力容量（功率）比例范围为0.2～5范围之间。

（3）储能系统容量设置合适，满足负荷变化要求，储能总容量小于 10 倍的平均每天耗电量。

4. 任务成果及考核评价

（1）系统设计满足指标要求，成功运行、数据界面运行数据正确，能记录运行数据，布局合理，占 90%。

（2）操作过程展现较好职业素养，做到 7S 管理，占 10%。

【练习】

1. 测风设备及要求是什么？
2. 风电场微观选址及修正技术有哪些？

任务 5.2　选 址 风 电 场

【学习目标】

知识目标：掌握风电场选址的要素。

能力目标：能选址风电场。

素质目标：树立清洁低碳意识；培养严谨细致的职业品质。

重点：风电场选址目标。

难点：风电场选址技术。

【任务分析】

风电场选址除主要考虑气象方面的参数外，还要综合考虑包括场址所在地对电网要求、交通、地质、环境、电力等诸多因素。

依托智慧新能源仿真规划软件平台，开展区域能源工程项目整体的项目需求分析、能源系统分析、产能分析、耗能分析、项目可行性分析、能源供电选址、系统设计等，完成风电场等能源规划设计。

【知识学习】

风电场选址考虑因素包括风资源情况、项目建设许可、获得场址海域使用权（针对海上风电场）、附近电网基本情况（包括陆地变电站位置、电压等级、可接入的最大容量及电网规划等）、场址基本情况（包括范围、水深、风资源及海底地质条件）、环境制约（包括当地旅游业、水中生物、鸟类、航道、渔业和海防等负面影响）等。

1. 地质地形环境与风电机组选型

（1）风电机组技术经济分析。风电机组选型时除了考虑风电机组本身的特性外，还必须考虑很多外部因素的影响，包括气候、环境、电力系统约束（接收风电能力、电网安全稳定约束等）。例如，我国气候条件差距很大，包括Ⅱ类风区及寒冷运行环境条件，根据《电工电子产品自然环境条件　温度和湿度》（GB/T 4797.1—2005），表 5.4 列出了气候条件定义，相应的机型见表 5.5。

表 5.4　　　　　　　　　气 候 条 件 定 义

气　候	温度值/℃	气　候	温度值/℃
寒冷	-50	寒温Ⅱ	-26
寒温Ⅰ	-33	暖温	-15

表 5.5　　　　　气候温度适合机型

机　型	温度值/℃
低温Ⅱ型	-40
低温Ⅰ型	-30
常温型	-20

为了确保风电场安全可靠运行，环境、电力和地表等因素都应该在风电机组选型时予以考虑，针对不同类型的风电机组特性，从技术指标和经济因素两方面综合分析各类型风电机组的特点，提出不同环境下风电机组的适用情况。同时，符合 IEC 61400-1 标准及其他国际标准要求。

（2）复杂地质、地形环境下风电场机组的选型。结合实际地质、地形实际，提出典型地形环境下风电机组的选型原则。通常，采用在平坦地形环境风电机组选型方法再分析复杂地质、地形环境下风资源对风、电机组选型的影响，重点考虑风速分布、普通风廓线模型、普通湍流模型等，再结合极端条件下的风速模型（EWM）、脉动风速模型（EOG）、湍流模型（ETM）、风向变化模型（EDC）及风切变模型（EWS）等因素的分析，提出不同地质、地形环境下风电机组选型的依据和方法建议。同时，还针对除风资源外的其他环境因素对风电机组选型的影响进行分析，包括温度、湿度、空气密度、阳光辐射、雨、雪、冰雹、盐度、地震等。另外，分析海上风电场选用风电机组时应考虑渔业、航运、通信、国防等特殊环境因素的影响。

（3）电网因素对风电机组选型的影响。从电力系统的角度研究电网因素对风电机组选型的影响，主要考虑电网对风电场接入点电压的限制、电网对风电场接入点频率的限制、电网可接纳风力发电容量的限制、电网停运对风电场的影响、风电场与电网间协调控制对风电机组选型的影响等。

2. 风电场微观选址

（1）风电场微观选址的目标。如何在风电场内布置风力发电机，才能得到最大的发电量，获得最佳的经济效益，一直是微观选址工作的焦点。目前，国内风电场建设过程中的微观选址工作主要依赖各电力设计院和设备供应商，各家的实力相差不多，大多都是在近几年内接触此项工作，主要采用丹麦国家实验室编制的风资源应用及分析软件——WAsP 软件，分析风电场的风资源，然后运用各种风电场优化设计软件，如 WindPro、WindFarmer 等优化设计风场机组的排布。由于 WAsP 根据欧洲的地形特点开发的，其能否准确计算我国各地的风资源情况一直没有明确的说明。WAsP 软件也不能准确地计算复杂地区的风资源状况。但目前国内没用应用较广泛的风资源分析软件，微观选址工作还是一直依赖 WAsP 软件，分析平坦地区和复杂地形，无法对软件的参数或计算结果进行修正。因此，开发适用于我国各种地形的风资源分析软件或研究 WAsP 软件的修正方法工作已迫在眉睫。

由于国外的风电技术起步早，技术相对成熟。无论是陆地上的风电场还是海上风电场，均有大量的统计数据作为参考，并且针对各种应用软件如 WAsP，开发者均做过大量的实验，可以根据具体的应用场合进行准确的修正或参数调整，得出准确的计算结果。

目前，除丹麦国家实验室开发 WAsP 风资源应有分析软件外，国内某软件公司也开发出了风电场风能及发电量分析计算软件，主要功能接近于 WAsP 软件。该软件以风电场测风数据验证系统为基础，通过模式计算可以求得风电场区域内任意空间位置的风资源参数，为建设风电场提供理论依据。风电场优化设计软件应用较广泛的是 WindFarmer 软件，主要用于设计、分析、优化风电场，能够计算风电场的能量产出和模拟地形及尾流对能里产出的影响。通过优化风力发电机在风电场的排布来使得在电场的能量产出最大化的同时使得能量损失降到最小。但该软件基于 WAsP，计算或设计的结果主要取决于 WAsP 软件的结果。

国内目前也有用大型流场分析软件来做复杂地区的风资源分析工作，但是其计算十分耗费时间。

（2）风电场微观选址技术。

1）风电场复杂地形风资源情况研究。根据不同地形（如平原、山区、海上等）风电场安装的测风塔获得的数据和地形、地貌特征来研究对风速变化规律的影响。

2）风电场经济性建设研究。根据安装的风电机组特征（数量、容量、类型、高度等参数），利用风电场微观选址软件，修正估算发电量的各个相关参数，完成风电机组的最优布局，达到充分利用资源，获得最大发电量的目的。

3）风电场安全运行研究。通过风电场经济性建设研究，优化整个风电场。但是，考虑已确认的微观选址方案中的个别相邻两台风电机组行距过小（指小于 5 倍的叶轮直径）而导致的沿主流风向前面风电机组尾流对后面风电机组的影响，必须对后面的风电机组进行安全可靠性分析。

拟解决的技术难点如下：

a. 测风数据的不完备性，各类风电场原始风资源数据补充修正方法的研究。

b. 在计算复杂地形时的误差，对不同地区、不同风资源情况如何对计算结果进行修正，确定各修正参数的研究。

c. 确定风电场上网电量估算时各项修正系数值，以准确地估算不同风力发电场的发电量。

d. 分别选择沿海风力发电场、山区风力发电场、平原风力发电场进行微观选址的验证工作。

e. 评价风电机组间的作用对风电机组安全可靠运行的影响程度研究。

（3）微观选址分析软件技术及不同地质地形环境对微观选址的影响。现有风力发电场微观设计软件有适用于平原地形的 WAsP 软件，以及基于 WAsP 风能资源计算的 WindFarmer、WindPro、WindFarm 风电机组布置优化软件，适用于丘陵和低山地形的 Windsim 和 Meteodyn 软件等。

针对不同地质地形环境，结合不同风资源分布计算软件的特点进行优化设计。实际地形测量和地质勘测不仅与实际风力评估有直接关系，还对风电机组的优化排列、架设安装有直接的影响。

【任务实施】

1. 任务准备

智慧新能源仿真规划软件平台1个、电脑主机和显示器1套。

2. 任务内容及步骤

任务：仿真能源分析与系统设计

任务内容：完成仿真能源分析与系统设计。

任务步骤：

(1) 分析耗能需求，合理设计能源种类和容量。

(2) 调试系统在供电不足天数、风能偏差等相关参数上综合设计方案最优，风机发电机参数扫一扫二维码表格。

任务5.2 相关任务实施图表

(3) 完成包括风力发电产能在内的四个能源产出分析。

(4) 完成单位面积风机容量选型、单位面积风力发电系统输出功率分析设计。

(5) 完成区域能源综合规划与优化，导出结果表格。

3. 技能要求

(1) 各种类型能源布局设计合理。

(2) 光伏发电容量与风力容量（功率）比例范围为0.2~5之间。

(3) 储能系统容量设置合适，满足负荷变化要求，储能总容量小于10倍的平均每天耗电量。

4. 任务成果及考核评价

(1) 系统设计满足指标要求，成功运行、数据界面运行数据正确，能记录运行数据，布局合理，占90%。

(2) 操作过程展现较好职业素养，做到7S管理，占10%。

【练习】

1. 测风设备及要求是什么？
2. 风电场微观选址及修正技术有哪些？

Project 5　Survey on Wind Resources and Selecting Sites for Wind Farms

Task 5.1　Survey on Wind Resources

【Learning objectives】

　　Knowledge objective: To master prediction and calculation methods of wind speed for wind farms

　　Ability objective: To be able to evaluate wind resources

　　Qualification objective: To develop the awareness of low-carbon life; to cultivate the professional quality of meticulousness

　　Learning priority: Classification of wind scales

　　Learning challenge: Measurement of wind resources in wind farms

【Task analysis】

　　The economic benefits of wind farms depend on a variety of factors, e.g., wind energy resources, grid connectivity, transport, geological conditions, topography & geomorphology, and socio-economics.

【Knowledge learning】

　　The construction of wind farms is an effective way to make full use of wind energy resources. It is also a profound manifestation of the practice of the initiative proposed at the 20th CPC National Congress: promoting clean, low-carbon, and high-efficiency energy use.

　　Table 5.1 lists the scale classification and energy characteristics of wind. According to the wind power generation design standard IEC 61400-1, there are three types of wind zones: Ⅰ, Ⅱ and Ⅲ, as shown in Table 5.2. IEC wind energy zoning can also be adopted, as shown in Table 5.3.

Table 5.1　　　　Scale classification and energy characteristics of wind

Levels of Typhon	Wind power/scale	Wind speed/(m/s)	Energy characteristics of wind
—	5	9-10	The force blowing on the surface of an object reaches 98 Pa

Project 5 Survey on Wind Resources and Selecting Sites for Wind Farms

Continued Table

Levels of Typhon	Wind power/scale	Wind speed/(m/s)	Energy characteristics of wind
Tropical depression	6 – 7	10.8~17.1	—
Tropical storm	8 – 9	17.2~24.4	The force blowing on the surface of an object reaches approximately 490 Pa
Severe tropical storm	10 – 11	24.5~32.6	—
Typhoon	12 – 13	32.7~41.4	—
Severe typhoon	14 – 15	41.5~50.9	The pressure on the surface of an object is 1.96×10^5 Pa or more; waves stirred up by the wind have a considerable impact on the coast, up to 5.88×10^5 Pa.
Super typhoon	16 – 17	>51.0	—

Table 5.2　　Wind zone classification according to wind power generation design standard IEC 61400-1

Wind zone	Annual average wind speed: V_{avg}/(m/s)	3-second average extreme wind speed: V_{avgm}/(m/s)	Characteristics
Class I wind zone	$8.5 < V_{avg} \leqslant 10$	$59.5 < V_{avgm} \leqslant 70$	At height of wind turbine generator system hub
Class II wind zone	$7.5 < V_{avg} \leqslant 8.5$	$52.5 < V_{avgm} \leqslant 59.5$	At height of wind turbine generator system hub
Class III wind zone	$V_{avg} \leqslant 7.5$	$V_{avgm} \leqslant 52.5$	At height of wind turbine generator system hub

Table 5.3　　　　　　　　　　IEC wind energy zoning　　　　　　　　　　Unit: m/s

IEC standard	Average wind speed	Annual maximum wind speed	Maximum gust	50-year maximum wind	50-year maximum gust
Class I wind zone	10	37.5	52.5	50	70
Class II wind zone	8.5	31.9	44.6	42.5	59.5
Class III wind zone	7.5	28.1	39.4	37.5	52.5
Class IV wind zone	6	22.5	31.5	30	42

1. Survey on wind resources

The preliminary evaluation of wind resources is mainly conducted with the help of observation data obtained from meteorological stations, oil drilling platforms, satellites and ships to estimate power generation capacity. Wind resources in China are concentrated in the grasslands and Gobi deserts in North China, Northwest China and Northeast China, as well as in the coastal areas and islands in eastern China. These areas lack coal and conventional energy sources. Wind speed is high in winter and spring, with little rainfall, whereas wind speed is low in summer, with much rainfall. Thus, wind energy and water energy can complement each other seasonally. The

Code for design of wind farm

Project 5 Survey on Wind Resources and Selecting Sites for Wind Farms

Poyang Lake area in Jiangxi Province, Tongshan area in Hubei Province, Xinjiang, Gansu, Ningxia, especially Inner Mongolia Autonomous Region, have abundant wind resources; there are also abundant wind resources along the long coastlines of Bohai Sea, Yellow Sea and Taiwan Strait. China can double its existing electricity production capacity by wind power generation alone.

2. Selection of wind resource survey equipment and anemometer tower location

(1) Wind resource survey equipment. Anemometer towers with a height of 50 – 100 m or buoy wind measurement equipment with a height of 10 m are installed in wind farms; long-term data obtained by buoy equipment and short-term data obtained by anemometer towers are combined and analyzed to reduce the uncertainties of wind energy resources evaluation. In addition, ultrasonic radar anemometers and laser radar anemometers can be used for wind measurement. Wind resources at high altitude can be measured simply by installing these anemometers on low-altitude planes and mobile platforms.

In Shanghai, for example, the height of the anemometer tower installed in the early days was 70 m. In March 2009, the Climate Center of Shanghai Meteorological Service built the first domestic offshore anemometer tower. With a height of 100 m, this anemometer tower was equipped with 12 NRG anemometers and could measure wind speed at heights of 100 m, 90 m, 80 m, 60 m, 40 m and 20 m. Moreover, it could measure wind direction, temperature, atmospheric pressure, and relative humidity at heights of 100 m and 20 m.

Traditional anemometers are mainly divided into two categories: mechanical and electronic. Among them, mechanical anemometers mainly adopt wind cups and wind turbines. Since the rotor is a movable element in mechanical anemometers, mechanical friction, sediment and dust accumulation, and other factors affect the reliability of such anemometers, resulting in a large error. Electronic anemometers mainly adopt thermal (hot-wire and hot-ball), ultrasonic, and other elements. When the thermal probe is used in turbulent flow, the airflow from all directions impacts on the thermal element at the same time, which affects measurement accuracy. In addition, thermal anemometers have poor long-term stability and non-linear output characteristics, and ultrasonic anemometers are relatively expensive.

(2) Airfoil solid-state anemometer.

1) Solid-state wind measurement technology. In solid-state wind measurement technology, there is no rotating part in wind measurement devices. This eliminates measurement errors caused by equipment's wear and tear, and enables long-term use without affecting accuracy. This wind measurement technology is currently recommended by the World Meteorological Organization (WMO). Figure 5.1 shows the block diagram of an airfoil solid-state anemometer system, which consists of three parts: wind measurement components, the data acquisition system, and the upper monitoring system.

Project 5 Survey on Wind Resources and Selecting Sites for Wind Farms

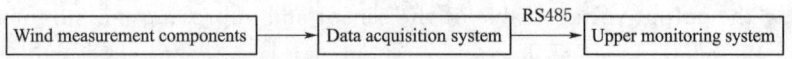

Figure 5.1 Block diagram of airfoil solid-state anemometer system

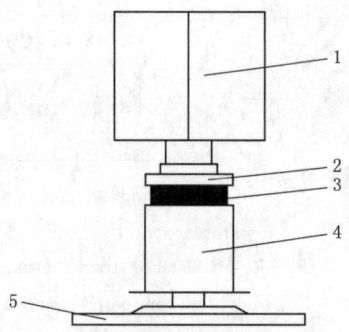

Figure 5.2 Wind measurement components of anemometers
1—Windward body; 2—Connecting sleeve; 3—Hose; 4—Protective sleeve 3; 5—Base

Wind measurement components are shown in Figure 5.2. The external structure is composed of the windward body, the connecting sleeve, and the base. Among them, the windward body consists of four identical metal blades welded at 90°; the connecting sleeve contains a resistance strain pressure sensor, a temperature sensor, and a humidity sensor. The resistance strain pressure sensor is connected to the windward body via the connecting rod, so that it can feel the pressure exerted on the windward body. The sensor output voltage signal is amplified and sent to the single-chip microcomputer.

2) Measurement principle. The natural wind acts on the windward body to generate force, and the scale of the wind determines the magnitude of the force. This force can be decomposed into the force acting on the two blades. Thus, the magnitude of the force generated by the wind can be obtained by calculating the values of the forces acting on the two blades. Then, wind speed can be obtained via the relationship between the force of the wind and the wind speed. Similarly, wind direction can be obtained by calculating the ratio of the forces on the two blades.

The resistance strain pressure sensor produces elastic deformation via the elastomer under the action of external force, and the resistance strain gauge (conversion element) pasted on the surface of the sensor is also deformed, resulting in a change in the resistance value. Then, the change in the resistance value is converted into an electrical signal (voltage or current) via the corresponding measurement circuit.

Commonly used bridge circuits of resistance strain sensors are shown in Figure 5.3. When the resistance of the bridge arm in the bridge circuit changes, the bridge circuit loses balance and the output starts to change from the zero potential of the initialized state, and the amount of this change (ΔV) reflects the amount of change in pressure. The direction of the force can be confirmed by determining whether ΔV is positive or negative. Similarly, the voltage output of two perpendicularly placed resistance strain sensors can be used to discern east-west and north-south directions of the force to obtain the exact wind direction. Since the force of the wind is generally a constant, small force is exerted on objects, the effect of the wind can be converted into a deformation of the metal to which the solid-state anemometer is attached, by mounting a long pole and aerofoils, thus changing the output voltage value of the sensor and improving measurement sensitivity.

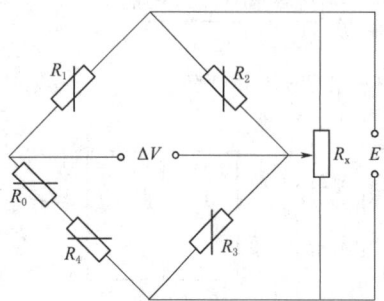

Figure 5.3 Bridge circuit of resistance strain sensors
$R_1 - R_4$: Resistance strain gauges;
R_x: Multi-turn zero potentiometer;
R_0: Temperature compensation resistor;
E: Sensor bridge; ΔV: Sensor output voltage

(3) Selection of anemometer tower location. Generally, the preliminary selection of installation location for wind turbine generator systems is based on the terrain of the site and the topographical map. The principle for determining the installation locations of anemometer towers is as follows: Anemometer towers should be installed in places where many wind turbine generator systems are planned to be installed; in case of complex terrain, anemometer towers should be installed in different locations; anemometer towers should not stand in wind speed separation zones; there should be no obstacles, e.g., tall buildings and trees, or steep terrain in the vicinity of anemometer towers; the distance between an anemometer tower and a single obstacle should be greater than 3 times the height of the obstacle, and the distance between an anemometer tower and a row of obstacles should be maintained at 10 times the maximum height of the obstacles; anemometer towers should be upwind of the main wind direction of the wind farm; the wind measurement height should be no less than 2/3 of the height of the wind turbine hub; wind measurement is generally carried out in three layers.

3. Evaluation of wind resources

(1) Characteristics of wind resources. Characteristics of wind resources include representativeness, consistency and integrity. Wind measurement time of anemometer towers should be guaranteed to be at least one year; among obtained wind measurements, the integrity rate of valid data should be more than 90%. However, in actual planning of wind farms, wind measurement equipment is often installed late at wind farm sites. Due to the lack of sufficient on-site measurement of wind speed, wind direction and other information, measured data from neighboring sites or regions is often used for calculation and analysis, resulting in a large error.

Wind resource evaluation is a key step in site selection of wind farms. Its accuracy is crucial to the benefits of future operation of wind farms. Traditional wind resource evaluation is based on interpolation or extrapolation of meteorological observation data, as well as 1 to 2 years of observations from meteorological observation towers installed at locations where wind farms have been built or are to be built. This often results in inaccurate or overrated evaluations. Nowadays, it has been recognized that the application of mesoscale numerical models to simulate wind conditions in a certain region is a more feasible approach, and that simulation results can be used as ancillary information for wind resource census, which can not only fill the gap in the uncertainty of wind resource status of regions with no wind records, but also provide some guidance on macro and micro site selection of wind farms. In addition to its feasibility, this method only requires computer simulation and a small investment, and has been widely adopted by the industry.

(2) Software application in wind resource evaluation. Wind resource evaluation is an essential part of the construction and operation of wind farms as a whole. It is the key to obtaining good economic benefits from the construction of wind farms. At present, commonly used softwares in China for calculating wind resource distribution includes WAsP, WindFarm, MS-MICRO, WindFarmer and WindPro. In actual application, these software have certain limitations, including a large calculation error when the slope is greater than 5 °. To overcome the limitation of a large calculation error, CFD technology can be used to numerically simulate various typical terrains, analyze simulation results combined with actual results, verify the credibility of numerical simulation, and analyze the distribution of wind energy in various terrains, so as to propose appropriate correction methods for wind resource evaluation and quantification based on modeling-related errors in existing wind resource evaluation results.

(3) Errors in wind resource evaluation results.

1) Differences between airflow characteristics and standard models. Unlike actual airflow characteristics, standard models of wind speed profile/wind shear generally adopt logarithmic law or exponential distribution.

2) Traditional linear evaluation methods. These methods are mainly parametric methods such as annual mean wind speed and the degree of fit of Weibull frequency distribution.

3) Mapping level of topographic maps. At present, most topographic maps used in micro site selection of wind farms in China are at a scale of 1 : 10,000, whereas when such site selection is carried out in hilly and low mountainous terrains, topographic maps at a scale of 1 : 5,000 should generally be used for wind farm measurement. To improve the accuracy of micro site selection of wind farms, the resolution of grid charts should be as large as possible when calculating wind resource distribution, generally 10 - 50 m.

4) Environmental factors such as noise and shadow flicker. Currently, in terms of the configuration of wind turbine generator systems, the environmental protection department generally requires that the distance between wind turbine generator systems and residential areas should be greater than 500 m to prevent noise, shadow flicker and other impacts on residents. Depending on the actual situation, if a village is in the upwind direction, the distance between wind turbine generator systems and the village should be greater than 300 m; if the village is in the downwind direction of wind turbine generator sys-

tems, the distance between the wind turbine generator systems and the village should be greater than 500 m. In terms of shadow flicker, when wind turbine generator systems are on the south side of the village, the distance between the wind turbine generator systems and the village should be greater than 500 m; when wind turbine generator systems are on the north side of the village, the distance between the wind turbine generator systems and the village should be greater than 300 m.

(4) Correction of errors in wind resource evaluation results.

Influence of slope, roughness and boundary layer thickness on flow fields around complex terrains. Generally, wind energy density increases with the increase in slope; the leeward side is affected by vortex and wake turbulence, and wind energy distribution near the ground in complex terrains is poorer than that in flat terrains; the smaller the roughness is, the better the wind energy distribution is; roughness only has a negligible effect on wind energy when it changes within a small range, but when the change is large, areas with larger friction coefficients should be avoided as much as possible when installing wind turbine generator systems; the selection of boundary layer thickness affects both the capturing of wind speed and the distribution of turbulence intensity, with a greater effect on velocity distribution.

CFD numerical simulation is used to analyze the effects of typical terrain geometry (slope) and atmospheric boundary layer characteristics (surface roughness and boundary layer thickness) on wind energy distribution, wind speed capture, and turbulence intensity. The results are then compared with evaluation results obtained from engineering methods to analyze causes of errors in engineering evaluation methods.

(5) Correction of numerical simulation methods for wind farms. Currently, most wind resource evaluation software, such as WAsP, WindFarm, MS-MICRO, WindFarmer and WindPro, adopts wind flow linearized models (assuming the presence of only small wind disturbances). Such models involve low computational effort, but are not applicable to wind resource evaluation in complex terrains (mountains, forests, mudflats, etc). With a history of more than 2 decades, the WAsP software is used for wind energy resource evaluation and wind farm design. As the world's most used software for wind resource analysis, its functionality for wind resource analysis of flat terrains has been widely recognized. However, the WAsP software uses standard linear models to simulate wind farms. When it is used for complex terrains, prediction evaluation of wind resources will have a large deviation. CFD simulation is a promising alternative to conventional tools, which represent effects of terrain, roughness and obstacles as parameters, and directly solves flow equations numerically to calculate airflow changes in three-dimensional directions. It can also calculate three-dimensional roughness effects, three-dimensional turbulence, and wind shear, etc, in complex environments such as woods. Compared with existing software, i. e. WAsP, CFD can calculate wind farm turbulence in

three dimensions with high computational accuracy, thus reducing the uncertainties of wind resource evaluation.

【Task implementation】

Ⅰ. Task preparations

1 software platform for intelligent simulation and planning of new energy, and 1 set of computer mainframe and monitor.

Ⅱ. Task content and procedures

(i) Task: Simulation of energy analysis and system design

Task content: Complete simulation of energy analysis and system design

Task procedures:

(1) Analyze the energy consumption demand; reasonably design the type and capacity of energy sources.

Task 5.1 Related task implementation charts

(2) Use the commissioning system to develop optimal integrated design schemes focusing on power supply shortage days, wind energy deviation, and other related parameters; scan the QR code to download the table for wind power generator parameters.

(3) Complete the analysis of four energy outputs including wind power generation capacity.

(4) Complete the selection of fan capacity per unit area and the analysis and design of the output power of wind power generation systems per unit area.

(5) Complete integrated planning and optimization of regional energy sources; export the result table.

Ⅲ. Skill requirements

(1) The layout of various types of energy sources is well designed.

(2) The ratio of photovoltaic power generation capacity to wind power capacity (power) ranges from 0.2 to 5.

(3) The capacity of the energy storage system is appropriately set to meet the load change requirements; the total energy storage capacity is less than 10 times the average daily electricity consumption.

Ⅳ. Task results, appraisal and evaluation

(1) System design meets indicator requirements; the system operates successfully; the data screen is well laid out and runs correctly; operation data are recorded (accounting for 90%);

(2) The operator exhibits good professional quality during the operation process and follows 7S management model (accounting for 10%).

Project 5 Survey on Wind Resources and Selecting Sites for Wind Farms

Task 5.2 Selecting Sites for Wind Farms

【Learning objectives】

　　Knowledge objective: To master key elements of wind farm site selection

　　Ability objective: To be able to select proper sites for wind farms

　　Qualification objective: To develop the awareness of low-carbon life; to cultivate the professional quality of meticulousness.

　　Learning priority: Site selection objectives for wind farms

　　Learning challenge: Site selection technology for wind farms

【Task analysis】

　　In addition to the main consideration of meteorological parameters, site selection of wind farms should also take into account a number of factors, including site location, power grid requirements, traffic, geology, environment, power supply, etc.

　　This task relies on the software platform for intelligent simulation and planning of new energy. It involves various implementation tasks such as overall project demand analysis for regional energy related engineering projects, energy system analysis, production capacity analysis, energy consumption analysis, project feasibility analysis, wind energy power supply site selection, and system design, and aims at completing energy planning and design of wind farms.

【Knowledge learning】

　　During site selection of wind farms, various factors need to be taken into account, including availability of wind resources, project construction permit, obtaining the right to use the sea area for the site (for offshore wind farms), basic conditions of the nearby power grid (including the locations of onshore transformer stations, voltage class, maximum accessible capacity, power grid planning, etc.), basic conditions of the site (including boundaries, water depth, wind resources, and seabed geological conditions), and environmental constraints (including negative impacts of the local tourism industry, aquatic organisms, birds, waterways, fishery, coast defense, etc.).

　　1. Geological and topographical environments and selection of wind turbine generator systems

　　(1) Technical and economic analysis of wind turbine generator systems. When selecting wind turbine generator systems, in addition to considering the characteristics of wind turbine generator systems, the impacts of many external factors must also be taken into account, including climate, environment, and power system constraints (ability to receive wind power, grid security, stability constraints, etc). For example, there is a

significant variation in the climatic conditions of China, including Class II wind zone and cold operating environment conditions. According to *Environmental conditions appearing in nature of electric and electronic products-Temperature and huvnidity* (GB/T 4797.1-2005), Table 5.4 lists the definition of climatic conditions, and the appropriate models are shown in Table 5.5.

Table 5.4   Definition of climate conditions   Unit: ℃

Climate	Temperature value
Cold	-50
Cold temperature I	-33
Cold temperature II	-26
Warm temperature	-15

Table 5.5   Models adapted to climatic temperatures   Unit: ℃

Model	Temperature value
Low temperature (Type II)	-40
Low temperature (Type I)	-30
Normal temperature	-20

To ensure safe and reliable operation of wind farms, factors such as environment, power supply and the earth's surface should be taken into consideration in the selection of wind turbine generator systems. In view of the characteristics of different types of wind turbine generator systems, technical indicators and economic factors should be combined to analyze the characteristics of each type of wind turbine generator system and determine the applicability of wind turbine generator systems in different environments. Meanwhile, requirements of IEC 61400-1 and other international standards should be met.

(2) Selection of wind turbine generator systems in complex geological and topographical environments. The principle of selecting wind turbine generator systems in typical topographical environments should be proposed based on actual geological and topographical conditions. Generally, methods for selecting wind turbine generator systems in flat terrains are used to analyze the impact of wind resources on the selection of wind turbine generator systems in complex geological and topographical environments. This analysis focuses on wind speed distribution, common wind profile models, common turbulence models, etc., and combining with the analysis of wind speed models (EWM), wind speed pulsation models (EOG), turbulence models (ETM), wind direction change models (EDC), wind shear models (EWS) and other factors in extreme conditions. The aim is to put forward rationale and methodological recommendations for the selection of wind turbine generator systems in different geological and topographical environments. Meanwhile, the influence of environmental factors other than wind resources on the selection of wind turbine generator systems is analyzed, including temperature, humidity, air density, solar radiation, rain, snow, hail, salinity, earthquake, etc. In addition, the influence of special environmental factors, e.g., fishery, shipping, communication, and national defense should be considered when selecting wind turbine generator systems for offshore wind farms.

(3) Influence of grid factors on selection of wind turbine generator systems. The influence of grid factors on the selection of wind turbine generator systems is studied from the perspective of the power system. This includes considering grid restraints on voltage and frequency at the access points of wind farms, grid restraints on acceptable wind power generation capacity, the impact of grid outages on the wind farms, and the influence of coordination and control between wind farms and the grid on the selection of the wind turbine generator systems.

2. Micro site selection of wind farms

(1) Objectives of micro site selection of wind farms. How to configure wind power generators in wind farms to get maximum power generation capacity and optimal economic benefits is the focus of micro site selection. Currently, the task of micro site selection in the construction process of domestic wind farms mainly relies on power design institutes and equipment suppliers, each of which has similar capabilities, and has only recently started engaging in this work. They mainly use WAsPwind resource application and analysis software developed by the Danish National Laboratory, to analyze wind resources of wind farms, and then use various optimization design softwares for wind farms, e.g., WindPro and WindFarmer, to optimize the layout design of wind turbine generator systems. Since WAsP is developed based on the terrain characteristics of Europe, there has been no clear indication whether it can accurately calculate wind resources in different regions of China. In addition, the WAsP software cannot accurately calculate wind resources in regions with complex terrains. However, there is no widely used wind resource analysis software in China, and micro site selection has been relying on the WAsP software to analyze regions with both flat and complex terrains. Moreover, it is not possible to correct software parameters or calculation results. Therefore, it is urgent to develop a wind resource analysis software that is applicable to various terrains in China or to investigate correction methods for the WAsP software.

Overseas wind power technology started early, so the technology is relatively mature. A large amount of statistical data is available for both onshore and offshore wind farms, and developers have performed numerous experiments on various application softwares like WAsP, which enables accurate correction and parameter adjustment based on specific application scenarios. In this way, accurate calculation results are obtained.

Currently, besides WAsPwind, a wind resource application and analysis software developed by the Danish National Laboratory, a domestic software company has also developed a similar analysis and calculation software for wind energy and power generation capacity of wind farms, it aims on replacing the WAsP software. The software is based on the wind measurement data verification system for wind farms, and adopts model calculation to obtain wind resource parameters at any spatial location within wind farm areas, thus providing a theoretical basis for the construction of wind farms. The Wind Farmer software is a widely used optimization design software for wind farms. It is mainly used for designing, analyzing and optimizing wind farms, and is able to calculate the energy output of wind farms and simulate the influence of terrain and wake on the energy output. By optimizing the layout of wind power generators in wind farms, the energy output of wind farms is maximized, while energy loss is minimized. However, the software is based on WAsP, and results of calculation or designs mainly depend on the results obtained by the WAsP software.

Currently, analysis software for large flow fields is also domestically available for wind resource analysis for regions with complex terrains, but its calculation is very time-consuming.

(2) Technology of micro site selection of wind farms.

1) Research on wind resources in wind farms with complex terrains. Data obtained from anemometer towers installed at wind farms with different terrains (such as plains, mountains, sea, etc), as well as topographic and geomorphological characteristics, are used to investigate the influence on the change pattern of wind speed.

2) Research on economic construction of wind farms. According to the characteristics of installed wind turbine generator systems (number, capacity, type, height, and other parameters), the software for micro site selection of wind farms is used to correct each parameter related to estimated power generation capacity, and to complete the optimal layout of wind turbine generator systems, so as to make full use of resources and achieve maximum power generation capacity.

3) Research on safe operation of wind farms. Wind farms as a whole are optimized through the research on economic construction of wind farms. However, in individual cases within identified micro site selection schemes, the row spacing between two neighboring wind turbine generator systems is too small (less than 5 times the impeller diameter), resulting in the wake of the wind turbine generator system at the front affecting the wind turbine generator system at the back along the prevailing wind direction. In view of this fact, safety and reliability analysis must be performed for the wind turbine generator system at the back.

Technical difficulties to be solved are as follows:

a. Incompleteness of wind measurement data. Research on various methods of supplementing and correcting raw wind resource data for wind farms.

b. Errors in the calculation of complex terrains: Research on correction of calculated results and determination of correction parameters according to different regions and different wind resources.

c. Determine values of correction coefficients when estimating power generation capacity of wind farms to accurately estimate the power generation capacity of different wind power generation farms.

d. Select coastal, mountainous, and plain wind power generation farms respectively to carry out the verification of micro site selection.

e. Evaluate the research on the extent to which the interaction between wind turbine generator systems influences the safe and reliable operation of wind turbine generator systems.

(3) Software and technology for micro site selection analysis and influence of different geological and topographical environments on micro site selection. Existing micro design software for wind power generation farms includes the WAsP software for plain terrains, WindFarmer based on WAsP wind energy resource calculation, WindPro, WindFarm for layout and optimization of wind turbine generator systems, as well as Windsim and Meteodyn software for hilly and low mountainous terrains.

Optimization design is carried out by combining different geological and topographical environments with the characteristics of different software for wind resource distribution calculation. Actual terrain measurement and geological survey are not only directly related to actual wind power evaluation, but also have a direct impact on the optimization layout and erection & installation of wind turbine generator systems.

【Task implementation】

Ⅰ. Task preparations

1 software platform for intelligent simulation and planning of new energy, and 1 set of computer mainframe and monitor.

Ⅱ. Task content and procedures

(ⅰ) Task: Simulation of energy analysis and system design

Task content: Complete simulation of energy analysis and system design

Task 5.2 Related task implementation charts

Task procedures:

(1) Analyze the energy consumption demand; reasonably design the type and capacity of energy sources.

(2) Use the commissioning system to develop optimal integrated design schemes focusing on power supply shortage days, wind energy deviation, and other related parameters; scan the QR code to download the table for wind power generator parameters.

(3) Complete the analysis of four energy outputs including wind power generation capacity.

(4) Complete the selection of fan capacity per unit area and the analysis and design of the output power of wind power generation systems per unit area.

(5) Complete integrated planning and optimization of regional energy sources; export the result table.

Ⅲ. Skill requirements

(1) The layout of various types of energy sources is well designed.

(2) The ratio of photovoltaic power generation capacity to wind power capacity (power) ranges from 0.2 to 5.

(3) The capacity of the energy storage system is appropriately set to meet the load change requirements; the total energy storage capacity is less than 10 times the average daily electricity consumption.

IV. Task results, appraisal and evaluation

(1) System design meets indicator requirements; the system operates successfully; the data screen is well laid out and runs correctly; operation data are recorded (accounting for 90%).

(2) The operator exhibits good professional quality during the operation process and follows 7S management model (accounting for 10%).

【Exercises】

1. What are the devices and requirements for wind measurement?

2. What technologies are available for micro site selection and correction for wind farms?

项目 6　认识与选型风力发电机组

任务 6.1　掌握风力发电系统组成

【学习目标】

知识目标：了解风力发电系统的组成；掌握双馈变速变桨距风电机组原理；掌握风力发电系统并网控制过程。

能力目标：能正确搭建小型风力发电系统。

素质目标：培养团队协作、刻苦钻研的职业品质。

重点：风力发电系统的组成。

难点：风力发电系统搭建与运行。

【任务分析】

现代的风力发电系统是由风能资源、风力发电机组、控制装置、蓄能装置、监测显示装置及用户电能负荷等组成，而风力发电机组是主要发电设备，其性能优劣直接影响系统发电效率。

依托全国职业院校技能大赛设备平台，完成风力发电机桨叶安装，以及风力发电系统数据采集、运动控制的接线，调试并运行风力发电系统。

【知识学习】

风力发电相关装置是将风能转换成电能的设备，在国家能源工业技术改革中，是党的二十大关于推动形成绿色低碳的生产方式和生活方式的生动展现。

6.1.1　风力发电系统组成

现代风力发电技术是涉及空气动力、机械传动、电机、自动控制、力学、材料、量测、气象、环境保护等多学科的综合性高技术系统工程。现代的风力发电系统是由风能资源、风力发电机组、控制装置、蓄能装置、监测显示装置及用户电能负荷等组成（有的风力发电系统中还包括有备用电源），如图 6.1 所示。

1. 风力发电机组

风力发电机组是实现能量转换的设备，它是将风能转换成电能的机械、电气及其控制设备的组合，通常包括风轮机、发电机、变速器及控制装置等。国际上通常按照机组容量

项目6　认识与选型风力发电机组

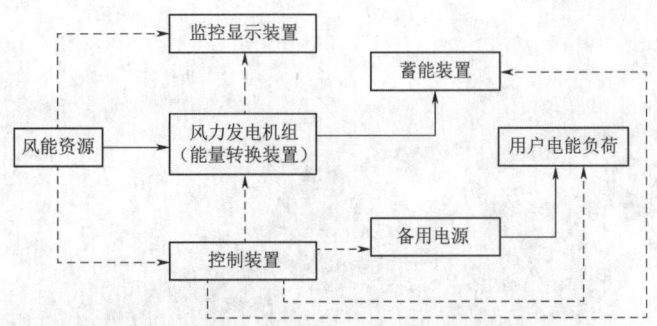

图 6.1　风力发电系统的组成

的大小，将风力发电机组分为大型（容量在兆瓦以上）、中型（容量在 100kW 以上至 1MW）、小型（容量在 1kW 以上至 100kW）。我国将容量小于 1kW 的机组列为微型。

　　风力发电机组中的风轮机是将通过风轮旋转面的流动空气的一部分动能转变为其轴上输出有用机械能的装置，即实现将风能转换为机械能的装置。根据风轮机旋转轴在空间为水平方向的及垂直方向的，风轮机可分为水平轴风轮机及垂直轴风轮机两大类。水平轴风轮机有调向机构并且风轮必须放置在塔架的顶端；垂直轴风轮机的风轮则不需要调向机构并且可安置在靠近地面处。

风力发电机组设计要求

　　无论哪种型式的风轮机皆需通过齿轮增速传动装置（即变速齿轮箱）来将风轮机轴上的低速旋转变换为较高的转速，以便与高速旋转的发电机转轴相连接。只有在微型和小容量的风力发电机组中或采用低速发电机的风力发电机组中才不包括变速齿轮箱。图 6.2（a）和图 6.2（b）分别表示水平轴及垂直轴风力发电机组中风轮机、齿轮箱及发电机的连接布置情况。图 6.3 表示现代中型水平轴风力发电机的结构。

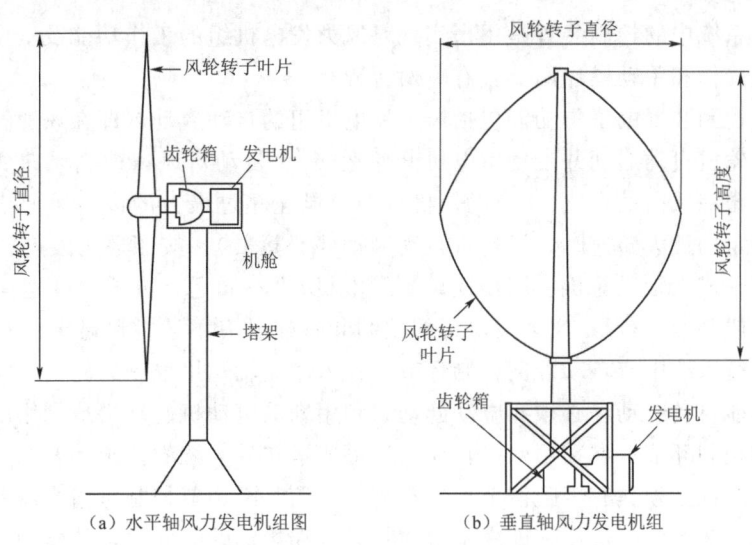

(a) 水平轴风力发电机组图　　(b) 垂直轴风力发电机组

图 6.2　风力发电机组中风轮机

177

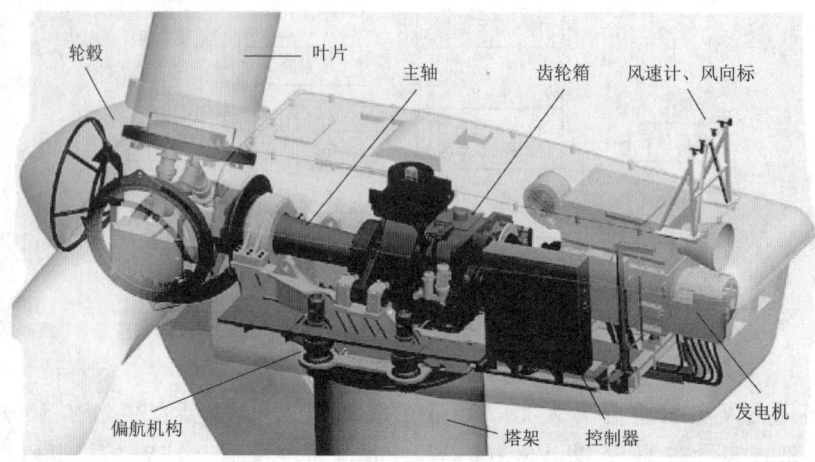

图 6.3　现代中型水平轴风力发电机组结构示意图

风力发电机组中的发电机对于在独立运行的小容量发电系统中大多采用永磁式或自励式交流发电机，对于在并网运行的发电系统中普遍采用同步发电机或异步（感应）发电机。在风力发电系统中采用同步发电机和异步发电机各有其优缺点。采用同步发电机时，通过调节励磁可以调节发电机的电压，并可向电网提供无功功率，改善电网的功率因数。但同步发电机需要风轮机有调速装置，以便维持恒速旋转（即以同步转速旋转），同时还需要复杂的并网设备。此外，在阵风时同步发电机的瞬态稳定也是必须考虑的问题。异步发电机的结构较简单，并允许转速在一定的限度范围内有所变化，以吸收瞬态阵风的能量，故不需要严格的复杂并网装置。但采用异步发电机时，发电机需要从电网获得励磁，使电网的功率因数变坏。

2. 控制装置

风力发电系统中的控制装置是用来实现对风力发电机组的工作功能及安全保护功能的控制。分自动操作和手动操作两类，有时两者皆有。

自动操作控制装置的工作功能包括风力发电机组的自动启动（即在风速达到设定的启动风速时，风轮机自动启动并带动发电机开始运转）、自动对风（即当风向变化时，水平轴风轮机自动跟踪风向的变化）、自动停机（即当风速超过最大的设定风速或风轮机的风轮转速超过规定的最大转速时，风轮机自动制动停止运转）。按照风力发电机组的不同结构型式（水平轴或立轴风轮机、同步或异步发电机）、不同运行方式（变速运转或恒速运转，独立运行或并网运行）。风力发电机的控制装置还具有下述控制环节。在采用同步发电机的并网运行系统中有自动并网控制环节；在采用立轴达里厄型风轮的系统中，由于达里厄型风轮不能自动起动，必须有电动起动（利用辅助电动机起动）或利用萨沃尼厄斯风轮气动起动的控制环节；在采用水平轴风轮机恒速运转的系统中，由于要在变化的风速情况下维持恒速，则必须具有桨距调节控制环节。所谓桨距调节控制是指当风速变化致使风轮机风轮转速偏离规定的数值（即额定转速）时，在规定的时间内，使借助液压控制或电液控制的桨距控制器动作，改变风轮机风轮叶片攻角，调整风轮机的输出功率，以达到维持风轮机转速恒定，通常是以风速及风轮机转速作为桨距调节控制器动作的信号。另一种桨距调节是借助风轮叶片在不同旋转速度时离心力的变化，通过机械联动机构来改变风轮叶片的攻角，达到维持恒速运行。在独立运行的风力发电系统中，为了维持系统的功率平衡，以使交流发电机输出恒压恒频的电能，必须具有负载调节及耗能负载调节的控制环节，一般是采用发电机输出的频率作为负载调节的信号。

自动操作控制装置的安全保护功能包括大风保护、风轮超速保护、发电机过热（温升过高）保护、对风调向用伺服电动机及桨距调节用油泵电机的过载保护、发电机引出电缆线防扭绞保护（立轴风力发电机组不需要此种保护）、机舱振动保护、电网故障（电网电压、频率失常）保护等。各种安全保护功能皆以达到使风力发电机组停止运转（通过制动实行）、自动偏离对风方向（偏离风向90°，立轴风力发电机组无此要求），并与负载或电网脱离作为目标。

自动操作控制装置是利用各种传感器件获取信号。经微处理机或可编程控制器（PLC）对信号进行判断、分析、计算及处理，然后再由继电器、开关及伺服电动机等执行控制命令，完成控制功能。

手动操作的控制环节只是在小型风力发电系统中采用，而且只限于部分功能，如手动启动、停机、紧急制动等。

3. 监测显示装置

风力发电系统中的监测显示装置是用来自动显示系统的工作状况的，包括自动显示风速、风向，风轮转速，发电机转速，发电机电压、电流、频率、功率、累计发电量及累计运转时数等。

4. 蓄能装置

风能是随机性能源，具有间歇性，并且不能直接储存。即使在风能资源丰富的地区，若以风力发电作为获得电能的主要方式，也必须配备蓄能装置。在有风期间将多余的风能转换为其他形式的能量在蓄能装置中储存起来；在无风期间再将蓄能装置中储存的能量释放出来并转换成电能，实现稳定持续的供电。风力发电系统中的蓄能方式主要有以下几种：

（1）蓄电池蓄能。当风力发电机组将风能转换为电能后。除向负荷供电外，多余的电能可以向蓄电池充电，将能量储存在蓄电池内。风力发电系统中经常采用铅酸电池（亦称铅蓄电池）或镍镉电池（亦称碱性蓄电池）。

（2）飞轮蓄能。在风轮机与发电机之间安装一个飞轮，利用飞轮旋转时的惯性储能。当风力强时，风能即以动能的形式储存在飞轮中；当风力弱时，储存在飞轮中的动能被释放出来，带动发电机发电。一般长轮多由钢制成，近年来正在研究采用高强度而质量轻的纤维材料制造飞轮。

（3）抽水蓄能。在地形条件适合的地点可以采用这种蓄能方法。当风力强而负荷所需电能较少时，将风力发电机组发出的多余电能带动抽水机，将低处的水抽到高处的水库中储存起来；当无风或风力弱时，将高处水库中的水释放出来流向低处并推动水轮机转动，从而带动发电机发电。

（4）压缩空气蓄能。在用电负荷减小时，将风力发电机组提供的多余的电能驱动电动机，再由电动机带动空气压缩机将空气压缩后储存在地下岩洞或废弃的矿坑内；在无风期或用电负荷达到高峰时，则以储存的压缩空气为动力推动涡轮机并带动发电机发电。

(5) 电解氢蓄能。在用电负荷减小时,将风力发电机组提供的多余的电能用来电解水,使氢和氧分离,把氢储存起来;当用电负荷增加或无风时,把氢和氧在燃料电池中进行反应产生电能。

目前,在风力发电系统中最常用的蓄能装置是蓄电池。飞轮蓄能及电解氢蓄能仍处于实验研究阶段。抽水蓄能及压缩空气蓄能在技术上是成熟的,但受到地形及水和压缩空气的储存地点等条件的制约。

6.1.2 大型风电机组控制与并网技术

1. 系统结构

(1) 定速风力发电系统。双速感应发电机中的小功率低速感应发电机工作在低风速区,大功率高速感应发电机工作在高风速区。当风速超过额定风速时,通过叶片的失速来降低其风能利用系数,从而维持功率恒定。由于风力机转速不能随风速变化,因此其风能利用系数往往偏离最大值,风能利用率不高,风力机常常运行在低效率状态。20世纪80—90年代丹麦生产的风电机组主要采用定速风力发电系统,我国生产的600kW和750kW风电机组也采用这种发电系统。

(2) 变速风力发电系统。

1) 双馈变速变桨距风电机组。如图6.4所示为双馈变速变桨距风电机组工作原理图,发电机的定子直接和电网连接,绕线转子则通过滑环与变换器相连接。其中,变换器用于控制转子绕组电流,调节发电机输出功率和转矩。也有采取在转子回路外接电阻的方法,如丹麦Vestas公司就采用转子电流控制结构(OptiSlip)实现变速控制。

双馈异步发电机的定子电流频率、转子转速和转子电流频率的关系为

$$f_1 = \frac{P n_m}{60} + f_2 \tag{6.1}$$

式中,P为发电机的极对数;n_m为发电机转子转速,r/min;f_1为定子频率,即电网频率,Hz;f_2为发电机转子电流频率,Hz。

可见,当风速变化引起发电机转速发生变化时,只要改变通入发电机转子励磁电流的频率f_2就可以保持发电机定子侧输出频率f_1不变。电网侧变换器将电网的交流电整流为直流电,转子侧变换器将直流电逆变为交流电,逆变的交流电频率由发电机的转子转速决定,从而实现定子侧输出恒定频率的电流。

双馈感应发电机工作在一个有限的变速范围,该范围与变换器设计有关。

通常,变换器容量为发电机额定功率的20%~30%,变速范围也比转子外接电阻的调速

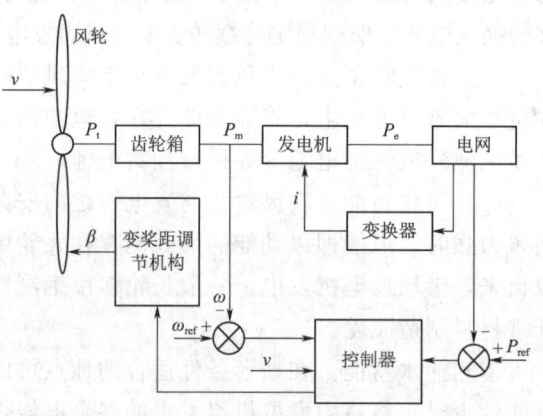

图6.4 双馈变速变桨距风电机组工作原理图
v—风速;P_t—风轮输出功率;P_m—机械功率;
P_e—电功率;β—桨距角;ω—角速度;
ω_{ref}—给定角速度;P_{ref}—给定功率

方式大。双馈变速变桨距风电机组会产生很大的电流峰值，因此，为了保证风电机组安全运行，需要采用先进的保护措施实现低电压穿越。

2）全功率变换器有增速齿轮箱风力发电系统。全功率变换器有增速齿轮箱风力发电系统采用全功率变换器实现全范围变速，发电机可以是感应发电机、同步发电机和永磁发电机，通过增速齿轮箱与风力机连接，再经变换器与电网连接。

对于电网发生故障时要求风电机组能够实现低电压穿越，全功率变换器的风力发电系统很容易实现。同时，该系统具有良好的控制性能，可实现多重目标控制，如电压稳定控制、无功控制等，应用范围更广。

3）全功率变换器无增速齿轮箱风力发电系统。全功率变换器无增速齿轮箱风力发电系统取消了增速齿轮箱，发电机为同步发电机或永磁发电机，设计成多极发电机形式。直接驱动永磁发电机，具有传动系统简单、效率高及控制鲁棒性好等特点。

（3）并网控制过程。

1）定速风力发电系统并网过程：采用晶闸管软切入，过渡过程结束后，立即切除变换器，该变换器并非整个系统的核心。

2）变速风力发电系统并网过程：变换器在变风速条件下，将频率随风速变化的交流电转换为与电网电压频率相同、与电网实现柔性连接的交流电，并通过调节风力机获取最大风能。

（4）变换器。

1）交-交变换器：变流效率高且可以四象限运行，功率可快速双向流动。但是因为采取相控方式，输出电压含大量谐波，尤其是低频时谐波含量大、功率因数低。经改进后的矩阵式交-交变换器采用全控器件和先进控制策略，输出电压灵活可控，低频谐波含量大大减小，电流为正弦形式等。

2）交-直-交电压型变换器：采用二极管不可控整流，输入电流发生畸变，谐波增大，输入功率因数低，并且能量无法双向流动。交-直-交电压型双 PWM 变换器主电路拓扑方案成熟，谐波含量非常低，并且可以调节功率因数。同时，通过 PWM 控制，易于实现变换器四象限运行，电路设计及控制系统设计均较矩阵式变换器简单。因此，目前得以大量采用。

2. 风电机组功率控制技术

（1）风力机变桨距控制。根据风力机叶片在轮毂的安装结构可将风电机组分为定桨距和变桨距风电机组两大类。其中，定桨距风电机组的叶片固定安装在轮毂上，当风速变化时，桨叶安装角不发生变化。

变桨距风电机组的叶片一与轮毂之间采用非刚性连接方式，允许叶片可以绕叶片纵梁调节节距，使得叶片相对于风向有不同的攻角。当风速持续变化时，叶片的攻角始终保持在最佳角度，从而使风电机组有可能在不同风速下始终保持最佳转换效率，获得最大输出功率。当风速大于切出风速时，风力机停止工作，叶片顺桨以保护风力机不受损坏。与定桨距风电机组相比，变桨距风电机组具有在额定风速以上输出功率平稳的特点。同时，变桨距风电机组叶片较薄，结构简单、质量轻，发电机转动惯量小，易于制造大型风电机组。因此，大型风电机组常采用变桨距技术。传统的变桨距方式主要有电液伺服和电气伺服两种形式。为了限制动态转矩，往往采取限制变桨距机构的输出节距角变化值，一般为 $5\sim 12°/s$。对于大型风电机组，叶片改变节距角时所需的驱动力相对比较大，对变桨距机构的强度和定位精度都有较高的要求。

同时，对于变桨轴承的要求更高，涉及材料和特殊加工工艺。例如，某企业生产的 1.5MW 变桨轴承采用合金材料，要求轴承滚道淬火层深度超过 4.5mm，轴承内外圈变形仅 0.05mm，内外齿轮对滚道径向跳动小于 $300\mu m$，滚道表面粗糙度为 $0.8\mu m$。

（2）风力机偏航控制。偏航控制系统是风电机组控制系统的重要组成部分，一般由偏航轴承、偏航驱动装置、偏航制动器、偏航计数器、扭缆保护装置、偏航液压回路等组成，主要作用有两个。

1）与风电机组的控制系统相互配合，使风力机叶片始终处于迎风状态，提高风电机组的发电效率。

2）保障风电机组的安全运行。风电机组的偏航控制系统主要分为两大类：被动迎风偏航系统和主动迎风偏航系统，前者多用于小型的独立风电机组，由尾舵控制，当风向改变时被动对风；后者多用于大型并网型风电机组，由位于下风向的风向标发出的信号进行主动对风控制。由于风向经常变化，因此必须通过不断转动机舱使得风力机叶片始终正面受风，增大风能的捕获率；但是，在实际应用中，因受风速仪及风向标传感器精度不高限制，再加上这些传感器往往安装在下风向位置受干扰，测量误差大，不能做到 100%对风，降低了风能捕获效率，同时因对称安装的风电机组叶片运行时受力不均，引起风电机组振动和加剧叶片的疲劳。因此，如何提高对风精度值得关注。

（3）风力发电机控制。双馈异步风力发电机的定子绕组接工频电网，转子绕组由具有可调节频率、相位、幅值和相序的交-直-交变换器激励，使得双馈发电机可以在不同的风速下运行，其转速随风速变化作相应调整，使风力发电机始终运行在最佳状态，提高了风能的利用率。同时，通过控制馈入转子绕组的电流参数，保持定子输出的电压和频率不变，同调节电网的功率因数，提高系统的稳定性。

（4）功率控制策略。

1）基于风速的风电机组输出功率控制方法：当风速在切入风速和额定风速之间变化时，采用变速控制方法，追踪最佳功率曲线，获得最大功率；当风速在额定风速和切出风速之间变化时，采用变桨距控制方法，调节风力机叶片桨距角，保持额定功率不变。该方法的特点是能根据风速的大小选用不同的控制方法，实现风力机最大功率的输出，提高了风电机组风能利用效率，同时提高了风力机运行的稳定性和可靠性。

2）基于风向标和输出功率的风力发电机偏航控制方法：在风向变化绝对值大于 15°时，采用风向标控制方法；在风向变化绝对值不大于 15°时，则采用功率控制方法。风向、风速变化势必引起风电机组的输出功率变化，通过功率检测仪测得风电机组输出功率，只有在风向变化时才进行偏航控制，风速变化对功率控制方法仅仅视为干扰信号。其中，功率控制方法又分为逆时针旋转、顺时针旋转和原位停止三种工况。该方法能缩短风力机对风时间，提高了风力机对风精度、风电机组风能利用效率和风力机使用寿命。

3. 低电压穿越技术

电力系统发生非永久性短路故障引起电网电压下降，危害极大。例如：我国东北某地在 2008 年就多次发生因小的电网故障造成方圆 200km 范围内的 400MW 风电机组同时全部切除的现象；在甘肃玉门风电场、甘肃安西中广核大梁子风电场、宁夏贺兰山风电场发生过类似的情况；某些电气化铁路附近的风电场在电气化机车经过时，也曾发生风电场内风电机组大部分甚至全部切除的现象。

风电机组在故障期间不脱离电网，并能及时向系统提供电压和无功支持，避免故障期间对风力发电机组齿轮传动机构和转子电力电子变流器的损伤。

综合考虑风电机组自身的安全和入网规程要求，针对风电机组提出如下要求：

1) 当发生三相对地短路故障（电压跌落至 15% 额定电压）时，风电机组升压变压器高压侧与电网的连接，至少应维持并网运行 625ms 低电压穿越能力。

2) 在发生不对称故障（如单相接地短路、两相相间或两相接地故障）时，风电机组必须能够抵御和穿越低电压，直到断路器清除故障。

发达国家风电运营商已开始要求新采购的风电机组具有低电压穿越能力（Low Voltagei Ride Through，LVRT）。同时，风电制造商为了保证产品顺利销售，也采取了很多改进措施，以提高风电机组的低电压穿越能力，并通过专门机构测试。但当前风电制造商大多凭经验采取增大转子侧变换器的容量，以及齿轮箱静态转矩余量的方式，结果将风电机组的电流、电压应力转移为齿轮箱及转轴的机械应力。由于齿轮箱及转轴有一定的疲劳寿命周期，因此不会在测试时立刻就损坏，但这种方法势必给风电机组造成潜在的危害。

【任务实施】

1. 任务准备

竞赛设备平台 1 个、一字螺丝刀 1 把、十字螺丝刀 1 把、剥线钳 1 把、U 形压线钳 1 把、管型压线钳 1 把、万用表 1 个、上电检查记录表 1 份、风力发电系统调试记录表 1 份、导线若干。

2. 任务内容及步骤

任务：风力发电系统的搭建与调试

任务内容：完成风力发电系统搭建与调试。

任务步骤：

(1) 完成风力发电机桨叶与尾舵的安装。

(2) 完成风力发电系统连接导线的制作。

(3) 按照接线图，完成风力供电控制单元的布线与接线。

(4) 根据 PLC 的配置，完成 PLC 的布线与接线。

(5) 按照继电器组的配置图，完成继电器组的布线与接线。

(6) 完成系统上电检查，正确调试与运行风力发电系统。

任务 6.1 相关任务实施图表

3. 技能要求

(1) 正确使用万用表档位进行不同参数的测量，操作规范，无短路、无错档测量。

（2）U形冷压端子在插入端子排时，U形部分应充分插入，并保证正面朝外。

（3）按照规范逐一完成设备安装固定、连接线情况检查、接地线检查等步骤检查，标准严格、无漏项、无错项。

（4）号码管在套入时，所有接线方向垂直于地面的套管，号码及字母组合读序从远离接线端至接线口，所有接线方向平行于地面的套管，号码及字母组合读序从左至右。

（5）在压接接线端子时，剥开的线芯插入接线端子套时，将所有的线芯全部插入端子中；采用压线钳压接接线端子时，应使压痕在接线端子套的底部（反面），压接后，压接部位不允许有导线外露。

3. 任务成果及考核评价

（1）系统调试正确且成功运行、数据界面运行数据正确，能记录运行数据，占90%；

（2）操作过程展现较好职业素养，做到7S管理，占10%。

【练习】

1. 风力发电系统中实现能量转换的设备是什么？
2. 风电机组低电压穿越LVRT技术特点是什么？
3. 风电机组功率控制技术有哪些？

任务6.2　选型风力发电机组

【学习目标】

知识目标：掌握双馈风力发电机组技术参数；理解直驱风力发电变换器产品及特点。
能力目标：能根据需求选型风力发电机组。
素质目标：树立民族自豪感；培养爱岗敬业、乐于奉献的精神品质。
重点：风力发电机组主要技术参数。
难点：风力发电机组的选型依据。

【任务分析】

风机选型要结合当地风能资源、气候特征、地形条件、地貌特征等，选择性价比最高的机型，使风电场在全寿命期内发电量最优，效益最好。在技术先进、运行可靠的前提下，选择经济上切实可行的风力发电机组，需要根据风场的风能资源状况和所选的风力发电机组，测算风场的年发电量，选择综合指标最佳的风力发电机组。

依托智慧新能源仿真规划软件平台，给定风电场需求指标，完成风力发电机组的选型设计。

【知识学习】

我国风电机组的装备制造技术进步显著，一批一批国产化风机落地祖国的大江南北，我国风电装机容量增长率居全球首位。

6.2.1 双馈风电机组

表 6.1　　　　　　　　　　双馈风电机组主要技术参数

技 术 参 数	型　号	
	国内产品 WD77-1500	国外产品 MD70
机组	变距变速型	变距变速型
变距机构	全翼展变距调速	全翼展独立变距
额定功率/kW	1000	1500
切入风速/(m/s)	2.5	3.0
额定风速/(m/s)	12.5	12.8
切出风速/(m/s)	25	25
叶轮直径/m	60.62	70
叶轮转速/(r/min)	12~21.5	10.6~19
额定电压/V	690	690
并网方式	IGBT 变流同步并网	IGBT 变流同步并网
功率因数调节	变流补偿（感、容性）	变流补偿（感、容性）
安全等级	IEC IIA	IEC IIA

1. 双馈风电机组技术关键及技术参数

(1) 技术关键。双馈变速恒频风电机组采用 3 叶片、水平轴、上风向、主动偏航方式，零部件均符合 ISO 9001 和 IEC 质量标准。双馈风电机组的关键技术如下：

1) 整机设计集成技术，系统的可靠性设计、防雷设计、各种恶劣环境下的适用性设计。

2) 叶片设计、制造、试验技术，全翼展变距、速度环、位置环、桨距角、功率流柔性调整技术。

3) 齿轮箱设计、制造、试验技术。

4) 双馈异步发电机设计、制造、试验技术。

5) 变流及控制系统设计技术，通过变速巨频控制实现变速全过程无冲击并网。

6) 机组其他主要部件的选型设计和技术条件要求，加工制造技术。

7) 整机和部件的动、静载荷计算，结构强度、疲劳及动力学分析。

8) 多点位在线振动监测、机组远程监控，通过控制电励磁阻尼抑制机组振动，优化运行性能。

9) 总体设计技术，涉及叶轮、传动系统、发电机及变流系统、变距系统、偏航系统、机舱、塔架、液压系统、冷却系统和联轴器等关键部件的结构参数、可靠性、载荷强度分析等。

(2) 主要技术参数。表 6.1 列出了我国自主设计的 1.0MW 和国外某 1.5MW 变速恒频双馈风电机组的主要技术与参数。

2. 双馈发电机

（1）双馈发电机的特点。

双馈发电机具有质量轻、造价低、运行稳定、功率因数调节可控性好、发电状态速度范围宽等特点。例如，我国生产的 YSBFF 系列双馈发电机的技术特点如下：

1) 采用散布绕组技术，有效提高输出波形质量。

2) 嵌装式定子结构，降低定子的质量约 20%。

3) 滚动轴承结构及轴承绝缘技术，提高轴承运行可靠性。

4) 滑环结构，提高可靠性。

5) C 级绝缘技术应用。

6) 主机采用 IC 666 冷却结构，改进通风结构，提高冷却效率，降低发电机温升 5～10℃。同时，通过完善生产工艺，降低了质量，制造成本降低 10%～15%，提高了发电机低速运行安全性。

7) 改进"三防"（防水、防尘、防腐）涂料配方，形成适合我国沿海不同风电场发电机涂覆方案。

8) 优化电磁方案，提高发电机自身效率超过 97.2%。

（2）主要技术参数。表 6.2 列出了我国设计生产的 2MW 双馈发电机和国外某公司生产的 2MW 双馈发电机的主要技术参数。

表 6.2　　　　　　　　　　2MW 双馈发电机主要技术参数

技 术 参 数	型　号	
	YSBFF 2.0-16	SIEMENS 2MW
波形畸变率/%	恒速 2.5	恒速 3.1
绝缘等级	C	H
冷却方式	IC 666	IC 616
噪声/dB(A)	98	97
振动/(mm/a)	1.2	1.5
效率/%	96.72	96.75
功率因数	-0.9～+0.9	-0.9～+0.9
最大转矩/倍	2.1	2
质量/kg	12500	13900

6.2.2　直驱型风电机组

这里主要介绍直驱风力发电变换器。

（1）直驱风力发电变换器产品及特点。国内外生产直驱风力发电变换器的厂家有很多，如 ABB、SIEMENS、AMSC、南车株洲、九州、许继和合肥阳光等，其技术特点如下：

1) 柔性并网控制：根据电网电压变化情况和电网调度要求，动态调节无功输出，提高电网支撑能力和电网稳定性。

2) 变步长自适应最大功率点跟踪技术,有效消除最大功率点偏差,提高算法稳定性。

3) 电网侧变换器采用错相控制及最小开关损耗的综合优化 FV 技术(Flux Vector,矢量控制),等效开关频率提高一倍,降低了并网电流中的开关纹波。

4) 独特的有源阻尼技术,抑制滤波电路谐振,减小并网电流波形畸变〔THD(Total Harmonic Distortion,总谐波畸变率)小于 3%〕。

5) 主从控制功率动态平衡控制方法,解决变换器并联时的"环流"问题。

6) 低电压穿越,在系统电压跌落至 1% 时,变换器持续运行 350ms 不脱网。

(2) 主要技术参数。表 6.3 所列为我国生产的直驱风力发电变换器和国外某直驱风力发电变换器的主要技术参数。

表 6.3　　　　　　　直驱风力发电变换器主要技术参数

技术参数	国内产品	国外产品	产品特点分析比较
功率器件	SKIIP	IGBT	国内产品采用高集成度功率模块
拓扑结构	双 PWM	双 PWM	一致
直流母线电压/V	1100	1100	一致
开关频率/kHz	3,错相并联	3	开关损耗不变情况下,国内产品等效开关频率提高一倍
效率/%	>97	>97.5	同一量级
发电机侧控制	矢量控制,转矩直接调节,功率可控	矢量控制,转矩直接调节,功率可控	一致
最大功率点跟踪	变步长、自适应控制	查表、定步长爬山法	国内产品减小对叶轮功率特性依赖,消除功率点偏差
电网侧控制	4 象限矢量控制,实时检测电网,快速动态无功支持	4 象限矢量控制	国内产品对电网支持性能更优
滤波电路	LCL 滤波、有源阻尼	LCL 滤波、有源阻尼	相同滤波效果下,国内产品省去无源阻尼支路损耗,效率提高了
THD/%	<3	<3	一致
最大无功功率/MVar	1.5	0.83	国内产品具有优势
低电压穿越	15% 剩余电压维持在网 350ms	20% 剩余电压维持在网 500ms	国内产品具有优势
冷却系统	水冷	空冷或水冷	相当
运行环境温度/℃	-30~+50	0~+40	相当

6.2.3　风力发电机组选型方法及流程

1. 机型选择的原则

(1) 选择适用安全等级机组。IEC61400-1 第三版标准规定,风电机组等级界定的基本参数见表 6.4。

表 6.4　　　　　　　　　　　风电机组界定等级

等级	I	II	III	S
v_{ref}/(m/s)	50	42.5	37.5	设计者确定
A I_{ref}/(m/s)	0.16			
B I_{ref}/(m/s)	0.14			
C I_{ref}/(m/s)	0.12			

注　各种参数值是指轮毂高度的数值。
　　v_{ref}：50年一遇参考风速10min平均值，一般称最大风速。（ve50＝1.4v_{ref}，ve50为50年一遇风速以3秒钟平均值，一般称极端风速。）
　　A：较高湍流强度特征值；B：中等湍流强度特征值；C：较低湍流强度特征值；I_{ref}：在风速15m/s时，湍流强度的平均值。

（2）选择可靠机组。机组可靠性包括：设计可靠性，制造可靠性，运维的可靠性。

1）设计及设计计算，是否标准，如性能计算，载荷计算，疲劳寿命等，一般应有设计认证证书。

2）制造工艺，产品试验。尤其是静动试验结果一般要有产品认证证书。

3）商品化生产后，运维可靠性，主要看故障率，以可利用指标来衡量。

（3）发电量。在选定机组应根据特定风电场风况和风频分布，选型时主要看运行功率曲线和满发小时数，是否具有一定的经济效益。

（4）使用、维护性能好。①便于使用维护；②全寿命期备品、备件是否能满足要求。

（5）选用于特定风电场气候条件的机组。如：低温、积冰、沙尘暴、雷暴等。

（6）用于特定风电场地形条件的机组交通，安装情况，及是否适合山地复杂地形的要求。

（7）性价比高的机组。考虑全寿命期，规定回收期后，计算各种费用，其内部收入大小来衡量其性价比。

（8）市场成熟化度高的商品化机组，并充分考虑其实际运行情况。

2. 机组选型的基本要求

（1）对质量认证体系的要求：风电机组制造必须具备 ISO9001 系列质量管理体系的认证。

（2）对机组功率曲线的要求：功率曲线是反映风力发电机组发电输出性能好坏的最主要曲线之一。

（3）对机组制造厂家业绩考查：业绩是评判一个风电制造企业水平的重要指标之一。

（4）对特定环境要求：积冰、积雪、低温、雷暴、沙尘等特殊环境都会对风力发电机组造成影响。

3. 机组选型的方法

风力发电机组的选型分为单机容量的选择和机型的选择。

（1）单机容量的选择。根据目前国内外风机市场的现状以及国内已建风电场的装机情况，按照单机容量的大小通常可以将风机分为3个级别。①kW级机组（小于1000kW）；

②MW级机组，目前我国 1.5～2MW 级的机组已经成为主流成熟机型；③多MW级机组，主要安装在海上风电场，尚未大规模投入商业运行。

(2) 机型的选择。根据目前国内外风力发电机组的发展趋势及当前国内装机的类型、制造水平、技术成熟度，并结合场区的风资源情况、地形地貌、安装条件，进行初步选择。

4. 机组选型基本流程

机组选型基本流程如图 6.5 所示。

对于特定的风电场，机组选型还需考虑以下几个因素：机组的安全等级应满足项目极端风况的要求；风轮直径应适合项目年平均风速的要求；轮毂高度选择应考虑项目风切变指数大小；根据项目气候条件，地形条件选择机组。

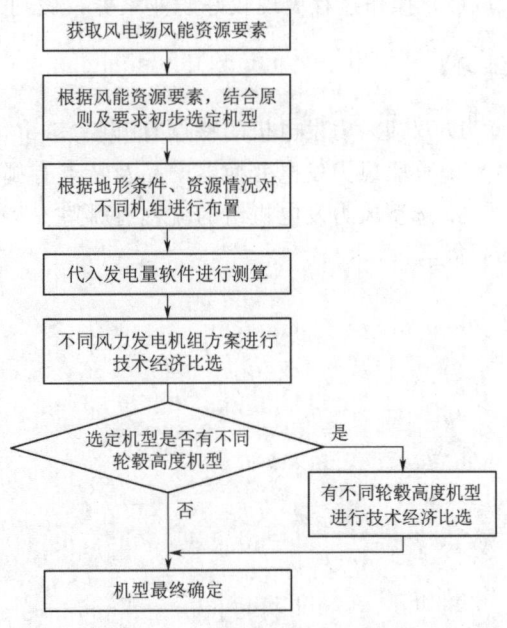

图 6.5 机组选型基本流程图

【任务实施】

1. 任务准备

智慧新能源仿真规划软件平台 1 个、电脑主机和显示器 1 套。

2. 任务内容及步骤

任务：仿真风力发电机组选型与设计

任务内容：完成仿真风力发电机组选型与设计。

任务步骤：

(1) 完成仿真海岛模型设计。

(2) 设定风电场比例指标，分析风电场资源。

(3) 完成风力发电机组间距排布分析。

(4) 完成风力发电机组额定功率分析，填写选型数据表格。

(5) 完成风电场综合规划与优化，导出结果表格。

任务 6.2 相关任务实施图表

3. 技能要求

(1) 各种类型能源布局设计合理。

(2) 光伏发电容量与风力容量（功率）比例范围为 0.2～5。

(3) 储能系统容量设置合适，满足负荷变化要求，储能总容量小于 10 倍的平均每天耗电量。

4. 任务成果及考核评价

(1) 系统设计满足指标要求，成功运行、数据界面运行数据正确，能记录运行数据，布局合理，占 90%。

(2) 操作过程展现较好职业素养,做到 7S 管理,占 10%。

【练习】

1. 双馈风力发电机的特点有哪些?
2. 直驱风力发电变换器产品及特点有哪些?
3. 选型风力发电机组的流程有哪些?

Project 6　Understanding Selecting Sites for Wind Turbine Generator Systems

Task 6.1　Mastering Composition of Wind Power Generation

【Learning objectives】

　　Knowledge objective: To understand the composition of wind power generation systems; to master the principles of doubly-fed variable-speed variable-pitch wind turbine generator systems; to master the grid-connected control process of wind power generation systems.

　　Ability objective: To be able to correctly construct a small wind power generation system.

　　Qualification objective: To cultivate professional qualities of teamwork and diligence.

　　Learning priority: Composition of wind power generation systems.

　　Learning challenge: Construction and operation of wind power generation systems.

【Task analysis】

　　Modern wind power generation systems are composed of wind energy resources, wind turbine generator systems, control devices, energy storage devices, monitoring and display devices, user electric loads, etc. Among these, wind turbine generator systems are the main devices used for power generation, whose performance has a direct impact on system power generation efficiency.

　　This task relies on the equipment platform of the National Vocational College Skills Competition and involves various tasks, such as completing the installation of paddle blades of wind power generators, the wiring of wind power generation systems for data acquisition and motion control, and the commissioning and operation of wind power generation systems.

【Knowledge learning】

　　Wind power generation devices convert wind energy into electrical energy. They are a vivid demonstration of the 20th CPC National Congress on promoting a green and low-carbon mode of production and lifestyle in the technological reform of the national energy industry.

6.1.1 Composition of wind power generation systems

Modern wind power generation technology is a comprehensive high-tech engineering system involving aerodynamics, mechanical transmission, electrical machinery, automatic control, mechanics, materials, measurement, meteorology, environmental protection, and other disciplines. Modern wind power generation systems are composed of wind energy resources, wind turbine generator systems, control devices, energy storage devices, monitoring and display devices, user electric loads, etc. (some wind power generation systems are also equipped with standby power supply), as shown in Figure 6.1.

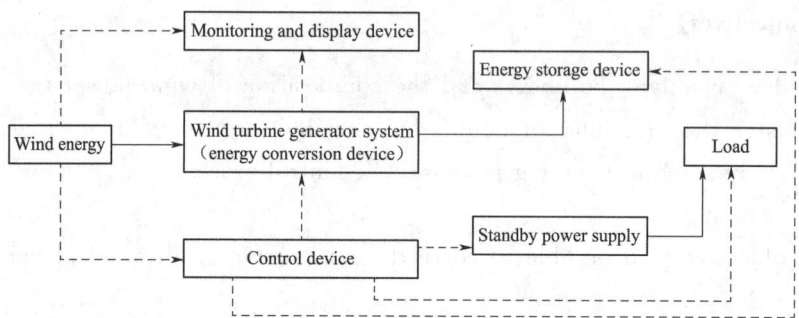

Figure 6.1 Composition of wind power generation systems

1. Wind turbine generator systems

Wind turbine generator systems are devices for energy conversion. They are a combination of mechanical, electrical and control devices that convert wind energy into electrical energy, generally consisting of wind turbines, generators, transmissions, control devices, etc. Internationally, wind turbine generator systems are generally classified into large (capacity above MW), medium (capacity above 100 kW to 1 MW), and small (capacity above 1 kW to 100 kW) according to the capacity of the generator systems. In China, wind turbine generator systems with a capacity of less than 1 kW are classified as micro.

In a wind turbine generator system, the wind turbine is a device that converts a portion of the kinetic energy of the air flowing through the rotating surface of the wind turbine into useful mechanical energy output from the shaft, i.e. a device that realizes the conversion of wind energy into mechanical energy. Depending on whether the rotation shaft of the wind turbine is horizontal or vertical in space, wind turbines can be divided into two categories: horizontal-shaft wind turbines and vertical-shaft wind turbines. Horizontal-shaft wind turbines have a direction-regu-

Design requirements for wind turbine generator systems

lating mechanism and wind turbines must be placed on the top of the tower; vertical-shaft wind turbines do not need a direction-regulating mechanism and can be placed near the ground.

Both types of wind turbines require a gear-increasing transmission device (i. e., a variable speed gearbox) to convert low-speed rotation of the wind turbine shaft to higher-speed rotation to connect with the generator shaft rotating at high speed. Variable speed gearboxes are excluded only in micro- and small-capacity wind turbine generator systems or in wind turbine generator systems with low-speed generators. Figures 6. 2 (a) and 6. 2 (b) show the connection and configuration of the wind turbine, gearbox and generator in horizontal-shaft and vertical-shaft wind turbine generator systems, respectively. Figure 6. 3 displays the structure of modern medium-sized horizontal-shaft wind power generators.

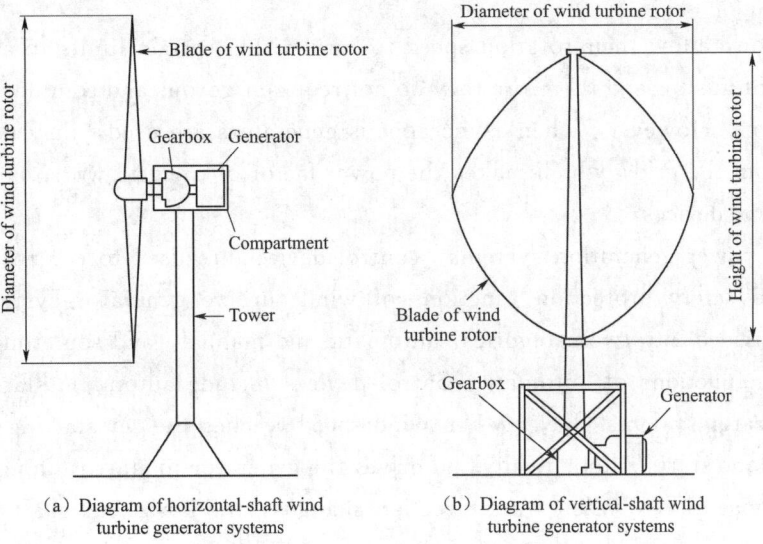

(a) Diagram of horizontal-shaft wind turbine generator systems

(b) Diagram of vertical-shaft wind turbine generator systems

Figure 6. 2 Wind turbine in wind turbine generator systems

Generators in wind turbine generator systems mostly consist of permanent magnet or self-excited AC generators for stand-alone small-capacity power generation systems, and synchronous or asynchronous (induction) generators for grid-connected power generation systems. Both synchronous and asynchronous generators used in wind power generation systems have their own advantages and disadvantages. When synchronous generators are used, generator voltage can be regulated by adjusting excitation, and reactive power can be supplied to the grid to improve the power factor of the grid. However, synchronous generators require a speed regulating device in the wind turbine to maintain constant-speed rotation (i. e., rotation at a synchronous speed), and they also require complex grid-connection equipment. Moreover, the transient stability of synchronous generators during wind gusts is also an issue that must be considered. Asynchronous generators are simpler

Project 6　Understanding Selecting Sites for Wind Turbine Generator Systems

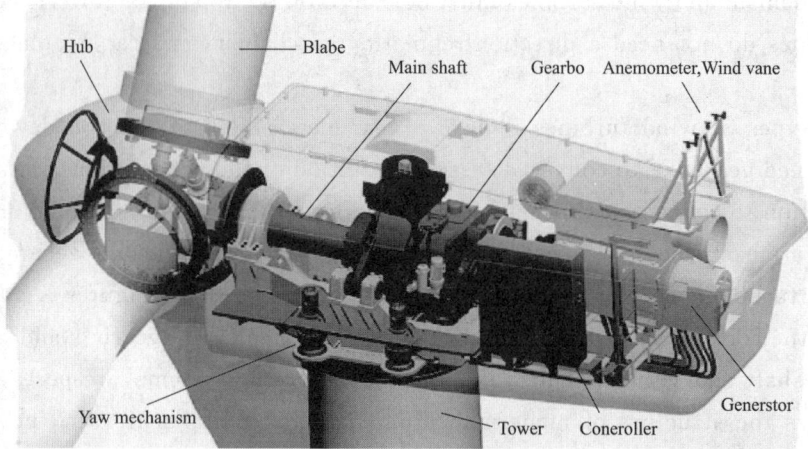

Figure 6.3　Structure schematic diagram of horizontal-shaft wind turbine generator systems

in construction, allow their rotation speed to vary within certain limits to absorb energy from transient gusts, and therefore they do not require rigorous and complex grid-connection equipment. However, when asynchronous generators are used, they need to obtain excitation from the grid, which makes the power factor of the grid worse.

2. Control devices

In wind power generation systems, control devices are used to control the working functions and safety protection functions of wind turbine generator systems. Control devices are divided into two categories: automatic and manual, and sometimes both.

Working functions of automatic control devices include automatic starting of wind turbine generator systems (i. e., when wind speed reaches the set starting wind speed, the wind turbine starts automatically and drives the generator to start running), automatic wind response (i. e., when wind direction changes, the horizontal-shaft wind turbine automatically tracks the change of wind direction), and automatic shutdown (i. e., when wind speed exceeds the maximum set wind speed, or when the rotation speed of the wind turbine exceeds the specified maximum rotation speed, the wind turbine automatically brakes and stops running). Depending on different structural types (horizontal-shaft or vertical-shaft wind turbines; synchronous or asynchronous generators) and operation modes (variable-speed or constant-speed running; stand-alone or grid-connected operation) of wind turbine generator systems, control devices of wind turbine generators also have the following control links. In grid-connected systems with synchronous generators, there is an automatic grid-connection control link; in systems with vertical-shaft Darrieus wind turbines, there must be a control link for electric starting (using an ancillary electric motor) or for pneumatic starting using a Savonius wind turbine, as Darrieus wind turbines cannot start automatically; in systems with horizontal-shaft wind turbines running at constant speed, there must be a pitch regulation control link, as constant speed has to be maintained in the presence of varying wind speeds. The pitch regulation control means that when the change in wind speed causes the rotation speed of the wind turbine to deviate from the specified value (i.e., rated rotation speed), the pitch controller operates, within a specified time period, via the action of hydraulic or electro-hydraulic control to change the attack angle of the wind turbine blade and regulate the output power of the wind turbine, so as to maintain the constant rotation speed of the wind turbine. Generally, wind speed and wind turbine rotation speed are used as action signals for the pitch regulation controller. There is another type of pitch regulation: The mechanical linkage mechanism is used via the change in the centrifugal force of the wind turbine blade at different rotation speeds to change the attack angle of the wind turbine blade, so as to maintain constant-speed operation. In stand-alone wind power generation systems, to maintain power balance of the system, and to make the AC generator's output electrical energy with constant voltage and frequency, there must be a control link for load regulation and energy-consuming load regulation. Generally, generator output frequency is used as load regulation signals.

Safety protection functions of automatic control devices include gale protection, wind turbine overspeed protection, generator overheating (high temperature rise) protection, overload protection of servo motors for wind response regulation, overload protection of oil pump motors for pitch regulation, anti-twisting protection of generator outgoing cables (not required for vertical-shaft wind turbine generator systems), compartment vibration protection, grid fault (grid voltage and frequency malfunction) protection, etc. All safety protection functions are aimed at stopping wind turbine generator systems from running (by applying brakes), automatically deviating from wind response direction (90° from wind direction; not required for vertical-shaft wind turbine generator systems), and disconnecting from loads or the power grid.

Automatic control devices use various sensor devices to obtain signals. Microprocessors or programmable controllers (PLCs) are used to determine, analyze, calculate and process signals. Then, relays, switches, servo motors, etc. are used to execute the control commands to complete the control functions.

The manual control link is only used in small wind power generation systems, and is only limited to some functions, such as manual start, shutdown, and emergency braking.

3. Monitoring and display devices

In wind power generation systems, monitoring and display devices are used to automatically display working conditions of the system, including the automatic display of wind speed, wind direction, rotation speed of wind turbines, rotation speed of the generators, generator voltage, current, frequency, power, cumulative power generation capacity, and cumulative running hours.

4. Energy storage devices

Wind energy is random and intermittent energy, and cannot be stored directly. Even in regions with abundant wind energy resources, energy storage devices must be equipped if wind power generation is the primary modality for obtaining electrical energy. During windy periods, excess wind energy is converted into other forms of energy and stored in energy storage devices; during windless periods, energy stored in energy storage devices is released and converted into electrical energy, so as to achieve stable and continuous power supply. Main modalities for energy storage in wind power generation systems are as follows:

(1) Storage by storage batteries. When wind turbine generator systems convert wind energy into electrical energy, power is first supplied to loads. Then, excess power is used to charge the storage batteries. Lead-acid batteries (also known as lead storage batteries) or nickel-cadmium batteries (also known as alkaline storage batteries) are often used in wind power generation systems.

(2) Flywheel energy storage. A flywheel is installed between the wind turbine and the generator to use the inertia of the flywheel as it rotates to store energy. When the wind is strong, wind energy is stored in the flywheel in the form of kinetic energy; when the wind is weak, kinetic energy stored in the flywheel is released, driving the generator to generate electricity. Generally, long flywheels are made of steel. In recent years, research is being conducted on using high-strength lightweight fiber materials to manufacture flywheels.

(3) Pumped energy storage. This energy storage method can be adopted at sites with suitable topographical conditions. When the wind is strong and the load requires less electrical energy, excess electrical energy generated by wind turbine generator systems is used to drive the pumping machine to pump water from a low place to a higher reservoir for storage; when there is no wind or the wind is weak, water in the higher reservoir is released to flow to the lower place and cause the hydraulic turbine to rotate, which in turn drives the generator to generate electricity.

(4) Compressed-air energy storage. When the electricity consumption load decreases, excess electrical energy provided by the wind turbine generator systems is used to drive an electric motor, which then drives the air compressor to compress the air and store it in an underground caverns or abandoned pits; when there is no wind or when the electricity consumption load reaches its peak, the stored compressed air is used as the driving force to drive the turbine and the generator to generate electricity.

(5) Hydrogen electrolysis energy storage. When the electricity consumption load decreases, excess electrical energy provided by wind turbine generator systems is used to electrolyze water, separating hydrogen and oxygen, and storing hydrogen; when the electricity consumption load increases or when there is no wind, hydrogen and oxygen are

reacted in fuel cells to generate electricity.

Currently, the most commonly used energy storage devices in wind power generation systems are storage batteries. Flywheel energy storage and hydrogen electrolysis energy storage are still in the experimental research phase. Pumped energy storage and compressed-air energy storage are technically mature, but are constrained by various conditions such as terrains and storage locations for water and compressed air.

6.1.2 Control and grid connection technology for large wind turbine generator systems

1. System structure

(1) Fixed-speed wind power generation system. In a dual-speed induction generator, the low-power, low-speed induction generator operates in regions with low wind speed, while the high-power, high-speed induction generator operates in regions with high wind speed. When the wind speed exceeds the rated wind speed, the blade's stall is used to reduce its wind energy utilization coefficient, thereby maintaining constant power. Since the wind turbine's rotational speed cannot change with the wind speed, its wind energy utilization coefficient often deviates from the maximum value, resulting in low wind energy utilization efficiency and causes the wind turbine to often operate in a low-efficiency state. Wind turbines produced in Denmark from the 1980s to the 1990s mainly adopted the fixed-speed wind power generation system, and China's 600kW and 750kW wind turbines also use this system.

(2) Variable-speed wind power generation system.

1) Doubly-fed, variable-speed, variable-pitch wind turbine

Figure 6.4 shows the working principle of a doubly-fed, variable-speed, variable-pitch wind turbine. The stator of the generator is directly connected to the grid, while the wound rotor is connected to the converter through slip rings. The converter is used to control the rotor winding current, adjusting the generator's output power and torque. Some systems employ the method of connecting an external resistor in the rotor circuit, such as the rotor current control structure (OptiSlip) used by Denmark's Vestas company to achieve variable-speed control.

The relationship between the stator current frequency, rotor speed, and rotor current frequency of a doubly-fed asynchronous generator is given by

$$f_1 = \frac{Pn_m}{60} + f_2 \tag{6.1}$$

where P is the number of pole pairs of the generator; n_m is the rotor speed of the generator, r/min; f_1 is the stator frequency, which is the grid frequency, Hz; f_2 is the rotor current frequency of the generator, Hz. It can be seen that when the wind speed variation cause the generator speed to change, adjusting the frequency f_2 of the excitation current into the generator rotor can maintain the constant output frequency f1on the stator side of

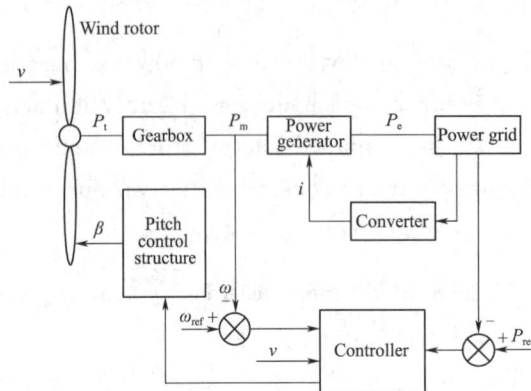

Figure 6.4　Working principle of doubly-fed, variable-speed, variable-pitch wind turbine

the generator.

The grid-side converter rectifies the grid AC power to DC power, and the rotor-side converter inverts the DC power back to AC power. The frequency of the inverted AC power is determined by the rotor speed of the generator, thus achieving a constant frequency output current on the stator side.

Doubly-fed induction generators operate within a limited variable-speed range, which is determined by the converter design. Typically, the converter capacity is 20%-30% of the generator's rated power, and the variable-speed range is larger than that of the speed regulation method using an external rotor resistor. Doubly-fed, variable-speed, variable-pitch wind turbines generate large current peaks; therefore, advanced protection measures are required to ensure the safe operation of the wind turbine and achieve low voltage ride through (LVRT).

2) Full-power converter with gearbox wind power generation system. The full-power converter with gearbox wind power generation system uses a full-power converter to achieve full-range variable speed. The generator can be an induction generator, synchronous generator, or permanent magnet generator, connected to the wind turbine through a gearbox and then to the grid through a converter.

During grid faults, the wind turbine is required to achieve LVRT, which is easily accomplished by the full-power converter wind power generation system. This system also has an excellent control performance, enabling multi-objective control, such as voltage stability control and reactive power control, making it widely applicable.

3) Full-Power Converter without Gearbox Wind Power Generation System. The full-power converter without gearbox wind power generation system eliminates the gearbox, by using a synchronous generator or permanent magnet generator designed as a multi-pole generator. Direct-drive permanent magnet generators feature simple transmission systems, high efficiency, and a robust control.

(3) Grid connection control process.

1) Grid connection process of fixed-speed wind power generation system: Uses thyristor soft cut-in. After the transition process ends, the converter is immediately disconnected, as it is not the core of the entire system.

2) Grid connection process of variable-speed wind power generation system: The converter, under variable wind speed conditions, converts the AC power with a variable frequency to an AC power with the same voltage frequency as the grid, achieving flexible

grid connection and maximizing wind energy capture by adjusting the wind turbine.

(4) Converters.

1) AC-AC converters: These have high conversion efficiency and can operate in four quadrants, allowing power to flow quickly in both directions. However, due to the use of phase control, the output voltage contains significant harmonics, especially at low frequencies, with high harmonic content and low power factor. Improved matrix AC-AC converters use fully controlled devices and advanced control strategies, with flexible and controllable output voltage, greatly reduced low-frequency harmonic content, and sinusoidal current form.

2) AC-DC-AC voltage source converters: These converters use diode uncontrolled rectification, causing input current distortion, increased harmonics, low input power factor, and unidirectional energy flow. The mature topology of the AC-DC-AC voltage source dual PWM converter main circuit has very low harmonic content and adjustable power factor. Through PWM control, four-quadrant operation of the converter is easily achieved, and the circuit and control system design is simpler than matrix converters. Therefore, they are widely used.

2. Wind turbine power control technology

(1) Wind turbine pitch control. Based on the installation structure of the wind turbine blades on the hub, wind turbines are divided into fixed-pitch and variable-pitch wind turbines. In fixed-pitch wind turbines, the blades are fixedly installed on the hub, and the blade pitch angle does not change with wind speed variation.

Variable-pitch wind turbines have blades connected to the hub in a non-rigid manner, allowing the blades to adjust their pitch around the blade's longitudinal axis, achieving different angles of attack relative to the wind direction. When the wind speed changes continuously, the blade's angle of attack remains optimal, enabling the wind turbine to maintain optimal conversion efficiency and achieve maximum output power at different wind speeds. When the wind speed exceeds the cut-out wind speed, the wind turbine stops, and the blades feather to protect the wind turbine. Compared to fixed-pitch wind turbines, variable-pitch wind turbines have stable output power above rated wind speed. The blades are thinner, with a simple structure, light weight, and low rotational inertia, making it easier to manufacture large wind turbines. Therefore, variable-pitch technology is commonly used in large wind turbines. Traditional pitch control methods mainly include electro-hydraulic servo and electric servo forms. To limit dynamic torque in the pitch mechanism the output pitch angle change is typically limited to 5°/s to 12°/s. For large wind turbines, the driving force required to change the pitch angle is relatively large, demanding high strength and positioning accuracy of the pitch mechanism.

The requirements for pitch bearings are also higher, involving specific materials and special processing techniques. For example, a company producing 1.5MW pitch bearings

Project 6　Understanding Selecting Sites for Wind Turbine Generator Systems

uses alloy materials, with bearing raceway quenching depth over 4.5mm, bearing inner and outer ring deformation of only 0.05mm, and radial runout of inner and outer gears relative to the raceway of less than $300\mu m$, and raceway surface roughness of $0.8\mu m$.

(2) Wind turbine yaw control. The yaw control system is a crucial part of the wind turbine control system, generally consisting of a yaw bearing, yaw drive, yaw brake, yaw counter, cable twist protection device, and yaw hydraulic circuit. It mainly serves two functions:

1) Cooperating with the wind turbine control system to keep the wind turbine blades always facing the wind, thereby improving the wind turbine's power generation efficiency.

2) Ensuring the safe operation of the wind turbine. Wind turbine yaw control systems are mainly divided into passive upwind yaw systems and active upwind yaw systems. The former is used in small standalone wind turbines, controlled by a tail vane, passively facing the wind when the wind direction changes; the latter is used in large grid-connected wind turbines, actively facing the wind, and controlled by signals from a downwind wind vane. Due to frequent wind direction changes, the nacelle must constantly rotate to keep the wind turbine blades facing the wind, thereby increasing wind energy capture rate. However, in practical applications, due to the low accuracy of anemometer and wind vane sensors, and because these sensors are often installed downwind and are subjected to interference, measurement errors are large and the wind turbine fails in achieving 100% wind facing, thereby reducing wind energy capture efficiency. Also, asymmetric loading on the wind turbine blades during operation causes vibration and accelerates blade fatigue. Thus, improving wind facing accuracy is essential.

(3) Wind turbine generator control. The stator winding of a doubly-fed asynchronous wind turbine generator is connected to the power grid, while the rotor winding is excited by an AC-DC-AC converter with adjustable frequency, phase, amplitude, and phase sequence, allowing the generator to operate at various wind speeds. Its speed adjusts with wind speed variations, ensuring the wind turbine generator always operates optimally, thereby enhancing wind energy utilization efficiency. Simultaneously, by controlling the current parameters fed into the rotor winding, and ensure that the stator output voltage and frequency remains constant, synchronizing with the grid's power factor and improving system stability.

(4) Power control strategy.

1) Wind speed-based wind turbine output power control method: When wind speed varies between cut-in wind speed and rated wind speed, variable-speed control is used to track the optimal power curve, obtaining maximum power. When wind speed varies between rated wind speed and cut-out wind speed, variable-pitch control is used to adjust the blade pitch angle, maintaining constant rated power. The advantage of this method is

that it selects different control methods based on wind speed, maximizing wind turbine power output, enhancing wind energy utilization efficiency, and improving wind turbine operational stability and reliability.

2) Wind vane and output power-based wind turbine yaw control method: When the absolute value of wind direction change exceeds 15°, the wind vane control method is used; when the absolute value is ≤15°, the power control method is used. Wind direction and speed changes inevitably and cause fluctuations in wind turbine output power, detected by power meters. Yaw control is only performed when the wind direction changes, and the wind speed changes are considered as interference signals. The power control method includes three conditions: counterclockwise rotation, clockwise rotation, and stopping in place. This method shortens wind turbine facing time, improves wind facing accuracy, wind energy utilization efficiency, and wind turbine lifespan.

3. Low voltage ride through (LVRT) technology

Non-permanent short-circuit faults in the power system cause grid voltage drops, posing significant risks. For example, in 2008, minor grid faults in a region in Northeast China caused simultaneous disconnection of 400MW of wind turbines within a 200km radius multiple times. Similar incidents also occurred in GansuYumen Wind Farm, Gansu Anxi CGN Daliangzi Wind Farm, and Ningxia Helanshan Wind Farm. Wind farms near electrified railways also experienced most or all wind turbines disconnecting when electric locomotives passed by.

Wind turbines must not disconnect from the grid during faults and must provide voltage and reactive power support to the system, preventing damage to the wind turbine's gear transmission mechanism and rotor power electronics converters during faults.

Considering the safety of wind turbines and grid code requirements, the following requirements are proposed for wind turbines:

1) During a three-phase ground short-circuit fault (voltage drop to 15% of rated voltage), the connection between the wind turbine's step-up transformer high-voltage side and the grid must maintain grid connection for at least 625ms LVRT capability;

2) For asymmetrical faults (e.g., single-phase ground short-circuit, two-phase short-circuit, or two-phase ground faults), wind turbines must withstand and ride through low voltage until the circuit breaker clears the fault.

Developed countries' wind power operators have begun requiring newly procured wind turbines to have LVRT capability. At the same time, wind turbine manufacturers have implemented various improvement measures to enhance the LVRT capability of wind turbines, and these improvements have been tested by specialized institutions to ensure smooth product sales. However, many manufacturers rely on experience to increase the capacity of the rotor-side converter and the static torque margin of the gearbox, transferring electrical and voltage stress to mechanical stress on the gearbox and shaft. Due to the fatigue life cycle of the gearbox and shaft, they will not be immediately damaged during testing, but this method will inevitably pose potential hazards to wind turbines.

【Task implementation】

Ⅰ. Task preparation

1 competition equipment platform, 1 slotted screwdriver, 1 philips screwdriver, 1 wire stripping plier, 1 U-shaped crimping pliers, 1 tube-shaped crimping pliers, 1 multimeter, 1 copy of record sheet for power-up inspection, 1 copy of record sheet for wind power generation system commissioning and a number of wires.

Task 6.1 Related implementation charts

Ⅱ. Task content and procedures

Task: Wind power system installation and commissioning

Task content: Complete the installation and commissioning of the wind power system.

Task procedures:

(1) Complete the installation of the wind turbine blades and tail vane.

(2) Complete the preparation of the connecting wires for the wind power system.

(3) According to the wiring diagram, complete the wiring and connection of the wind power supply control unit.

(4) Complete the wiring and connection of the PLC according to its configuration.

(5) Complete the wiring and connection of the relay group according to the configuration diagram of the relay group.

(6) Complete the system power-up inspection and correctly commission and operate the wind power system.

Ⅲ. Skill requirements

(1) Correctly use the multimeter range to measure different parameters, ensuring proper operation without short circuits or incorrect measurements.

(2) When inserting U-shaped cold-pressed terminals into the terminal block, ensure the U-shaped part is fully inserted with the front side facing outward.

(3) Follow the standard procedure to complete equipment installation and fixation, check the connection lines, and inspect grounding lines. Ensure strict standards without any omissions or errors.

(4) When inserting wire markers, all vertically oriented markers should be read from the far end to the connection port, and all horizontally oriented markers should be read from left to right.

(5) When crimping the wire terminals, insert all stripped wire strands into the terminal sleeve completely. Use the crimping tool to crimp the wire terminal with the crimping mark on the bottom (reverse side) of the terminal sleeve. After crimping, ensure no

wire strands are exposed.

Ⅳ. Task results, appraisal and evaluation

(1) The system is correctly commissioned and successfully connected to the grid; the data screen runs correctly; operation data are recorded (accounting for 90%).

(2) The operator exhibits good professional quality during the operation process and follows 7S management model (accounting for 10%).

【Exercises】

1. What equipment in the wind power system is responsible for energy conversion?

2. What are the characteristics of LVRT (Low Voltage Ride Through) technology in wind turbine systems?

3. What power control technologies are available for wind turbines?

Task 6.2 Selecting Wind Turbine Generator Systems

【Learning objectives】

Knowledge objective: To master the technical parameters of doubly-fed wind turbine generator systems and understand the products and characteristics of direct-drive wind turbine converters.

Ability objective: To be able to select wind turbine generator systems according to the requirements.

Qualification objective: To cultivate national pride, foster dedication, professional commitment and willingness to contribute.

Learning priority: Major technical parameters of wind turbine generator systems.

Learning challenge: Criteria for selecting wind turbine generator systems.

【Task analysis】

The selection of wind turbines should consider local wind energy resources, climate characteristics, terrain conditions, and topographic features to choose the most cost-effective model, ensuring optimal power generation and benefits over the entire life cycle of the wind farm. Based on advanced technology and reliable operation, the selected wind turbine generator systems should be economically feasible. It is necessary to calculate the annual power generation of the wind farm based on its wind energy resource conditions and the selected wind turbine generator systems to determine the best comprehensive indicators.

This task relies on the smart new energy simulation planning software platform to complete the selection design of wind turbine generator systems given the wind farm's demand indicators.

Project 6　Understanding Selecting Sites for Wind Turbine Generator Systems

【Knowledge learning】

China's wind turbine equipment manufacturing technology has made significant progress, with a series of domestically produced turbines installed across the country. The growth rate of China's installed wind power capacity ranks first in the world.

6.2.1　Doubly-fed wind turbine generator systems

Table 6.1　Main technical parameters of doubly-fed wind turbine generator systems

Technical parameters	Model	
	Domestic product WD77-1500	Foreign product MD70
Unit	Variable pitch and variable speed type	Variable pitch and variable speed type
Pitch control Mechanism	Full wingspan variable pitch speed regulation	Full wingspan independent variable pitch
Rated Power/kW	1000	1500
Cut-in wind speed/(m/s)	2.5	3.0
Rated wind speed/(m/s)	12.5	12.8
Cut-out wind speed/(m/s)	25	25
Impeller diameter/m	60.62	70
Impeller rotation speed/(r/min)	12 – 21.5	10.6 – 19
Rated voltage/V	690	690
Grid-connection method	IGBT converter synchronous grid-connection	IGBT converter synchronous grid-connection
Power factor adjustment	Converter compensation (inductive, capacitive)	Converter compensation (inductive, capacitive)
Safety level	IEC IIA	IEC IIA

1. Key technologies and technical parameters

(1) Key technologies. Doubly-fed, variable speed constant frequency wind turbine generators adopt a 3-blade, horizontal axis, upwind, active yaw mode, with components meeting ISO 9001 and IEC quality standards. Key technologies include:

1) Integrated design technology, system reliability design, lightning protection design, and suitability design for various harsh environments.

2) Blade design, manufacturing, testing technology, full span pitch, speed loop, position loop, pitch angle, and flexible power flow adjustment technology.

3) Gearbox design, manufacturing, and testing technology.

4) Doubly-fed asynchronous generator design, manufacturing, and testing technology.

5) Converter and control system design technology, achieving seamless grid connec-

tion through variable speed control.

6) Selection and technical requirements for other main components, processing and manufacturing technology.

7) Dynamic and static load calculation, structural strength, fatigue, and dynamic analysis of the entire machine and components.

8) Multi-point online vibration monitoring, remote monitoring of the unit, vibration suppression through control excitation damping, thereby optimizing operational performance.

9) Overall design technology, involving key component structural parameters, reliability, load strength analysis, including rotor, drive system, generator and converter system, pitch system, yaw system, nacelle, tower, hydraulic system, cooling system, and coupling.

(2) Main technical parameters. Table 6.1 lists the main technical parameters of domestically designed 1.0MW and a foreign 1.5MW doubly-fed constant speed wind turbine generators.

2. Doubly-fed generators

(1) Characteristics. Doubly-fed generators are light in weight, low in cost, stable in operation, have good power factor adjustment controllability, and a wide speed range in the generating state. For example, the technical characteristics of the YSBFF series doubly-fed generators produced in China include:

1) Adoption of distributed winding technology to effectively improve output waveform quality.

2) Embedded stator structure, reducing stator weight by about 20%.

3) Rolling bearing structure and bearing insulation technology to improve bearing reliability.

4) Slip ring structure to enhance reliability.

5) Application of Class C insulation technology.

6) The main engine adopts IC 666 cooling structure, improving ventilation structure, enhancing cooling efficiency, and reducing generator temperature rise by 5~10℃. Improved production processes reduce weight and manufacturing costs by 10%~15%, improving the generator's low-speed operation safety.

7) Improved "three-proof" (waterproof, dustproof, anti-corrosion) coating formula suitable for different coastal wind farms in China.

8) Optimized electromagnetic scheme, increasing generator efficiency to over 97.2%.

(2) Main technical parameters. Table 6.2 lists the main technical parameters of both the 2MW doubly-fed generators designed and produced in China, and a 2MW doubly-fed generator produced by a foreign company.

Table 6.2   Main technical parameters of the 2MW doubly-fed generators

Technical parameters	Model	
	YSBFF 2.0-16	SIEMENS 2MW
Waveform distortion Rate/%	Constant speed 2.5	Constant speed 3.1
Insulation class	C	H
Cooling method	IC 666	IC 616
Noise/dB(A)	98	97
Vibration/(mm/a)	1.2	1.5
Efficiency/%	96.72	96.75
Power factor	$-0.9 \sim +0.9$	$-0.9 \sim +0.9$
Maximum torque/Times	2.1	2
Mass/kg	12500	13900

6.2.2 Direct-drive wind turbine generator systems

Here we mainly introduce the direct-drive wind turbine converter.

(1) Characteristics. Domestic and foreign manufacturers of direct-drive wind turbine converters include ABB, SIEMENS, AMSC, CSR Zhuzhou, Jiuzhou, XJ Electric, and Hefei Sunshine. Their technical characteristics are:

1) Flexible grid connection control: dynamically adjusts reactive power output based on grid voltage changes and grid scheduling requirements, improving grid support capability and stability.

2) Variable step adaptive maximum power tracking technology, which effectively eliminates maximum power point deviation and improves algorithm stability.

3) Grid-side converter adopts phase-shift control and optimized FV technology with minimum switching loss, doubling the equivalent switching frequency and reducing switching ripple in the grid-connected current.

4) Unique active damping technology suppresses filter circuit resonance, reducing grid-connected current waveform distortion (THD less than 3%).

5) Dynamic Power Balance Control Method for Master-Slave Control to Address the "Circulating Current" Issue in Converter Parallel Operation.

6) Low voltage ride-through capability: the converter continues to operate for 350ms without tripping off the grid when the system voltage drops to 1%.

(2) Main technical parameters. Table 6.3 lists the main technical parameters of direct-drive wind turbine converters produced in China and a foreign direct-drive wind turbine converter.

Table 6.3 Main technical parameters of direct-drive wind turbine converters

Technical parameters	Domestic products	Foreign products	Product features comparison
Power devices	SKIIP	IGBT	Domestic products use highly integrated power modules
Topological structure	Dual PWM	Dual PWM	Consistent
Dc bus/V	1100	1100	Consistent
Switching Frequency /kHz	3, Phase parallel	3	Domestic products have twice the effective switching frequency under unchanged switching loss conditions
Efficiency/%	>97	>97.5	Same magnitude
Generator side control	Vector control, direct torque control, controllable power	Vector control, direct torque control, controllable power	Consistent
Maximum power tracking	Variable step size, adaptive control	Look-up table, fixed step size hill-climbing method	Domestic products reduce dependency on impeller power characteristics, and eliminate power point deviation
Grid side control	Four-quadrant vector control, real-time grid detection, rapid dynamic reactive support	Four-quadrant vector control	Domestic products have better grid support performance
Filter circuit	LCL filter, active damping	LCL filter, active damping	With the same filtering effect, domestic products eliminate passive damping branch losses, improving efficiency
Thd/%	<3	<3	Consistent
Maximum Reactive Power/MVar	1.5	0.83	Domestic products have an advantage
Low voltage ride-through	15% residual voltage maintained for 350ms	20% residual voltage maintained for 500ms	Domestic products have an advantage
Cooling system	Water cooling	Air cooling or water cooling	Comparable
Operating ambient temperature/℃	−30~+50	0~+40	Comparable

6.2.3 Methods and processes for selecting wind turbine generator systems

1. Principles for selecting models

(1) Selecting suitable safety level units. Table 6.4 lists the basic parameters for defining wind turbine classes according to the IEC61400-1 third edition standard.

Project 6 Understanding Selecting Sites for Wind Turbine Generator Systems

Table 6.4　　　　Basic parameters for defining wind turbine classes

Classes	I	II	III	S
v_{ref}/(m/s)	50	42.5	37.5	Decided by the designer
A I_{ref}/(m/s)		0.16		
B I_{ref}/(m/s)		0.14		
C I_{ref}/(m/s)		0.12		

In this table, various parameter values refer to the hub height values.

v_{ref} represents the 50-year reference wind speed 10-minute average value, commonly referred to as maximum wind speed. (ve50＝1.4 v_{ref}, ve50 is the 50-year wind speed with a 3-second average value, commonly referred to as extreme wind speed.) A represents high turbulence intensity characteristic value; B represents moderate turbulence intensity characteristic value; C represents low turbulence intensity characteristic value; I_{ref} represents the average value of turbulence intensity at a wind speed of 15m/s.

(2) Selecting reliable units. Design reliability, manufacturing reliability, and operational reliability.

1) Design and design calculation, whether standard, such as performance calculation, load calculation, fatigue life, etc., should generally have design certification.

2) Manufacturing process, product testing, especially the static and dynamic test results should generally have product certification.

3) After commercial production, operational reliability is generally measured by failure rate and availability indicators.

(3) Power generation capacity. The selected unit should be based on the specific wind farm's wind conditions and wind frequency distribution, mainly looking at the operating power curve and full load hours, to ensure certain economic benefits.

(4) Good usage and maintenance performance. ①Easy to use and maintain; ②Full life cycle spare parts and accessories should meet requirements.

(5) Selecting units for specific wind farm climate conditions.

Climate conditions such as low temperature, ice accretion, sandstorm, thunderstorm, etc. should be considered.

(6) Selecting units for specific wind farm terrain conditions

Terrain conditions should be considered while selecting the unit, such as traffic, installation conditions, and ensure whether the unit meets the requirements of complex mountain terrain.

(7) Cost-effective units

Considering the entire life cycle, after the specified payback period, calculate various costs and measure the cost-effectiveness by the amount of internal income.

(8) Market matured commercial units, fully considering actual operating conditions.

2. Basic requirements for unit selection

(1) Quality certification system requirements: wind turbine manufacturers must have ISO9001 series quality management system certification.

(2) Power curve requirements: the power curve is one of the most important curves reflecting the power output performance of a wind turbine.

(3) Manufacturer performance review: performance is an important indicator to judge the level of a wind turbine manufacturer.

(4) Special environmental requirements: ice accretion, snow accumulation, low temperature, thunderstorm, sandstorm, and other special environments can affect wind turbines.

3. Methods for selecting units

The selection of wind turbine generators involves choosing both the single unit capacity and the model.

(1) Selection of single unit capacity.

According to the current situation of the wind turbine market locally and abroad, and the installed capacity of domestic wind farms, wind turbines can generally be divided into three levels by unit capacity: ①kW-level units (less than 1000kW); ②MW-level units: currently, 1.5 - 2MW units have become the mainstream mature model in China; ③Multi-MW-level units: mainly installed in offshore wind farms, not yet widely commercialized.

(2) Selection of model. Conduct preliminary selection based on the development trend of wind turbine generators locally and abroad, the current types of installed capacity in China, manufacturing level, technology maturity, and combined with wind resource conditions, topography, installation conditions.

4. Basic selection process

Basic selection process is shown in Figure 6.5.

For specific wind farms, the selection of units also needs to consider the following factors: the safety level of the units should meet the requirements of the project's extreme wind conditions; the rotor diameter should match the project's annual average wind speed; the hub height should consider the project's wind shear index; based on the project's climate conditions and ter-

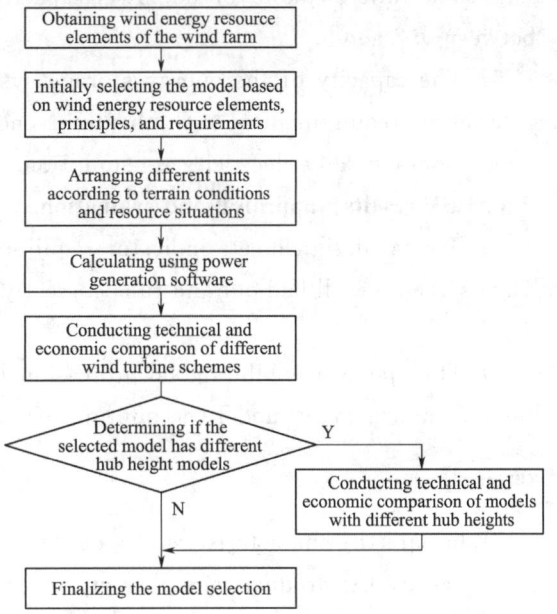

Figure 6.5 Basic selection process diagram for wind turbine generators

rain conditions, choose suitable units.

【Task implementation】

Ⅰ. Task preparation

1 software platform for intelligent simulation and planning of new energy, 1 set of computer mainframe and monitor.

Ⅱ. Task content and procedures

Task 6.2 Related implementation charts

Task: Simulation wind turbine generator selection and design

Task content: Complete the selection and design of the simulation wind turbine generator.

Task procedures:

(1) Complete the design of the simulation island model.

(2) Set the wind farm scale indicators and analyze the wind farm resources.

(3) Complete the analysis of the spacing layout of the wind turbine generators.

(4) Complete the analysis of the rated power of the wind turbine generators and fill out the selection data form.

(5) Complete the comprehensive planning and optimization of the wind farm and export the results table.

Ⅲ. Skill requirements

(1) Reasonable layout design for various types of energy.

(2) The ratio of photovoltaic power capacity to wind power capacity (power) should be between 0.2 and 5.

(3) The capacity of the energy storage system should be appropriately set to meet load variation requirements, with the total energy storage capacity being less than 10 times the average daily electricity consumption.

Ⅳ. Task results, appraisal and evaluation

(1) System design meets indicator requirements; the system operates successfully; the data screen is well laid out and runs correctly; operation data are recorded (accounting for 90%).

(2) The operator exhibits good professional quality during the operation process and follows 7S management model (accounting for 10%).

【Exercises】

1. What are the characteristics of a doubly-fed wind turbine?
2. What are the products and characteristics of direct-drive wind turbine converters?
3. What is the process for selecting wind turbine generators?

项目 7　调节与安装风力发电机组

任务 7.1　掌握风轮机的调向、调速和保护装置

【学习目标】

　　知识目标：掌握风轮机的调向、调速和保护装置的组成及其功能。
　　能力目标：能检测与处理小型风机调速偏航系统。
　　素质目标：培养专注认真、团队协作的职业品质。
　　重点：风机调速、保护装置的功能。
　　难点：风机调速故障的检测与处理。

【任务分析】

　　风轮机的调向装置、调速装置和保护装置是风力发电系统的重要组成部分，对风力发电机组的正常稳定运行具有重要作用，是系统不可缺少的部分。
　　依托全国职业院校技能大赛设备平台，完成风机调速偏航系统的故障检测与处理。

【知识学习】

7.1.1　风轮机的调向装置

　　风轮机的调向装置是指当风向改变时能随时调整风轮机的风轮叶片旋转平面与风向（即气流方向）的相对位置，使风轮机在正常工作时基本上迎着风向（即是使风轮叶片旋转平面与气流方向相垂直）的机构。众所周知，当风轮叶片旋转平面与风向正好垂直时，风轮机的机械输出功率最大，因而可以更充分地利用风能。因此调向装置又称为迎风装置。调向装置是水平轴风轮机不可缺少的装置之一，垂直轴风轮机则不需要调向装置。水平轴风轮机中常用的调向装置，其结构依风轮机功率的大小有多种不同型式，如尾舵（亦称尾翼）、尾车（亦称侧风轮）和伺服电动机驱动的齿轮传动调向装置等。

　　1. 尾舵

　　尾舵多用于小型风轮机中，尾舵由翼柄和翼叶组成，如图 7.1 所示，图中 L 代表翼柄长度（即从风轮叶片旋转面到尾舵最末端的距离），翼叶的形状可以有各种不同的形状，图 7.2 表示几种面积相同而形状各异的翼叶图形。

　　尾舵翼柄的长度与翼叶的面积应当能够保证当风向偏侧时（一般按 10°~20°），尾舵上

由于所受到的风压作用而产生的力矩能够足以使风轮机头转动，从而使风轮转到迎风位置。

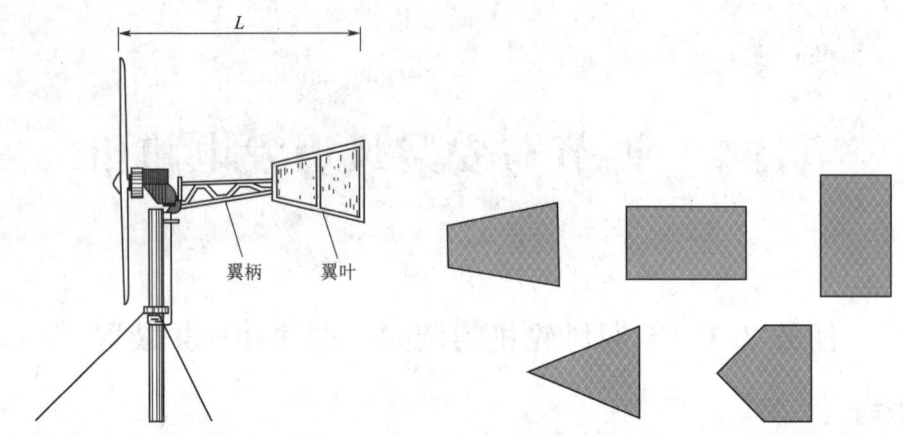

图 7.1　水平轴风轮机的尾舵　　　　图 7.2　常见的尾舵翼叶形状

根据经验，在采用尾舵作为调向装置的风轮机中，尾舵翼柄的 Y 度取与风轮叶片直径相等；而翼叶的面积可取为风轮叶片旋转面积的 1/8 左右。尾舵翼柄一般皆制成与地面平行，但也有将尾舵翼柄做成上翘式的。翼叶一般多由金属材料制成。

2. 尾车

在容量大于 15～20kW 的风轮机中，经常采用尾车型式的调向装置。所谓尾车，是指安装在风轮机机舱侧面的小风轮，其转轴与风轮机主轴相垂直（也即其旋转面与主风轮旋转面互相垂直）。当主风轮叶片旋转平面与风向垂直时，尾车旋转面正好平行于风向，因而侧风轮并不旋转；当主风轮偏离风向时（即主风轮叶片旋转面与风向不垂直时），则侧风轮在风力的作用下旋转，并通过蜗轮蜗杆的传动让主风轮机头旋转，使毛风轮旋转面重新达到迎风位置。

3. 伺服电动机驱动的齿轮传动调向装置

在中大型风轮机中多采用由伺服驱动电动机驱动的齿轮传动装置来进行调向，如图 7.3 所示。伺服电动机在风向标及与风轮主轴联接的测速发电机给出的信号控制下转动，电动机带动齿轮传动装置，当大齿轮盘转动时，即可实现调向。由于伺服电动机可以正反转，因此可以实现两个方向的调向。为了避免伺服电动机连续不断地工作，一般规定当风向偏离风轮主轴±10°～±15°时，调向机构才开始动作。此外，调向速度还受到风轮陀螺效应引起的应力限制，一般为 1°/s。

7.1.2　风轮机的调速装置

风轮机的调速装置是用来调节风轮

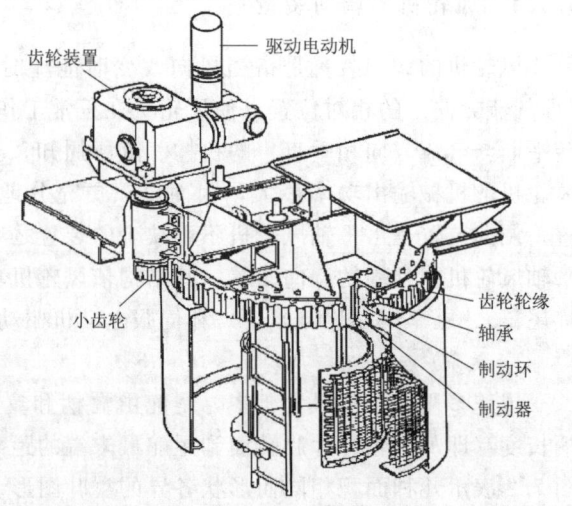

图 7.3　伺服电动机的齿轮传动调向装置

机转速的机构。由前述风轮机的功率-转速特性可知,当风速变化时,风轮机的转速也将变化。风轮机转速的变化将导致发电机输出电压及频率的变化,这对风力发电机无论是向用电负荷供电或是向电网送电,皆是不允许的。因此必须有风轮机的调速机构,使之在变化的工作风速范围内起到调节风轮机功率,从而达到稳定风轮机转速的作用。当然,在高风速时它还可以起到限速保护的作用。

风轮机的调速方法及装置有多种多样,常用的有以下几种:

(1) 风轮偏侧调速。这种调速方法的依据是当风速变化使风轮转速超过额定值时,借助一定的机械机构动作,使风轮叶片的旋转平面及时偏离垂直迎风位置(即偏侧),使风轮从风能中吸收的功率减少,从而使转速减小到规定的额定值。

使风轮偏侧的方法有两种:

1) 借助于一个与风轮机机体固定联接的侧翼及机体与尾舵间的连接弹簧。其工作原理如图 7.4 所示。所谓侧翼,是指在风轮叶片旋转平面之后机体上安装的一个叶片,该叶片处于风轮旋转面之外,并与风轮旋转面平行,而其叶柄则与地面平行。因其位于风轮机机身一侧,故称侧翼。

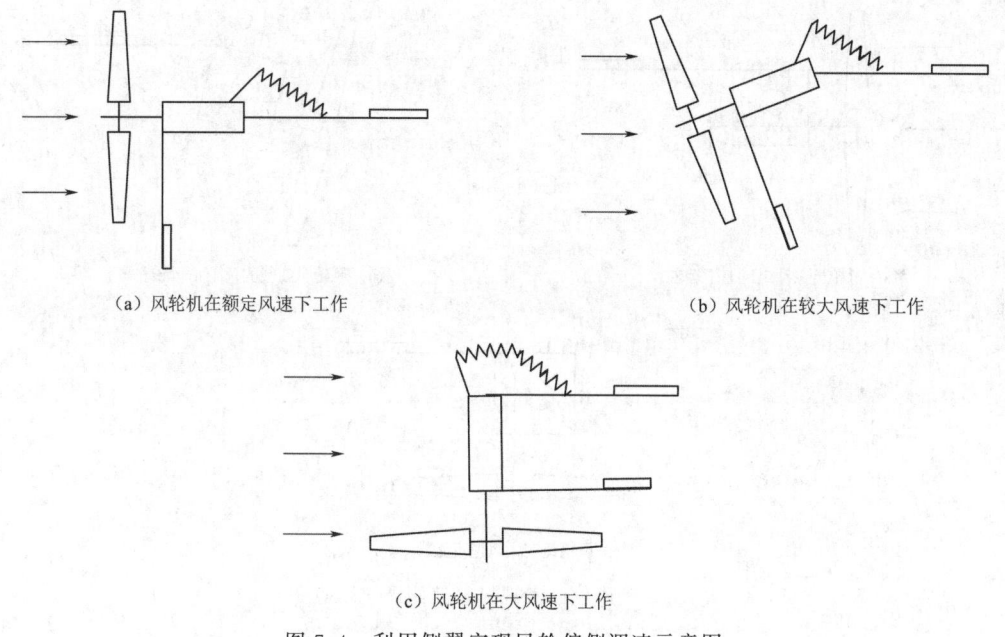

(a) 风轮机在额定风速下工作　　　　　(b) 风轮机在较大风速下工作

(c) 风轮机在大风速下工作

图 7.4　利用侧翼实现风轮偏侧调速示意图
(向南走线 T 接 10kV 平丝线)

图 7.4 (a) 表示风轮在额定风速下工作的情况,此时由于风轮机尾舵的作用,风轮机的风轮旋转平面正对准风向。风轮机的侧翼虽然也受到一定风力的作用企图使风轮偏侧,但由于弹簧的作用(拉力),使之不能动作。当风速大于额定风速时,风轮的转速升高,同时侧翼受到的风压也比以前增大,风轮必定要偏转一定的角度到有侧翼的一边,如图 7.4 (b) 所示。这样,由于风轮旋转平面与风向不再处于垂直方向,风轮机的功率减小,风轮转速也就跟着减小下来。当然,此时弹簧被拉开的程度要较前增大了。当风速一旦减小,则它又会将风轮拉回到先前的位置(即风轮旋转面与风向垂直的位置)。由此可

以看出，正确地选择弹簧的拉力及侧翼面积的大小是影响调速精确性的重要因素，通常根据试验确定。当大风时，则风轮旋转平面处于图 7.4（c）所示的位置，风轮叶片旋转平面与风向平行，风轮停止转动，从而达到在大风时对风轮机的保护作用。

2）利用偏心的办法使风轮实现偏侧以达到调速的目的，其工作原理如图 7.5 所示。所谓偏心，是指风轮机的主轴与风轮机机舱座下的垂直转轴不相交（也即不在同一平面内），如图 7.5 所示，在带动机舱座旋转的垂直立轴与风轮水平方向的主轴间有一定的距离 D，此距离即称为偏心距。当风轮机在额定风速下运转时，虽然此时风轮由于风的作用所受到的正面压力对机枪座下垂直轴（图 7.5 中的 A）有一个力矩的作用（此力矩的力臂就等于偏心距的距离），但由于风轮机尾舵的定向与平衡作用，风轮并不偏侧，风轮旋转平面处于迎风位置，如图 7.5（a）所示。当风向不变而风速增大时，由于风压面产生的对风轮的压力增强，因而对垂直轴的力矩也随着增大，风轮就会产生偏侧，如图 7.5（b）所示。当风轮偏侧后，由于风轮叶片旋转面不再处于迎风位置，风轮机的功率减小，转速也跟着减小下来。当风速非常高时，风轮机叶片的旋转面将偏侧 90°，处于与风向平行的位置，如图 7.5（c）所示，也即是处于停转的状态。

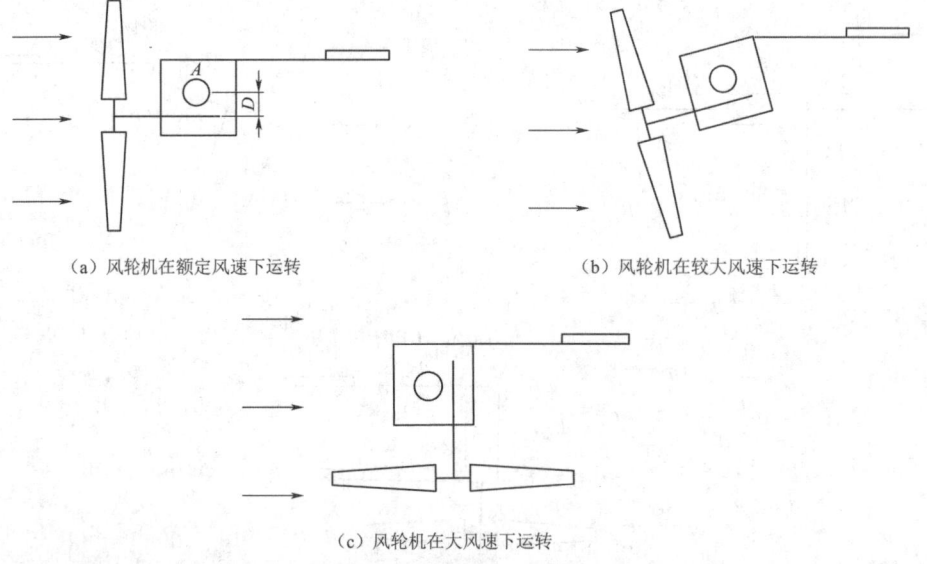

(a) 风轮机在额定风速下运转　　　(b) 风轮机在较大风速下运转

(c) 风轮机在大风速下运转

图 7.5　利用偏心实现风轮偏侧调速示意图

上述的风轮偏侧调速方法适用于具有固定桨距叶片的风轮机。

（2）改变风轮叶片桨距调速。众所周知，任何一种翼型风轮机的桨叶（叶片）在风力的作用下都同时受到升力与阻力两种作用。升力推动叶片在风轮平面内旋转，而阻力则起阻止的作用。改变风轮叶片桨距调速就是使叶片可以根据要求绕叶柄转过一个角度来改变叶片的冲角，从而改变叶片的升力与阻力，如升力增大则转速增加，如阻力增大则转速降低。所以这种调速方式又称为桨叶（叶片）偏侧调速法。

风力发电机组变速恒频控制系统　第2部分：试验方法

要使旋转的桨叶能够绕叶柄自动偏侧可以通过不同的方式来实现。现代中大型风轮机多是借助液压控制系统来实现桨叶绕叶柄的自动偏侧，但对中小型风轮机较多的还是利用离心力的办法。由动力学知道，物体在高速旋转时，其离心力也较大，而且离心力和运动物体的质量成正比。因此如果在风轮叶片上附加固定某一定的重物，或者就借助叶片本身的重力，那么当叶片高速旋转时，就有一定的离心力产生。这样，如果使此离心力与装设在风轮上的一些可使叶片偏侧的机械部件（如弹簧、杠杆等）发生联系，只要配合恰当，对应于不同的风轮转速，就可使叶片自动改变本身的冲角，从而改变叶片上受到的升力与阻力，达到调速的目的。

7.1.3 风轮机保护装置

当风轮机工作时，如果风速超过风轮机的工作风速范围，或是发电机突然甩掉负荷，则都会导致风轮机超速，甚至造成风轮机的损坏。因此风轮机都装有能自动防止风轮机超速的保护装置，以达到限制风轮超速的目的。限制风轮超速的方法主要有两种，一是利用空气动力阻力的方法；二是设法减小风轮的迎风面积（也即是使风轮偏侧）。水平轴风轮机的保护装置有叶尖阻尼板、扰流器、顺桨机构以及风轮侧偏或上仰机构等；垂直轴风轮机的保护装置主要是阻尼板。

（1）叶尖阻尼板。叶尖阻尼板是安装在水平轴风轮叶片尖部的阻尼装置。当风轮正常运转时，它与叶片的作用相同，能产生升力；当风轮超速时，则围绕风轮叶片纵向轴线转90°角，与风轮旋转平面成垂直位置，故能产生阻力，从而使风轮转速降下来。

（2）扰流器。扰流器是安装在风轮叶片上距叶尖叶片长度的1/3位置上的阻尼装置。当风轮正常运转时，扰流器的两个端面分别与叶片上下表面重合，当风轮超速时，则张开延伸到叶片外面，这样由于它与风轮旋转平面垂直，产生了阻力，从而使风轮转速降下来。

上述两种阻尼装置的动作一般靠的是风轮转动时的离心力，也有根据风轮转速信号由液压传动系统或机械传动系统使阻尼装置动作的。前者称为被动式的，后者称为主动式的。

（3）顺桨机构。所谓顺桨是指风轮叶片弦长方向与风向一致，也即风轮叶片的冲角趋近零升力的状态。风轮叶片顺桨也属于风轮变桨距控制的一部分，即根据风速或转速的信号，通过液压变距或机械变距机构来实现。风轮的顺桨既可用在大风或甩负荷时的紧急停车起保护作用，也可用于风轮机正常运行时的停机。

（4）风轮侧偏或上仰机构。水平轴风轮机也有利用风轮偏侧机构、风轮上仰机构或安装在风轮机传动轴上的紧急制动闸来实现超速保护。关于风轮偏侧的方法前面已介绍过。风轮上仰机构一般只用于小型风轮机中。紧急制动闸在小型风轮机中分手动和自动制动两种，两者皆是利用抱闸刹车的原理。图7.6表示这两种抱闸刹车的原理。

图7.6（a）是手动停车，人手向下拉刹车绳，则制动刹车带将刹车鼓紧紧抱住而实现停车；图7.6（b）是自动停车，当风速超过限定的最大风速时，此时刹车风板被大风有力地推动（如图中箭头所示方向），从而带动了刹车杠杆，而杠杆则拉动刹车绳向下并使制动刹车带紧紧抱住刹车鼓而实现自动停车。刹车风板面积的大小与限定的最大风速值之间的配合关系可通过试验方法确定。

在中型或大型水平轴风轮机中的制动闸是由液压供油系统、制动卡钳以及安装在风轮主轴上的制动盘组成。当大风超速时，由液压驱动的制动卡钳动作将制动盘卡住。从而实现风轮机的自动停车。

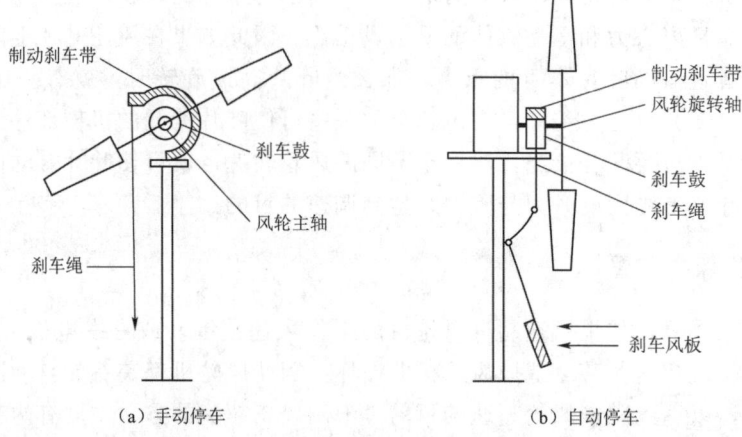

图 7.6 小型风轮机紧急制动闸示意图

（5）阻尼板。垂直轴风轮机（例如达里厄型）的保护装置主要是安装在风轮传动轴上就紧急制动闸及风轮叶片上的阻尼板。垂直轴风轮机的制动闸系统与水平轴的制动闸系统原理相同，但除用液压驱动外，有时也用电驱动方式。阻隔板是靠离心力动作的，当大风超速时，离心力增大到足以克服阻尼板背面的弹簧拉紧力时，则阻尼板打开，产生阻力，从而使风轮转速降低。一般达里厄风轮有 2 个或 3 个叶片，因此这种风轮机上可有 2 个或 3 个阻尼板（一般每个叶片上装 1 个阻尼板），但每个阻尼板的弹簧拉紧力可以调整得不一样，这样阻尼板可以随着风速增大（转速增高）而逐个打开。

【任务实施】

1. 任务准备

竞赛设备平台 1 个、一字螺丝刀 1 把、十字螺丝刀 1 把、剥线钳 1 把、U 形压线钳 1 把、管型压线钳 1 把、万用表 1 个、上电检查记录表 1 份、风机调速偏航故障处置数据记录表 1 份、导线若干。

任务 7.1 相关任务实施图表

2. 任务内容及步骤

任务 1：风力调速偏航控制系统搭建

任务内容：完成风力调速偏航控制系统的搭建。

任务步骤：

（1）完成风力调速偏航控制系统连接导线的制作。

（2）按照接线图，完成风力调速偏航控制 PLC 模块的布线与接线。

（3）按照接线图，完成风力调速偏航控制继电器模块的布线与接线。

（4）完成系统上电检查，正确调试与运行风力调速偏航控制系统。

任务 2：风力调速偏航控制系统故障排除

任务内容：完成风力调速偏航控制系统的故障检测与处理。

任务步骤：

（1）检测风力调速偏航控制系统的供电模块。

(2) 检测风力调速偏航控制系统的 PLC 控制模块。
(3) 检测风力调速偏航控制系统的继电器组模块。
(4) 检测风力调速偏航控制系统的电机驱动模块。
(5) 根据各个模块功能的完整性，完成故障排除，并填写机调速偏航故障处置数据记录表。

3. 技能要求

(1) 正确使用万用表挡位进行不同参数的测量，操作规范，无短路、无错挡测量。
(2) 正确测量各个模块功能的故障点。
(3) U 形冷压端子在插入端子排时，U 形部分应充分插入，并保证正面朝外。
(4) 号码管在套入时，所有接线方向垂直于地面的套管，号码及字母组合读序从远离接线端至接线口，所有接线方向平行于地面的套管，号码及字母组合读序从左至右。
(5) 在压接接线端子时，剥开的线芯插入接线端子套时，将所有的线芯全部插入端子中；采用压线钳压接接线端子时，应使压痕在接线端子套的底部（反面），压接后，压接部位不允许有导线外露。
(6) 对设备运行数据观察到位，记录正确，记录参数数据包含数值和单位。

4. 任务成果及考核评价

(1) 系统调试正确且成功运行、数据界面运行数据正确，能记录运行数据，曲线绘制平滑，布局合理，占 90%。
(2) 操作过程展现较好职业素养，做到 7S 管理，占 10%。

【练习】

1. 水平轴风轮机中常用的调向装置，其结构依风轮机功率的大小有哪些不同型式？
2. 风轮机的调速方法及装置有多种多样，常用的有哪几种？
3. 水平轴风轮机的保护装置有哪些？它们分别起到什么作用？

任务 7.2　安装风力发电机组

【学习目标】

知识目标：了解风力发电装置安装地点相关考虑要素；掌握风力发电机组的安装流程。

能力目标：能安装小型风力发电设备。

素质目标：培养团队协作、认真细致的职业精神。

重点：风力发电机组安装要素。

难点：风力发电机组安装流程。

【任务分析】

风机的建设，都是模块化运输和装配，通过宏观和微观选址，确定具体机位（会预留 1～2 机位）。然后踩点，主要通过运输和施工难度进行讨论，敲定最终机位位置。土建等由施工单位进行，进行道路和风机基础施工。同时确定设备运输中转场地。设备按套装数量分批次运往现场。风场规模按照5万kW计算的话，不会同一时间运输单种设备，会匹配几套完整风机的设备为单位，运往中转场地，再由中转场地运往现场。最后大型吊车、挖掘机等配合风机吊装作业，完成系统安装。

依托全国职业院校技能大赛设备平台，完成风机机的安装与调试，并完成能源互联网云平台的搭建，设置网络通讯参数实现云平台与设备正常通讯。

【知识学习】

7.2.1 风力发电装置安装地点的选择

1. 选择风力发电装置安装地点时应考虑的因素

众所周知，风力发电装置能否发挥作用，充分利用风能是和其安装地点的风况、地形及其他一些气象因素密切相关的。无论哪种风力发电装置，尽管其性能优越，但如果安装地点选择不合适，则其技术上的性能就不能充分发挥出来，利用这种装置的经济效益也将受到影响，因此，正确选择风力发电装置的安装地点是非常重要的。

风力发电机组装配和安装规范

一般来说，风力发电装置可安装在开阔平坦的地方，也可安装在山岳的山顶上，小型风力发电机还可安装在靠近住宅附近或房屋顶上口近年来有些国家为了更充分地利用海上风能，将风力发电装置安装在靠近海岸的海上。但无论选择哪种地方安装风力发电装置，对下列这些因素都必须加以认真仔细的考虑：

（1）对拟安装风力发电装置地点的风力资源的大小及风况特性应有比较精确的了解与掌握，这里所说的风力资源大小系指风能功率密度（W/m^2），年平均风速（m/s），全年3～20m/s风速吹风总时数等；风况特性系指风向变化，风速频率分布等。只有这样才能准确地估算风力发电机组的全年发电量及风电机组的动态特性，并进而估价安装这台风电装置是否有经济价值。

（2）对于对风力发电装置的正常运行及维护可能造成伤害的气象现象应有充分的了解及掌握。这些气象问题包括紊流、大风、冰雪、盐雾、沙尘、雷电等。

所谓紊流是指空气流速度的急剧变化及风向的变动，而且这两种变化经常同时发生。气流中存在的这种紊流会影响到风力发电机组的输出功率，同时还会使整个风电装置产生振动，严重时会使风电装置损坏。因此，风电装置不应设置在经常发生紊流的地点。

对于风力发电装置来说，自然应该选择安装在风力较强的地点，这样才能充分利用风能资源。但是风力强的地区也往往是大风经过的地区，大风风速可达20～30m/s；特别是我国东南沿海地区，在台风出现时，风速更高，最高可接近40～50m/s。因此在这些地区安装风力发电装置，风电装置本身要有足够的强度，并有可靠的安全保护装置。

在气候干燥的地区，风中往往有灰尘或沙粒，我国内蒙古、甘肃、青海等地即属于这种情况。风中携带尘沙，将使安装在这些地区的风轮机叶片受到磨损而缩短寿命，因此对于安装在这种气象条件下的风轮机叶片要进行防止风沙磨损的处理。

在沿海地区或海岛上选择风力发电装置的安装地点时，还要考虑风电装置防盐雾腐蚀的措施。盐雾腐蚀能使金属制造的风轮叶片及塔架受到损坏,同时还将使发电机的绝缘受到破坏以及使继电器、接触器等电器的触头动作失灵,因此,对安装在这种地区的风电装置的部件必须进行防盐雾处理。

在春夏季多雷的地区安装风力发电装置必须考虑有完善的避雷装置,对于安装在凸出的山顶上的风电装置更应慎重采取可靠的防雷措施。

对于安装在冬季寒冷地区的风力发电机,必须考虑在冰冻季节时风轮叶片上可能结冰,使叶片质量发生变化而产生振动;另外由于气温很低,还可能会造成润滑油冻结从而导致发生机械故障。

总之,这些气象现象有的确能对风电装置的安全构成损坏性的后果,有的虽不能造成大的损坏,却会使风电装置的投入及维护的费用增加或是使装置的运行时间(寿命)缩短。

(3) 要考虑风力发电机组占用土地费用及安装工程费用,特别是对于安装多台风力发电机组(风电场)更要仔细比较,应选择离公路道路较近,宜于设备运输和距离电力输电线路较近,宜于联网的地点。

(4) 要考虑对环境的影响。风力发电装置对环境的影响一般说来是不大的,主要应考虑的是风轮机叶片旋转时发出的噪声及旋转的叶片(特别是金属制造叶片)可能反射电磁波而造成电磁干扰。研究表明,大型水平轴风轮机无论在起动、停机或是运行过程中产生的噪声实际上并不比风本身的声音大多少,中小型风轮机发出的噪声就更低些。但是,随着人们对环境污染认识的提高,风力发电装置安装地点还是应该离开居民点一定的距离,以降低到达居民点的噪声水平。对电磁波的干扰可能是风轮机产生的一个潜在的环境问题,目前对这个问题的研究主要集中在对电视广播的干扰上。

2. 在开阔平地上安装风力发电机

在平地上安装风力发电机组应满足下列情况:

(1) 在开阔平坦的土地上安装单台风力发电机组时,离开机组安装地点半径为1km的面积内应无障碍物。

(2) 在有障碍物的开阔土地上安装单台风力发电机组时,风力发电机组的安装地点应远离障碍物,离开的距离应为障碍物高度的15~20倍,如图7.7所示。这是因为风在遇到障碍物时,风速就要减慢;但是风越过障碍物一段距离之后,风速又逐渐加大起来,在离开障碍物的距离大约为障碍物高度的15倍左右处,风速又恢复到越过障碍物前的大小。因此使风力发电机组安装地与障碍物之间的距离大于障碍物高度的15~20倍,就可充分地利用风能,使风轮机的输出功率增大。

3. 在山顶上安装风力发电机

当流动的空气接近山脊时,由于伯努利效应,气流跨过山顶时使其被压缩并加速,而这种加速能极大地增加一可能获得的能量。图7.8表示跨过山脊顶端的空气流被压缩后气流层变薄的情况。图7.9表示空气流跨过一个理想化的山脊时,气流在山脊和山顶处被加速的情况(理想化的山脊是指山脊的走向与空气流的方向恰成直角)。从图7.9可以看出,山顶上的风速比远离山脚下地面处的风速高了一倍,因此山顶上是安装风力发电机组的有利位置。

项目7 调节与安装风力发电机组

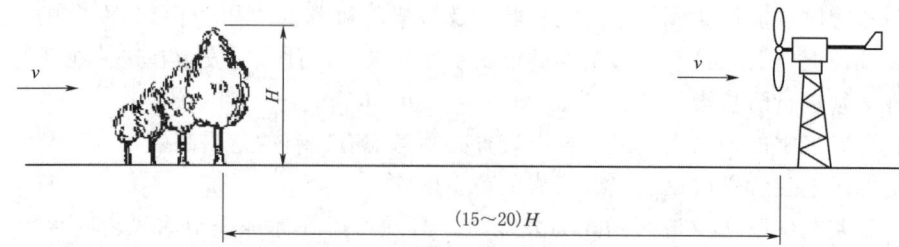

图 7.7 障碍物高度与风力发电机与障碍物距离示意图

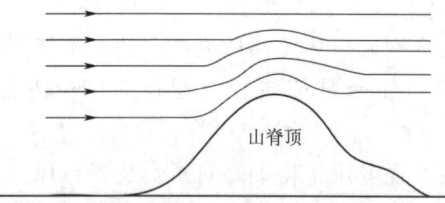

图 7.8 气流越过山脊时被压挤的情况

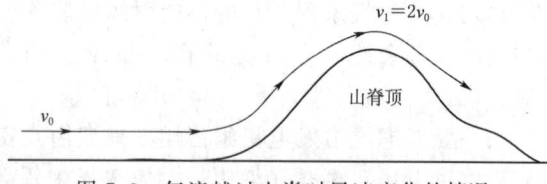

图 7.9 气流越过山脊时风速变化的情况

4. 在建筑物附近或建筑物上安装风力发电机

虽然风力发电机最好安装在远离建筑物的开阔平坦的土地上或山顶上，但有时却需要安装在城镇的住宅或建筑物附近，甚至就在建筑物上安装风力发电机。在这种情况下，就需要了解建筑物对气流的影响，因为气流的变化将影响风力发电机的功率输出。如果安装地点选择不合适，甚至会造成装置的损坏及安全事故。

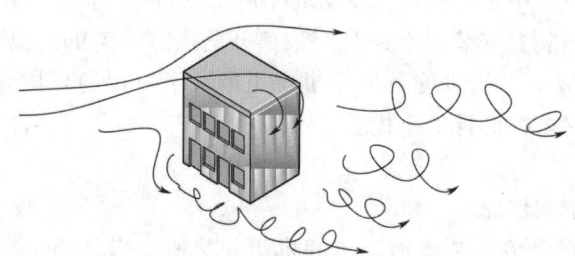

图 7.10 建筑物对气流的影响

建筑物对于气流所引起的影响如图 7.10 所示，从图中可见，沿气流前进方向，在建筑物后的气流是紊乱的。也即是产生了紊流；在建筑物的前面也产生了一些紊流，但是其范围不如建筑物后面产生的紊流范围大。图 7.11 表示建筑物高度与气流经过该建筑物时产生的紊流范围的关系，由图 7.11 可以得知，在架设风力发电机组时应避开产生紊流的区域，因为紊流不仅使风力发电机组的功率输出受影响，而且还会造成机组振动。因此，如果风力发电机组安装在沿气流前进方向建筑物后面时，则安装地点离开建筑物的距离至少要有建筑物高度的 15～20 倍；如果风力发电机组安装在建筑物前面时，则安装地点离开建筑物的距离至少要有建筑物高度的 2 倍；如果风力发电机组就安装在建筑物上，则风力发电机塔架（或风轮机轮毂中心）距建筑物顶的距离至少等于建筑物的高度。如图 7.11 所示。由图中可看出，若风力发电机离地面高度小于 $2H$，则不能利用气流加速（伯努利效应）的效果了。

7.2.2 海上风电机组安装

1. 风力发电机组分体安装

分体安装包括塔架、机舱和叶轮的安装。分体安装过程比较复杂，应根据安装程序，合理安排设备运输及安装施工顺序,并针对塔架、机舱、叶轮的结构特点,充分考虑工程工期、设备配置及气象水文因素,制定相应的吊装措施,确保吊装作业安全、可靠、有序进行。

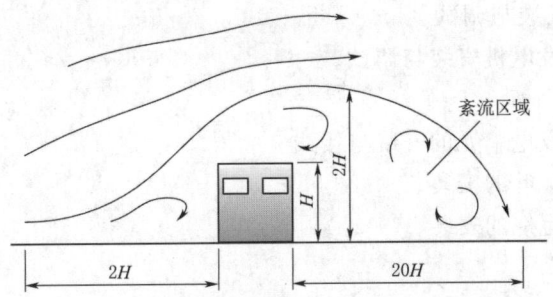

图 7.11 建筑物附近产生紊流的情况

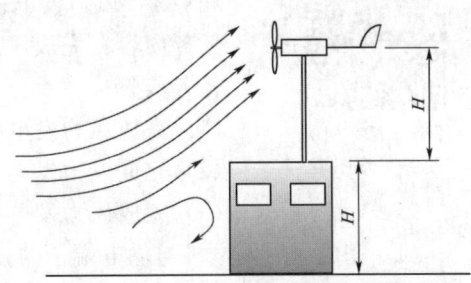

图 7.12 在建筑物上安装风力发电机示意图

2. 风电机组整体安装

整体安装包括整体组装、整体移位、整体运输和整体吊装等过程。由于海上风电机组设备尺寸较大,质量较大,陆地组装和整体移位装船的难度较大,应进行精心的设计与准备,选用的起吊、转运设备应足够满足机组设备组装与转运要求。组装与转运过程中应遵守操作规程,确保组装与转运装船安全、有序进行。

海上风力发电工程施工规范

风电机组设备整体运输至风电场区域经检查合格后,通过专用的安装船舶吊装设备缓慢移动就位,在确保准确对接后,再固定连接法兰上的连接螺栓。由于风电机组整体质量较重,重心较高,其安装过程受风、浪、海流影响的效应将被放大。因此,在风电机组设备整体吊装作业时,应采取措施,确保风电机组塔架法兰与基础顶部法兰对接准确,螺栓连接紧密,受力均匀,安装精度在规定允许的范围内。安装完成后,应对安装工作进行检验,以确保安装作业的可靠性。

3. 海上风电场变电站安装

海上变电站构件及设备较多,若全部在海上完成安装作业,施工难度极大,容易造成设备受损,也不经济。因此,海上变电站构件宜在陆地完成部分或全部设备组装后运输至风电场场址处进行吊装作业。

在海上变电站吊装前,应根据变电站尺寸及质量选用合适的吊装设备。并在尽量减少海上作业时间的前提下,确定与变电站规模相适宜的吊装方式。海上变电站体积、质量均较大,对吊装设备及操作均要求较高,起吊前应做好充分准备。吊具及加固件应保证吊装过程中结构受力及稳定性,并加强保护,防止各构件在吊装过程中受损。

目前,国内外均未制定关于海上变电站高压设备的规范,也没有海上风电场高压变电站的规范。设备安装可参照现有的海上采油平台、DNV、IEC 船舶电气设备规范的相关规定进行。由于海上变电站设备安装要求大部分与陆上设备一样,因此,也可参照现有的陆上设备安装规范进行,同时注意海上设备的防腐、防潮等措施。

【任务实施】

1. 任务准备

竞赛设备平台 1 个、一字螺丝刀 1 把、十字螺丝刀 1 把、剥线钳 1 把、U 形压线钳 1

把、管型压线钳1把、万用表1个、上电检查记录表1份、导线若干。

2. 任务内容及步骤

任务7.2 相关任务实施图表

任务1：风力发电机安装与调试

任务内容：完成风力发电机安装与调试。

任务步骤：

（1）完成风力发电机发电单元的安装与接线。

（2）完成风力发电机桨叶的安装。

（3）完成风力发电机尾舵的安装。

（4）完成风力发电机与供电端子的接线。

（5）完成系统上电检查，正确调试与运行风力发电机。

任务2：能源互联网云平台的组网与通信

任务内容：完成能源互联网云平台的组网与通信。

任务步骤：

（1）完成网络连接线的制作。

（2）按照接线图，完成终端设备与能源互联网云平台的连接。

（3）完成网络通信参数设置。

（4）建立物联管理模板，完成物联设备配置，实现通信数据采集。

（5）完成云平台能源管理应用组态设计。

3. 技能要求

（1）正确使用万用表档位进行不同参数的测量，操作规范，无短路、无错档测量。

（2）正确采集连接至能源互联平台的各个终端设备运行参数。

（3）U形冷压端子在插入端子排时，U形部分应充分插入，并保证正面朝外。

（4）号码管在套入时，所有接线方向垂直于地面的套管，号码及字母组合读序从远离接线端至接线口，所有接线方向平行于地面的套管，号码及字母组合读序从左至右。

（5）在压接接线端子时，剥开的线芯插入接线端子套时，将所有的线芯全部插入端子中；采用压线钳压接接线端子时，应使压痕在接线端子套的底部（反面），压接后，压接部位不允许有导线外露。

（6）对设备运行数据观察到位，记录正确，记录参数数据包含数值和单位。

4. 任务成果及考核评价

（1）系统调试正确且成功运行、数据界面运行数据正确，能记录运行数据，曲线绘制平滑，布局合理，占90%。

（2）操作过程展现较好职业素养，做到7S管理，占10%。

【练习】

1. 选择风力发电装置安装地点时应考虑哪些因素？
2. 在开阔平地上安装风力发电机有哪些情况？
3. 海上风力发电机组分体安装包括哪些？

Project 7　Adjusting and Installing Wind Turbine Generator Systems

Task 7.1　Mastering the Yaw, Speed Control, and Protection Devices of Wind Turbines

【Learning objectives】

　　Knowledge objective: To master the components and functions of the yaw, control speed and protect devices of wind turbines.

　　Ability objective: To be able to detect and handle the failures of speed control and yaw system of small wind turbines.

　　Qualification objective: To cultivate professional qualities of focus, diligence, and teamwork.

　　Learning priority: Functions of wind turbine speed control and protection devices.

　　Learning challenge: Detection and handling of wind turbine speed control failures.

【Task analysis】

　　Yaw devices, speed control devices, and protection devices are crucial components of a wind power generation system. They play an important role in the stable and normal operation of wind turbine generators and are indispensable parts of the system.

　　This task relies on the equipment platform of the National Vocational College Skills Competition, complete the detection and handling of faults in the wind turbine speed control and yaw system.

【Knowledge learning】

7.1.1　Yaw devices of wind turbines

　　The yaw device of a wind turbine refers to the mechanism that can adjust the relative position of the wind turbine blade's rotation plane to the wind direction (i.e., the airflow direction) when the wind direction changes, allowing the wind turbine to face the wind direction during normal operation. It is well known that when the rotation plane of the wind turbine blades is perpendicular to the wind direction, the mechanical output power of the wind turbine is maximized, thereby utilizing wind energy more effectively. Therefore, the yaw device is also called the wind-facing device. It is an indispensable device for horizontal axis wind turbines, but vertical axis wind turbines do not require a yaw device. Common yaw devices in horizontal axis wind turbines vary in structure depending on the power of the wind turbine, such as tail vanes (also known as tail wings), tail cars (also known as side vanes), and servo motor-driven gear transmission yaw devices.

1. Tail vanes

Tail vanes are mostly used in small wind turbines. The tail vane consists of a vane arm and a vane blade. In Figure 7.1, The length of the vane arm (L) represents the distance from the rotation plane of the wind turbine blades to the furthest end of the tail vane. The shape of the vane blade can vary, with some common shapes shown in Figure 7.2.

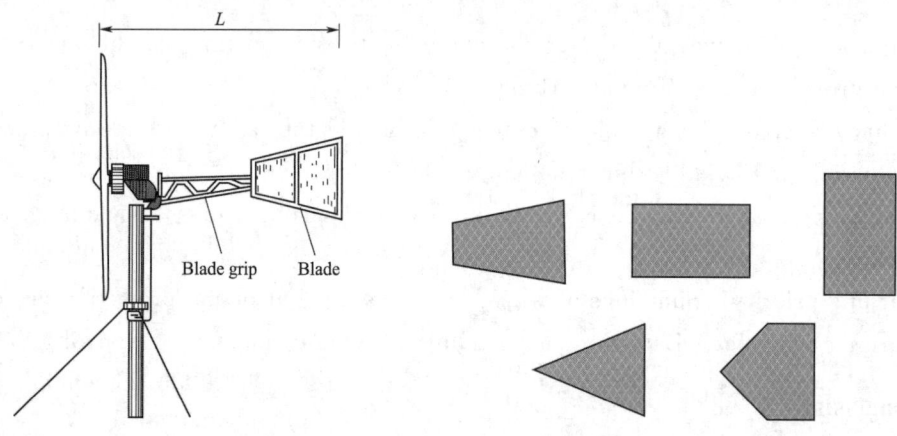

Figures 7.1 Tail vane of a horizontal axis wind turbine

Figure 7.2 Common shapes of tail vane blades

The length of the vane arm and the area of the vane blade should ensure that, when the wind direction deviates (typically by 10° to 20°), the torque generated by the wind pressure on the tail vane is sufficient to turn the wind turbine head, thereby aligning the wind turbine to face the wind direction.

Empirically, the length of the vane arm in wind turbines using tail vanes is equal to the diameter of the wind turbine blades, and the area of the vane blade can be about 1/8 of the rotational area of the wind turbine blades. The vane arm is generally parallel to the ground, but can also be angled upwards. The vane blade is usually made of metal materials.

2. Side vanes

In wind turbines with a capacity greater than 15-20 kW, side vanes are often used as yaw devices. The side vane is a small wind vane installed on the side of the wind turbine nacelle, with its rotation axis perpendicular to the main axis of the wind turbine. When the main wind turbine blade's rotation plane is perpendicular to the wind direction, the side vane's rotation plane is parallel to the wind direction and does not rotate. When the main wind turbine deviates from the wind direction, the side vane rotates under wind force, driving the main wind turbine's head to rotate back to the wind-facing position through a worm gear mechanism.

3. Servo motor-driven gear transmission yaw devices

In medium to large wind turbines, a gear transmission device driven by a servo motor is commonly used for yaw control, as shown in Figure 7.3. The servo motor rotates according to the control signals from the wind vane and the tachogenerator connected to the main shaft of the wind turbine. The motor drives the gear transmission device, and when the large gear rotates, yaw control is achieved. Since the servo motor can rotate in both directions, yaw control in both directions can be achieved. To prevent the servo motor from working continuously, it is generally stipulated that the yaw mechanism only starts to act when the wind direction deviates from the wind turbine's main shaft by $\pm 10°$ to $\pm 15°$. Additionally, the yaw speed is limited by the stresses induced by the gyroscopic effect of the wind turbine, typically set at $1°/s$.

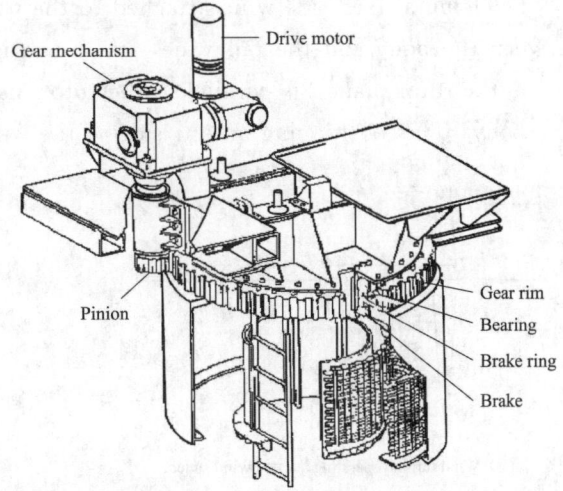

Figure 7.3 A gear transmission yaw device driven by servo motor

7.1.2 Speed regulation mechanisms of wind turbines

The speed regulation mechanism of a wind turbine is used to adjust the rotational speed of the wind turbine. As previously mentioned, according to the power-speed characteristics of wind turbines, when the wind speed changes, the rotational speed of the wind turbine will also change. This change in rotational speed will lead to variations in the output voltage and frequency of the generator, which is unacceptable for wind power generators whether supplying power to an electrical load or feeding into the grid. Therefore, a speed regulation mechanism is necessary for the wind turbine to regulate the turbine's power within a range of operating wind speeds, thereby stabilizing the rotational speed of the wind turbine. Additionally, it can also ensure speed limit protection in high wind speeds.

There are various methods and devices used for wind turbine speed regulation, commonly used ones include:

(1) Yawing speed regulation. This method is based on the principle that when the wind speed changes causing the turbine's rotational speed to exceed the rated value, a certain mechanical mechanism is activated. This mechanism causes the rotor blades to deviate from the perpendicular wind-facing position (i.e., yaw), reducing the power absorbed from the wind and thus decreasing the rotational speed to the rated value.

There are two methods to achieve rotor yaw:

1) Using a fixed side wing attached to the wind turbine body and a spring connection between the body and the tail vane, as shown in Figure 7.4. The side wing, installed behind the rotor plane, is parallel to the rotor plane but positioned on one side of the turbine body. This positioning on one side of the wind turbine body is called a flank.

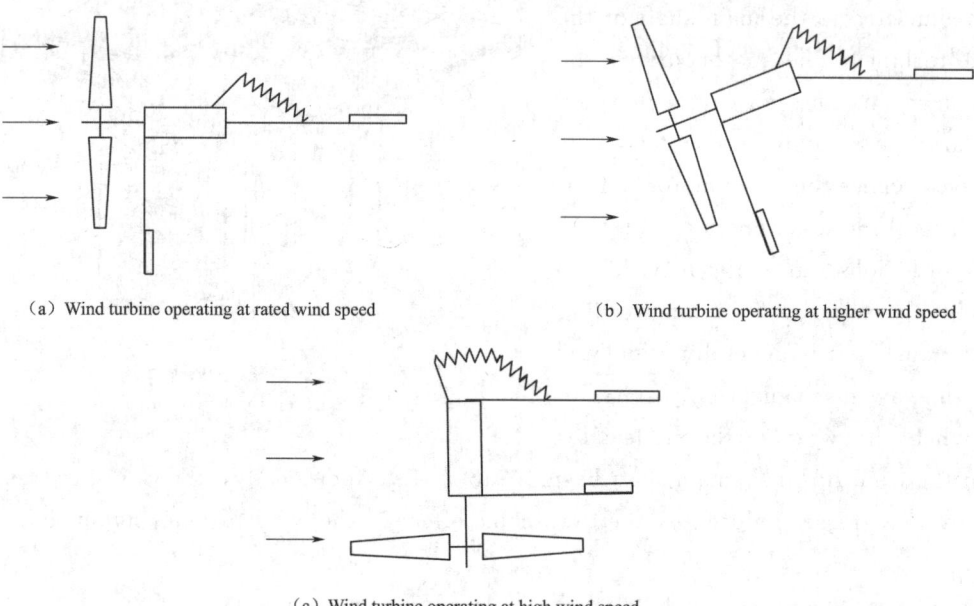

(a) Wind turbine operating at rated wind speed
(b) Wind turbine operating at higher wind speed
(c) Wind turbine operating at high wind speed

Figure 7.4 Schematic diagram of yawing speed regulation using a side wing
(Southbound T - connection of 10kV flat wire)

Figure 7.4 (a) shows the wind turbine operating at rated wind speed, where the rotor plane is facing the wind due to the action of the tail vane. The side wing is subjected to some wind force trying to yaw the rotor, but due to the spring's tension, it does not move. When the wind speed exceeds the rated speed, the rotor speed increases, and the wind pressure on the side wing also increases, causing the rotor to yaw to the side with the side wing, as shown in Figure 7.4 (b). As a result, since the rotational plane of the wind rotor is no longer perpendicular to the wind direction, the power output of the wind turbine decreases, and the rotor speed correspondingly slows down. Naturally, at this point, the spring is stretched further than before. When the wind speed decreases, the spring pulls the rotor back to its original position (i.e., the position where the rotor's rotational plane is perpendicular to the wind direction). Therefore, it is evident that the correct selection of the spring's tension and the size of the side vane area are crucial factors affecting the accuracy of speed regulation, typically determined through experimentation. During high winds, the rotor's rotational plane will be in the position shown in Figure 7.4 (c), where the rotor blades' rotational plane is parallel to the wind direction, causing the rotor to stop, thus protecting the wind turbine in high wind conditions.

2) Using an eccentric method to achieve rotor yaw for the purpose of speed regulation is illustrated in Figure 7.5. Eccentricity refers to the non-coincidence of the main shaft of the wind turbine with the vertical axis beneath the nacelle (i.e., they are not in the same plane). As shown in Figure 7.5, there is a certain distance D between the vertical shaft that rotates the nacelle and the horizontal main shaft of the rotor, known as the eccentric distance. When the wind turbine operates at its rated wind speed, although the wind exerts a forward pressure on the vertical shaft beneath the nacelle (point A in Figure 7.5), creating a torque (with the moment arm equal to the eccentric distance), the directional and stabilizing effect of the wind turbine's tail vane keeps the rotor aligned with the wind direction, as shown in Figure 7.5 (a). When the wind speed increases without a change in wind direction, the pressure on the rotor increases, thereby increasing the torque on the vertical shaft, causing the rotor to yaw, as shown in Figure 7.5 (b). After the rotor yaws, its rotational plane is no longer aligned with the wind direction, reducing the turbine's power output and rotor speed. When the wind speed is extremely high, the rotational plane of the rotor blades will yaw 90° to a position parallel to the wind direction, as

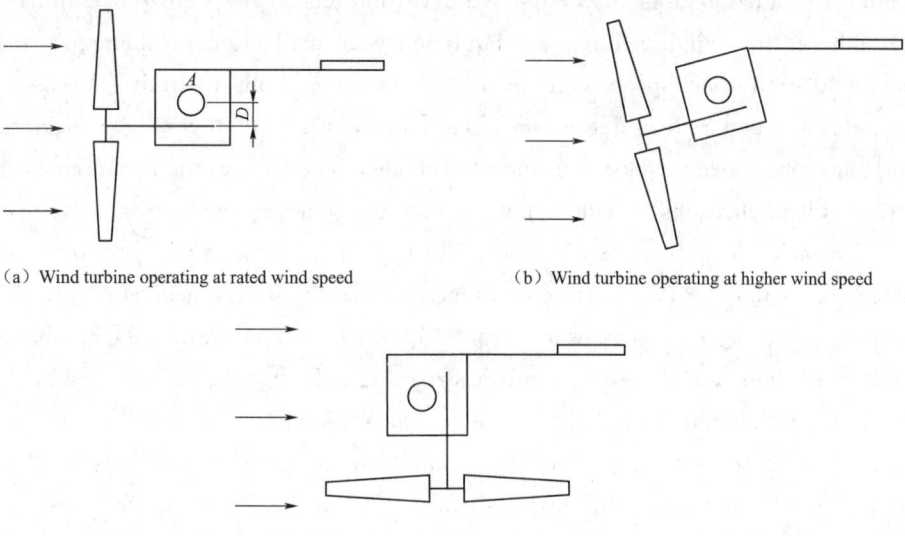

(a) Wind turbine operating at rated wind speed

(b) Wind turbine operating at higher wind speed

(c) Wind turbine operating at high wind speed

Figure 7.5　Schematic diagram of yawing speed regulation using eccentric method shown in Figure 7.5 (c), effectively bringing the rotor to a stop.

Wind turbine generator system variable speed constant frequency control system-Part 2: Test method

The above yawing speed regulation methods are suitable for fixed-pitch blade wind turbines.

(2) Changing blade pitch for speed regulation. It is well known that paddles (blades) of any type of airfoil-type wind turbine are subjected to both lift and drag forces under wind action. Lift drives the blade to rotate in the rotor plane, while drag opposes it. Changing the blade pitch for speed regulation involves rotating the blade around its axis to alter the angle of attack, thereby changing the lift and drag forces. Increasing lift increases rotational speed, while increasing drag decreases rotational speed. This method is also known as paddle (blade) pitch speed regulation.

Various methods can be used for enabling rotating blades to automatically adjust pitch. Modern, medium to large wind turbines often use hydraulic control systems to achieve automatic blade pitch adjustment. In contrast, small and medium wind turbines often use centrifugal force. From dynamics, it is known that an object in high-speed rotation generates a large centrifugal force proportional to its mass. By attaching a fixed mass to the blade or using the blade's own weight, centrifugal force is generated during high-speed rotation. This centrifugal force, along with mechanical components (e.g., springs, levers) installed on the wind turbine to adjust blade pitch, allows the blade to change its angle of attack automatically, achieving speed regulation.

7.1.3 Wind turbine protection mechanisms

When a wind turbine operates, if the wind speed exceeds the operating range, or if the generator suddenly loses load, the wind turbine can overspeed, potentially causing damage. Therefore, wind turbines are equipped with protection mechanisms to prevent overspeed and limit their speed. There are two main methods to limit overspeed: using aerodynamic drag and reducing the wind-facing area of the rotor (yawing). Horizontal axis wind turbine protection mechanisms include tip brakes, spoilers, feathering mechanisms, and rotor yaw or tilt mechanisms, while vertical axis wind turbines mainly use damping plates.

(1) Tip brake. A tip brake is a damping device installed at the tip of horizontal axis wind turbine blades. During normal operation, it functions like the blade, generating lift. When the wind turbine overspeeds, it rotates 90° around the blade's longitudinal axis, aligning perpendicularly to the rotor plane, generating drag and reducing the rotor speed.

(2) Spoiler. A spoiler is a damping device installed on the wind turbine blade at one-third of its length from the tip. During normal operation, the two ends of the spoiler overlap with the blade's upper and lower surfaces. When the wind turbine overspeeds, the spoiler extends outward, perpendicular to the rotor plane, generating drag and reducing the rotor speed.

Both damping devices typically operate using centrifugal force from the rotor rotation but can also be actuated by hydraulic or mechanical systems based on rotor speed signals. The former is passive, while the latter is active.

(3) Feathering mechanism. Feathering refers to aligning the blade chord with the wind direction, minimizing the angle of attack and lift. Blade feathering is a part of blade pitch control, achieved through hydraulic or mechanical pitch systems based on wind speed or rotational speed signals. Feathering can be used for emergency shutdown in high winds or load rejection and for normal shutdown of the wind turbine.

(4) Rotor yaw or tilt mechanism. Horizontal axis wind turbines may also use rotor yaw, tilt mechanisms, or emergency brakes on the transmission shaft for overspeed protection. The yaw method has been previously described. The tilt mechanism is typically used in small wind turbines. Emergency brakes in small wind turbines can be manual or automatic, both using a friction brake principle, as shown in Figure 7.6.

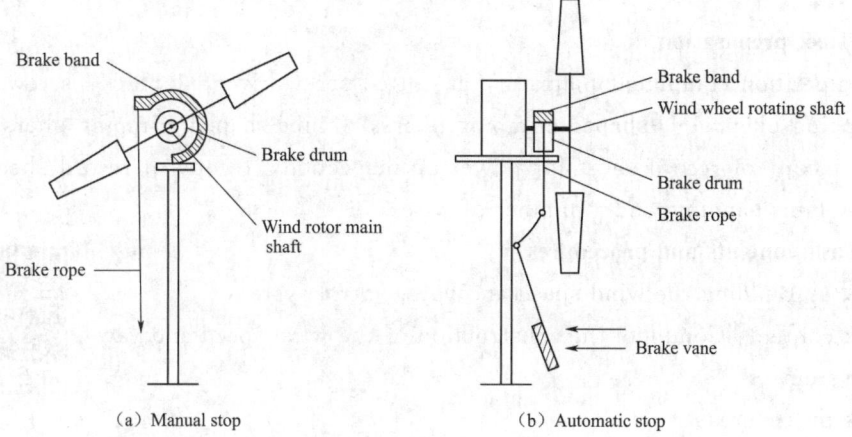

Figure 7.6 Principles of Manual and Automatic Friction Brakes

Figure 7.6 (a) depicts manual braking, where pulling the brake rope downward causes the brake band to tightly grip the brake drum, thereby stopping the wind turbine. Figure 7.6 (b) shows automatic braking, where the brake vane is pushed forcefully by high winds (as indicated by the arrow in the diagram) when the wind speed exceeds the maximum limit. This action drives the brake lever, which in turn pulls the brake rope downward, causing the brake band to grip the brake drum tightly, thereby achieving automatic braking. The relationship between the size of the brake vane and the maximum wind speed limit can be determined through experimentation.

In medium or large horizontal axis wind turbines, the braking system consists of a hydraulic oil supply system, brake calipers, and a brake disc mounted on the main shaft of the wind turbine. When overspeeding due to high winds occurs, the hydraulically driven brake calipers engage the brake disc, thus achieving automatic braking of the wind turbine.

(5) Damping plate. The protective devices of vertical axis wind turbines (e. g., Darrieus type) mainly include emergency brakes installed on the wind turbine's transmission shaft and damping plates mounted on the wind turbine blades. The braking system of a vertical axis wind turbine operates on the same principle as that of a horizontal axis wind turbine, but it can be driven hydraulically or electrically. The damping plate operates based on centrifugal force: when the wind speed exceeds a certain limit, the centrifugal force increases enough to overcome the spring tension behind the damping plate, causing the damping plate to open and create resistance, thereby reducing the turbine's rotational speed. Generally, Darrieus wind turbines have 2 or 3 blades, so they can be equipped with 2 or 3 damping plates (typically one per blade). The spring tension of each damping plate can be adjusted differently so that the damping plates open successively as the wind speed increases.

【Task implementation】

Ⅰ. Task preparation

1 competition equipment platform, 1 slotted screwdriver, 1 philips screwdriver, 1 wire stripping plier, 1 U-shaped crimping pliers, 1 tube-shaped crimping pliers, 1 multimeter, 1 copy of record sheet for power-up inspection, 1 copy of record sheet for fan speed yaw fault handling and a number of wires.

Ⅱ. Task contents and procedures

Task 1: Building the wind speed and yaw control system

Task content: Complete the construction of the wind speed and yaw control system.

Task 7.1 Related implementation charts

Task procedures:

(1) Fabricate the connection wires for the wind speed and yaw control system.

(2) Complete the wiring and connection of the wind speed and yaw control PLC module according to the wiring diagram.

(3) Complete the wiring and connection of the wind speed and yaw control relay module according to the wiring diagram.

(4) Perform power-up checks, correct debugging, and operation of the wind speed and yaw control system.

Task 2: Troubleshooting the wind speed and yaw control system

Task content: Complete the fault detection and handling of the wind speed and yaw control system.

Task procedures:

(1) Inspect the power module of the wind speed and yaw control system.

(2) Inspect the PLC control module of the wind speed and yaw control system.

(3) Inspect the relay group module of the wind speed and yaw control system.

(4) Inspect the motor drive module of the wind speed and yaw control system.

(5) Based on the completeness of each module's function, complete the fault elimination and fill in the wind speed and yaw fault handling data record sheet.

III. Skill requirements

(1) Correctly use the multimeter range for measuring different parameters, operate standardly, without short circuits or incorrect range measurements.

(2) Accurately measure the fault points of each module's function.

(3) When inserting U-shaped cold-pressed terminals into terminal blocks, ensure the U-shaped part is fully inserted with the front facing outward.

(4) When inserting number tubes, all wiring directions perpendicular to the ground should have the numbers and letter combinations read from the terminal end to the connection port; for wiring directions parallel to the ground, the numbers and letter combinations should be read from left to right.

(5) When crimping the terminal, insert all stripped wire cores fully into the terminal; use a crimping tool to crimp the terminal so that the crimp mark is on the bottom (back) of the terminal, with no exposed wires after crimping.

(6) Thoroughly observe and record the equipment's operating data, ensuring accuracy and including values and units.

IV. Task results, appraisal and evaluation

(1) The system is correctly commissioned and successfully operating; the data screen is well laid out and runs correctly; operation data are recorded; curves are drawn smooth (accounting for 90%).

(2) The operator exhibits good professional quality during the operation process and follows 7S management model (accounting for 10%).

【Exercises】

1. What are the different types of yaw devices commonly used in horizontal axis wind turbines, depending on the turbine's power size?

2. What are the various methods and devices for wind turbine speed regulation?

3. What are the protective devices in horizontal axis wind turbines, and what roles do they serve?

Task 7.2　Installing Wind Turbine Units

【Learning objectives】

Knowledge objective: To understand the factors to be considered when selecting wind turbine installation sites and master the installation process of wind turbine units.

Ability objective: To be able to install small wind power equipment.

Qualification objective: To develop teamwork and meticulous professional spirit.

Learning priority: Elements of wind turbine unit installation.

Learning challenge: Installation process of wind turbine units.

【Task analysis】

The construction of wind turbines involves modular transportation and assembly. Through macro and micro site selection, specific turbine positions are determined (with 1-2 positions reserved). Site inspection is then conducted, mainly discussing transportation and construction difficulties to finalize the turbine location. Civil engineering is handled by the construction unit, including road and turbine foundation construction, while also determining equipment transfer sites. Equipment is transported to the site in batches based on the number of sets, not all at once. For a wind farm with a capacity of 50,000 kW, different sets of complete wind turbine equipment are transported to transfer sites, then to the installation site. Large cranes, excavators, and other machinery assist the turbine installation, and completing the system installation.

This task relies on the national vocational college skills competition equipment platform, complete the installation and debugging of wind turbines, and set up the Energy Internet cloud platform, configure network communication parameters to achieve a normal communication between the cloud platform and the equipment.

【Knowledge learning】

7.2.1 Selection of wind power equipment installation sites

1. Factors to consider when choosing wind power equipment installation sites

As is well known, the effectiveness of wind power equipment in optimally utilizing wind energy is closely related to the wind conditions, terrain, and other meteorological factors at the installation site. No matter how advanced is the performance of the wind power equipment, if the installation site is not suitable, its technical performance cannot be fully utilized, and the economic benefits are also affected. Therefore, it is crucial to choose the correct installation site for wind power equipment.

Generally, wind power equipment can be installed in open, flat areas, on mountain tops, or even near residential areas or rooftops for small wind turbines. In recent years, some countries have been installing wind power equipment offshore near the coast to fully utilize marine wind energy. Regardless of the location chosen for installation, the following factors must be carefully considered:

Assembling and installation regulation for wind turbine generator systems

(1) A precise understanding of the wind resources and wind condi-

tions at the proposed installation site for the wind power device is essential. The term "wind resource" here refers to the wind power density (W/m^2), the annual average wind speed (m/s), and the total number of hours per year with wind speeds between 3 and 20 m/s. "Wind conditions" refer to factors such as wind direction variability and wind speed frequency distribution. Only with this information can the annual energy production of the wind turbine and its dynamic characteristics be accurately estimated, and further, assess whether the installation of this wind power device is economically viable.

(2) Have a full understanding of meteorological phenomena that could affect the normal operation and maintenance of the wind power equipment, such as turbulence, strong winds, snow, salt spray, dust, and lightning.

Turbulence refers to the rapid changes in air flow velocity and variations in wind direction, which often occur simultaneously. This turbulence in the airflow can affect the output power of wind turbines and cause vibrations throughout the entire wind power installation. In severe cases, it can even damage the wind power equipment. Therefore, wind power installations should not be placed in locations where turbulence frequently occurs.

Wind power generation devices should be installed in locations with strong wind power in order to fully utilize wind energy resources. However, in areas with strong winds, wind speeds can increase up to 20-30 m/s; especially in the southeast coast of China, where typhoons can increase wind speeds up to 40-50 m/s, the wind power equipment must be strong enough and equipped with reliable safety devices in such conditions.

In arid regions where the wind carries dust or sand, such as Inner Mongolia, Gansu, and Qinghai, wind turbine blades may suffer abrasion, reducing their lifespan. Therefore, the blades should be treated for sand abrasion resistance.

In coastal or island areas, wind power equipment must be protected against salt spray corrosion, which can damage metal blades and towers and affect the insulation of generators and the functionality of electrical components like relays and contactors. Therefore, anti-salt spray treatment is necessary for the components of wind power installations installed in such areas.

In regions with frequent lightning in spring and summer, wind power equipment must have a robust lightning protection, especially for those installed on prominent mountain tops.

For wind turbines in cold and winter regions, considerations should include potential icing on the blades, which could cause vibrations due to changes in blade mass, and low temperatures, which might also freeze lubricating oil, leading to mechanical failures.

In short, these meteorological phenomena can indeed have destructive consequences on the safety of wind power plants. Although some may not cause significant damage, they can increase the investment and maintenance costs of wind power plants or shorten their operating time (lifespan).

(3) To consider the land occupation cost and project installation cost of wind turbines, especially for the installation of multiple wind turbines (wind farms), a careful comparison should be made. A location that is close to highways, suitable for equipment transportation, close to power transmission lines, and suitable for networking should be selected.

(4) Consider the environmental impact. Generally, the environmental impact of wind power installations is minimal. The main concerns are the noise produced by the rotating blades and the potential electromagnetic interference caused by the reflection of electromagnetic waves by the rotating blades (especially metal blades). Research indicates that the noise generated by large horizontal axis wind turbines during startup, shutdown, or operation is not significantly louder than wind itself. The noise produced by small and medium-sized wind turbines is even lower. However, with increasing awareness of environmental pollution, wind power installations should be located at a certain distance from residential areas to reduce noise levels reaching the inhabitants. Electromagnetic interference is a potential environmental issue associated with wind turbines, with current research primarily focusing on interference with television broadcasts.

2. Installing wind turbines on open flat land

When installing wind turbines on flat land, the following conditions should be met:

(1) For a single wind turbine installation on an open, flat land, there should be no obstacles within a 1-kilometer radius of the installation site.

(2) For a single wind turbine installation on an open land with obstacles, the installation site should be at a distance that is 15-20 times the height of the obstacles, as shown in Figure 7.7. This is because when the wind encounters an obstacle, its speed decreases; however, after a certain distance, the wind speed gradually increases again. At a distance approximately 15 times the height of the obstacle, the wind speed returns to its previous level. Thus, positioning the wind turbine installation site at a distance greater than 15-20 times the height of the obstacle allows for optimal wind energy utilization, thereby increasing the wind turbine's output power.

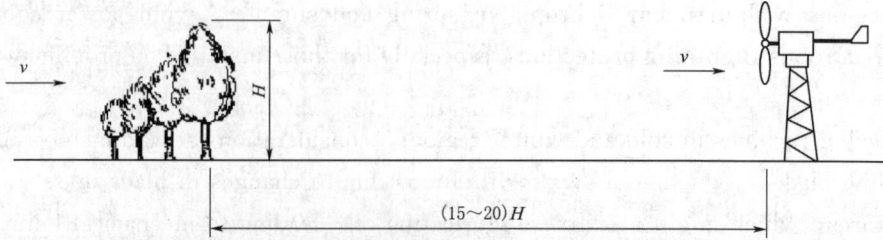

Figure 7.7 Relationship between obstacle height and the distance of the wind turbine from the obstacle

3. Installing wind turbines on mountain tops

When moving air approaches a ridge, the Bernoulli effect causes the airflow to compress and accelerate as it crosses the mountain top, significantly increasing the potential energy that can be harnessed. Figure 7.8 shows the thinning of the airflow layer after compression as it crosses the ridge top. Figure 7.9 shows the situation where the airflow is accelerated at the ridge and mountaintop when crossing an idealized ridge (the idealized ridge refers to the direction of the ridge being at a right angle to the direction of the airflow). As shown in Figure 7.9, the wind speed at the mountain top is twice that at the base, making mountain tops advantageous locations for wind turbine installations.

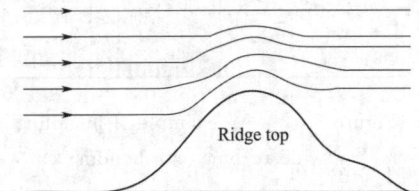
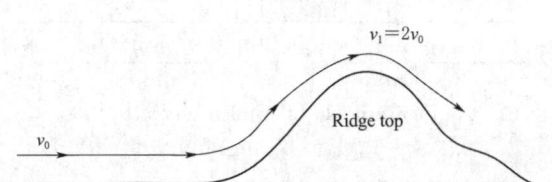

Figure 7.8 Compression of airflow over a ridge

Figure 7.9 Changes in wind speed as the airflow crosses a ridge

4. Installing wind turbines near or on buildings

While wind turbines are ideally installed on open, flat land or mountain tops, there are conditions when installation near residential or other buildings, or even directly on buildings, is necessary. In such cases, it is essential to understand the impact of the building on the airflow, as changes in airflow can affect the wind turbine's power output. An inappropriate installation site can even lead to equipment damage and safety incidents.

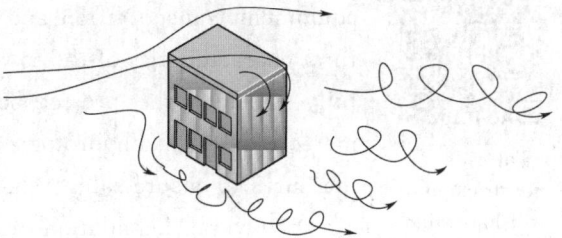

Figure 7.10 Impact of buildings on airflow

The impact of buildings on airflow is shown in Figure 7.10. From the figure, it is evident that the airflow behind the building is turbulent. Some turbulence also occurs in front of the building, but it is not as extensive as the turbulence behind the building. Figure 7.11 illustrates the relationship between building height and the extent of turbulence caused by the airflow over the building. From Figure 7.11, it is clear that wind turbines should be installed away from turbulent areas, as turbulence not only affects power output but also causes vibrations in the turbine. Therefore, if a wind turbine is to be installed behind a building in the direction of airflow, the installation site should be at least 15-20 times of the building heights away from the building. If the turbine is to be installed in front of the building, the site should be at least twice the building height away. If the turbine is to be installed on the building itself, the tower (or the hub center) should be at least as high as the building's top, as shown in Figure 7.11. From the figure, it can be seen that if the wind turbine's height above the ground is less than 2H, the airflow acceleration (Bernoulli effect) cannot be utilized effectively.

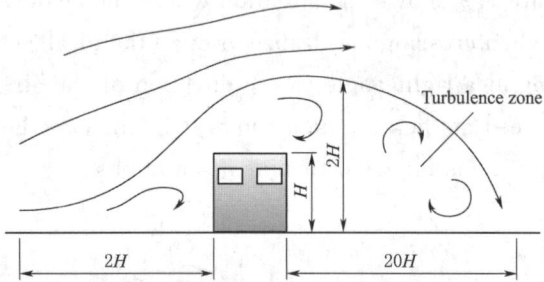

Figure 7.11 Turbulence created near buildings

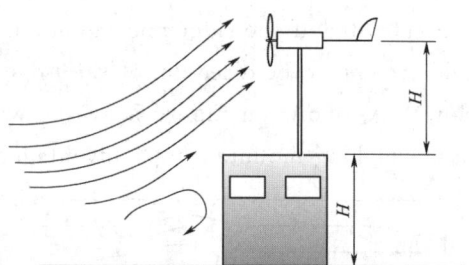

Figure 7.12 An example of installing a wind turbine on a building

7.2.2 Offshore wind turbine installation

1. Component installation of wind turbines

Component installation includes the installation of the tower nacelle, and rotor. This process is relatively complex and requires careful planning of equipment transportation and installation sequence. Given the structural characteristics of the tower, nacelle, and rotor, it is essential to fully consider the project schedule, equipment configuration, and meteorological and hydrological factors to develop corresponding lifting measures to ensure safe, reliable, and orderly lifting operations.

The code for construction of offshore wind power project

2. Overall installation of wind turbines

Overall installation includes processes such as assembly, relocation, transportation, and lifting. Due to the large size and weight of offshore wind turbine equipment, assembling and relocating them onto the vessel or land poses significant challenges. Therefore, meticulous design and preparations are necessary, and the selected lifting and transport equipment must meet the assembly and transport requirements of the turbine equipment. During assembly and transport, operation procedures must be followed to ensure safety and orderliness.

Once the wind turbine equipment has been transported to the offshore wind farm area and has passed inspection, it is slowly moved into position using specialized installation vessel lifting equipment. After ensuring accurate alignment, the connecting bolts on the flanges are fixed. Due to the heavy weight and high center of gravity of the wind turbine, the installation process is highly susceptible to the effects of wind, waves, and currents. Therefore, measures must be taken during the overall lifting of wind turbine equipment to ensure accurate alignment of the tower flange with the top foundation flange, tight bolt connections, uniform stress distribution, and installation precision within the allowable range. After installation, inspections should be carried out to ensure the reliability of the installation work.

3. Installation of offshore wind farm substations

Offshore substations involve numerous components and equipment. Completing all the installation work offshore is highly challenging, prone to equipment damage, and not economical. Therefore, it is preferable to complete partial or full assembly of offshore substation components on land before transporting them to the wind farm site for lifting operations.

Before lifting an offshore substation, suitable lifting equipment should be selected based on the substation's size and weight. The lifting method should be chosen to minimize the offshore operation time while matching the scale of the substation. Due to the large size and weight of offshore substations, there are high demands of the lifting equipment and operations. Adequate preparations should be made before lifting. Lifting gear and reinforcements should ensure structural stability and protection during lifting to prevent damage to components.

At present, neither domestic nor international standards have been established for high-voltage equipment in offshore substations, nor are there any regulations specifically for high-voltage substations in offshore wind farms. Equipment installation can refer to existing offshore oil platform standards, DNV, and IEC marine electrical equipment standards. Since the installation requirements for most offshore substation equipment are similar to those for onshore equipment, existing onshore equipment installation standards can also be followed, with additional attention to measures used for corrosion and moisture protection of the offshore equipment.

【Task implementation】

Ⅰ. Task preparation

1 competition equipment platform, 1 slotted screwdriver, 1 philips screwdriver, 1 wire stripping plier, 1 U-shaped crimping pliers, 1 tube-shaped crimping pliers, 1 multimeter, 1 copy of record sheet for power-up inspection and a number of wires.

Ⅱ. Task contents and procedures

Task 1: Wind turbine installation and commissioning

Task content: Complete the installation and commissioning of the wind turbine.

Task procedures:

(1) Complete the installation and wiring of the wind turbine generating unit.

(2) Complete the installation of the wind turbine blades.

(3) Complete the installation of the wind turbine tail rudder.

(4) Complete the wiring of the wind turbine to the power supply terminals.

(5) Perform a power-on inspection, correct commissioning, and operation of the wind turbine.

Task 7.2 Related implementation charts

Task 2: Networking and communication of the energy internet cloud platform

Task content: Complete the networking and communication of the energy internet cloud platform.

Task procedures:

(1) Complete the production of network connection cables.

(2) According to the wiring diagram, complete the connection of terminal equipment to the Energy Internet cloud platform.

(3) Complete the network communication parameter settings.

(4) Establish an IoT management template, complete the configuration of IoT devices, and achieve data collection.

(5) Complete the configuration design of the energy management application on the cloud platform.

Ⅲ. Skill requirements

(1) Correctly use the multimeter range to measure different parameters with standard operation, avoiding short circuits and incorrect measurements.

(2) Correctly collect the operational parameters of each terminal device connected to the Energy Internet platform.

(3) When inserting U-type cold-pressed terminals into the terminal block, ensure that the U-type part is fully inserted and facing outward.

(4) When sliding the number tube into place, all wiring directions perpendicular to the ground should have the number and letter combination readable from the end farthest from the connection to the connection point. For wiring directions parallel to the ground, the number and letter combination should be readable from left to right.

(5) When crimping the connection terminal, insert all stripped wire cores into the terminal. Use the crimping tool to ensure the crimping mark is at the bottom (back) of the terminal sleeve. After crimping, no wire cores should be exposed.

(6) Accurately observe and record equipment operation data, including both values and units.

Ⅳ. Task results, appraisal and evaluation

(1) The system is correctly commissioned and successfully operating; the data screen is well laid out and runs correctly; operation data are recorded; curves are drawn smooth (accounting for 90%).

(2) The operator exhibits good professional quality during the operation process and

follows 7S management model (accounting for 10%).

【Exercises】

1. What factors should be considered when choosing the installation site for wind power devices?

2. What are the conditions for installing wind turbines on open flat land?

3. What does component installation of offshore wind turbines include?

项目 8　运行与维护风力发电系统

任务 8.1　掌握风电场变电站倒闸操作

【学习目标】

　　知识目标：理解风力发电机组监控系统的原理和构成；掌握风电场监控系统的功能。
　　能力目标：能完成风电场变电站倒闸操作。
　　素质目标：培养自主创新、追求卓越的精神品质。
　　重点：风电场运行的操作票和工作票制度。
　　难点：风电场变电站倒闸操作。

【任务分析】

　　风电场变电站的工作票和操作票制度是保证风电场现场生产管理，规范各类工作人员的工作行为的重要制度，作业人员必须能够正确填写操作票和工作票，并按照流程实施倒闸操作任务。
　　依托全国职业院校技能大赛设备平台，完成配电系统的倒闸操作任务。

【知识学习】

　　为加强风电场现场生产管理，规范各类工作人员的工作行为，保证人身、电网设备安全，依据《电业安全工作规程　第1部分：热力和机械》(GB 26164.1—2010)、《风力发电场运行规程》(DL/T 666—2012)等有关规章制度，在风电场运行与维护过程中实施工作票和操作票制度。
　　工作票是保证生产现场、设备、系统上进行检修维护作业安全的技术措施与组织措施，是检修、运行人员双方共同持有、共同强制遵守的书面安全约定。操作票是运行人员改变设备、系统运行方式的指令及操作步骤，是运行人员从事现场操作的书面依据。在表现形式上，两者都是表格，需要相关执行的人员填写，责任管理人员签字审批。

1. 工作票

风电场的工作票分为以下几种：
(1) 电气第一种工作票：在风电场区内及场内线路、风机变作业，需要高压设备全部停电、部分停电或做安全措施的工作。
(2) 电气第二种工作票：带电作业和在带电设备外壳上的工作；二次接线回路上无须

将高压设备停电的工作；低压配电盘、配电箱回路上的工作；更换生产区域及相关区域照明灯泡的工作；在升压站、变压器、配电室、控制室区域等危险重要场所进行动土、植（除）草、粉刷墙壁、屋顶修缮、搭（拆）脚手架等，或在配电间进行粉刷墙壁、搭（拆）脚手架、保洁等，不需要将高压设备停电或做安全措施的工作。

（3）风机工作票：在风力发电机组本体进行的巡检、消缺、定检、技改等作业；风机巡检需要办理风机工作票，巡检过程中可对风机进行日常维护，如加水、加脂、加油、连接部位紧固、照明修复、补充标示牌、打扫卫生等工作。

（4）风力机械工作票：在机械设备及系统（生活水、消防水系统）上进行检修、维护工作；在生活水泵房、消防水泵房等生产区域内进行粉刷墙壁、屋顶修缮、整修地面、保洁（地面保洁除外）、搭（拆）脚手架等不需要做系统隔离措施的工作。

工作票编号共12位，由"风电场编号＋票种类＋年＋月＋月度序号"组成，含义如下：

1/2/3	4/5	6/7	8/9	10/11/12
风电场编码	票种类	年	月	月度序号

1~3位为风电场编码，按投产时间排序，从001开始，收购风电场按收购时间算。

4~5位为工作票种类，D1：电气第一种工作票；D2：电气第二种工作票；FJ：风机工作票；FL：风力机械工作票；H1：一级动火工作票；H2：二级动火工作票；DT：生产区域动土工作票；YX：有限空间作业安全措施票；JD：继电保护措施票。

6~7位表示年，如22表示2022年。8~9位表示月，如06表示6月。

10~12位表示当月工作票顺序排列号，每月从001开始。

如001D12206001表示某某电场2022年6月第1份电气第一种工作票。

工作票涉及人员有工作票签发人、工作负责人、工作许可人、工作协调人、第二监护人、工作班成员、工作票接收人、值班负责人、专责监护人、外包队伍业主带班人员等。电气工作票的执行流程有工作任务的派发、工作票的填写、工作票的签发、工作票的送达、工作票的接收、运行安全措施的落实、工作票运行许可、工前会、工作票检修许可、工作及工作监护、工作任务增加、工作间断和转移、工作负责人变更、工作成员变更、工作延期、检修设备试运、工作结束、工作票终结、安全措施恢复方面。风力机械工作票的派发、填写、签发、送达、接收、运行许可、工前会、工作负责人及成员变更、延期、试运、终结与电气工作票相同。风机工作票执行流程与电气工作票相同。

2. 操作票

电气倒闸操作票适用于风电场内一般电气操作和复杂电气操作。

操作票编号共12位，由"风电场编号＋票种类＋年＋月＋月度序号"组成，含义如下：

1/2/3	4/5	6/7	8/9	10/11/12
风电场编码	票种类	年	月	月度序号

1~3位为风电场编码，按投产时间排序，从001开始，收购风场按收购时间算。4~5位为操作票种类，DQ表示电气倒闸操作票。

6~7 位表示年，如 22 表示 2022 年。

8~9 位表示月，如 06 表示 6 月。

10~12 位表示当月操作票顺序排列号，每月从 001 开始。

风力发电机组
运行及维护要求

如 001DQ2206001 表示某某风电场 2022 年 6 月第 1 份电气倒闸操作票。

每份电气操作票由《电气倒闸操作前标准检查项目表》《电气倒闸操作票》和《电气倒闸操作后应完成的工作表》三部分组成。每份操作票应附有针对该项操作的危险点分析与控制措施内容，应使用统一格式。

操作票涉及人员有操作人、监护人、值班负责人、风电场管理人员。操作票执行流程包括接受操作预令、生成操作票、分析危险点，制定控制措施、票面审核、发布和接受操作命令、操作前准备、模拟操作、实际操作、终结等内容。根据要求，已执行的纸质操作票由风电场收存，保存六个月。

【任务实施】

1. 任务准备

竞赛设备平台 1 个、倒闸操作工具套装 1 份、工作票 1 份、操作票 1 份。

任务 8.1 相关
任务实施图表

2. 任务内容及步骤

任务：运行转检修倒闸操作

任务内容：完成运行转检修倒闸操作。

任务步骤：

（1）完成工作票填写。

（2）完成操作票填写。

（3）完成运行转检修倒闸操作任务。

3. 技能要求

（1）正确填写工作票。

（2）正确填写操作票。

（3）工作负责人角色正确履行职责任务。

（4）操作人角色正确履行职责任务。

（5）倒闸操作任务完成流畅，记录正确。

4. 任务成果及考核评价

（1）工作票填写正确、操作票填写正确，执行流畅，协作有序合理，占 90%。

（2）操作过程展现较好职业素养，做到 7S 管理，占 10%。

【练习】

1. 什么是工作票，其编号的含义是什么？

2. 什么是操作票，其编号的含义是什么？

任务 8.2　运行风力发电系统

【学习目标】

知识目标：理解风力发电机组变桨系统的巡视和检查；理解风力发电机组齿轮箱的巡视和检查；掌握风力发电机组的运行管理。

能力目标：能够正确巡视和检查风力发电机组的运行状态。

素质目标：培养自主创新、追求卓越的精神品质。

重点：风力发电机组变桨系统、齿轮箱的巡视和检查。

难点：风力发电机组的运行系统和运行管理。

【任务分析】

风力发电机组的正常运行影响着整个风电场的运行效益，在风力发电机组的巡视和检查过程中，需要完成对风力发电机组变桨系统、齿轮箱、机舱及附件机舱的巡视和检查，以保证风力发电机组设备正常运行，同时对风力发电机组运行状况进行实时监视，加强风力发电机组运行管理，促进风力发电系统在最优工况下运行。

依托全国职业院校技能大赛设备平台，完成风力发电系统实时运行管理监控系统设计，实现对发电参数采集与显示、远程控制功能与状态显示，以及身份认证登录。

【知识学习】

8.2.1　变桨系统巡视和检查

（1）叶片：通过目视、耳听方式，主要检查叶片表面是否无破损、无裂纹、无雷击，以及痕迹、无油污的情况；运转时，叶片是否无异常声音（如哨声），力矩线标识线清晰、连续覆盖螺母、垫片及基础，同一颗螺栓力矩线不能超过三条；叶片/轮毂连接螺栓有无松动、有无断裂情况。

（2）叶片轴承：通过目视、测试、耳听等方式，主要检查表面漆膜无龟裂、起泡、剥落情况；叶片变桨时，轴承应无异响；分油器有无漏油。

（3）叶轮机械锁：通过目视、手摸等方式，主要检查变桨系统数量齐全、无变形、无断裂、连接可靠的情况。

（4）轮毂及导流罩：通过目视方式，主要检查轮毂外观有无腐蚀、有无裂纹情况；导流罩有无破损、有无裂纹；导流罩支架有无裂纹、有无腐蚀、有无变形、螺栓有无松动；轮毂进入口是否固定牢靠（轮毂内工作完成后紧固）；轮毂内照明是否正常点亮、固定牢靠。

（5）变桨控制柜、超级电容：通过目视方式，主要检查是否关闭紧密、部件紧固牢固、电缆无放电痕迹。

（6）变桨电机：通过目视、鼻闻、测试等方式，主要检查漆膜是否完好、无锈蚀、接线牢固，无异味；连接螺栓是否无松动，无断裂；风扇是否可以正常运行。

项目8 运行与维护风力发电系统

(7) 变桨齿圈和驱动小齿轮：通过目视方式，主要检查润滑是否良好，无崩齿、无裂纹，无异常磨损。

(8) 螺栓：通过目视方式，主要检查力矩线标识线是否清晰、连续覆盖螺母、垫片及基础，同一颗螺栓力矩线不能超过三条。

(9) 其他检查方面：通过目视方式，主要检查各柜间连接电缆是否固定良好，无破损、放电痕迹；变桨轴承渗油情况是否无大量渗油积累；轮毂内表面是否无油污，无锈蚀，无裂纹；轮毂内叶片盖板是否无油污，无锈蚀，无裂纹，固定牢靠；雷击卡及引雷线是否固定牢靠，无雷击痕迹。

8.2.2 齿轮箱运行技术和巡视检查

1. 齿轮箱运行技术

(1) 齿轮箱工作时要求其内部的齿轮油温不得低于$-15℃$。即当温度低于$-15℃$时，先通过齿轮箱中的加热系统，将齿轮油加热到$-15℃$再启动机器。

(2) 当齿轮油温度在$-15\sim+45℃$时，油泵装置要求保证40（L/min）油流量，用于齿轮箱润滑。

(3) 齿轮油温度在$45\sim60℃$范围内时冷却齿轮箱所需油量为80（L/min）。

(4) 齿轮油油温超过$60℃$时则经热交换器对齿轮油进行强制冷却。

(5) 齿轮箱油温最高不应超过$80℃$，超过$80℃$将故障报警并作用于停机，不同轴承间的温差不得超过$15℃$。

(6) 运行温度：环境温度（指机舱内齿轮箱附近的空气温度）。

常温型：生存温度$-20\sim50℃$。

工作温度$-10\sim40℃$。

齿轮箱运转在机舱内的最低温度是$-30℃$，低于这个温度禁止运行，齿轮箱在机舱内的存储温度是$-40℃$，最高不超过$50℃$。

(7) 油池温度：正常运转时的油池温度低于$70℃$，如果油池温度超过$90℃$，并且持续时间超过30分钟，风机必须停止运转，如果温度超过$80℃$，风机应立即停止运转，经历高温停止的风机再启动前，应进行内部检查。

(8) 轴承温度：正常运转时的轴承温度低于$90℃$，如果轴承温度超过$90℃$持续超过30min，风机必须停止运转，如果超过$95℃$，风机应当立即停止运转，经历高温停止的风机再启动前，应进行内部检查。

2. 巡视检查内容

(1) 检查齿轮箱表面的防腐涂层是否有脱落现象。

(2) 检查齿轮箱表面清洁度。

(3) 检查齿轮箱低速端、高速端、各联结处是否有漏油、渗油现象。

(4) 检查润滑冷却油油位、油色是否正常。

(5) 检查齿轮箱空气过滤器。

(6) 检查齿轮箱噪声。

(7) 检查齿轮箱振动情况。

(8) 检查轮齿啮合及齿轮表面情况。
(9) 检测齿轮箱上所有的温度、压力传感器，查看其连接是否牢固。
(10) 检查单个齿轮箱轴承温度。
(11) 检查齿轮箱油冷回路中的压力。
(12) 检查管路连接情况。
(13) 检查热交换器上电动机的接线情况及风扇是否有过多的污垢以及旋转方向是否正常。
(14) 热交换器与其支架的各连接部位的连接情况。
(15) 检查热交换器的整体运转情况是否正常，是否存在震动、噪声过大等现象。
(16) 检查冷却润滑油泵与过滤器的连接处是否漏油。
(17) 检查两个手动阀，检查其工作是否正确，有无漏油现象。

8.2.3 机舱及附件机舱

1. 自动消防

风力发电机机组都必须配备自动消防装置。如远景 EN121-2200 机组配备一套 FFX-ACT5 自动灭火系统，储存有 2 罐 8kg 干粉灭火器，存于塔顶位置，当检测到火灾信号时，干粉自动释放，扑灭火灾。

2. 逃生包

(1) 检查装置是否放置在机舱尾部的规定位置，如没有在规定位置需将装置归位。
(2) 检查逃生装置和救援装置是否在正常的质量范围内。
(3) 检查逃生包内的绳子是否杂乱无序，如果存在杂乱现象需重新整理绳子。
(4) 检查主装置外观是否良好，无锈蚀，紧固件无松动。

3. 底座

底座传递所有影响叶轮、发电机或塔架的静态和动态载荷。底座通过偏航轴承与塔架连接，机舱在偏航机构的驱动下使叶轮对准风向。

4. 基础

基础是机组安全和稳定的最基本保证。基础设计为钢筋混凝土基础，叶轮的载荷通过各段塔架相继传送到基础。基础环是一个较短的与基础连接在一起的钢制圆筒。

5. 防雷系统

防雷系统是机组安全运行的重要保障，它有多种避雷装置组成。风电机组的机舱整体主要包括机舱罩、轮毂、齿轮箱、发电机、控制柜等主要部件。布置机舱的防雷接地系统，主要是建立正确合理的雷电流泄放通道，实现强弱电分开，使雷电流瞬间以最短路径导入大地，有效保护舱内的各个设备和电器元件。

8.2.4 运行系统的说明

1. 运行状态

风力发电机的运行模式是指，风机状态参数在某种特定条件的逻辑组合下，能构成一个风机运行过程中必然经历的模式，那么此种状态就可定义为一种运行模式，例如待机、等风、自检、启动、停止等不同运行工况。风机所有模式的组合，可包含机组全部行为，不同运行模式之间都有特定切换条件。

风机在无故障等待状态下时，高速刹车松开，桨距角为89°，风机空转。

当风速不小于设定风速时，自动偏航启动，风机将自动对风。

风机对风后，桨距角会逐步降低，风机平稳升速，当转速升至某个特定值时，就会自动并网。

风机的发电过程中，会有两个闭环控制器介入风机的运行：

（1）风速低于额定风速时，风机欠负荷运行，通过双馈异步发电机的变频器来控制发电机的转矩，从而根据转矩转速特性来优化发电机的输出功率。风机会在不同的转速下并网运行。

（2）风速高于额定风速时，通过调整叶片角度来限制发电功率。此时，发电机输出功率会通过变频器控制保持在额定值。当有暴风时，风机的第一反应是风轮加速，然后会通过升高桨距角来降低转速，从而使风轮转速保持在设定转速（根据叶片直径不同转速也会不同）。风机会在变桨变速下并网运行风速太低时，转子不动，等待风起来时自动运转。

2. 风电机组在投入运行前应具备的条件

（1）电源相序正确，三相电压平衡。

（2）调向系统处于正常状态，风速仪和风向标处于正常运行的状态。

（3）制动和控制系统的液压装置的油压和油位在规定范围。

（4）变速箱油位和油温在正常范围。

（5）各项保护装置均在正确投入位置，且保护定值均与批准设定的值相符。

（6）控制电源处于接通位置。

（7）控制计算机显示处于正常运行状态。

（8）手动启动前叶轮上应无结冰现象。

（9）长期停用和新投运的风电机组在投入运行前应检查绝缘，合格后才允许启动。

（10）经维修的风电机组在启动前，所有为检修而设立的各种安全措施应已拆除。

（11）检查SCADA通信系统是否处于正常状态。

（12）动力电源处于接通位置，且冷却电机、加热电机、偏航电机、液压电机能够正常运转。

3. 风电机组的启动和停机

风电机组的启动和停机有手动和自动两种方式。

风电机组应能自动启动和停机。

风电机组的自动启动：风电机组处于自动状态，当风速达到启动风速范围时，风电组按计算机程序自动启动并入电网。

风电机组的自动停机：风电机组处于自动状态，当风速超出正常运行范围时，风电机组按计算机程序自动与电网解列、停机。

风电机组的手动启动和停机手动启动和停机有四种操作方式，其操作条件为：

1）主控室操作：在主控室操作计算机启动键和停机键。

2）就地操作：断开遥控操作开关，在风电机组的控制盘上，操作启动或停机按钮，操作后再合上遥控开关。

3) 远程操作：在远程终端操作启动键或停机键。

4) 机舱上操作：在机舱的控制盘上操作启动键或停机键，但机舱上操作仅限于调试时使用。

5) 风电机组的手动启动：当风速达到启动风速范围时，手动操作启动键或按钮，风电机组按计算机启动程序启动和并网。

6) 风电机组的手动停机：当风速超出正常运行范围时，手动操作停机键或按钮，风电机组按计算机停机程序与电网解列、停机。

7) 凡经手动停机操作后，须再按"启动"按钮，方能使风电机组进入自启状态。

8) 故障停机和紧急停机状态下的手动启动操作。

9) 风电机组在故障停机和紧急停机后，如故障已排除且具备启动的条件，重新启动前必须按"重置"或"复位"就地控制按钮，方能按正常启动操作方式进行启动。

8.2.5 风电机组运行管理

巡视人员对监控风电场安全稳定运行负有直接责任，应按要求定期（每3个月）到现场通过目视观察等直观方法对风电机组的运行状况进行巡视检查。应当注意的是，所有外出工作出于安全考虑均需两人或两人以上同行。检查工作主要包括风电机组在运行中有无异常声响、叶片运行的状态、偏航系统动作是否正常、塔架外表有无油迹污染等。巡检过程中要根据设备近期的实际情况，有针对性地重点检查，尤其是重点检查重新投入运行的机组。重点检查启停频繁的机组，重点检查负荷重、温度偏高的机组，重点检查带病运行的机组，重点检查重新投入运行的机组。若发现故障隐患，则应及时报告处理，查明原因，从而避免事故发生，减少经济损失。同时做好相应巡视检查记录。风电机组故障停机原因未查明，禁止运行人员盲目远程复位风电机组。发现风电机组反复自动复位（3次以上）应立即手动停机，查明原因。

8.2.6 风电场运行监视

(1) 风电场运行人员每天应按时收听和记录当地天气预报，做好风电场安全运行的事故预想和对策。

(2) 运行人员每天应定时通过主控室计算机的屏幕监视风电机组各参数变化情况。

(3) 运行人员应根据计算机显示的风电机组运行参数，检查分析各项参数变化情况，发现异常情况应通过计算机屏幕对该机组进行连续监视，并根据变化情况作出必要处理。同时在运行日志上写明原因，进行故障记录与统计。

(4) 风机的检查。运行人员应定期对风电机组、风电场测风装置、场内高压配电线路进行巡回检查，发现缺陷及时处理，并登记在缺陷记录本上。

1) 检查风电机组在运行中有无异常响声、叶片运行状态、调向系统动作是否正常，电缆有无绞缠情况。

2) 检查风电机组各部分是否渗油。

3) 当气候异常、机组非正常运行、或新设备投入运行时，需要增加巡回检查内容及次数。

4）风电机组故障停机原因未查明，禁止运行人员盲目远程复位风电机组。发现风电机组反复自动复位（3次以上）应立即手动停机，查明原因。

5）风电场综合后台、风机 SCADA 系统必须具备音响报警功能。

6）主控室每小时与作业现场联络机制等。

【任务实施】

1. 任务准备

竞赛设备平台 1 个、万用表 1 个、上电检查记录表 1 份、风力发电系统实时监控记录表 1 份。

2. 任务内容及步骤

任务：风力发电实时监控系统设计

任务 8.2 相关任务实施图表

任务内容：完成风力发电实时监控系统设计。

任务步骤：

（1）完成不同管理权限的身份登录管理界面设计与制作。

（2）完成风力电站设备检测与控制界面设计与制作。

（3）完成负载设备检测与控制界面设计与制作。

（4）完成通信配置，实现界面数据采集。

（5）完成系统上电检查，正确调试与运行风力发电系统实时监控，填写风力发电系统实时监控记录表。

3. 技能要求

（1）正确使用万用表档位进行不同参数的测量，操作规范、无短路、无错档测量。

（2）正确采集连接至风力发电实时监控系统的各个终端设备运行参数。

（3）界面元件尺寸合理、布局整齐、色彩搭配美观。

（4）界面功能齐全，具有界面登录、转换等按钮。

（5）界面实时数据显示正确，能够实现对设备的远程控制及状态显示。

（6）对设备运行数据观察到位，记录正确，记录参数数据包含数值和单位。

4. 任务成果及考核评价

（1）系统调试正确且成功运行、数据界面运行数据正确，能记录运行数据，曲线绘制平滑，布局合理，占 90%。

（2）操作过程展现较好职业素养，做到 7S 管理，占 10%。

【练习】

1. 齿轮箱巡视检查内容有哪些？
2. 风电机组在投入运行前应具备哪些条件？
3. 风电机组运行管理内容有哪些？
4. 风机的检查内容有哪些？

任务 8.3 维护风力发电系统

【学习目标】

知识目标:理解风电机组的检查维护内容;掌握风电机组的日常维护事项;掌握风电机组日常事故内容与要求。

能力目标:能完成风电机组日常维护;能处理风电机组日常事故。

素质目标:培养自主学习、开创进取的精神品质。

重点:风电机组的日常维护内容。

难点:风电机组日常事故内容与处理。

【任务分析】

风电机组是一种复杂的机器设备,需要经常进行各种维护和保养工作,以确保其高效、稳定、安全地运转。风电机组的定期检修维护可以使设备保持最佳状态,并延长风电机组的使用寿命,减少维修成本和停机时间,提高发电效率。正确的风电机组维护方法包含定期检查风电机、维护和更换润滑油、清理和更换过滤器、做好安全工作等方面。

依托全国职业院校技能大赛设备平台,完成风力发电系统搭建,实现多能源、多负载能源调度运营,完成风力发电系统的运行与维护任务。

【知识学习】

8.3.1 风电机组检查维护

1. 风电机组检查维护事项

风电机组的定期登塔检查维护应在手动"停机"状态下进行。戴安全帽、穿安全鞋。零配件及工具必须单独放在工具袋内,工具袋必须与安全绳联结牢固,以防坠塔。

(1) 检查风电机组液压系统和齿轮箱以及其他润滑系统有无泄漏,油面、油温是否正常,油面低于规定时要及时加油。

(2) 对设备螺栓应定期检查、紧固。

(3) 对液压系统、齿轮箱、润滑系统应定期取油样进行化学分析,对轴承润滑点定时注油。

(4) 对爬梯、安全绳、照明设备等安全设施应定期检查。

(5) 控制箱应保持清洁,定期进行清扫。

(6) 对主控室计算机系统和通信设备应定期进行检查和维护。

2. 停机的几种原因

下面给出了几种风机停机的原因和控制系统所作的相应的操作,遇到如下情况时,风机执行正常停机:

(1) 风速过高,伴随强阵风,10min 后系统判断是否重启。

(2) 电网波动。

(3) 环境温度低于-30℃，温度回升后自动重启。

(4) 油位低于设定值。

(5) 理论和实际的功率曲线偏差太大，不自动重启。

(6) 零部件损坏，零部件过热。

(7) 扭缆，解缆后自动重启。

(8) 偏航系统故障，根据不同的故障，系统判断是否重启。

(9) 速度检测故障（无紧急停机速度），自动重启。

3. 接近风电机组时的安全要求

(1) 雷电天气，禁止人员进入或靠近风机，至少在雷电过去1h后再进入。

(2) 车辆靠近风电机组需停在上风向20m以外。

(3) 靠近风电机组时，正确佩戴安全帽。

(4) 用提升机吊物时应使用导向绳，同时确保此期间无人在塔架周围，避免坠物伤人。

4. 在风电机组内工作的安全要求

(1) 工作人员攀爬塔架时，应戴好安全帽、脚工作鞋、装备并挂好专用安全带。攀爬之前，必须仔细检查梯架、安全带和安全绳，如果发现任何损坏，应在修复之后方可攀爬。平台窗口盖板在通过后应当立即关闭。

(2) 塔筒内无照明时，原则上不允许攀爬风机。确因工作需要必须攀爬风机时，应携带必要的照明设备。攀爬风机时，随身携带的小工具或小零件必须放在工具包中，防止意外坠落伤人。不方便随身携带的重物应使用提升机输送。

(3) 风速≥12m/s时，禁止在机舱外作业，不得打开机舱盖；风速≥14m/s时，应关闭机舱盖；风速≥18m/s时，禁止在机舱内工作。

(4) 工作人员进入风机维护操作时，应先将启停开关打至"停机"状态，然后将切换开关扳到"维护"或"维修"状态。

(5) 任何人员需要在机舱外部工作时，必须系上安全带并将安全带挂好，防止意外坠落。

(6) 一般情况下，一项工作应由两个或以上的人员来共同完成。相互之间应能随时保持联系，超出视线或听觉范围，应使用对讲机或移动电话等通讯设备来保持联系。只有在特殊情况下，工作人员方可单独进行工作，但必须保证与控制室人员有可靠的通信联系。

5. 运动部件的危险性

(1) 机舱是运动部件，机舱通过偏航轴承与塔架连接，在此区域里，塔架和机舱的相对运动是一个危险因素，不允许在偏航齿轮附近逗留，以免被偏航驱动夹伤。

(2) 偏航刹车闸安装在机舱底座下部，闸片贴着偏航刹车盘运动，不允许接触偏航刹车装置内部以免被偏航刹车夹伤。

(3) 在主轴、集电环、弹性联轴器等转动部件附近作业过程中应确保整个传动系统不会被无意识启动，以防操作人员被转动部件伤害。

(4) 进入轮毂前必须将液压刹车打至刹车状态并锁定风轮机械锁；在轮毂内作业过程

中未经许可,不得擅自进行变桨操作,如果误操作,可能会导致严重的设备损坏或人身伤害,只有通过专业培训的维修人员才能进入轮毂内部作业。

6. 风电机组的保护措施

风力发电机组必须具备一套逻辑上独立于控制系统的安全(链)系统。在运行过程中有关安全的极限值被超过以后,或者如果控制系统不能使机组保持在正常的运行范围内时,则安全系统动作,使机组最终停止转动。

允许采取间接的方法验证安全系统在出现下列情况时可靠动作:超速;功率超限;发电机短路;机舱过度振动;由于机舱偏航转动造成电缆的过度缠绕;控制系统功能失效;紧急停机;其他与安全系统有关的故障。

控制功能试验。控制系统的功能应满足在规定的运行条件下都能使风力发电机组的运行参数保持在其正常运行范围内。

控制系统的控制功能控制功能试验项目如下:机组的启动和停止;发电特性;偏航稳定性;转速变化的平稳性;功率因数的自动调节;扭缆限制;电网异常或负载丢失时的停机等;制动功能(正常刹车和紧急刹车)。

上述控制功能应满足设计要求。

控制系统的检测和监控功能。应测试控制系统对风力发电机组运行参数和状态的检测和监控功能,包括:①风速和风向;②风轮和发电机转速;③电气参数,包括电网电压和频率、发电机输出电流、功率和功率因数;④温度,包括发电机绕组温度和轴承温度、齿轮箱油温、控制柜温度和环境温度等;⑤制动设备状况;⑥电缆缠绕;⑦机械零部件故障;⑧电网失效等。

7. 风电机组的被动保护系统

被动保护系统能保护风机免受外部环境的影响,如雷电、重载荷等。叶片里安装有雷电感应器,内部的导电系统可以防止叶片受到雷击。另外,变桨系统可以一直保持正常工作,即便是在风机受到雷击的时候。

顺桨刹车时,叶轮的自由运转产生的扭矩很小,因此,风机受到的载荷也很小,这就是不锁定叶轮(即便是紧急停机)的原因。

8.3.2 风电机组的日常维护

维护工作是机组安全、正常、可靠运行的保障,为了保证风电机组的安全稳定运行,延长使用寿命,对机组的检查和维护工作是必不可少的,因此我们应定期对机组进行维护,根据维护时间的不同,维护可分为首次维护、500小时维护和定期维护几种,下面就根据维护周期不同具体说明。

1. 首次维护与500h维护

在风电机组正常安装调试过程中,应在机组第一次并网一周后对风机塔筒进行检查,并在第一次并网四周后进行500h维护。

风机并网一周后,应对风机塔筒做初次检查,内容包括:①检查法兰连接处所有螺栓;②检查接口焊缝是否有裂缝;③检查塔筒内各层平台是否稳固。

如果检查时发现有损坏,依据有关"塔筒"的内容做详细检查。如果没有,在检查文档中记录下来，风机没有出现损坏。

500h维护指的是首检后，机组运行的500h或1个月后，做并网后的第二次最终检查。它应对每一点、每一个设置以及第一次并网的工作，进行第二次最终检查。检查内容包括：①按照螺栓力矩表检查所有的螺栓力矩并将其打至额定力矩；②对油滤系统（齿轮箱、液压站）滤芯检查，如有必要进行更换；③检查液压回路是否泄漏；④检查主轴、叶轮轴承等部位轴承的润滑油是否正常；⑤检查机舱或轮毂内和转动部件是否有异响；⑥检查齿箱冷却系统是否泄漏。

2. 定期维护

风机正常投入运行后，经过相应的时间间隔应做定期保养维护，以检查机组运行过程中可能产生的潜在问题，并将之消除在萌芽状态，防止问题的继续扩大，对风机的运行和使用寿命造成影响。

当维护人员进入风机时，有些维护是每次都要进行的，即对一些重要，易损坏的部件加强维护。

在特殊情况下进行的消缺维护也要详细记录。例如，雷击、更换旧零件等。之后必须遵循正常的维护周期。如果有任何疑虑，可以选择更保守、更短的维护周期。

(1) 日常维护。日常维护的间隔与时间无关（所有风机3个月至少完成一次），每次进入风机（无论什么原因）时，都要进行日常维护项目的检查。这些维护检查点列出了进入风机时必要的步骤（开门、开灯、停机、进入安全模式等等），还列出了离开风机时必要的步骤（运行测试、检查所有工具、清理工作地点、填写记录）。

日常维护需要进行常规的肉眼检查和噪声检查。例如：油的颜色是否正常、塔筒平台或机架上是否有油或冷却水泄漏的痕迹、是否有断裂的螺栓、是否有闪电击中的迹象、是否有东西发出咔哒声或嘶嘶声等。

(2) 半年维护。两个维护期间隔半年。需要准确完成半年内的定期维护检查及维护工作项。

(3) 整年维护。每年维护要做彻底的检查和维护。每12个月一次，该项工作与机组运行小时数无关，即使上次维护后没有运行也要进行。

8.3.3 风力发电设备事故处理

1. 风电场异常运行与事故处理基本要求

(1) 当风力设备出现异常运行或发生事故时，当班值长应组织运行人员尽快排除异常，恢复设备正常运行，处理情况记录在运行日志上。

(2) 事故发生时，应采取措施控制事故不再扩大并及时向有关领导汇报，在事故原因查清前，运行人员应保护好事故现场和损害的设备，特殊情况例外（如抢救人员生命）。如需立即进行抢修的，必须经领导同意。

(3) 当事故发生在交接班过程中，应停止接班，交班人员必须坚守岗位、处理事故，接班人员应在交班值长指挥下协助事故处理。事故处理告一段落后，交接双方值长决定是否继续交接班。

(4) 事故处理完毕后，当班值长应将事故发生的经过和处理情况，如实记录在交班簿上。事故发生后应根据计算机记录，对保护、信号及自动装置动作情况进行分析，查明事故发生的原因，并写出书面报告，汇报上级领导。

2. 风电机组异常运行及故障处理

(1) 对于标志机组有异常情况的报警信号，运行人员要根据报警信号提供的部位进行现场检查和清理。

(2) 测风仪故障。风电机组显示输出功率与对应风速有偏差时，检查风速仪、风向仪的传感器有无故障，如有故障则予以排除。

(3) 风电机组在运行中发现有异常声音，应查明响声部位，分析原因，并做出处理。

(4) 风电机组在运行中发生设备和部件超过运行温度而自动停机的处理。风电机组在运行中发电机温度、变频柜温度、控制箱温度、机械制动刹车片温度、冷却器温度超过规定值均会造成自动停机。运行人员应查明设备温度上升原因，如检查冷却系统、刹车片间隙、刹车片温度传感器及变送回路。待故障排除后，才能再启动风电机组。

(5) 风电机组液压控制系统油压过低而自动停机的处理。运行人员应检查油泵工作是否正常。如油压不正常应检查油泵、油压缸及有关阀门，待故障排除后再恢复机组自启动。

(6) 风电机组因调向故障而造成自动停机的处理。运行人员应检查调向机构电气回路、偏航电动机与缠绕传感器工作是否正常，电动机损坏应予更换，对于因缠绕传感器故障致使电缆不能松线的应予以处理。待故障排除后再恢复自启动。

(7) 风电机组振动超过允许振幅而自动停机的处理。风电机组运行中，由于喘振或变桨系统失灵会造成风电机组振动超过极限值。以上情况发生均使风电机组安全停机，运行人员应检查振动的原因，经处理后，才允许重新启动。

(8) 当风电机组运行中发生系统断电或线路开关跳闸的处理。当电网发生系统故障造成断电或线路故障导致线路开关跳闸时，运行人员应检查线路断电或跳闸原因（若逢夜间应首先恢复主控室用电），待系统恢复正常，则重新启动机组并通过计算机并网。

3. 风电机组因异常需要立即进行停机操作的顺序

(1) 利用主控室计算机进行遥控停机。

(2) 当遥控停机无效时，则就地按下停机按钮并将"参观/运行/检修维护"钥匙置于"参观"位置。

(3) 当正常停机无效时，使用紧急停机按钮停机。

(4) 仍然无效时，断开箱变低压测断路器或连接此台机组的线路断路器。

4. 风力发电机典型事故处理

发生下列事故之一者，应立即停运风力发电机组：

(1) 明显的叶片破损。

(2) 风电机组主要保护装置拒动或失灵时。

(3) 风电机组因雷击损坏时。

(4) 风电机组因发生叶片断裂等严重机械故障时。

(5) 制动系统故障时。

当机组发生起火时，运行人员应立即停机并切断电源，迅速采取灭火措施，防止火势蔓延；当机组发生危机人员和设备安全的故障时，值班人员应立即断开该机组箱变低压侧断路器。

风电机组主开关发生跳闸时，要先检查主回路变频装置、发电机绝缘是否击穿，主开关整定动作值是否正确，确定无误后才能重合开关，否则应退出运行进一步检查。

风电机组液压控制系统油压过低而自动停机的处理：运行人员应检查油泵工作是否正常。如油压不正常，应检查油泵、油压缸及有关阀门，待故障排除后再恢复机组自启动。

风电机组因调向故障而造成自动停机的处理：运行人员应检查调向机构电气回路、偏航电动机与缠绕传感器工作是否正常，电动机损坏应予更换，对于因缠绕传感器故障致使电缆不能松线的应予处理。待故障排除后再恢复自启动。

风电机组转速超过极限或振动超过允许振幅而自动停机的处理：风电机组运行中，由于变桨系统失灵会造成风电机组超速；机械不平衡，则造成风电机组振动超过极限值。以上情况发生均使风电机组安全停机。运行人员应检查超速、振动的原因，经处理后，才允许重新启动。

风电机组运行中发生系统断电或线路开关跳闸的处理：当电网发生系统故障造成断电或线路开关跳闸时，运行人员应检查线路断电或跳闸原因（若逢夜间应首先恢复主控室用电），待系统恢复正常，则重新启动机组并通过计算机并网。当箱变高压侧开关或低压侧熔丝熔断时，则应根据变压器故障的分析处理，待正常后并网。

当机组发生火灾时，运行人员应立即停机并切断电源，迅速采取灭火措施，防止火势蔓延；当机组发生危机人员和设备安全的故障时，值班人员应立即拉开该机组线路侧的断路器。

风电机组主开关发生跳闸，要先检查主回路可控硅、发电机绝缘是否击穿，主开关整定动作值是否正确，确定无误后才能重合开关。否则应退出运行进一步检查。

机组出现振动故障时，要先检查保护回路，若不是误动，应立即停止运行做进一步检查。

【任务实施】

1. 任务准备

竞赛设备平台1个、一字螺丝刀1把、十字螺丝刀1把、剥线钳1把、U形压线钳1把、管型压线钳1把、万用表1个、上电检查记录表1份、多能源与多负载系统协调运行记录表1份、导线若干。

2. 任务内容及步骤

任务8.3 相关任务实施图表

任务：多能源与多负载系统搭建与运行维护

任务内容：完成多能源与多负载系统搭建与运行维护。

任务步骤：

(1) 完成多能源与多负载系统连接导线的制作。

(2) 按照接线图，完成多能源与多负载系统控制 PLC 和继电器模块的布线与接线。

(3) 按照接线图，完成多能源与多负载系统本地控制模块的布线与接线。

(4) 按照接线图，完成工控机多能源与多负载系统电控制界面设计。

(5) 完成系统上电检查，正确调试与运行多能源与多负载系统控制系统。

3. 技能要求

(1) 正确使用万用表档位进行不同参数的测量，操作规范，无短路、无错档测量。

(2) 正确测量多能源与多负载系统运行电压、电流等参数。

(3) U 形冷压端子在插入端子排时，U 形部分应充分插入，并保证正面朝外。

(4) 号码管在套入时，所有接线方向垂直于地面的套管，号码及字母组合读序从远离接线端至接线口，所有接线方向平行于地面的套管，号码及字母组合读序从左至右。

(5) 在压接接线端子时，剥开的线芯插入接线端子套时，将所有的线芯全部插入端子中；采用压线钳压接接线端子时，应使压痕在接线端子套的底部（反面），压接后，压接部位不允许有导线外露。

(6) 对设备运行数据观察到位，记录正确，记录参数数据包含数值和单位。

4. 任务成果及考核评价

(1) 系统调试正确且成功运行、数据界面运行数据正确，能记录运行数据，曲线绘制平滑，布局合理，占 90％。

(2) 操作过程展现较好职业素养，做到 7S 管理，占 10％。

【练习】

1. 风电机组检查维护事项有哪些？
2. 在风电机组内工作的安全要求有哪些？
3. 机组运行的 500 小时或 1 个月后，做并网后第二次最终检查的内容有哪些？
4. 风电场异常运行与事故处理基本要求有哪些？
5. 当发生哪些事故时，应立即停运风力发电机组？

Project 8　Operation and Maintenance of Wind Power Systems

Task 8.1　Mastering Switching Operations in Wind Farm Substations

【Learning objectives】

Knowledge objective: To understand the principles and composition of the wind turbine monitoring system and master the functions of the wind farm monitoring system.

Ability objective: To be able to complete the switching operations in wind farm substations.

Qualification objective: To cultivate a spirit of independent innovation and the pursuit of excellence.

Learning priority: The work ticket and operation ticket system in wind farm operations.

Learning challenge: Switching operations in wind farm substations.

【Task analysis】

The work ticket and operation ticket system in wind farm substations is a crucial system to ensure on-site production management and standardize the behavior of various personnel. Operators must be able to correctly fill out work and operation tickets and perform switching operations according to the procedures.

This task relies on the equipment platform of the National Vocational College Skills Competition, complete the switching operation tasks of the distribution system.

【Knowledge learning】

To strengthen on-site production management in wind farms, standardize the behavior of various personnel, and ensure the safety of personnel and power grid equipment, the work ticket and operation ticket system is implemented during the operation and maintenance of wind farms based on relevant regulations such as the *Safety code of electric power industry-Part*1: *Thermal and machine* (GB 26164.1-2010) and *Code on operation of wind farm* (DL/T 666-2012).

Project 8   Operation and Maintenance of Wind Power Systems

Work tickets are technical and organizational measures to ensure safety during maintenance operations on production sites, equipment, and systems. They are a written safety agreement jointly held and enforced by both maintenance and operational personnel. Operation tickets are written instructions and steps for operators to change the operating mode of equipment and systems and are the basis for on-site operations. Both are in the form of forms that need to be filled out by relevant personnel and approved by responsible management personnel.

1. Work ticket

There are several types of work tickets in wind farms:

(1) Electrical work ticket type 1: For work in the wind farm area, including lines and turbine transformations, requiring total or partial power outages or safety measures for high-voltage equipment.

(2) Electrical work ticket type 2: For live work and work on live equipment enclosures; work on secondary wiring circuits without needing to power down high-voltage equipment; work on low-voltage distribution panels and circuits; replacing lighting bulbs in production and related areas; for activities such as ground excavation, planting or removing grass, painting walls, roof repairs, and erecting or dismantling scaffolding in critical and hazardous areas like substations, transformer stations, distribution rooms, and control rooms, or for painting walls, erecting or dismantling scaffolding, and cleaning in distribution rooms, without needing to de-energize high-voltage equipment or implement safety measures.

(3) Wind turbine work ticket: This ticket is required for inspections, defect corrections, regular maintenance, and technical modifications performed on the wind turbine itself. When conducting inspections, a wind turbine work ticket must be obtained. During the inspection, routine maintenance tasks such as adding water, grease, or oil, tightening connections, repairing lighting, adding signage, and cleaning can be performed.

(4) Wind mechanical work ticket: For maintenance on mechanical equipment and systems (such as domestic water and fire water systems); work in areas like water pump rooms and fire pump rooms, including painting walls, roof repairs, floor repairs, and cleaning (excluding floor cleaning) without needing system isolation measures.

The work ticket number consists of 12 digits, composed of "Wind Farm Number + Ticket + Type + Year + Month + Monthly Sequence Number" as follows:

1/2/3	4/5	6/7	8/9	10/11/12
Ticket	Type	Year	Month	Monthly Sequence Number

Digits 1 – 3: Wind farm code, sorted by commissioning time, starting from 001. Acquired wind farms are coded by acquisition time.

Digits 4 – 5: Work ticket type, with D1 for Electrical Work Ticket Type 1, D2 for Electrical Work Ticket Type 2, FJ for Turbine Work Ticket, FL for Wind Mechanical

Work Ticket, H1 for First-Level Hot Work Ticket, H2 for Second-Level Hot Work Ticket, DT for Production Area Earthwork Work Ticket, YX for Confined Space Operation Safety Measures Ticket, JD for Relay Protection Measures Ticket.

Digits 6 – 7: Year, e.g., 22 for 2022.

Digits 8 – 9: Month, e.g., 06 for June.

Digits 10 – 12: Monthly sequence number, starting from 001 each month.

For example, 001D12206001 indicates the first Electrical Work Ticket Type 1 in June 2022 for a particular wind farm.

Work tickets involve personnel such as the ticket issuer, work supervisor, work permit issuer, work coordinator, second supervisor, work team members, ticket receiver, on-duty supervisor, dedicated supervisor, and external team owner representatives. The execution process for electrical work tickets includes task assignment, ticket filling, ticket issuance, ticket delivery, ticket receipt, implementation of safety measures, work permit issuance, pre-work meeting, maintenance permit, work and supervision, task addition, work interruption and transfer, change of work supervisor, change of work members, work extension, trial operation of equipment, work completion, ticket closure, and safety measure restoration. The distribution, completion, issuance, delivery, receipt, operation permit, pre-job meeting, changes in work supervisor and team members, extension, trial operation, and termination of wind turbine work tickets are the same as those for electrical work tickets. The execution process for wind turbine work tickets is identical to that of electrical work tickets.

2. Operation ticket

Electrical switching operation tickets are applicable for general and complex electrical operations within wind farms.

The operation ticket number consists of 12 digits, composed of "Wind Farm Number + Ticket + Type + Year + Month + Monthly Sequence Number" as follows:

1/2/3	4/5	6/7	8/9	10/11/12
Ticket	Type	Year	Month	Monthly Sequence Number

Digits 1 – 3: Wind farm code, sorted by commissioning time, starting from 001. Acquired wind farms are coded by acquisition time.

Digits 4 – 5: Operation ticket type, with DQ indicating Electrical Switching Operation Ticket.

Digits 6 – 7: Year, e.g., 22 for 2022.

Digits 8 – 9: Month, e.g., 06 for June.

Digits 10 – 12: Monthly sequence number, starting from 001 each month.

For example, 001DQ2206001 indicates the first Electrical Switching Operation Ticket in June 2022 for a particular wind farm.

Each electrical operation ticket consists of three parts: the "Standard Inspection

Checklist for Electrical Switching Operation," the "Electrical Switching Operation Permit," and the "Post-Operation Work Completion Checklist." Each operation ticket should include a risk analysis and control measures content specific to the operation, using a unified format.

Operation tickets involve personnel such as operators, supervisors, on-duty supervisors, and wind farm management personnel. The execution process includes accepting pre-operation orders, generating operation tickets, analyzing risk points, formulating control measures, reviewing tickets, issuing and accepting operation commands, pre-operation preparations, simulated operations, actual operations, and ticket closure. Paper operation tickets that have been executed are stored by the wind farm for six months as required.

Operation and maintenance requirement for wind turbines

【Task implementation】

I. Task preparation

1 competition equipment platform, 1 set of electrical switching operation tools, 1 work ticket, 1 operation ticket

Task 8.1 Related implementation charts

II. Task content and procedures

Task: Switching operations from operation to maintenance

Task content: Complete the switching operations from operation to maintenance.

Task procedures:

(1) Complete the work ticket filling.

(2) Complete the operation ticket filling.

(3) Complete the switching operation task from operation to maintenance.

III. Skill requirements

(1) Correctly fill out work tickets.

(2) Correctly fill out operation tickets.

(3) The work supervisor must correctly fulfill their duties.

(4) The operator must correctly fulfill their duties.

(5) The switching operation task should be completed smoothly, with accurate records.

IV. Task results, appraisal and evaluation

(1) Both the work ticket and operation ticket are filled in correctly, the execution is smooth, and the collaboration is orderly and reasonable (accounting for 90%);

(2) The operator exhibits good professional quality during the operation process and follows 7S management model (accounting for 10%).

【Exercises】

1. What is a work ticket, and what is the significance of its numbering?

Project 8 Operation and Maintenance of Wind Power Systems

2. What is an operation ticket, and what is the significance of its numbering?

Task 8.2   Operation of Wind Power Generation Systems

【Learning objectives】

Knowledge objective: To understand the inspection and maintenance of the pitch system of wind turbines, understand the inspection and maintenance of the gearbox of wind turbines and master the operational management of wind turbines.

Ability objective: To be able to correctly inspect and maintain the operational status of wind turbines.

Qualification objective: To cultivate the spirit of independent innovation and pursuit of excellence.

Learning priority: Inspection and maintenance of the pitch system and gearbox of wind turbines.

Learning challenge: Operational system and management of wind turbines.

【Task analysis】

The normal operation of wind turbines affects the operational efficiency of the entire wind farm. During the inspection and maintenance of wind turbines, it is necessary to complete the inspection and maintenance of the pitch system, gearbox, nacelle, and auxiliary nacelle to ensure the normal operation of the wind turbine equipment. At the same time, real-time monitoring of the operational status of wind turbines should be strengthened to promote the operation of the wind power generation system under optimal conditions.

This task relies on the equipment platform of the National Vocational College Skills Competition, complete the design of a real-time operational management and monitoring system for the wind power generation system, achieving the collection and display of generation parameters, remote control functions, and status display, as well as identity authentication login.

【Knowledge learning】

8.2.1 Inspection and maintenance of the pitch system

(1) Blades: Visually and audibly check for surface damage, cracks, lightning strikes, and oil stains; check for abnormal sounds during operation (such as whistling); ensure clear and continuous torque line markings covering nuts, washers, and bases; ensure that the torque line of the same bolt does not exceed three lines; check for looseness and breakage of the blade/hub connection bolts.

(2) Blade bearings: Visually, test, and audibly check for cracking, blistering, and peeling of the surface paint film; ensure no abnormal noise during pitch adjustment; check for oil leaks in the oil separator.

(3) Mechanical lock of the rotor: Visually and manually check for completeness, deformation, breakage, and reliable connections of the pitch system.

(4) Hub and spinner: Visually check for corrosion and cracks on the hub surface; check for damage and cracks on the spinner; check for cracks, corrosion, and deformation on the spinner support, and for loose bolts; ensure the hub entry is securely fixed (after work inside the hub is completed, secure it); ensure the hub interior lighting is functioning and securely fixed.

(5) Pitch control cabinet and super capacitor: Visually check for tight closure, firm components, and no discharge marks on cables.

(6) Pitch motor: Visually, by smell, and through testing, check for intact paint film, no rust, firm connections, and no abnormal odor; ensure bolts are not loose or broken; ensure the fan can operate normally.

(7) Pitch gear ring and drive pinion: Visually check for good lubrication, no broken teeth, no cracks, and no abnormal wear.

(8) Bolts: Visually check for clear and continuous torque line markings covering nuts, washers, and bases, ensuring the torque line of the same bolt does not exceed three lines.

(9) Other checks: Visually check that cables between cabinets are well secured, undamaged, and free of discharge marks; check for no significant oil accumulation in the pitch bearings; ensure the hub interior surface is clean, rust-free, and crack-free; ensure the blade cover inside the hub is clean, rust-free, crack-free, and securely fixed; check that the lightning arresters and lightning leads are securely fixed and free of lightning marks.

8.2.2 Inspection and maintenance of the gearbox

1. Gearbox operation technology

(1) The internal gear oil temperature of the gearbox should not be lower than $-15℃$ during operation. If the temperature is below $-15℃$, the gear oil must be heated to $-15℃$ using the heating system before starting the machine.

(2) When the gear oil temperature is between $-15℃$ and $+45℃$, the oil pump device should ensure a flow rate of 40 (L/min) for gearbox lubrication.

(3) When the gear oil temperature is between $45℃$ and $60℃$, the required oil flow for cooling the gearbox is 80 (L/min).

(4) When the gear oil temperature exceeds $60℃$, forced cooling of the gear oil is done through a heat exchanger.

(5) The maximum gear oil temperature should not exceed $80℃$; if it does, a fault

alarm will be triggered, leading to a shutdown. The temperature difference between different bearings should not exceed 15℃.

(6) Operating temperature: Ambient temperature (the air temperature near the gearbox inside the nacelle).
- Normal type: Survival temperature range: -20℃ to 50℃.
- Operating temperature range: -10℃ to 40℃.
- The minimum operating temperature of the gearbox inside the nacelle is -30℃. Operation is prohibited below this temperature. The storage temperature of the gearbox inside the nacelle is -40℃, and it should not exceed 50℃.

(7) Oil pool temperature: During normal operation, the oil pool temperature should be below 70℃. If the oil pool temperature exceeds 90℃ for more than 30 minutes, the wind turbine must stop operating. If the temperature exceeds 80℃, the wind turbine should immediately stop operating. Before restarting a wind turbine that has stopped due to high temperature, an internal inspection must be performed.

(8) Bearing temperature: During normal operation, the bearing temperature should be below 90℃. If the bearing temperature exceeds 90℃ for more than 30 minutes, the wind turbine must stop operating. If it exceeds 95℃, the wind turbine should immediately stop operating. Before restarting a wind turbine that has stopped due to high temperature, an internal inspection must be performed.

2. Inspection contents

(1) Check for peeling of the anti-corrosion coating on the gearbox surface.

(2) Check the cleanliness of the gearbox surface.

(3) Check for oil leakage or oil seepage at the low-speed end, high-speed end, and various connection points of the gearbox.

(4) Check the oil level and color of the lubrication cooling oil.

(5) Check the gearbox air filter.

(6) Check the noise of the gearbox.

(7) Check the vibration of the gearbox.

(8) Check the meshing and surface condition of the gear teeth.

(9) Inspect all temperature and pressure sensors on the gearbox and check the firmness of their connections.

(10) Check the temperature of individual gearbox bearings.

(11) Check the pressure in the oil cooling circuit of the gearbox.

(12) Check the connection of pipelines.

(13) Check the wiring condition and fan cleanliness of the electric motor on the heat exchanger, and ensure the fan rotation direction is correct.

(14) Check the connection conditions of the heat exchanger with its support structure.

(15) Check the overall operation of the heat exchanger for any abnormal vibrations or

excessive noise.

(16) Check for oil leaks at the connections of the cooling lubrication oil pump and filter.

(17) Check the working condition of the two manual valves and for any oil leaks.

8.2.3 Nacelle and auxiliary nacelle

1. Automatic fire protection

Wind turbines must be equipped with an automatic fire protection system. For example, the Envision EN121-2200 turbine is equipped with an FFX-ACT5 automatic fire extinguishing system, storing two 8kg dry powder extinguishers at the tower top. When a fire signal is detected, the dry powder is automatically released to extinguish the fire.

2. Escape pack

(1) Check if the device is placed in the specified position at the rear of the nacelle. If not, return the device to the specified position.

(2) Check if the escape and rescue devices are within the normal quality range.

(3) Check if the ropes in the escape pack are tangled. If so, reorganize the ropes.

(4) Check if the main device is in good condition, free of rust, and if the fasteners are tight.

3. Base

The base transfers all static and dynamic loads affecting the rotor, generator, or tower. The base is connected to the tower through the yaw bearing, allowing the nacelle to align the rotor with the wind under the drive of the yaw system.

4. Foundation

The foundation is the most fundamental guarantee of the unit's safety and stability. The foundation is designed as a reinforced concrete structure, transmitting the loads from the rotor through various sections of the tower to the foundation. The foundation ring is a short steel cylinder connected to the foundation.

5. Lightning protection

The lightning protection system is an important guarantee for the safe operation of the unit. It consists of multiple lightning protection devices. The main components of the wind turbine nacelle include the nacelle cover, hub, gearbox, generator, control cabinet, etc. The lightning protection grounding system in the nacelle establishes a proper and reasonable lightning current discharge path, separating strong and weak currents, and leading the lightning current to the ground through the shortest path to effectively protect the equipment and electrical components inside the nacelle.

8.2.4 Description of the operating system

1. Operating status

The operating mode of wind turbines refers to the logical combination of turbine status parameters under certain conditions, forming a mode that the turbine inevitably experiences during operation. This state can be defined as an operating mode, such as standby, waiting for wind, self-check, start-up, stop, etc. The combination of all modes can include all the unit's behaviors, with specific switching conditions between different operating modes.

In a fault-free waiting state, the high-speed brake is released, the pitch angle is 89°, and the turbine idles.

When the wind speed reaches or exceeds the set wind speed, the automatic yaw starts, and the turbine automatically aligns with the wind.

After the wind turbine starts to face the wind, the blade pitch angle will gradually decrease, and the turbine will smoothly increase its speed. When the speed reaches a certain value, it will automatically connect to the grid.

During the power generation process, two closed-loop controllers will be involved in the operation of the wind turbine:

(1) When the wind speed is below the rated wind speed, the turbine operates in an underloaded state. The variable frequency drive of the doubly-fed induction generator controls the generator's torque, optimizing the generator's output power according to the torque-speed characteristics. The turbine will operate in grid-connected mode at different speeds.

(2) When the wind speed exceeds the rated wind speed, the blade angle is adjusted to limit the power generation. The generator's output power is controlled by the frequency converter to remain at the rated value. During a storm, the turbine's first response is to accelerate the rotor, then increase the pitch angle to reduce the speed, thereby keeping the rotor speed at the set value (which varies with blade diameter). The turbine will operate in grid-connected mode with pitch adjustment and speed variation. When the wind speed is too low, the rotor will remain stationary and will automatically start when the wind picks up.

2. Conditions that must be met before the wind turbine is put into operation

(1) The power supply phase sequence is correct, and the three-phase voltage is balanced.

(2) The yaw system is in normal condition, and the anemometer and wind vane are operating correctly.

(3) The hydraulic pressure and oil level of the braking and control system are within the specified range.

(4) The gearbox oil level and temperature are within the normal range.

(5) All protection devices are in the correct position, and their settings match the approved values.

(6) The control power supply is on.

(7) The control computer display is functioning normally.

(8) The rotor blades should be free of icing before manual start-up.

(9) Wind turbines that have been idle for a long time or newly commissioned should have their insulation checked and confirmed before starting.

(10) All safety measures implemented for maintenance should be removed before starting the wind turbine.

(11) Check that the SCADA communication system is functioning normally.

(12) The power supply should be on, and the cooling motor, heating motor, yaw motor, and hydraulic motor should be operating normally.

3. Starting and stopping the wind turbine

Wind turbines can be started and stopped both manually and automatically.

Automatic start: When the wind turbine is in automatic mode and the wind speed reaches the start-up range, the turbine will automatically start and connect to the grid according to the computer program.

Automatic stop: When the wind turbine is in automatic mode and the wind speed exceeds the normal operating range, the turbine will automatically disconnect from the grid and stop according to the computer program.

Manual start and stop. Four methods for manual start and stop:

1) Main control room operation: Use the computer in the main control room to press the start and stop buttons.

2) Local operation: Disconnect the remote control switch, use the control panel on the wind turbine to press the start or stop button, and then reconnect the remote control switch.

3) Remote operation: Use the remote terminal to press the start or stop button.

4) Cabin operation: Use the control panel in the cabin to press the start or stop button; however, this method is only for debugging purposes.

5) Manual start: When the wind speed reaches the start-up range, manually press the start button or switch, and the wind turbine will start and connect to the grid according to the computer program.

6) Manual stop: When the wind speed exceeds the normal operating range, manually press the stop button or switch, and the wind turbine will disconnect from the grid and stop according to the computer program.

7) After manual stopping, the start button must be pressed again to allow the wind turbine to enter auto-start mode.

8) Manual start operation under fault and emergency shutdown conditions.

9) After fault and emergency shutdown, if the fault has been resolved and start-up conditions are met, press the "reset" or "reboot" local control button before starting the wind turbine as per the normal start-up procedure.

8.2.5 Wind turbine operation management

Inspectors are directly responsible for monitoring the safe and stable operation of the wind farm and should regularly (every 3 months) visit the site for visual inspections and other direct methods to check the operational status of the wind turbines. It is important that all field work is carried out by at least two people for safety reasons. The inspection mainly includes checking for abnormal noises during operation, the condition of the blades, the functionality of the yaw system, and any oil stains on the tower. Inspections should be focused on recent equipment conditions, especially for turbines that have been re-commissioned after fault repair. Special attention should be given to turbines with frequent starts and stops, heavy loads, high temperatures, or those running with known issues. If faults are found, they should be reported and addressed promptly to prevent accidents and minimize economic losses. Relevant inspection records should be maintained. Do not blindly reset the wind turbine remotely if the fault cause is unknown. If the turbine repeatedly resets automatically (more than 3 times), it should be manually stopped immediately to determine the cause.

8.2.6 Wind farm operation monitoring

(1) Wind farm operators should listen to and record local weather forecasts daily, and prepare for potential accidents and countermeasures for the wind farm's safe operation.

(2) Operators should regularly monitor the parameters of wind turbines through the computer screen in the main control room.

(3) Operators should analyze the changes in wind turbine parameters displayed on the computer, continuously monitor the turbine if anomalies are detected, and make necessary adjustments. The reasons for any changes should be noted in the operation log for fault recording and statistics.

(4) Wind turbine inspection. Operators should periodically inspect the wind turbines, wind measurement devices, and high-voltage distribution lines within the site, address any defects promptly, and record them in the defect logbook.

1) Check for abnormal noises during turbine operation, the condition of the blades, the functionality of the yaw system, and if any cables are tangled.

2) Check for oil leaks in various parts of the wind turbine.

3) Increase inspection frequency and content during abnormal weather, abnormal turbine operation, or when new equipment is put into use.

4) Do not blindly reset the wind turbine remotely if the cause of a fault is unknown. If the turbine repeatedly resets automatically (more than 3 times), it should be manually stopped immediately to determine the cause.

5) The wind farm integrated self-monitoring and control system and wind turbine SCADA system must have an audible alarm function.

6) The liaison mechanism between the main control room the main control room and the operation site every hour, etc.

【Task implementation】

Ⅰ. Task preparation

1 competition equipment platform, 1 multimeter, 1 copy of record sheet for power-up inspection, 1 copy of record sheet for wind power generation system real time protection.

Task 8.2 Related implementation charts

Ⅱ. Task content and procedures

Task: Design of wind power real-time monitoring system

Task content: Complete the design of the wind power real-time monitoring system.

Task procedures:

(1) Design and create a login management interface with different management permissions.

(2) Design and create the equipment detection and control interface for the wind power station.

(3) Design and create the load equipment detection and control interface.

(4) Complete communication configuration to achieve data collection from the interface.

(5) Perform system power-on checks, correctly debug, and operate the wind power system real-time monitoring. Fill out the wind power system real-time monitoring record form.

Ⅲ. Skill requirements

(1) Correctly use the multimeter to measure different parameters, with proper operation, no short circuits, and no incorrect settings.

(2) Correctly collect operational parameters from various terminal devices connected to the wind power real-time monitoring system.

(3) Interface components should be appropriately sized, neatly arranged, and aesthetically colored.

(4) The interface should be fully functional, with login, switching, and other buttons.

(5) Real-time data display on the interface should be accurate, capable of remote control of devices, and display their status.

(6) Observation of device operation data should be thorough, with accurate recording, including both numerical values and units.

Ⅳ. Task results, appraisal and evaluation

(1) The system is correctly commissioned and successfully operating; the data screen is well laid out and runs correctly; operation data are recorded; curves are drawn

smooth (accounting for 90%).

(2) The operator exhibits good professional quality during the operation process and follows 7S management model (accounting for 10%).

【Exercises】

1. What are the inspection contents for the gearbox?
2. What conditions must be met before a wind power unit is put into operation?
3. What are the contents of wind power unit operation management?
4. What are the inspection contents for the wind turbine?

Task 8.3 Maintenance of Wind Power Systems

【Learning objectives】

Knowledge objective: To understand the inspection and maintenance of wind turbine units, master daily maintenance tasks for wind turbine units and master the content and requirements of daily wind turbine accidents.

Ability objectives: To be able to complete daily maintenance of wind turbine units and be able to handle daily accidents of wind turbine units.

Qualification objective: To cultivate the spirit of independent learning and pioneering.

Learning priority: Daily maintenance of wind turbine units

Learning challenge: Content and handling of daily accidents in wind turbine units

【Task analysis】

Wind turbine units are complex mechanical equipment that require regular maintenance and servicing to ensure efficient, stable, and safe operation. Regular maintenance can keep the equipment in optimal condition, extend the life of the turbine, reduce maintenance costs and downtime, and improve power generation efficiency. Proper maintenance methods include regular inspections, lubrication maintenance and replacement, cleaning and replacing filters, and ensuring safety measures.

This task relies on the equipment platform of the National Vocational College Skills Competition, complete the construction of the wind power system, realize multi-energy, multi-load energy dispatch operation, and complete the operation and maintenance tasks of the wind power system.

【Knowledge learning】

8.3.1 Wind turbine inspection and maintenance

1. Wind turbine inspection and maintenance tasks

Regular tower inspections and maintenance of wind turbines should be conducted in manual "shutdown" state. Wear a safety helmet and safety shoes. Spare parts and tools must be placed in a tool bag and securely fastened with a safety rope to prevent falling.

(1) Inspect the hydraulic system, gearbox, and other lubrication systems for leaks, check if oil levels and temperatures are normal, and refill oil if levels are below specified.

(2) Regularly check and tighten equipment bolts.

(3) Regularly take oil samples from hydraulic systems, gearboxes, and lubrication systems for chemical analysis and lubricate bearing points on time.

(4) Regularly inspect safety facilities such as ladders, safety ropes, and lighting equipment.

(5) Keep control boxes clean and conduct regular cleaning.

(6) Regularly check and maintain the main control room's computer system and communication equipment.

2. Reasons for shutdown

The following are reasons for wind turbine shutdowns and corresponding control system actions:

(1) Excessive wind speeds accompanied by strong gusts; the system will decide whether to restart after 10 minutes.

(2) Grid fluctuations.

(3) Ambient temperature below -30℃; the system will automatically restart when the temperature rises.

(4) Oil level below the set value.

(5) Significant deviation between theoretical and actual power curves; no automatic restart.

(6) Damaged parts or overheating parts.

(7) Cable twisting; the system will automatically restart after untwisting.

(8) Yaw system fault; the system will decide whether to restart based on the fault.

(9) Speed detection fault (no emergency stop speed); the system will automatically restart.

3. Safety requirements when approaching wind turbine units

(1) Do not approach or enter the turbine during thunderstorms; wait at least one hour after the thunderstorm has passed.

(2) Vehicles should stop at least 20 meters upwind of the wind turbine unit.

(3) Wear a safety helmet when approaching wind turbine units.

(4) When lifting objects with a hoist, use guide ropes and ensure no one is around the tower during this time to avoid injuries from falling objects.

4. Safety requirements for working inside wind turbine units

(1) Workers climbing the tower should wear a safety helmet, work shoes, and secure a special safety belt. Check the ladder, safety belt, and safety rope carefully

before climbing. If any damage is found, repairs must be made before climbing. Close platform window covers immediately after passing.

(2) Climbing the wind turbine is generally not allowed without lighting in the tower. If necessary, bring lighting equipment. Tools and small parts should be placed in a tool bag to prevent falling injuries. Heavy items should be lifted using a hoist.

(3) Do not work outside the nacelle when wind speeds are $\geq 12 \text{m/s}$; do not open the nacelle cover when wind speeds are $\geq 12 \text{m/s}$; close the nacelle cover when wind speeds are $\geq 14 \text{m/s}$; do not work inside the nacelle when wind speeds are $\geq 18 \text{m/s}$.

(4) When performing maintenance operations inside the wind turbine, switch the start-stop switch to the "stop" position and then turn the switch to the "maintenance" or "repair" position.

(5) Anyone working outside the nacelle must wear a safety harness and secure it properly to prevent falling.

(6) Generally, tasks should be performed by two or more people who can keep in contact. If out of sight or hearing range, use a walkie-talkie or mobile phone to maintain communication. In special cases, a worker may work alone but must maintain reliable communication with the control room.

5. Hazards of moving parts

(1) The nacelle is a moving part connected to the tower through the yaw bearing. Relative movement between the tower and the nacelle is a danger; avoid staying near the yaw gear to prevent injuries from yaw drive.

(2) The yaw brake is located at the bottom of the nacelle, and brake pads move with the yaw brake disc; avoid contact with the internal yaw brake to prevent injuries.

(3) Ensure the entire transmission system cannot start unintentionally when working near rotating parts such as the main shaft, slip rings, and elastic couplings to prevent injuries.

(4) Before entering the hub, engage the hydraulic brake and lock the wind wheel mechanical lock; unauthorized pitch operations are not allowed during work in the hub to prevent severe equipment damage or personal injury. Only professionally trained personnel should work inside the hub.

6. Wind turbine protection measures

Wind turbine units must have a safety (chain) system logically independent of the control system. When safety limits are exceeded or the control system cannot keep the unit within normal operating range, the safety system will stop the unit.

The safety system should be verified to operate reliably under conditions such as overspeed, power limit, generator short circuit, excessive nacelle vibration, cable over-twist due to yaw, control system failure, emergency shutdown, and other safety-related faults.

Control function tests. Control function should ensure that the control system keeps the wind turbine's operating parameters within the normal range under specified conditions, including start and stop of the unit, power characteristics, yaw stability, smooth speed changes, automatic power factor adjustment, cable twist limitation, and stopping under grid failure or load loss. Brake functions (normal and emergency brakes) must meet design requirements.

The above control functions should meet the design requirements.

The detection and monitoring functions of the control system. The control system should be tested for its ability to detect and monitor the operating parameters and status of wind turbines, including: ①wind speed and direction; ②rotor and generator speeds; ③electrical parameters (grid voltage and frequency, generator output current, power, and power factor); ④temperatures (generator winding temperature, bearing temperature, gearbox oil temperature, control cabinet temperature, and ambient temperature); ⑤brake equipment status; ⑥cable twisting; ⑦mechanical part failures; ⑧and grid failures.

7. Passive protection system for wind turbine units

The passive protection system protects the wind turbine from external environmental impacts, such as lightning and heavy loads. Blades are equipped with lightning sensors, and the internal conductive system protects the blades from lightning strikes. The pitch system remains operational even during lightning strikes.

During feathering braking, the torque generated by the free rotation of the rotor is minimal, thus reducing the load on the turbine, which is why the rotor is not locked even during emergency stops.

8.3.2 Maintenance of wind turbines

Maintenance work is essential to ensure the safe, normal, and reliable operation of wind turbines. To guarantee the stable and safe operation of the wind turbines and extend their service life, regular inspection and maintenance of the turbines are indispensable. Therefore, we should carry out maintenance on the turbines periodically. Maintenance can be divided into initial maintenance, 500-hour maintenance, and regular maintenance according to different maintenance intervals. Below is a detailed explanation based on the maintenance cycle.

1. Initial maintenance and 500-hour maintenance

During the normal installation and commissioning process of a wind turbine, the turbine tower should be inspected one week after the first grid connection of the unit, and 500-hour maintenance should be carried out four weeks after the first grid connection.

One week after the turbine is connected to the grid, an initial inspection of the turbine tower should be carried out, including: ①checking all bolts at the flange connections; ②inspecting weld seams at the interfaces for cracks; ③ensuring that all platforms inside the tower are stable.

If any damage is found during the inspection, a detailed inspection should be carried out according to the relevant "tower" content. If no damage is found, it should be recorded in the inspection document, indicating that the turbine is undamaged.

The 500-hour maintenance refers to the second final inspection after the unit has operated for 500 hours or one month after the first inspection. It involves a thorough check of every point, every setting, and every task done during the second grid connection. The inspection items include: ①checking the torque of all bolts according to the bolt torque table and adjusting them to the rated torque; ②inspecting the filter elements of the oil filtration system (gearbox, hydraulic station) and replacing them if necessary; ③checking for leaks in the hydraulic circuit; ④checking the lubrication oil of bearings in parts such as the main shaft and rotor to ensure it is normal; ⑤checking for any abnormal sounds inside the nacelle or hub and around rotating parts; ⑥checking for leaks in the gearbox cooling system.

2. Regular maintenance

After the turbine is put into normal operation, regular maintenance should be carried out at appropriate intervals to inspect and eliminate potential issues that may arise during operation, preventing further problems from affecting the turbine's performance and lifespan.

Some maintenance tasks should be performed every time the maintenance personnel enter the turbine, focusing on key, easily damaged parts.

Detailed records should be kept for maintenance conducted under special circumstances, such as lightning strikes or replacement of old parts. Subsequent maintenance should follow the normal cycle, and a more conservative, shorter cycle may be chosen if there are any doubts.

(1) Daily maintenance. Daily maintenance intervals are not time-based (each turbine must be checked at least once every three months). Every time the maintenance personnel enter the turbine (for any reason), they must inspect the daily maintenance items. These tasks list the necessary steps when entering the turbine (opening the door, turning on the lights, stopping the machine, entering safety mode, etc.) and the necessary steps when leaving the turbine (running tests, checking all tools, cleaning the work area, filling out records).

Daily maintenance involves regular visual and noise checks, such as checking whether the oil color is normal, whether there are oil or cooling water leakage marks on the tower platform or frame, whether there are broken bolts, signs of lightning strikes, or any unusual noises.

(2) Semi-annual maintenance. Semi-annual maintenance should be carried out accu-

rately every six months, ensuring that all maintenance tasks and checks are completed within this period.

(3) Annual maintenance. Annual maintenance involves a thorough inspection and maintenance, conducted once every12 months, regardless of the turbine's operating hours. Even if the turbine has not operated since the last maintenance, the annual maintenance should still be performed.

8.3.3 Wind power equipment accident handling

1. Basic requirements for handling abnormal operation and accidents at wind farms

(1) When wind power equipment operates abnormally or an accident occurs, the on-duty supervisor should organize the operators to quickly resolve the abnormality and restore the equipment to normal operation, recording the handling situation in the operation log.

(2) In the event of an accident, measures should be taken to control the incident and prevent it from escalating. The incident should be reported to the relevant authorities promptly. Before the cause of the accident is identified, operators should protect the accident site and damaged equipment, except in special circumstances (e.g., rescuing lives). Immediate repairs must be approved by the authorities.

(3) If an accident occurs during shift handover, the handover should be suspended. The outgoing staff must stay at their posts to handle the accident, while the incoming staff assist in accident handling under the direction of the outgoing supervisor. After the incident is handled, the supervisors of both shifts will decide whether to continue the handover.

(4) After handling the accident, the on-duty supervisor should record the accident's occurrence and handling details truthfully in the handover log. Following the accident, computer records should be used to analyze the actions of protections, signals, and automatic devices to identify the cause of the accident and prepare a written report for higher authorities.

2. Handling abnormal operation and faults in wind turbines

(1) For alarm signals indicating abnormal conditions in the turbine, operators should inspect and address the specific areas indicated by the alarms.

(2) In the event of an anemometer fault, when the turbine's displayed output power deviates from the corresponding wind speed, check the sensors of the anemometer and wind vane for faults and address them if any.

(3) If abnormal noises are detected during turbine operation, the source of the noise should be identified, analyzed, and addressed.

(4) Handling automatic shutdowns due to equipment and component temperatures exceeding operational limits: If temperatures in the generator, frequency converter cabi-

net, control box, mechanical brake pads, or cooler exceed specified values, leading to an automatic shutdown, operators should identify the cause of the temperature rise, such as inspecting the cooling system, brake pad gaps, temperature sensors, and related circuits. The turbine should only be restarted after resolving the fault.

(5) Handling automatic shutdowns due to low oil pressure in the hydraulic control system: Operators should check the oil pump's operation. If oil pressure is abnormal, inspect the oil pump, oil cylinders, and relevant valves, and only restart the turbine after resolving the fault.

(6) Handling automatic shutdowns due to yaw system faults: Operators should check the electrical circuits of the yaw system, the yaw motors, and the winding sensors. Faulty motors should be replaced, and issues with winding sensors should be resolved before restarting the turbine.

(7) Handling automatic shutdowns due to excessive vibration: If turbine vibrations exceed limits due to surging or pitch system failures, causing a safety shutdown, operators should identify and address the cause of the vibration before restarting the turbine.

(8) Handling system power outages or line switch trips: If a system fault or line fault causes a power outage or switch trip, operators should identify the cause (restoring main control room power first if the incident occurs at night). The turbine should be restarted and reconnected to the grid via computer once the system is normal.

3. Procedure for immediate shutdown of turbines due to abnormal conditions

(1) Use the main control room computer for remote shutdown.

(2) If remote shutdown fails, press the shutdown button on-site and set the "Visit/Operation/Maintenance" key to "Visit."

(3) If normal shutdown fails, use the emergency shutdown button.

(4) If still ineffective, disconnect the low-voltage circuit breaker in the transformer box or the line circuit breaker connected to the turbine.

4. Handling typical wind turbine accidents

Immediate shutdown of the wind turbine is required if any of the following occur:

(1) Significant blade damage;

(2) Failure or malfunction of the primary protection system of the turbine;

(3) Damage due to lightning strikes;

(4) Severe mechanical faults such as blade breakage;

(5) Brake system failure.

In case of a fire in the turbine, operators should immediately shut down the turbine, cut off the power, and take swift measures to extinguish the fire and prevent it from spreading. If faults endanger personnel or equipment safety, the operator should immediately disconnect the low-voltage side circuit breaker of the transformer for the affected turbine.

If the main switch of the turbine trips, first check if the main circuit frequency converter and generator insulation are intact and if the main switch setting action value is correct. Reclose the switch only after confirming no issues; otherwise, withdraw the turbine from operation for further inspection.

Handling automatic shutdown of wind turbines due to low hydraulic pressure: Operators should check whether the hydraulic pump is functioning properly. If the oil pressure is abnormal, they should inspect the hydraulic pump, pressure cylinders, and relevant valves. Restart the turbine's automatic system only after the fault has been resolved.

Handling automatic shutdown of wind turbines due to yaw system faults: Operators should check the electrical circuit of the yaw mechanism, the operation of the yaw motor, and the winding sensor. If the motor is damaged, it should be replaced. If the winding sensor fault causes the cable to be unable to unwind, it should be addressed. Restart the automatic system only after the fault has been cleared.

Handling automatic shutdown of wind turbines due to excessive speed or vibration: During operation, if the pitch control system fails, it may lead to the turbine exceeding its speed limit. Mechanical imbalance can cause the turbine to vibrate beyond allowable limits. In both cases, the wind turbine will automatically shut down for safety. Operators should investigate the causes of excessive speed or vibration and address them before allowing a restart.

Handling power outages or circuit breaker trips during wind turbine operation: In the event of a power outage or circuit breaker trip due to a system fault, operators should check the cause of the power loss or breaker trip (if it occurs at night, prioritize restoring power to the main control room). Once the system is restored to normal, restart the turbine and reconnect it to the grid via the computer. If the high-voltage side switch or low-voltage side fuse of the transformer is blown, analyze and address the transformer fault. Reconnect to the grid only after the issue is resolved.

If a fire occurs in the turbine, operators should immediately shut down the turbine, cut off the power, and take swift measures to extinguish the fire and prevent it from spreading. If faults endanger personnel or equipment safety, the operator should immediately disconnect the circuit breaker on the line side of the turbine.

If the main switch of the turbine trips, first check if the main circuit's silicon-controlled rectifier and generator insulation are intact and if the main switch setting action value is correct. Reclose the switch only after confirming no issues; otherwise, withdraw the turbine from operation for further inspection.

If vibration faults occur, first check the protection circuits. If it's not a false alarm, immediately stop the turbine for further inspection.

【Task implementation】

I. Task preparation

Task 8.3 Related implementation charts

1 competition equipment platform, 1 slotted screwdriver, 1 philips screwdriver, 1 wire stripping plier, 1 U-shaped crimping pliers, 1 tube-shaped crimping pliers, 1 multimeter, 1 copy of record sheet for power-up inspection, 1 copy of record sheet for wind power generation system real time protection and a number of wires.

II. Task content and procedures

Task: Construction and maintenance of multi-energy and multi-load systems

Task content: Complete the construction and maintenance of multi-energy and multi-load systems.

Task procedures:

(1) Complete the production of connection wires for the multi-energy and multi-load system.

(2) According to the wiring diagram, complete the wiring and connection of the PLC and relay module for the multi-energy and multi-load system.

(3) According to the wiring diagram, complete the wiring and connection of the local control module for the multi-energy and multi-load system.

(4) According to the wiring diagram, complete the design of the electrical control interface for the multi-energy and multi-load system on the industrial computer.

(5) Complete the system power-on inspection, correctly debug and operate the multi-energy and multi-load system control system.

III. Skill requirements

(1) Correctly use the multimeter to measure different parameters, ensuring proper operation without short circuits or incorrect measurements.

(2) Accurately measure the operating voltage, current, and other parameters of the multi-energy and multi-load system.

(3) When inserting U-type cold-pressed terminals into the terminal block, the U-shaped part should be fully inserted and face outward.

(4) When fitting number tubes, for wires oriented vertically, the number and letter combination should be read from the end away from the connection terminal to the terminal; for wires oriented horizontally, the number and letter combination should be read from left to right.

(5) When crimping the connection terminals, ensure that all strands of the stripped wire are inserted into the terminal sleeve. When using the crimping plier, the crimp mark

should be at the bottom (reverse side) of the terminal sleeve. After crimping, no wires should be exposed at the crimped area.

(6) Observing and recording equipment operating data accurately, including both values and units.

Ⅳ. Task results, appraisal and evaluation

(1) The system is correctly commissioned and successfully operating; the data screen is well laid out and runs correctly; operation data are recorded; curves are drawn smooth (accounting for 90%).

(2) The operator exhibits good professional quality during the operation process and follows 7S management model (accounting for 10%).

【Exercises】

1. What are the maintenance items for wind turbines?
2. What are the safety requirements for working inside wind turbines?
3. What are the contents of the second final inspection after 500 hours or one month of turbine operation?
4. What are the basic requirements for handling abnormal operation and accidents in wind farms?
5. What accidents require the immediate shutdown of wind turbines?

参 考 文 献

[1] [美] 瑞安·梅菲尔德. 太阳能光伏发电系统设计与安装 [M]. 刘长浥,许晓艳,译. 北京:人民邮电出版社,2012.
[2] 廖明夫,R. Gasch,J. Twele. 风力发电技术 [M]. 西安:西北工业大学出版社,2009.
[3] 黄汉云. 太阳能光伏发电应用原理 [M]. 北京:化学工业出版社,2013.
[4] 李安定,吕全亚. 太阳能光伏发电系统工程 [M]. 北京:化学工业出版社,2012.
[5] 王志新. 现代风力发电技术及工程应用 [M]. 北京:电子工业出版社,2010.